LAW AS JUSTICE

THE MORAL IMPERATIVE OF OWEN FISS'S SCHOLARSHIP

Irwin P. Stotzky

Professor of Law and Director,
Center for the Study of Human Rights,
University of Miami School of Law

Cover photograph: Civil Rights Protesters Being Sprayed by Fire Hoses in Birmingham

© Bob Adelman/Corbis

"No man is an island, Kelly Ingram Park, Birmingham, Alabama. 1963 The police and firemen used a brute show of force to try to stop the ongoing demonstrations. It didn't work on this day. Rather than fleeing, the protestors hung on to each other and were able to stand up to the full fury of the water, though not without casualties. I have never witnessed such cruelty. There was almost as much moisture behind the lens as in front. I gave a print of this picture to Dr. King. He studied it and said, I am startled that out of so much pain some beauty came."

Image: © Bob Adelman/Corbis
Collection: Historical Standard RM
Photographer: Bob Adelman
This image is part of these set(s): The African-American Experience

Twelve Tables Press, LLC
462 Broome Street, Suite 4W
New York, NY 10013
www.twelvetablespress.com

To Audrey, Jacob, and Joshua,
The Lights of My Life

Acknowledgments

The idea for this book first occurred to me in 2003, when I organized a symposium on Owen Fiss's work. The project took shape after discussions with Steve Errick. He showed great enthusiasm for the project and has continued to be extremely supportive of it. I thank him for his support. I also thank Jay Tidmarsh for his excellent editing suggestions and good humor during the entire process. Sharon Ray has done an excellent job of putting the book into printable form. Kevin Muth's cover design is exceptional.

In addition, there were several students whose energy and talent eased my research and proofing burdens as the work progressed: Cathy Dorvil, Sylvia-Rebecca Gutiérrez, Jennifer Hochstadt, Corey Lazar, and Michael Pieciak deserve special praise.

The University of Miami Library Staff was always helpful. I am deeply grateful to all the library staff. In particular, I am indebted to Pamela Lucken and Robin Schard, whose research was indispensable.

Finally, Shannon Maharajh deserves special mention. She combined intelligence with competence and hard work and almost single-handedly typed several drafts of the book while inputting numerous changes.

Contents

LAW AS JUSTICE

THE MORAL IMPERATIVE OF OWEN FISS'S SCHOLARSHIP

Introduction[*]

This is a book about the scholarship of Owen Fiss and the impact and importance of his ideas. For the past four decades, Fiss has stood for the idea of achieving justice through law. His work is particularly significant today as a response to the Bush Administration's powerful attack on the rule of law.

While there is great hope that the election of Barack Obama will put an end to this attack, it is by no means a certainty. During the presidential campaign, a constant theme for President Obama was the need to restore American values in the fight against terrorism. He pledged to banish secret interrogation rules and to follow military guidelines set out in the Army Field Manual on Interrogation.[1] But he also stated that

---

[*] Each part of the book, starting with the Introduction, uses its own footnote numbers. Each of Owen Fiss's articles uses the footnote numbers and citation form of that particular journal.

[1] In his early days in office, he did indeed live up to some of his pledges. On January 22, 2009, only two days after his inauguration, President Obama signed three executive orders reversing some of the Bush Administration's interrogation and detention policies. The first executive order directs the closure of the prison at Guantánamo Bay within one year. Exec. Order No. 13,492, 74 Fed. Reg. 4897 (Jan. 27, 2009). A second order calls for the creation of a Special Task Force to review detainee policy and to determine whether it should go forward. Exec. Order No. 13,493, 74 Fed. Reg. 4901 (Jan. 27, 2009). A third order establishes the United States Army Field Manual as the standard for interrogation for all prisoners captured during armed conflict, grants the International Committee of the Red Cross access to prisoners detained in armed conflict, and eliminates all Central Intelligence Agency (C.I.A.) detention centers. The order also calls for a Special Task Force to review Army Field Manual practices and rendition policies. Exec. Order No. 13,491, 74 Fed. Reg. 4893 (Jan. 27, 2009). But even as he reversed the Bush Administration's most disputed counterterrorism policies, President Obama postponed for at least six months difficult decisions on the details. He ordered a cabinet-level review on the most challenging questions his administration faces—what to do with dangerous prisoners who cannot be tried in American courts; whether some interrogation methods should remain secret to keep Al Qaeda from training to resist them; and how the United States can make sure prisoners transferred to other countries will not be tortured. Moreover, even as the Obama Administration has pursued policies to end some of the most blatant violations of the rule of law by the Bush Administration, it has been signaling continued support for other major elements of Bush's approach to fighting terrorism. When appearing before Congressional committees, Obama nominees have endorsed the C.I.A.'s program of transferring prisoners

he would consider allowing the Central Intelligence Agency (C.I.A.) to continue holding prisoners in overseas jails.[2] And it is not clear what kind of trials would take place for these prisoners or for how long they would be held before being charged with a crime or released. Many of these issues, as well as questions about the general powers of the Executive Branch—including questions about the extensive surveillance policies of the Bush Administration—will surely invite additional constitutional challenges. Fiss's work and the moral force of his ideas, if adhered to by the courts and by our democratic, governmental institutions, will help to overcome any significant attack on the rule of law and aid the Obama Administration in its mission to restore our national values.

Owen Fiss is one of the great constitutional scholars and teachers of his generation. Indeed, it is no exaggeration to claim that he is a hero of the law. His writings have had a profound impact on the work of thousands of students, scholars, practitioners, judges, and, of course, on the law itself. His view of family and friendship, broad and all encompassing, including students and colleagues alike, has made him an even more important and varied role model than any scholarship would suggest.

His credentials are impeccable. He is Sterling Professor of Law at Yale University. He was educated at Dartmouth (B.A. 1959, with valedictory standing), Oxford (B.Phil 1961) and Harvard (LL.B 1964), where he served as an editor on the Harvard Law Review. From 1964-1965, he clerked for Thurgood Marshall (when Marshall was a judge on the United States Court of Appeals for the Second Circuit) and later (1965-1966) for Justice William J. Brennan, Jr. on the United States Supreme Court. He then served as a Special Assistant to John Doar, Assistant

---

to other countries without legal rights, and indefinitely detaining terrorism suspects without trials even if they are arrested outside of a war zone. The Obama Administration has even agreed with the Bush legal team's arguments that a lawsuit by former C.I.A. detainees should be stopped based on the "state secrets" doctrine. Charlie Savage, *Obama's War on Terror May Resemble Bush's in Some Areas*, N.Y. TIMES, Feb. 18, 2009, at A19. The Obama Administration has also left the door open to resuming military commission trials. Indeed, on May 15, 2009, President Obama announced that his Administration would prosecute some detainees being held at the prison in Guantánamo Bay, Cuba in a military commission system. The Obama Administration said, however, that it would make changes in the system to grant detainees expanded legal rights. The proposed changes would limit the use of hearsay evidence, ban evidence obtained from cruel and harsh treatment, and give defendants more latitude to select their own lawyers. Nevertheless, retaining the military commission system—the much-criticized centerpiece of the Bush Administration's strategy for fighting terrorism—is a stunning reversal of President Obama's position. William Glaberson, *Vowing More Rights for Accused, Obama Retains Tribunal System*, N.Y. TIMES, May 16, 2009, at A1.

[2] Mark Mazetti & Scott Shane, *After Sharp Words on C.I.A., Obama Faces a Delicate Task*, N.Y. TIMES, Dec. 3, 2008, at A1.

Attorney General in charge of the Civil Rights Division of the Department of Justice (1966-1968). Before coming to Yale, Fiss taught at the University of Chicago (1968-1974).

In this book, I celebrate his many contributions to legal scholarship, but not only because of the high quality of his work. I celebrate his contributions because of the powerful moral force he brings to that scholarship and because the personal and professional integrity and the intellectual rigor with which he approaches his tasks are beyond reproach. Perhaps even more important is the power of his ideas. His work advances a principle that is extremely relevant, even crucial, to the constitutional crises we often face as a nation and to the role of law in our society. Owen Fiss's position is a powerful one: law is an expression of public reason and the practice of constitutional adjudication is crucial in determining the quality of our social life. Indeed, law brings structure to our public life. The role of the judge is to embody that reason and to measure practical reality against the authoritative values produced by the law and then to seek ways to bring that reality into accord with those values.

These attributes and ideas are especially significant today, when much of the population, particularly members of the bar and academic lawyers, feels so alienated from the historic function played by the federal courts in perpetuating a highly moral body of learning known as constitutional law. Fiss's position is, however, quite unfashionable in today's legal and political climate. But with the recent election of Barack Obama, it is possible that Fiss's vision may be reinvigorated.

Lawyers who came of age in previous generations, such as Owen Fiss, saw the Supreme Court of the United States, as well as the federal circuit and district courts, and even some state courts, as institutions worthy of their highest respect, admiration, and support. Presently, however, federal courts are often seen as hostile and uncommitted to our most prized national ideals of equality and justice under the law.[3] They are frequently seen as institutions dedicated to protecting the status quo and increasing the power of those who serve it, such as officials of the Executive Branch.[4]

---

[3] Many would cite Bush v. Gore, 531 U.S. 98 (2000), as one of the most egregious examples. Unfortunately, I do not believe that case is so out of the ordinary, certainly not in its methodology. *See* Owen Fiss, *The Fallibility of Reason, in* BUSH V. GORE, THE QUESTION OF LEGITIMACY (B. Ackerman, ed., 2000). The decision stopped Florida's ballot recount, allowing Florida's Secretary of State's previous certification of George W. Bush as the winner of the State's 25 electoral votes to stand.

[4] The protracted litigation over the terrorism cases is a prime example. *See* Owen Fiss, *In the Shadow of War*, 58 U. MIAMI L. REV. 449 (2003).

It is, therefore, not an exaggeration to say that Owen Fiss is an important scholar who possesses qualities that have long since gone out of style, but which are integrally related to the fragile art of constitutional adjudication and to the pursuit of substantive justice. He represents the best ideals of the legal institutions that created the impetus for the most significant changes in the history of the republic, including, not least of all, the quest for racial equality. Being entirely cynical, even hostile, about the positive role that courts may play in assuring justice in our society, a view I have certainly held and I suspect many members of the academy and the bar hold, jeopardizes the significant achievements of constitutional scholars and of federal courts in profound ways. Owen Fiss is so important, both as a scholar and as a moral force, because he constantly confronts that cynicism and attacks it in ways that are difficult to ignore. His work forces us to "stand within the law and test the government's actions by the law."[5]

My views about the importance of Owen Fiss's work are best understood if I set the context for my conclusions. On many significant levels—intellectual, political, and social—Owen Fiss came of age in his conceptions of the role the judiciary should play in our society in the 1960s and early to mid-1970s. This was, of course, during the hey-day of the Warren Court, a remarkable era of Supreme Court history that can be said to have started with *Brown v. Board of Education*[6] in the mid-1950s, and to have reached its most dazzling heights during the early to mid-1960s when the progressive wing of the Court achieved a strong majority. This was the *golden age* of American law, the era of Justices Warren, Black, Brennan, Douglas, Fortas, Goldberg, and Marshall, among others. Although Chief Justice Earl Warren retired in 1969, this extraordinary phase of legal history that bears his name continued into the early 1970s. Owen Fiss played an important role in this *golden age*. His timing for being involved in great events was—and still is—impeccable. Indeed, his clerkships with Judge Marshall[7] and Justice Brennan and his two-

---

[5] *Id.* at 470.

[6] Brown v. Bd. of Educ., 347 U.S. 483 (1954) (eliminating state-mandated or deliberately maintained dual school systems).

[7] Thurgood Marshall was sworn in as a federal judge on October 23, 1961. He was the first African-American to serve on the United States Court of Appeals for the Second Circuit. During his first several years on the bench, he relied extensively on his law clerks because the bulk of his case assignments dealt with "big business" issues. His practice experience, of course, was concerned with civil rights issues. Marshall believed that he needed the very best law students to compensate for his lack of experience. He hired clerks only from the top law schools. Owen Fiss was one of the best students from one of the top law schools. *See* JUAN WILLIAMS, THURGOOD MARSHALL: AMERICAN REVOLUTIONARY 304-05 (1998).

year stint at the Civil Rights Division of the Justice Department placed him directly in the most important events of his time. For example, he worked on several important civil rights cases both as a clerk and as an attorney in the Civil Rights Division of the Justice Department. He lived and participated directly in these amazing times and events. He worked directly with great judges and with first rate lawyers all of whom fought the battle of assuring equal justice under the law. Fiss's theories came directly out of these experiences.

The foundation of the Warren Court jurisprudence had its antecedents in earlier Supreme Court periods. Most particularly, these foundations are reflected in some of the decisions of the Supreme Court in the 1930s. During the Warren Court period, for example, the Court took the dissents written by Justices Holmes and Brandeis and turned them into majority positions, thus elevating the principle of freedom of speech into a significant set of values of American society.[8] Simultaneously, the Court began to intervene in criminal proceedings to assure a minimum level of procedural fairness.

Even with these roots as background, however, the Warren Court represented an almost completely new experiment in judicial decision-making. There was clearly something unique, indeed special, about that Court. *Brown*, for example, undertook the most daunting of all constitutional jobs: making America's historic promise of racial equality in all aspects of political and social life a reality. But *Brown* stood for even more than this incredible challenge. It stood for an entirely new vision of constitutional law that grew into a set of cases that resulted in significant constitutional reform of the entire institutional structure of our state and federal governments.

In *Brown*, the Supreme Court declared the idea of "separate but equal" unconstitutional and then sought to transform the Jim Crow school systems into unitary, nonracial ones. Indeed, the Warren Court attempted to live up to the Constitution's promises and used its authority to achieve that purpose. The Court's emphasis, however, did not stop with public school systems. It extended to the entirety of the modern state, including employment agencies, hospitals, housing, the police and prisons. While equality was the centerpiece of its revolutionary reform program, the Court's vision extended to the entire scope of the Bill of Rights. In pursuit of this vision, the Warren Court used the Civil War

---

[8] It was not until this period that the Supreme Court began to create and take seriously the tradition of protecting citizens from prosecution for seditious libel. The idea that democracy demands a right to criticize government became the central meaning of the First Amendment. *See, e.g.*, N.Y. Times Co. v. Sullivan, 376 U.S. 254 (1964).

Amendments, particularly the Fourteenth Amendment, and the Bill of Rights as the basis for evaluating the then accepted order. By so doing, it changed the entire range of relationships between the citizen and the state and federal governments.

The Warren Court nationalized a set of rights reflected in these amendments. For example, no longer could a man charged with a crime in State A be given virtually no procedural protections or be treated with fewer procedural protections than one charged with the same crime in State B. Both would now have to be treated with an equivalent minimum of procedural protections. Convictions would no longer be based on evidence seized in violation of the Fourth Amendment or on statements physically or psychologically coerced from the accused in violation of the Fifth Amendment. Criminal trials would no longer be allowed without the right to counsel or the right to a jury of the accused's peers. In addition, the Warren Court placed legal barriers on the death penalty, made sure the welfare system was not administered in an arbitrary and capricious manner, stopped the state governments from imposing poll taxes, protected "radical" speech, and allowed the dissemination of information concerning contraception. Indeed, many government practices of the 1950s and early 1960s disproportionately affected the poor and otherwise disadvantaged. The Warren Court attacked this invidious discrimination with vigor.

These were only some of the extremely difficult challenges faced by the Warren Court. The Court not only spoke to these issues, but attacked them systematically and, by and large, successfully. In dealing with these matters, the Supreme Court acted with the strong support of many sectors of society, such as the civil rights and welfare rights movements. It did not, and could not, act without such political and social support. Law reflects and is reflected in social movements. Indeed, the federal courts often looked to the executive and legislative branches for support during the most critical times of change.

Nevertheless, in my opinion, it was the Warren Court and the lower federal courts of that era that acted as a catalyst for these bold reforms. The federal courts inspired and protected the people who sought to implement those changes. To put it another way, constitutional and statutory law became both an object as well as a subject. Employing that law, the federal judiciary created a centrifugal force for change, and was itself inspired and empowered by those political and social changes. Owen Fiss's scholarship can surely be seen as deriving from many of the Warren Court's decisions, and especially from the vision of judicial decision-making created by that Court.

Today, it is almost impossible to conceive of law in these terms. The Fissian argument—a heroic position to be sure—that profound social change, justice, can be accomplished through judicial action, has taken a serious beating. Even many people who originally held this view have come to doubt the ability of courts to change the world of social reality. The tension is acute between the vision of constitutional interpretation as an engine of social progress, on the one hand, and the fear that harnessing it through judicial action to serve that role is, on the other hand, seriously counterproductive. Faith in public reason has been destroyed. The strongly held belief that the judiciary can and should use reason to give concrete meaning to constitutional values has been discarded.

A constitutional program that was so revolutionary, as was the Warren Court's program, is certain to face powerful opposition. The assault began in the early 1960s. By 1980, the Warren Court's jurisprudence was essentially gutted. As only one example, the Burger and Rehnquist Courts attacked *Brown* and its progeny. Although the Court did not expressly overrule *Brown*, it ruled, for example, that it is constitutional in some circumstances for a school system to contain a large number of all-black and all-white schools.[9] The Rehnquist Court shifted the emphasis of *Brown*, indeed turned it topsy-turvy, and, in so doing, severely limited the nature of the remedy. As a result, *Brown* has lost much of its strength, energy, and moral power.

In other areas, such as freedom of speech, the Rehnquist Court created new power for the state and certain private interests. The Court's strong commitment to what Justice Brennan called "uninhibited, robust, and wide-open"[10] debate, for example, has been severely cut back, and even gutted.

In the criminal context, the Warren Court precedents have fared no better. The Rehnquist Court has shifted the balance of advantage in the criminal process strongly in favor of the state. For example, restrictions on the investigatory power of the police have been almost totally removed. Fourth Amendment protections against unreasonable searches and seizures and Fifth Amendment bars against self-incrimination have been narrowly construed. The Sixth Amendment right to counsel has also

---

[9] *See, e.g.*, Pasadena City Bd. of Ed. v. Spangler, 427 U.S. 424 (1976) (finding the District Court could not require the school district to rearrange its attendance zones annually to insure a desirable racial mix in the schools); Milliken v. Bradley, 418 U.S. 717 (1974) (busing public school students to effectuate desegregation could only extend across district lines where there was *actual evidence* that multiple districts deliberately engaged in a policy of segregation).

[10] *N.Y. Times Co.*, 376 U.S. at 270.

been severely compromised. The ban on the death penalty has essentially been removed. Moreover, Rehnquist, both as Chief Justice and as head of the Judicial Conference of the United States, attempted to institute a series of "procedural reforms" to speed up that process. To a large extent, he succeeded. Over 1,000 convicted persons have been executed from 1976 through 2006.[11]

These changes, of course, are only a sample of the success that the Rehnquist Court[12] had in destroying the vision and jurisprudence of the Warren Court. Unfortunately, the new Roberts Court has not missed a beat in following Rehnquist's lead. Mirroring the efforts of the Rehnquist Court, the Roberts Court continues to attempt to rid *Brown* of all of its moral, legal, and political strength. On June 29, 2007, for example, a bitterly divided Supreme Court, by a vote of 5 to 4, invalidated voluntary integration plans in the school districts of Seattle and metropolitan Louisville, ruling that using a student's race to govern the availability of a place at a desired public school, even for the purpose of preventing resegregation, violated the Fourteenth Amendment guarantee of equal protection.[13] Both programs had been upheld by lower federal courts and were similar to plans in place in hundreds of school districts around the country. Chief Justice Roberts, who wrote the opinion of the Court, claimed, in a bizarre and obviously incorrect statement, that his decision was "more faithful to the heritage of Brown"[14] than the dissenter's view. Justice Breyer, in his dissent, correctly argued that the decision was a radical step away from settled law and would strip local communities of the tools they need and have used for many years to prevent resegregation of other public schools. Predicting that the ruling would "substitute for present calm a disruptive round of race-related litigation,"[15] he said, "This is a decision that the Court and the nation will come to regret."[16]

The Roberts Court's 2007 decisions in other areas demonstrate a complete rejection of Fiss's vision of the role of courts in our society.

---

[11] *Executions Since 1976*, DEATH PENALTY INFORMATIONAL CENTER, Mar. 7, 2004, http://www.deathpenaltyinfo.org/article.php?&did=2026.#exe (last visited Mar. 7, 2004).

[12] In a biting critique published in *The New Republic* in 1982, Charles Krauthammer, the conservative essayist, and Owen Fiss charged that Rehnquist "repudiates precedents frequently and openly, and if that is impossible (because the precedent represents a tradition that neither the Court nor society is prepared to abandon), then he distorts them." Owen Fiss & Charles Krauthammer, *The Rehnquist Court*, THE NEW REPUBLIC, Mar. 10, 1982, at 15.

[13] Parents Involved in Cmty. Schs. v. Seattle Sch. Dist. No. 1, 127 S. Ct. 2738 (2007).

[14] *Id.* at 2767.

[15] *Id.* at 2800 (Breyer, J., dissenting).

[16] *Id.* at 2837.

On campaign finance, for example, the Court handed a major victory to corporations and wealthy individuals—again by a 5 to 4 vote.[17] The Court ruled that the restriction on corporate and union sponsored television advertising contained in the McCain-Feingold campaign finance law threatened to curb core political speech. The provision could be constitutional, Chief Justice Roberts argued, only if interpreted narrowly to apply exclusively to advertisements that are "susceptible of no reasonable interpretation other than as an appeal to vote for or against a specific candidate."[18] The dissenters correctly argued that the ruling would open the door to a flood of corporate and union money in the guise of the "sham" issue advertisements that the law was designed to stop. The case effectively overruled a major part of the Act as well as *McConnell v. Federal Election Commission*,[19] the 2003 Supreme Court decision that upheld it. The ruling will make it easier for corporations and lobbyists to purchase the policies they want from Congress.[20]

Unfortunately, another striking feature of the Roberts Court has been its often contemptuous attitude toward common people looking for justice. As only one example, the Court ruled that an individual who

---

[17] Fed. Election Comm'n v. Wis. Right to Life, Inc., 127 S. Ct. 2652 (2007).

[18] *Id.* at 2655.

[19] McConnell v. Fed. Election Comm'n, 540 U.S. 93 (2003).

[20] In other areas as well, the Roberts Court has certainly not been progressive. Corporations also won repeatedly over consumers and small stockholders. For example, the Court overturned a jury's award of $79.5 million in punitive damages against Philip Morris. Philip Morris USA v. Williams, 127 S. Ct. 1057 (2007). The Oregon Supreme Court had upheld the award, calling Philip Morris's forty years of denying the connection between smoking and cancer "extraordinarily reprehensible." Williams v. Philip Morris, Inc., 127 P.3d 1165, 1177 (Or. 2006). Justice Breyer's majority opinion found that the Oregon jury that gave the award to the widow of a lifelong smoker might have improperly calculated the figure to punish the cigarette maker for harm to other smokers as well.

Two other decisions made it even more difficult for investors to sue companies, executives, and underwriters when they suspect securities fraud or unlawful manipulation. In *Tellabs, Inc. v. Makor Issues & Rights, Ltd.*, 127 S. Ct. 2499 (2007), the Court, in an 8 to 1 opinion, ruled that shareholders must show "cogent and compelling evidence" of intent to defraud in order to withstand dismissal of their suit. In *Credit Suisse Sec. (USA) LLC v. Billing*, 127 S. Ct. 2383 (2007), the Court, in a 7 to 1 opinion, dismissed a shareholder's anti-trust suit that accused ten leading investment banks of conspiring to fix the price and terms for initial public offerings. The Court held that the challenged behavior fell within the regulatory domain of the Securities and Exchange Commission, thus making the banks generally immune from antitrust liability. Finally, in another example of a ruling that will enrich companies at the expense of consumers, the Court overturned—by a 5 to 4 vote—a ninety-six-year-old precedent under which it was always illegal for a manufacturer and a retailer to agree on minimum retail prices. The legality of price maintenance will now be judged case by case for its impact on competition. Leegin Creative Leather Prods. v. PSKS, Inc., 127 S. Ct. 2705 (2007).

filed his appeal within the deadline set by a federal judge was out of luck because the judge had mistakenly given the wrong date.[21] This is, of course, an unusually unjust and harsh decision that overturned two Supreme Court precedents from the 1960s on missed deadlines.[22] Those cases had supported a "unique circumstances" excuse for missing deadlines. Clearly, following an order from a federal judge has to be seen as a very "unique circumstance."

It is difficult to imagine, let alone remember, when the most privileged members of society—corporations, the wealthy, whites who want to attend school only with other whites—have had such a successful Supreme Court term. Indeed, Chief Justice Roberts's first term may even surpass many of the victories for these forces during the Rehnquist Court's reign.[23] These opinions, of course, are clear rejections of Fiss's heroic view of the judiciary and the constitutional demand for justice.

The Roberts Court's 2008 decisions, while not necessarily as offensive to the rule of law—in Fissian terms—as the Court's 2007 decisions, nevertheless demonstrate a striking disregard of Fiss's vision of constitutional adjudication.[24] Indeed, the 2008 term brought a spectacularly mixed set of results. Unlike the 2007 term, there was not a glut of 5 to 4 decisions. Only 11 cases out of 67 were decided by one-vote margins.[25] Moreover, Chief Justice Roberts did not get his way on several high profile cases.[26] For example, over the dissents of Chief Justice Roberts, the Supreme Court granted the Guantánamo detainees access to federal

---

[21] Bowles v. Russell, 127 S. Ct. 2360 (2007).

[22] Harris Truck Lines, Inc. v. Cherry Meat Packers, Inc., 371 U.S. 215 (1962) (*per curiam*) and Thompson v. INS, 375 U.S. 384 (1964) (*per curiam*).

[23] Editorial, *Justice Denied*, N.Y. TIMES, July 5, 2007, at A12.

[24] The 2008 term seems somewhat muddled. The Court issued some highly disturbing rulings on subjects like voting rights and gun control along with important decisions supporting our basic liberties in other areas, including the rights of detainees at Guantánamo Bay, Cuba. I believe the key to understanding the term lies in the fragility of the Court's center. Some of the most important decisions came on 5 to 4 votes.

[25] *See* Linda Greenhouse, *On Court that Defied Labeling, Kennedy Made the Boldest Mark*, N.Y. TIMES, June 29, 2008, at A1.

[26] Justice Kennedy, not Chief Justice Roberts, became the Court's most important actor. In the 2007 term, Justice Kennedy dissented only twice in 68 decisions and voted with the majority in all 24 cases decided by votes of 5 to 4. In the 2008 term, however, Justice Kennedy dissented 10 times (compared with the chief justice's seven dissents) including in four of the 5 to 4 decisions. In addition, there was less unanimity than in the 2007 term. The Court decided a little under 30 percent of the cases without dissent. In the 2007 term, the Court decided a little over 40 percent of the cases without dissent, and a little over half of the cases in 2005-2006 term. In the 2008 term, the Court decided the fewest cases since the 1953-54 term.

court[27] and rejected capital punishment for the rape of a child.[28] As horrible as that crime is, the Court wisely drew a clear line and said that capital punishment can only be imposed for crimes in which the victim's life was taken.

On the other hand, in the case for which history may ultimately remember the 2008 term—the decision interpreting the Second Amendment to protect the right to own a gun for private use—the Court's "conservative" block won a stunning victory. Justice Antonin Scalia, writing for the 5 to 4 majority, ruled that there is a constitutional right to keep a loaded handgun at home for self-defense.[29] In reaching this conclusion, the Court declared the District of Columbia's ban on handguns to be unconstitutional.[30]

In addition, the Court struck down a law meant to level the playing field when rich candidates pay for their campaigns.[31] The law at issue imposed special rules in races with candidates who finance their own campaigns. Those candidates are required to disclose more information, and their opponents are allowed to raise more money. The law allows opponents of candidates for the House who spend more than $350,000 of their own money to receive triple the usual amounts—$6,900 rather than $2,300—from individual contributors when a complex statutory formula is met. The law also waives expenditures from political parties.

Justice Samuel A. Alito, Jr., writing for the majority, found unacceptable the asymmetry imposed by the law. The law was a response to Supreme Court rulings that forbid limits on the amount that candidates can spend on their own behalf. But in *Davis v. Federal Election Commission*,[32] Justice Alito ruled that the legislative response was unconstitutional because it "imposes an unprecedented penalty on any candidate who robustly exercises [free speech rights guaranteed by the] First Amendment."[33] Rich candidates, Justice Alito wrote, must "choose between the First Amendment right to engage in unfettered political

---

[27] Boumediene v. Bush, 128 S. Ct. 2229 (2008).

[28] Kennedy v. Louisiana, No. 07-343, 2008 WL 2511282 (U.S. June, 25, 2008).

[29] Justice Scalia's opinion was signed by Chief Justice John G. Roberts, Jr., Anthony M. Kennedy, Clarence Thomas and Samuel A. Alito, Jr.

[30] District of Columbia v. Heller, 128 S. Ct. 2783 (2008).

[31] Davis v. Fed. Election Comm'n., 128 S. Ct. 2759 (2008).

[32] *Id.*

[33] *Id.* at 2764.

speech and subjection to discriminatory fundraising limitations."[34] To put it another way, money determines free speech rights.[35]

Two other major decisions of the term, in which the Court upheld Kentucky's method of execution by lethal injection,[36] and Indiana's law requiring voters to produce photographic identification at the polls,[37] can be described as denying the Fissian notion of justice.[38] Both decisions raise serious questions about whether the Supreme Court is searching for constitutional justice.

Baze v. Rees,[39] the lethal injection decision, is particularly disturbing. Despite evidence that the procedure Kentucky uses can cause excruciating pain, the Court ruled that it does not violate the Eighth Amendment prohibition on cruel-and-unusual punishment. This was a squandered chance to set rules requiring that executions be carried out as humanely as possible.

The Supreme Court abandoned its special role in protecting voter rights when it rejected a challenge to Indiana's harsh and undemocratic voter identification law. Critics warned that the law, which bans anyone without a government-issued photographic identification from voting, would disenfranchise poor people, minorities, and the elderly, all of whom disproportionably lack drivers' licenses. The critics, of course, are factually correct. In Indiana's presidential primary, shortly after this decision came out, many people were turned away at the polls for not having acceptable identification.

In these two cases, however, the Court did leave room for individual rebuttal. In both the lethal injection case and the voter identification case, the Court found the evidence insufficient to declare the challenged practices unconstitutional. But the Court left the door open, at least theoretically, for more fully substantiated lawsuits in the future.[40]

---

[34] *Id.*

[35] In addition, corporations fared especially well in the 2008 term. The Court reduced the punitive-damages award against Exxon Mobil for the 1989 Exxon Valdez spill from $2.5 billion to about $500 million, surely a pittance for the energy company. Exxon Shipping Co. v. Baker, 128 S. Ct. 2605 (2008). In the process, the Court decided that in maritime cases, punitive damages should not exceed the actual damages in a case. It is a rule that violates the very purpose of punitive damages: to punish and deter bad conduct.

[36] Baze v. Rees, 128 S. Ct. 1520 (2008).

[37] Crawford v. Marion County Election Bd., 128 S. Ct. 1610 (2008).

[38] The Court decided both cases by large, more comfortable margins than some of the other important cases. *Baze* was a 7 to 2 decision and *Crawford* was a 6 to 3 decision.

[39] *Baze*, 128 S. Ct. 1520.

[40] The term did include some positive, unanticipated developments. In the 2007 term, a 5 to 4 decision, *Ledbetter v. Goodyear Tire and Rubber Co.*, 127 S. Ct. 2162 (2007), im-

Even with some unpredictable decisions in the 2008 term on matters concerned with process and precedent, the Roberts Court demonstrated that in cases raising ideological questions—cases concerned with justice in the Fissian sense—the Court remains ideologically divided about its role and interpretive methods.

Indeed, to many, it is almost inconceivable to believe that the judiciary can continue to be a positive force in giving concrete meaning to our constitutional values through reasoned analysis. For many members of the profession, both in practice and in the academy, disaffection from the federal judiciary runs deep. Under such conditions, therefore, it is very difficult to pay respect to and admire the present body of constitutional law. It is difficult to see how the courts, particularly the federal courts, can continue to speak authoritatively to the burning issues that divide us, and can successfully attempt to ameliorate the great tensions in our society when many feel so alienated from the courts. Yet, for the most optimistic of us, it is always possible to believe that the federal courts will once again become a source of moral authority and hope. Can we create a new vision of what might be by looking at what was and what is?

In thinking about this predicament, I cannot help but think about Owen Fiss. While he means many things to many students, professors, and practicing lawyers, one of the most important aspects of his public life, which touches many of us deeply and pushes the cynicism away, is his loyalty to the federal courts both as an institution of justice and as an institution of limited power. As a constitutional scholar, he resists

---

posed unrealistically tight time limits on workers' ability to file pay discrimination cases. In that case, the Court issued a much criticized ruling against a woman who was discriminated against in pay, baselessly deciding that she had filed her complaint too late. The *Ledbetter* opinion caused a strong response. Indeed, the first bill the Obama Administration signed into law overturned the decision in *Ledbetter*. Christina Bellantoni, *Obama Signs His First Law on Equal Pay in Workplace*, WASH. TIMES, Jan. 30, 2009, at A06. Additionally, the plan to use *Ledbetter* by groups opposed to the Court's jurisprudence as a focal point about the lack of justice in the Roberts Court's rulings was weakened somewhat by several discrimination cases in the 2008 term that favored employees. For example, in two cases, the Court ruled that federal statutes cover claims of retaliation against employees who complain to management about retaliation. Gomez-Perez v. Potter, 128 S. Ct. 1931 (2008); CBOCS West, Inc. v. Humphries, 128 S. Ct. 1951 (2008).

The term also included several favorable rulings for criminal defendants. For example, the Court, in a 7 to 2 decision, overturned a Louisiana death row inmate's conviction and gave added strength to its rule against racial discrimination in jury selection. Snyder v. Louisiana, 128 S. Ct. 1203 (2008). Only Justices Scalia and Thomas dissented. In other cases, the Court limited the application of two federal money laundering statutes. Regaldo Cuellar v. United States, 128 S. Ct. 1994 (2008); United States v. Santos, 128 S. Ct. 2020 (2008); The Court also allowed federal judges added discretion to show leniency in sentencing defendants for crimes involving cocaine. Kimbrough v. United States, 128 S. Ct. 558 (2007).

these cynical views of constitutional law tenaciously. He always remains faithful to the prospect of achieving justice, even within the confines of this dilemma.

His scholarship is an attempt to convince those who now reject law that once again judges can and will perform their most important function—giving meaning to our public values through reason. By so doing, his scholarship confronts more modern jurisprudential movements, which in the face of these developments, have turned away from law altogether. Advocates of the Critical Legal Studies School denied the integrity of law and its unique claim to public reason, portraying law as politics. The scholarship of the Critical Race Theorists and the branch of the Law and Literature movement that reduced law to some form of storytelling had a similar approach. The Civic Republican School of the Burger-Rehnquist era, rejecting the judicial role, placed its trust in the more political agencies, including Congress, to give specific content to our public values. The Law and Economics Movement exalted the market and saw "law as efficiency." While more conservative in its approach than these other movements, it grew out of the same disenchantment with the Supreme Court as the other above-mentioned movements.

For the past four decades, Owen Fiss has analyzed the place of adjudication in American life and defended the role of the judge as the main instrument of public reason.[41] His achievements speak for the correctness of his views. His faith is the torch that leads our way and sustains us through these dark times.

There are, of course, other qualities of heart and mind that Owen Fiss possesses and that inspire many to use law both as an end in itself and as an instrument for achieving justice. Owen Fiss's contributions to constitutional law, to federal courts, and to the search for substantive justice have many levels. His writings span a broad range of issues—free speech, equality and desegregation, Supreme Court history, and various strands of jurisprudence. He believes passionately in the values we identify with freedom, liberty, and autonomy—such as equality, procedural fairness, freedom of speech and the like—and he has attempted to protect and perpetuate these values by writing and teaching about them and acting on them whenever the opportunity presents itself.

Moreover, Owen Fiss is thoroughly devoted to the federal courts as a co-equal branch of government. His articles and books reflect a set of skills that attest to the details that constitute the law in a manner

---

[41] For an analysis of his work, see, Symposium, *Fiss's Way: The Scholarship of Owen Fiss*, 58 U. Miami L. Rev. 1 (2003).

that is meant to strengthen the courts in the eyes of the public and the profession alike. To Owen Fiss, this is significant both constitutively and instrumentally. He believes that opinions should be written in a technically correct manner by employing the craft of law as an end in itself, and so that opinions will enhance a court's capacity to do its socially important work.

Perhaps even more significantly, Owen Fiss is, in the best sense of the phrase, a constitutional law diplomat. He is a person who is capable of grasping a multiplicity of conflicting principles, including some of which are concerned with the health of our system of constitutional law and the courts' role in protecting and perpetuating that system. At the same time, he pushes the vision that a judge's duty is not merely to speak to the law, but also to act on it. In his scholarship, Owen Fiss always takes the high road and lives his life through principled judgment and action. In his writings, he always selects his words in a way that will minimize the confrontation with other branches of government. Owen Fiss clearly understands that major reforms require a coordination of government powers. He also respects the traditions of law and, thus, follows the principle of stare decisis—but not in a wooden way. Justice always remains the overriding goal.

Owen Fiss is equally as much a great lawyer as a constitutional law diplomat. The mastery of the craft of law requires a mixture of the theoretical and the technical. Owen Fiss is a master of both sets of skills. He knows the cases, the statutes and the theories behind them, and how they interact. He also understands how the legal system works, how it ought to work, and how to make it better. In his distinguished public career as a constitutional scholar of the first order, Owen Fiss constantly blends all of these remarkable skills.

I first met Owen Fiss in the early 1970s when I was a first year student at the University of Chicago Law School in what was inappropriately labeled a property class. What I soon discovered, however, was that it was not a course in the technical aspects of property law, but rather a course in constitutional and moral theory. When I think about that course and other classes I took from him, and when I think about his scholarship, I am often reminded of a Platonic dialogue—*Gorgias*[42]—which I teach in my jurisprudence course. To me, and I suspect many others, the theory of that dialogue is another reason to celebrate Owen Fiss's work.

Gorgias himself is a professor of oratory, and the dialogue opens with a discussion between Socrates and Gorgias on the nature of his art.

---

[42] PLATO, GORGIAS (Walter Hamilton trans., Penguin Classics 1960).

It soon becomes clear, however, that the true concern of *Gorgias* is with ethics, and its scope cannot be better indicated than by a quotation from Socrates' concluding words.

> All the other theories put forward in our long conversation have been refuted, and this conclusion alone stands firm, that one should avoid doing wrong with more care than being wronged, and that the supreme object of [an individual's] efforts, in public and in private life, must be the reality rather than the appearance of goodness.[43]

The dialogue is in fact a passionate defense by Socrates of the ideals for which he gave his life: that man's business on earth is to discover and do what is right. To Socrates, therefore, it is better to suffer wrong than to do wrong. If we ask what this ideal has to do with oratory, the answer is that in Socrates' view it stands in direct opposition to the ends which the oratorical training of the day was adapted to serve. Indeed, to Socrates, a person will not be justified in embarking on a public career unless she possesses a knowledge of moral values and an appropriate vision which will enable her to improve the character of the community.

Owen Fiss is one of the few people I have ever known who actually attempts to live his life in harmony with the stringent moral and ethical requirements envisioned by Socrates. As his scholarship and teaching attest, he believes passionately in the importance of doing what is right and in treating each person he encounters with respect and dignity. He lives the Socratic ideal in all aspects of his public and private life. He is a role model for his students and colleagues alike.

Perhaps his most outstanding characteristic is that he cares so intensely. He cares about people, institutions, and ideas. Moreover, he values people not for what they can give him but for their individual, intrinsic worth. His loyalty to his friends is uncompromising and enduring. This is so not out of mere habit, but because of the intensity and depth of his feelings. He values ideas because they are good and important and affect human beings, not simply because of the intellectual puzzles they produce.

All of these positive attributes are reflected in his scholarship and even in the critical comments of his opponents. To Owen Fiss, constitutional law and adjudication is more than an object of scholarly pursuit; it is an ideal of behavior between the state and the individual. The adjudicative

---

[43] *Id.* at 148.

process is a method of giving meaning and content to our social values. This book honors Owen Fiss for all of his remarkable public and private qualities. The essays in this book offer a response to those who have lost faith in the Warren Court's conception of law.

The essays selected for this book, and Fiss's ideas as demonstrated in his scholarship, speak not only to the courts, but to all of our government institutions and to all of our citizens. They speak directly to our constitutional democracy. Fiss's ideas pose a significant barrier to the Bush Administration's severe attacks on the rule of law.[44] While the nation is generally happy about the new president-elect and his plans as disclosed in the recent presidential campaign, his administration faces severe challenges to the rule of law. Our nation remains in the "shadow of war," a war that raises serious questions as to whether President Bush falsely and intentionally convinced our nation of its necessity.[45] The Bush Administration has created and developed an Executive Branch that has

---

[44] The rule of law is a call to political justice and has remained, over the centuries, a vibrant ideal of democratic society. The central core of the principle embodies the enduring values of regularity and restraint—of treating like cases alike and inhibiting the arbitrary actions of government officials. These thoughts are traditionally captured in the slogan of "a government of laws, not men." When I refer to the rule of law, I also mean to refer to the Constitution, the document which creates and embodies the public morality of the nation. The rule of law includes both the words of the Constitution and its animating principles—those that are necessarily "inferred from the overall structure of the Constitution." Owen Fiss, *The Fragility of Law*, 54 YALE L. REP. 40 (2007). In addition, it includes specific congressional enactments, "that articulate the governing principles of American society. These principles are laden with a special normative value that derives from the role they play in defining our national identity—what it means to be American." *Id.*

[45] Indeed, two recently released United States Senate Select Committee on Intelligence reports conclude that the Bush Administration gave inaccurate assessments of the threat posed to the United States by Iraq and Iran. The reports followed five years of investigation by the committee into the Bush Administration's use of intelligence preceding the invasion of Iraq in March 2003. The first report, 170 pages in length, examines statements made by United States officials and finds that many of the comments were not supported by adequate intelligence. Report on Whether Public Statements Regarding Iraq by U.S. Government Officials were Substantiated by Intelligence Information Together with Additional and Minority Views, S. Rep. No. 110-345 (2008). It accuses President Bush, Vice-President Cheney and other high level executive branch officials of repeatedly overestimating the threat posed by Iraq following the September 11 attacks. All eight Democratic committee members and two Republican committee members endorsed the report. Senator John D. Rockefeller IV (Democrat from West Virginia), chairman of the committee, made the following statement: "In making the case for war, the Administration repeatedly presented intelligence as fact when in reality it was unsubstantiated, contradicted, or even non-existent. As a result, the American people were led to believe that the threat from Iraq was much greater than actually existed." Press Release, U.S. Senate Select Comm. on Intelligence, Senate Intelligence Committee Unveils Final Phase II Reports on Prewar Intelligence (June 5, 2008), *available at* http://intelligence.senate.gov/press/record.cfm?id=298775.

continuously attempted to dismantle our constitutional system of checks and balances; that has claimed the power and authority to torture prisoners in United States custody; and has held people in prison indefinitely without charging them with a crime or allowing them the right of habeas corpus. It is also alarming to realize the unprecedented frequency[46] with which President Bush has signed congressional enactments into law while brazenly signaling his position that giving those enactments their intended effect would cut impermissibly into his breathtakingly inflated conception of illimitable presidential power and prerogative. Indeed, virtually every one of these enactments are entirely constitutional exercises of Congress's power to structure the Executive Branch, regulate the branch's military and civilian investigations, prosecutions, or detentions, or engage in Congress's other undoubted heads of lawmaking authority.

It was Richard Nixon who said, "When the President does it, that means that it is not illegal." This Administration, led by President George W. Bush and his partner and fellow proponent of an imperial Executive Branch, Vice President Dick Cheney,[47] operating behind the imposing

---

The second report describes clandestine intelligence meetings by the Department of Defense's (DOD) Office of the Under Secretary of Defense for Policy, a group charged with gathering intelligence on Iraq and Iran. Report on Intelligence Activities Relating to Iraq Conducted by the Policy Counterterrorism Evaluation Group and the Office of Special Plans Within the Office of the Under Secretary of Defense for Policy Together with Additional and Minority Views, S. Rep. No. 110-346 (2008). It concludes that DOD officials failed to investigate sufficiently the intelligence gathered and that they conducted activities without the knowledge of the Intelligence Community or the State Department. See also, GORE VIDAL, IMPERIAL AMERICA (2004).

[46] President Bush has used the signing statements to assert a right to bypass more than 1,100 sections of laws. All previous presidents combined challenged about 600 sections of bills. Charlie Savage, Bush Declares Exceptions to Sections of Two Bills He Signed Into Law, N.Y. TIMES, Oct. 15, 2008, at A17.

[47] Vice President Cheney has not only placed himself above Congress and the courts, but even President Bush. For the past six years, he has been defying a presidential order requiring Executive Branch agencies to account for the classified information they handle. When the Federal agency that enforces this rule tried to do its job, the Vice President proposed abolishing the agency. Cheney then suggested that the Vice President is not a member of the Executive Branch but rather that he is the titular president of the Senate—a lawmaker—and thus does not have to answer to the Executive Branch. Cheney was, of course, invoking a double standard: frequently claiming executive privilege when accused of being overly secretive, and then claiming not to be a member of the Executive Branch. Mr. Cheney's office has regularly denied routine requests for data on its classifications of internal documents by the Information and Security Oversight Office of the National Archives, the agency that oversees the classification and declassification of data. The National Archives is required to collect this data under a presidential executive order. After a public outcry over this absurd argument, Cheney now claims that he is not required to cooperate with the National Archives officials seeking the data because he is a member of the Executive Branch with power vested in him by the President. Jim

barrier of national security, took this questionable and dangerous statement to heart and put it into widespread practice.

For the first time in American history, the Executive Branch claimed authority under the Constitution to set aside laws permanently, including the laws prohibiting torture and warrantless eavesdropping on Americans. The idea that a President, like a king, can do no wrong, an idea decisively rejected at the nation's birth, has reemerged to justify torture and indefinite detention when authorized by the President.

The courts have intervened to check some of these executive abuses, but only to a limited extent and certainly not in a manner that would satisfy the Fissian notion of law as justice. In June 2004, the Supreme Court ruled that prisoners at Guantánamo had the right to challenge the legal and factual basis of their detention in United States courts.[48] It held that the habeas corpus statute gives federal courts jurisdiction over territory that is functionally part of the United States. In 2006, the Supreme Court put a second roadblock in the way of unfettered executive power. That case,[49] brought by Salem Ahmed Hamdan, a Yemeni charged with conspiring to help Al Qaeda, reaffirmed, to a limited extent, that even in time of war, the law is what the Constitution, the statutes, and the Geneva Conventions say it is, and not what the President wants it to be. The Bush Administration argued that Hamdan and the other prisoners at Guantánamo are not covered by either Congressional laws governing military trials or by the Geneva Convention on treatment of prisoners of war.[50] Instead, Mr. Hamdan was put on trial before a military tribunal where defendants can be excluded from the proceedings and convicted on evidence kept secret from them and their lawyers. Prosecutors can also rely on hearsay, coerced testimony, and unsworn statements.

Rutenberg, *White House Drops Vice President's Dual Role Argument as Moot*, N.Y. TIMES, June 28, 2007, at A15. For a detailed analysis of Cheney's unprecedented assertions of power, see the four-part series in the Washington Post. Barton Gellman & Jo Becker, *A Different Understanding with the President*, WASH. POST, June 24, 2007, at A1; Barton Gellman & Jo Becker, *The Unseen Path to Cruelty*, WASH. POST, June 25, 2007, at A1; Barton Gellman & Jo Becker, *A Strong Push from Backstage*, WASH. POST, June 26, 2007, at A1; Barton Gellman & Jo Becker, *Leaving No Tracks*, WASH. POST, June 27, 2007, at A1.

[48] Rasul v. Bush, 542 U.S. 466 (2004) (remanding the case to the district court for reconsideration of the merits of the prisoners' claims in the first instance in accordance with the Supreme Court's decision).

[49] Hamdan v. Rumsfeld, 548 U.S. 557 (2006) (finding the structures and procedures of the military commissions set up by the Bush Administration to try Guantánamo Bay detainees violate the Uniform Code of Military Justice and Common Article 3 of the Third Geneva Convention).

[50] Geneva Conventions Relative to the Treatment of Prisoners of War, art. 3, Aug. 12, 1949, 6 U.S.T. 3316, 75 U.N.T.S. 135.

The Supreme Court held that these rules violate the standards that Congress set forth in the Uniform Code of Military Justice, which requires tribunals to offer the same protections, whenever practicable, as other military trials. The Court found that the military commissions were improperly established by the President without Congressional authorization. It also ruled that the tribunals fall short of the kind of trial required by the Geneva Conventions, rejecting the Bush Administration's claim that these venerable international standards cannot be invoked in an American court. Indeed, the Justices rejected the Administration's constant refrain—made in everything from its "enemy combatant" policies to its defense of the National Security Agency's domestic spying programs— that President Bush has the authority to trample on existing laws as he sees fit under 1) the congressional grant to use force after September 11, 2001; 2) the exigencies of wartime; or 3) simply the inherent power of the presidency.

In September 2006, in response to the *Hamdan* decision, and after a fierce campaign by the Bush Administration, Congress passed a bill to grant the President authorization for the establishment of military commissions. The bill also stripped the federal courts of jurisdiction over the pending as well as any new Guantánamo cases. In February 2007, the Court of Appeals for the District of Columbia Circuit ruled that the law, passed in September, had stripped the detainees of the right to habeas corpus.[51] In April 2007, the Supreme Court declined to review that federal appeals court decision. On June 29, 2007, however, the Supreme Court, in a surprise decision, rescinded that order and agreed to hear those claims.[52] The Court rarely grants such motions for reconsideration. There has not been a similar reversal by the Supreme Court in decades. The Court, of course, offered no explanation. The case set up a test of one of the central premises of the Bush Administration's detention policies: that it can hold "enemy combatants" without allowing them habeas corpus proceedings. It raised the question of whether the Constitution protects the people detained at Guantánamo Bay. This decision set the stage for a legal battle that would clearly shape debates in the Bush Administration about whether to close the detention center. The Supreme Court heard oral argument on December 5, 2007.[53]

---

[51] Boumediene v. Bush, 476 F. 3d 981 (D.C. Cir. 2007) (rejecting claims of Guantánamo detainees that they had a right to challenge their detention in American courts).

[52] *Id., cert. granted*, 127 S. Ct. 3078 (2007) (mem.).

[53] Linda Greenhouse, *Justices Ready to Answer Detainee Rights Question*, N.Y. Times, Dec. 6, 2007, at A32.

On June 12, 2008,[54] the Supreme Court handed down its opinion in this case and again delivered another—its third consecutive—rejection to the Bush Administration's handling of the detainees at Guantánamo Bay. In *Boumediene v. Bush*,[55] the Court ruled 5 to 4 that the prisoners there have a constitutional right to go to federal court to challenge their continued detention. In reaching this result, the Court declared unconstitutional a provision of the Military Commission Act of 2006 that had, at the Bush Administration's behest, stripped the federal courts of jurisdiction to hear habeas corpus petitions from the detainees seeking to challenge their designation as "enemy combatants."

Congress and the Bush Administration had passed a shortened alternative to a habeas procedure for the prisoners in the 2005 Detainee Treatment Act. But Justice Anthony M. Kennedy, writing for the majority, rejected that alternative procedure. He claimed that procedure "falls short of being a constitutionally adequate substitute"[56] because it failed to offer "the fundamental procedural protections of habeas corpus."[57] The decision, joined by Justices John Paul Stevens, David H. Souter, Ruth Bader Ginsburg, and Stephen G. Breyer, was categorical in its rejection of the Administration's basic arguments. Indeed, the Court went so far as to repudiate the fundamental legal basis for the Administration's strategy of housing prisoners captured in Afghanistan and elsewhere at the United States Naval base in Guantánamo, Cuba, where Justice Department lawyers advised the Bush White House that domestic law would never reach.[58]

In addition, in 2006, a federal district court judge ruled[59] that the President committed a serious felony and violated the Constitution by authorizing the National Security Council to monitor the phone calls and e-mail messages of Americans, which, at that time, he did for four

---

[54] In another case decided on June 12, 2008, a unanimous United States Supreme Court ruled that United States citizens detained by United States military forces in Iraq have the right to habeas corpus review by a United States federal court of the legality of their custody. But, because they are accused of terrorism crimes under Iraqi criminal law, the United States courts will not stop their transfer to Iraqi custody by United States military forces. Munaf v. Geren, 128 S. Ct. 2207 (2008).

[55] Boumediene v. Bush, 128 S. Ct. 2229 (2008).

[56] *Id.* at 2272.

[57] *Id.* at 2277.

[58] The decision, of course, left many important questions unanswered. *See infra* (Parts IV and V, The War Against Terrorism and the Rule of Law Section and the Fragility of Law Section).

[59] ACLU v. NSA, 438 F. Supp. 2d 754 (E.D. Mich. 2006).

years, without first obtaining warrants from the Foreign Intelligence Surveillance Court, as required by the Foreign Intelligence Surveillance Act (FISA). Justice Department lawyers argued that the National Security Council did not need warrants for what they called the Administration's "terrorist surveillance program" because of the President's "inherent powers" to order eavesdropping. Further rationalizing this practice, the Justice Department once again appealed to Congressional authorization to use military force against those responsible for the September 11, 2001 attacks.

On January 17, 2007, Attorney General Gonzalez unexpectedly declared that President Bush had ended the program and would again seek warrants in all cases. Exactly what kind of warrant—individual, as required by law, or broad-based, which is undoubtedly illegal—is as yet unknown. The action may have been designed to forestall a potentially adverse ruling by the Federal Appeals Court in Cincinnati (the Sixth Circuit), which had scheduled oral arguments for January 31, 2007. At that hearing, the Administration argued that the case is moot and should be dismissed, while reserving the right to restart the program at any time.

The judicial victory against the Executive Branch's extraordinarily broad assertion of power, however, proved short-lived. On July 6, 2007, a divided federal appeals court reversed the trial judge's order to shut down the National Security Agency's (NSA) program to wiretap the international communications of some Americans without warrants.[60] The majority, in a three-judge panel of the United States Court of Appeals for the Sixth Circuit, ruled on a narrow ground. The Court found that none of the plaintiffs—including lawyers and journalists—could show injury direct and concrete enough to allow them standing to sue. The majority did not rule on the merits of the case.

However, because it may be impossible for any plaintiff to demonstrate injury from the highly classified wiretapping program, the effect of the ruling is to insulate it from judicial scrutiny. Ironically, the program's secrecy is proving to be its best legal protection.[61]

Congress has not put up a decisive counter-force to this unprecedented assertion of presidential power.[62] Indeed, simultaneously with

---

[60] ACLU v. NSA, 493 F.3d 644 (6th Cir. 2007).

[61] Plaintiffs filed a petition for certiorari but the Supreme Court denied certiorari. ACLU v. NSA, 493 F.3d 644 (6th Cir. 2007), *petition for cert. filed*, 76 U.S.L.W. 3436 (U.S. Oct. 3, 2007), *cert. denied*, 76 U.S.L.W. 3438 (U.S. Feb. 19, 2008) (No. 07-468); *see also*, Linda Greenhouse, *Justices Will Hear Case on Evidence Suppression*, N.Y. TIMES, Feb. 20, 2008, at A15.

[62] At the end of June 2007, Congress, after six years of allowing the President to trample all legal and constitutional restraints on his power, finally asserted its authority. Congressional

this litigation over the warrantless monitoring of phone calls and e-mail messages, the Bush Administration continued pressuring Congress into passing legislation to legalize this clearly illegal practice. In August 2007, the Bush Administration seized on a secret court ruling that highlighted a technical way in which the 1978 law has allegedly not kept pace with the Internet era.

Under FISA, the government may freely monitor communications when both parties are outside the United States, but must get a warrant aimed at a specific person for communications that originate or end in this country. (The FISA court has rejected only one warrant request in the past several years.) On August 2, 2007, the Los Angeles Times reported that the FISA court had recently ruled that the law also requires that the government seek such a warrant for purely foreign communications that, nevertheless, move through American data networks.[63] The White House, instead of asking Congress to address this issue, sought to use it to destroy the 1978 spying law. It proposed giving the Attorney General absolute authority to order eavesdropping on any international telephone call or e-mail message, when he decides on his own that there is a "reasonable belief" that the target of the surveillance is outside of the United States. The Attorney General's decision would not be subject to court approval or any supervision. The Bush Administration insisted that Congress authorize this immediately. This is the same deliberate urgency it used to pressure Congress into passing the Patriot Act, without reading it, and the clearly dangerous Military Commissions Act of 2006. Both Senator Jay Rockefeller, the Chairman of the Senate Intelligence Committee, and Senator Russell Feingold, offered a reasonable alternative. Under that plan, in either case—international telephone calls or e-mail messages—the Attorney General would be able to get a broad warrant to intercept foreign communications routed through American networks for a limited period. At that point, he would be required to justify the spying in court. This proposal would have an expiration date so Congress could then consider what permanent changes, if any, might be needed to FISA. But, of course, the Bush Administration has had no interest in that

---

committees have issued subpoenas for documents and witnesses in two major cases and have asked for the first—and likely not the last—criminal investigation of an Executive Branch official who might have lied to Congress. The White House, of course, is claiming executive privilege and refusing to cooperate with these legitimate Congressional investigations. One of the investigations springs from Mr. Bush's decision to spy on Americans without a warrant and the other from the purge of United States attorneys. Editorial, *Abuse of Executive Privilege*, N.Y. TIMES, July 1, 2007, at 11.

[63] Greg Miller, *Special Court Restricts Spy Actions Overseas*, L.A. TIMES, Aug. 2, 2007, at A16.

constitutionally acceptable approach. Nevertheless, bowing to pressure from the Bush Administration, the Senate passed a bill that removed requirements for court approval when communications pass through the United States.[64]

On August 4, 2007, the House also approved the changes.[65] President Bush then signed the legislation into law.[66] The new law represented a power shift in terms of oversight and regulation of government surveillance. It required initial approval, not by the FISA court, but by the Director of National Intelligence, Mike McConnell, and the Attorney General, who at that time, was Alberto Gonzales. The FISA court's only role was to review and approve the procedures used by the government in the surveillance after it has been conducted. The Court would not scrutinize the cases of the individuals being monitored. The law also gave the Administration greater power to force the telecommunications companies to cooperate with spying operations.[67]

This new law for the first time provided a legal framework for much of the surveillance without warrants that was being conducted in secret by the NSA and outside FISA. It gave broad new powers to the Executive. Most telephone conversations to and from the United States are conducted over fiber-optic cables. The most efficient way for the government to eavesdrop on this traffic is to monitor giant telecommunications switches physically located in the United States. The new law changed the definition of what was considered "electronic surveillance" and thus allowed the government to eavesdrop on those conversations without warrants as long as the target of the government's surveillance was "reasonably believed" to be overseas. For example, if a person in Miami calls

---

[64] Greg Miller, *Senate Votes to Expand Spy Authority*, L.A. TIMES, Aug. 4, 2007, at A12.

[65] Carl Hulse & Edmund L. Andrews, *House Approves Changes in Eavesdropping Program*, N.Y. TIMES, Aug. 5, 2007, at A1.

[66] James Risen, *Bush Signs Law to Widen Reach for Wiretapping*, N.Y. TIMES, Aug. 6, 2007, at A1.

[67] The law, which was approved for a six month period, expired on February 16, 2008, when House Democrats allowed the law to lapse, and refused to grant the Bush Administration broader spying powers. Carl Huse, *House Leaves Surveillance Law to Expire*, N.Y. TIMES, Feb. 15, 2008, at A17. The expiration of the law in fact has little practical effect. Intelligence agencies are allowed to gather information for a year after initial eavesdropping authorization. Therefore, groups that have already been identified and authorized for surveillance continue to be monitored without a warrant. Intelligence agencies now only need to seek warrants under the original FISA laws for newly identified terrorist organizations. Eric Lichtblau, *Eavesdropping Law is Likely to Lapse*, N.Y. TIMES, Feb. 14, 2008, at A25.

someone in Paris, the NSA can eavesdrop on that conversation without a warrant as long as the NSA's target is the person in Paris.

Moreover, by redefining the meaning of "electronic surveillance," the new law narrowed the types of communications covered in FISA by indirectly giving the government the power to use intelligence collection methods far beyond wiretapping that previously required court approval if conducted inside the United States. These increased powers included the collection of business records, physical searches and so-called "trap and trace" operations that analyze specific calling patterns. The legislation, for example, allowed the government to demand the business records of an American in Detroit without a warrant if it claims that the search concerned its surveillance of a person who is in Berlin.[68]

The only encouraging notes are that the new law had a six-month expiration date and that the leaders of both houses of Congress claimed that they would start revising it immediately.[69] There is, however, a serious problem with this promise. None of the lawmakers have any idea of what eavesdropping is already occurring or what President Bush's justification was in the first place for ignoring the law and ordering warrantless spying after the September 11, 2001 attack.

The Bush Administration has refused to divulge how much warrantless spying it has been doing. Clearly, it is significantly more than President Bush has acknowledged. Americans have a right to know exactly how far their civil liberties have been breached and whether the warrantless spying included purely domestic eavesdropping. Moreover, Americans also have a right to know why President Bush felt compelled to create an illegal eavesdropping operation in the first place, other than to expand presidential power and evade the checks and balances of our constitutional system.

FISA, of course, does not make it too difficult to obtain a warrant. Indeed, the FISA court approves virtually every warrant request. Over the past thirty years, the FISA court has approved nearly 20,000 warrants

---

[68] James Risen & Eric Lichtblau, *Concerns Raised On Wider Spying Under the New Law*, N.Y. TIMES, Aug. 19, 2007, at A1.

[69] Carl Hulse & Edmund L. Andrews, *House Approves Changes in Eavesdropping Program*, N.Y. TIMES, Aug. 5, 2007, at A1. Despite the initial promises to oppose the Administration's wiretapping program, the Senate continues to pander to the Bush Administration's demands, striking down a measure that would have provided judicial oversight to government spying and supporting immunity for telecommunications companies that gave private information to intelligence officers. *See* Eric Lichtblau, *In Senate, A White House Victory on Eavesdropping*, N.Y. TIMES, Jan. 25, 2008, at A17; and Eric Lichtblau, *Senate Votes for Expansion of Spy Powers*, N.Y. TIMES, Feb. 13, 2008, at A17.

while rejecting perhaps a half dozen.[70] It is not a question of speed either. The law allows the government to initiate surveillance and get a warrant later if necessary.

Instead of answering these pertinent questions, the Administration has done its best to keep everyone confused. It has, for example, refused repeated requests by Senator Jay Rockefeller, the Democratic Chairman of the Senate Intelligence Committee, for documents relating to the President's order creating the spying program, and the Justice Department's legal justification for it. Moreover, President Bush continues to claim executive privilege for these documents.

But there seemed to be a ray of hope. Congress appeared ready to reject the Bush Administration's attempt to legalize its illegal surveillance activities. On October 10, 2007, for example, two congressional panels rejected President Bush's request to renew the government's broad eavesdropping authority, and instead adopted a measure that would give federal judges some oversight and more scrutiny over electronic surveillance conducted overseas by the NSA.[71]

Congress, however, backed down and gave the Bush Administration carte blanche to continue its unconstitutional surveillance activities. By doing so, Congress has silently agreed to protect President Bush from revealing his past illegal surveillance acts. On July 9, 2008, the Senate gave final approval by a 69 to 28 vote to a major expansion of the government's surveillance powers.[72] On July 10, 2008, President Bush signed the bill into law.[73] It is the biggest revamping of federal surveillance law in thirty years. Indeed, the bill needlessly expands the government's ability to spy on Americans and ensures that the country will never learn the full extent of President Bush's unlawful wiretapping.

The bill dangerously weakens the 1978 FISA. That law, of course, required the government to get a warrant to intercept communications between anyone in this country and anyone outside of it, and to dem-

---

[70] Editorial, *Compromising the Constitution,* N.Y. TIMES, July 8, 2008, at A22.

[71] Stephen Labaton, *House Panels Vote for More Scrutiny Over Foreign Eavesdropping,* N.Y. TIMES, Oct. 11, 2007, at A21.

[72] Eric Lichtblau, *Senate Approves Bill to Broaden Wiretap Powers,* N.Y. TIMES, July 10, 2008, at A1. Even with this unprecedented expansion of power to intercept communications, however, the NSA has repeatedly violated this law by intercepting private e-mail messages and phone calls of Americans that have gone beyond the broad legal limits established by Congress. Eric Lichtblau & James Risen, *Officials Say U.S. Wiretaps Exceeded Law,* N.Y. TIMES, Apr. 16, 2009, at A1, *available at* 2009 WLNR 7068775.

[73] Foreign Intelligence Surveillance Act of 1978 Amendments Acts of 2008, H.R. 6304, 110th Cong. (2008) (enacted) *available at* http://thomas.loc.gov/cgi-bin/bdquery/z?d110:HR6304.

onstrate that it is investigating a foreign power or the agent of a foreign power, that plans to harm America. The FISA law also created a court to issue the warrants quickly. FISA did not unduly burden law enforcement. It allowed the government to wiretap without a warrant in moments of crisis and to get the court's permission later.

This new bill makes it much easier to spy on Americans at home, substantially reduces the FISA court's powers, and grants immunity to the companies that turn over Americans' private communications without a warrant. The bill allows the government to bypass the FISA court and collect large amounts of Americans' communications without a warrant simply by declaring that it is doing so for reasons of national security. It deletes the vital "foreign power" provision from FISA, fails to even mention counterterrorism and defines national security so broadly that the term could be interpreted to mean almost anything a president wants it to mean.

Supporters of the bill argue, however, that the bill still requires a warrant for eavesdropping that targets an American. But that is a false argument. The bill does not require the government to name any target. The purpose of warrantless eavesdropping could be as vague as listening to all calls to a particular area code in any other country.

The legislation also expands the government's power to invoke emergency wiretapping procedures. While the NSA is allowed to seek court orders for broad groups of foreign targets, the law creates a new seven-day period for directing wiretaps at foreigners without a court order in "exigent" circumstances if government officials assert that important national security information would be lost. The law also expands to seven days, from three, the period for emergency wiretaps on Americans without a court order if the attorney general certifies there is probable cause to believe the target is linked to terrorism.

The bill also gives legal immunity to the telephone companies that gave the government the private communications of Americans without a warrant. American citizens filed more than forty cases in federal court against AT&T, Verizon, and the other major carriers charging these companies with violating their privacy by conducting wiretaps at the government's direction without valid court orders. This bill ends those lawsuits. It includes a narrow review by a federal district court to determine whether the companies being sued received formal requests or directives from the government to take part in the program. The Bush Administration has already stated that these directives exist. The bill requires the dismissal of the lawsuits once such a finding is made.

Proponents of this bill argue that companies should not be "punished" for cooperating with the government. But the purpose of withholding immunity is not to punish the companies. It is to preserve the only opportunity of unearthing the details of the Bush Administration's illegal eavesdropping. If Congress does not pass other legislation in the near future to counter this new, dangerous program, and once again allows itself to be intimidated by President Bush's fear mongering tactics, it must accept equal responsibility for undermining the democratic values that separate this nation from the terrorists that Bush claims to be fighting.[74]

In addition to this legislation giving the Bush Administration unprecedented authority to wiretap without warrants, Congress acceded to President Bush's imperial view of presidential power by meekly passing the appalling Military Commissions Act of 2006.[75] The Bush Administration used the Republican Party's fear of losing the 2006 mid-term elections and thus its majority in Congress to push through a set of extremely dangerous ideas about anti-terrorism that make American troops less safe, cause lasting damage to our 220-year-old nation of laws, and actually do nothing to protect the nation from terrorism.

Republicans claimed Congress had to act immediately to create procedures for charging and trying terrorists because the men accused of plotting the September 11, 2001 attacks were available for trial. However, that was pure propaganda. Those men could have been tried, and perhaps convicted, long ago but President Bush chose not to proceed with adjudication. He held them in illegal detention, had them questioned in ways that will make real trials very difficult, and invented a transparently illegal system of kangaroo courts to convict them.

It was only after the Supreme Court issued the ruling striking down President Bush's shadow penal system that he adopted this deliberate tone of urgency. Its purpose was to serve a cynical goal. Republican strategists thought they could win the 2006 mid-term election not by passing a good law, but by forcing Democrats to vote against a bad one so that they would look soft on terrorism.

The President and three Republican senators then announced a terrible agreement on this legislation that gave Mr. Bush most of what he wanted, including a waiver for crimes Americans may have committed (including torture) in the service of his anti-terrorist policies. Then Vice President Cheney and his willing "lawmakers" rewrote the rest of the measure to give Mr. Bush the power to imprison almost anyone he wants

---

[74] Immediately after President Bush signed the bill into law, the American Civil Liberties Union filed a lawsuit challenging its constitutionality. Amnesty International USA, et al. v. McConnell, No. 08-CV-6259 (S.D.N.Y. July 10, 2008).

[75] Military Commissions Act of 2006, Pub. L. No. 109-366, 120 Stat. 2600 (2006).

for as long as he wants without charging them; to unilaterally interpret the Geneva Conventions; to authorize torture; and to deny justice to hundreds of men captured in error.

There are many dangerous parts of the Military Commissions Act that violate our hard-earned principles of justice. An overbroad definition of "unlawful enemy combatant" in the bill could subject legal residents of the United States, as well as foreign citizens living in their own countries, to summary arrest and indefinite detention with no hope of appeal. The power to apply this label to anyone he chooses is entirely within the President's unfettered discretion.

The Act can be read to repudiate a half-century of international precedent by allowing the President to decide on his own what abusive interrogation methods he considers permissible. Moreover, his decision could remain secret—there is no requirement that these methods be published. Under this Act, detainees in United States military prisons lose their basic right to habeas corpus[76] and thus their right to challenge their imprisonment. The courts would have no power to review any aspect of this new system, except verdicts by military tribunals.

The Act limits appeals and bans legal action based on the Geneva Conventions, directly or indirectly. All the President would have to do to lock someone up forever is to declare him an enemy combatant without having a trial. In addition, coerced evidence is permissible if a

---

[76] *Boumediene v. Bush*, 128 S. Ct. 2229 (2008), of course, decided this issue, finding that section—section 7—of the Military Commission Act to be unconstitutional. On February 14, 2008, the Bush Administration filed an emergency appeal in the Supreme Court, seeking review of a decision from the United States Court of Appeals for the D.C. Circuit, which required that the government supply more information to defend its designation of a detainee as an enemy combatant. In *Bismullah v. Gates*, 501 F.3d 178 (D.C. Cir. 2007), *petition for cert. filed*, 76 U.S.L.W. 3456 (U.S. Feb. 14, 2008) (No. 07-1054), also dealing with the Military Commissions Act, the Court examined the adequacy of procedure within the special tribunals. In *Bismullah*, the detainee requested a more extensive record of his case than the Bush Administration is willing to supply. The Administration argued that to require the government to turn over relevant information in its possession that is reasonably available, including the evidence that leads to the original enemy combatant designation, imposed an intolerable burden. According to the Administration, the D.C. Circuit ruling posed a serious national security threat. The Bush Administration sought a stay of the lower court's ruling pending either an expedited review of the ruling or deferred action until the Supreme Court decided *Boumediene*. Both *Boumediene* and *Bismullah* overlap on the question of judicial review of the enemy-combatant designation. Linda Greenhouse, *Bush Appeals to Justices on Detainees Case*, N.Y. TIMES, Feb. 15, 2008, at A17. The Court has since vacated the judgment in *Bismullah* and remanded the case to the United States Court of Appeals for the District of Columbia Circuit for further consideration in light of its decision in *Boumediene*. Bismullah, *cert. granted, judgment vacated and remanded*, No. 07-1054 (07A677), 2008 WL 436938 (June 23, 2008) (mem).

judge considers it reliable—already a contradiction in terms—and relevant. Coercion is defined in a way that exempts anything done before the passage of the 2005 Detainee Treatment Act,[77] and anything else the President chooses. The Military Commissions Act also allows the use of evidence and testimony that is kept secret from the defendant. Finally, the Act's definition of torture is unacceptably narrow, a virtual reprise of the deeply cynical memoranda the Administration produced after September 11, 2001.[78] For example, rape and sexual assault are defined in a retrograde way that covers only forced or coerced activity, effectively eliminating the idea of rape as torture.

In the midst of this constitutional crisis—the crisis over protecting and perpetuating the rule of law—stands the work of Owen Fiss. Indeed, one of the articles in this book directly addresses the constitutional demands against torture and surveillance. Perhaps the Obama Administration will respond by banning these practices. But one can never be sure that the Executive Branch will live up to its constitutional requirements. Moreover, the unprecedented expansion of Executive Branch power under the Bush Administration may not be easily relinquished by any politician. Indeed, there will almost certainly be a great deal of pressure from the entrenched bureaucracy to retain this power for the Executive Branch. What we must depend upon is the legal and moral force of the ideas of

---

[77] Detainee Treatment Act of 2005, Pub. L. 109-148, 119 Stat. 2739 (2005).

[78] The debate around Guantánamo has intensified as investigations by the House Intelligence Committee have revealed that the C.I.A. illegally destroyed videotapes documenting the "harsh interrogation methods"—deemed to be torture by most standards except the Bush Administration's standards—of some detainees. *See The Right to Move on the C.I.A. Tapes*, N.Y. TIMES, Jan. 3, 2008, at A22. The initial findings of an incomplete review of videotaped interrogations at military facilities from Iraq to Guantánamo Bay identify nearly 50 tapes, including one that showed what a military spokesman described as the forcible gagging of a terrorism suspect. Mark Mazzetti & Scott Shane, *Pentagon Cites Tapes Showing Interrogations*, N.Y. TIMES, Mar. 13, 2008, at A1.

Ironically, the harsh interrogation techniques employed by the Bush Administration are borrowed from the interrogation methods used by the Chinese against American prisoners of war in Korea. In 2002, American intelligence officers, looking for more effective methods to interrogate prisoners in the "war on terror," studied government files. They discovered and reprinted a 1957 chart describing death threats, degradation, sleep deprivation and even worse inflicted by the Chinese against American prisoners of war. They incorporated the chart into a new handbook for interrogations at Guantánamo. The supreme irony is that Albert D. Biderman, the original author of the chart, concluded after interviewing 235 Air Force prisoners of war that these techniques mainly serve to "extort false confessions." He also concluded that these interrogation methods were a common practice at "other times and nations." Moreover, "inflicting physical pain is not a necessary nor particularly effective method" to persuade prisoners of war. Tim Weiner, *Remembering Brainwashing*, N.Y TIMES, July 6, 2008, at WR1.

people such as Owen Fiss. As he sees it, the Constitution reflects a commitment to a set of ideals about fairness, justice, and dignity. These ideals have been adopted previously because our government officials and the majority will be tempted during times of crisis to abandon them.

I

GROUPS AND THE EQUAL
PROTECTION CLAUSE[1]

Directly after his work at the Civil Rights Division, Owen Fiss began his academic career at the University of Chicago Law School. It was there that he started to explore in writing, and in great depth, his vision of equality—the meaning of and the interpretive method required by the Equal Protection Clause.

However, Fiss actually began to think seriously about the ideal of equality as a student. Indeed, even during his high school years at Stuyvesant High School in New York, Owen Fiss spent a great deal of time discussing and arguing about major public issues—particularly about equality—with his classmates. His intellectual journey—as expressed in writing—began in 1965, with an article he published in the Harvard Law Review while he was clerking—*Racial Imbalance in the Public Schools: The Constitutional Concepts.* His intellectual journey continued with a series of articles, related to the issues raised in *Brown,* including *Gaston County v. United States: Fruition of the Freezing Principle,* which appeared in the 1969 Supreme Court Review; *The Charlotte-Mecklenberg Case—Its Significance for Northern School Desegregation,* which was published in 1971 in the University of Chicago Law Review; *The Uncertain Path of the Law,* published in 1974 in Philosophy and Public Affairs; and *The Fate of An Idea Whose Time Has Come: Antidiscrimination Law in the Second Decade After Brown v. Board of Education,* published in 1974 in the University of Chicago Law Review. In all of these articles, one can see Fiss struggling with the ideal of equality—what it means and what it ought to mean. Perhaps his two most significant works dealing with equality theory before his *Groups and the Equal Protection Clause*

---

[1] Owen M. Fiss, *Groups and the Equal Protection Clause,* 5 PHIL. & PUB. AFF. 107 (1976).

article, however, are *A Theory of Fair Employment Laws,* published in 1971 in the University of Chicago Law Review, and *The Jurisprudence of Busing,* published in 1975 in Law and Contemporary Problems. Indeed, the seeds for *Groups* are clearly planted in these two articles. This is most striking in *A Theory of Fair Employment.* It is here that Fiss begins to puzzle over the shortcomings of the antidiscrimination principle and seeks to extend that principle beyond its logical boundaries to meet the stunning difficulties of that principle as applied to the serious real world problems then confronting our society. By the time he writes *Groups,* it is clear that he more fully understands the inadequacies of the anti-discrimination principle and thus tries to remedy those inadequacies by formulating an entirely new theory of equality.

In *Groups and the Equal Protection Clause,* Owen Fiss introduces the group disadvantaging principle (the antisubordination tradition)[2] to legal scholarship in the appropriately named Second Reconstruction Era. The article is an elegant, subtly argued brief that the Equal Protection Clause prohibits laws or official practices that "aggravate[ ] (or perpetuate[ ]?) the subordinate position of specially disadvantaged groups."[3] His group-disadvantaging principle is, of course, normative: to Fiss, the central command of the Equal Protection Clause is that the government shall not subordinate African-Americans (or similar social groups[4]) regardless of motive. As he forthrightly acknowledges, his theory is a "redistributive theory" on behalf of African-Americans that is not simply a policy option for government but one that is constitutionally required.[5] Stated otherwise, Fiss contends that the guarantees of equal citizenship cannot be realized under the present conditions of pervasive social stratification and that the law's function is to reform social practices and institutions that enforce the secondary social status of historically opposed groups, particularly African-Americans.

This article is a seminal article in constitutional law, certainly one of the best articles ever written on equality. Brilliantly conceived, elegantly constructed, and historically timely, the article has had a huge impact on the scholarly literature and on those working with the ideal of equality

---

[2] Fiss's group disadvantaging principle, in the decades following his promulgation of it, has been variously referred to as the anticaste, antisubjugation, and, more generally, the antisubordination principle.

[3] Fiss, *supra* note 1, at 157.

[4] Fiss would protect other similar social groups to the same degree if these other groups have the same characteristics as African-Americans—perpetual subordination and circumscribed political power. *Id.* at 155.

[5] *Id.* at 168-69, 171-72.

and, more specifically, the Equal Protection Clause. Indeed, Fiss's idea of distinguishing between "antidiscrimination" and "antisubordination" principles arose at a critical point in American race history. Directly after World War II, the intense battle for civil rights led to a fundamental transformation of American society and law. Constitutional and statutory antidiscrimination laws began to break down the entrenched segregation and antisubordination that had existed since the Civil War.

The legal system by itself, of course, could not make the necessary changes to allow for social and political equality. But the Civil Rights Movement, supported by the federal government's intervention, pushed the legal system in the right direction. The legal system responded in turn and this movement helped to improve the lives of African-Americans, and, of course, the nation as a whole. By the early to mid-1970s, American law and society had attacked and displaced Jim Crow laws, *de jure* racial segregation, and the directly related practices of overt racial segregation. *Brown v. Board of Education*[6] and the forces for change that it set loose were revolutionary. Revolutions, of course, often lead to counterattacks. The civil rights revolution certainly was no exception. The attack was political as well as legal and it was intense. The 1968 presidential campaign that led to the election of Richard Nixon began the retrenchment. This attack surely had a profound impact on the Civil Rights Movement, bringing an abrupt end to the Second Reconstruction. Richard Nixon, for example, appealed to the white working class voters by openly attacking the civil rights revolution and the Warren Court.[7] He claimed that the country needed to restore "law and order." This was, of course, a thinly veiled appeal to racial prejudice. The jurisprudential attack soon followed.

Nixon's assault on the Warren Court's jurisprudence and its noble view of law was certainly aided by a strange series of historical events.

---

[6] 347 U.S. 483 (1954).

[7] On Nixon's attacks on the Warren Court, see, e.g., DONALD GRIER STEPHENSON, JR., CAMPAIGNS AND THE COURT: THE U.S. SUPREME COURT IN PRESIDENTIAL ELECTIONS 180 (1999) (describing Nixon's opposition to busing to achieve racial balance, and his statement that "[o]ur schools are for education, not integration."). On Nixon's civil rights strategy, see, e.g., DAN T. CARTER, FROM GEORGE WALLACE TO NEWT GINGRICH: RACE IN THE CONSERVATIVE COUNTERREVOLUTION, 1963-1994, at 30 (1996) (describing Nixon's ability to present positions on crime, education, or public housing in such a way that a voter could "avoid admitting to himself that he was attracted by a racist appeal."); LEWIS L. GOULD, 1968: THE ELECTION THAT CHANGED AMERICA, 103-05, 140 (1993) ("[Nixon's] stance on civil rights was designed to position him between Humphrey and Wallace in a way that appealed to Southern voters"); IRWIN UNGER & DEBI UNGER, TURNING POST: 1968, at 439 (1988) (making the same point).

Prior to Nixon's election in 1968, Earl Warren tendered his resignation to President Johnson in an effort to have Johnson's choice, Abe Fortas, replace him as leader of the Court. But Fortas' nomination was withdrawn when the Senate refused to confirm him, and later, due to financial improprieties, he was forced to resign altogether. Following the 1968 election, Nixon appointed Warren Burger to replace Earl Warren as chief justice. In short order, John Harlan and Hugo Black resigned. President Nixon found himself with the opportunity to make three appointments during his first term in office. Over time, only one of those appointments, Harry A. Blackmun, grew into a justice whose constitutional vision could be said to be compatible with that of the Warren Court and, of course, Owen Fiss. The other two appointments, Lewis Powell and William Rehnquist, were clearly at odds with the Warren Court's jurisprudence of the sixties.

The final dissolution of the Warren Court came in 1975, with the resignation of William O. Douglas and his replacement by John Paul Stevens. Moreover, two other significant accidents of history occurred which secured this shift in power: President Carter did not have an opportunity to make any appointments to the Court (a distinction he shared with no other President in our history who completed a full term), while President Reagan had the opportunity to fill three vacancies during his term in office. He appointed Antonin Scalia to replace Justice Burger, Sandra Day O'Connor to replace Justice Stewart, and Anthony Kennedy to replace Justice Powell. In 1986, President Reagan elevated Rehnquist to the position of chief justice. Rehnquist, who actually led the Court intellectually and politically during the seventies and eighties in its counter-assault to the Warren Court's jurisprudence, finally assumed the formal, outward mantle of leadership. These changes led to an entirely new era of Supreme Court history.

Beginning in the 1970s, the federal courts applied the existing antidiscrimination doctrine to slow down the civil rights revolution. The danger, in Fiss's view, was that the virtues of judicial craft would be used as a form of attack not only to stop but also to dismantle the gains of *Brown*. Unfortunately, he was correct.[8] The judicial response went hand-in-hand with the political response. Large numbers of whites became convinced that the civil rights revolution had gone too far. The judiciary's response reflects a loss of political will to continue the work of the civil rights

---

[8] *See, e.g.*, Parents Involved in Cmty. Schs. v. Seattle Sch. Dist. No. 1, 127 S. Ct. 2738 (2007).

revolution. The distinctions in the case law[9] reflect this position and did indeed cause an abrupt halt to continuing racial reform.

It was in these circumstances—an extremely hostile political landscape and a judiciary unwilling to sustain the mandate of *Brown*—that Fiss developed his group disadvantaging theory. But it was not simply a legal or political struggle that was at issue. It was also a struggle over the memory of the principles and the culture that created and developed the Civil Rights Movement of the Second Reconstruction. It was a battle over ideas and policies and the immorality of unequal treatment under the law.

Fiss clearly believed that he had to show that this emerging body of constitutional law diverged from the commitments and understandings of the civil rights struggle. The Supreme Court had by this time discredited most overt forms of racial discrimination. At the same time, however, the controversy shifted to new, more polarizing issues. In particular, two major issues faced the Court. First, there were questions concerning the use of race-conscious remedies to integrate formerly segregated institutions. Second, the Court had to address facially neutral practices that perpetuated racial discrimination in most institutions of American life. The debate about these issues took the form of a dispute about the principles of and commitments to the Civil Rights Movement as embodied in *Brown*.

Fiss's article can be seen as addressing this debate. In his view, the judiciary refused to follow through on the promise of *Brown*. Federal judges, led by the Supreme Court, through their opinions, seemed to fear that the elimination of the caste system would require a total reconstruction of society. In their view, that responsibility simply would lie outside the competencies of the courts. The problem ran even deeper. Many believed that if the courts assumed the role of reconstructing society then the political reaction would undermine the legitimacy of the judiciary required for it to do its "ordinary work" of dispute resolution. By the mid-1970s, the federal courts, led by the Supreme Court, were in full retreat from the civil rights revolution. The flag under which the courts retreated was the antidiscrimination principle.

---

[9] *See, e.g.,* Washington v. Davis, 426 U.S. 229 (1976) (holding that *only* proof of specific intent to discriminate on the basis of race justifies strict scrutiny of government policies under the Equal Protection Clause); Milliken v. Bradley, 418 U.S. 717 (1974) (imposing strict limits on interdistrict desegregation plans); San Antonio School District v. Rodriguez, 411 U.S. 1 (1973) (holding that education is not a fundamental right and that inequalities of educational opportunity caused by unequal funding do not violate the Constitution).

Fiss's intervention at this particular historical moment was important in order to contest this vision. He disaggregated the principle of equality into antidiscrimination and group disadvantaging strands and claimed the latter as the constitutionally required principle precisely to capture and promulgate the true meaning of the civil rights tradition. To Fiss, equality is about the struggle against caste (subordination) in an American society of entrenched social hierarchies. It is not simply the formal principle that like cases be treated alike. It is a struggle against the practices and institutions that continue to aggravate or perpetuate the subordinate position of specially disadvantaged groups, particularly African-Americans.

In response to this judicial retreat under the authority of the antidiscrimination doctrine, Fiss offers a very sophisticated and intellectually challenging understanding of the judicial method (or craft). Fiss clearly understands that the argument is not one between adhering to the text and various interpretive claims. The text of the Equal Protection Clause is so vague—so radically indeterminate—that, as Fiss claims, "mediating principles" are required to properly apply the text to specific situations. As Fiss argues: "The ethical issue is whether the position of perpetual subordination is going to be brought to an end for our disadvantaged groups."[10] Moreover, because of the opaqueness of the Equal Protection Clause, "[a] judge must become a natural lawyer out of default."[11] The questions facing the Court contested the very meaning and importance of *Brown* and the Civil Rights Movement. If the Court read *Brown* as invalidating segregation on the ground that it violated the antidiscrimination principle, then affirmative action would be presumptively unconstitutional, while facially neutral practices with disparate impact on African-Americans (or other racial minorities) would be presumptively constitutional. However, if the Court read *Brown* as invalidating segregation because it violated the group disadvantaging principle, then affirmative action would be presumptively constitutional but facially neutral practices with a disparate impact on African-Americans (or other racial minorities) would be presumptively unconstitutional.

If the Equal Protection Clause is so opaque as not to state an intelligible rule of decision, then what Fiss calls "mediating principles" must be employed to apply the text to real cases (social situations). Thus, the judge's task must be one of interpretation. The issue then is, of course, which mediating principles should the judge choose. As Fiss recognizes,

---

[10] Fiss, supra note 1, at 173.

[11] *Id.*

the judge is not free simply to select the "mediating principle" that reflects her own preferences or those of any other individual or group, even if (or particularly if) the group is the majority of the population. Judges must simultaneously maintain the rule of law *and* do justice. Fiss's argument is clear. The two functions are not necessarily in conflict because the role of the judge under the Equal Protection Clause is to do justice. And to Fiss, that means protecting a specific disadvantaged group—African-Americans.

According to Fiss, judges have chosen the antidiscrimination principle over the group disadvantaging principle because it is more compatible with the virtues of the judicial craft. The antidiscrimination principle's appeal lies in its supposed "value neutrality," its quantitative or mechanical character, its "objectivity," its championing of a moral individualism, and its universality. Perhaps even more important, "the antidiscrimination principle embodies a conception of equality that roughly corresponds to the conception of equality governing the judicial process . . . . The over-arching obligation is to treat similar persons, similarly."[12] Fiss understands this choice as a natural one for judges. "It is natural for the Justices to seize upon the ideals of their craft in setting norms to govern others."[13] While Fiss acknowledges the seeming naturalness of this choice, he then proceeds to dismantle the antidiscrimination principle. He decisively demonstrates that its supposed promise to live up to the virtues of craft is a completely false one.

Fiss demonstrates in devastating detail that the antidiscrimination principle relies on a series of quantitative, substantive judgments, that it is not value neutral, that it cannot support its individualistic claim, and that it cannot be applied universally. The promise of what some may refer to as a "mechanical jurisprudence" is an illusion. The antidiscrimination principle requires the creation of even more elaborate and complex doctrinal innovations supported by the construction of a complicated secondary apparatus.

For example, Fiss shows that the antidiscrimination principle, which holds that classifications (means) that do not sufficiently fit legislative goals (ends), violate the Equal Protection Clause, must itself be supplemented. The principle needs a substantive theory of which legislative ends are legitimate, and a convincing argument about the level of generality at which they may be shown to be legitimate. Otherwise, any legislative means can always be justified tautologically. The theory that elaborates

---

[12] *Id.* at 119-20.

[13] *Id.* at 120.

which legislative ends are legitimate must also specify how weighty those ends are. This will, in turn, help judges determine whether those ends are "compelling" enough to justify particular inequalities. But the process is even more complicated. Legislative means often will not perfectly fit a given legitimate end, particularly if the end is created at a high enough level of generality to justify its legitimacy as an end. Thus, judges applying the antidiscrimination principle need a theory of legitimacy and weight of that mix of primary and secondary ends to account for the degree of over and under-inclusiveness of the means.

Therefore, to do its work, the antidiscrimination principle, with its strict attention to the fit between legislative means and legislative ends, must be supported by a normative theory that evaluates and weighs legislative ends and various mixes of such ends. However, this supplementation violates the alleged value neutrality of the antidiscrimination principle. And, as Fiss makes clear, one of the main attractions of the antidiscrimination principle to judges is its supposed value neutrality.

As he summarizes his critique:

> The appeal of the antidiscrimination principle may be unfounded. The ideals served by the principle may not have any intrinsic merit, or the connection between those ideals and the principle may be nothing more than an illusion. . . . But I believe the criticism runs deeper. The antidiscrimination principle has structural limitations that prevent it from adequately resolving or even addressing certain central claims of equality now being advanced. For these claims the antidiscrimination principle either provides no framework of analysis or, even worse, provides the wrong one. Conceivably, the principle might be adjusted by making certain structural modifications; and indeed, on occasion, over the last twenty-five years, that has occurred, through an ad hoc and incremental basis, and at the expense of severing the principle from its theoretical foundations and widening the gap between the principle and the ideals it is supposed to serve.[14]

Fiss demonstrates these problems with the antidiscrimination principle by looking at the issues of preferential treatment and disparate impact. The doctrinal innovations and compromises with the principle required to deal correctly with these issues, as he sees it, undermine the very craft virtues upon which the judges seek to rely under the antidis-

---

[14] *Id.* at 129.

crimination principle. The judges find themselves in a serious conflict. If the judges refuse to innovate and compromise under the antidiscrimination principle when dealing with preferential treatment and disparate impact cases, the courts will allow the systemic injustices perpetuated against African-Americans to be constitutionally acceptable. In point of fact, the antidiscrimination principle leads judges in the wrong direction. It has been used for this very purpose—to allow the most significant issues of justice to be resolved against the most disadvantaged group (African-Americans).[15]

Fiss's destruction of the antidiscrimination principle demonstrates that the supposed virtues of craft offer only a false promise. To Fiss, the judge's role is to search for justice despite the doctrinal problems. If this is his task, his role requires him to adjust the doctrine to concrete action. This means abandoning the antidiscrimination principle and replacing it with the group disadvantaging principle, a principle that will allow him to do justice.

The judge must, therefore, take the lead in the obligation of doing justice when and where the political process fails the least powerful in our society. As Fiss puts it: "The injustice of the political process must be corrected, and perhaps as a last resort, the task falls to the judiciary."[16] Moreover, the special disadvantaged status of the group adds to the necessity of judicial intervention. "The socioeconomic position of the group supplies an additional reason for the judicial activism and also determines the content of the intervention—improvement of the status of that group."[17] The role of the judiciary under the group disadvantaging principle is clearly redistributive. Judges must not only bring justice to the disadvantaged but also demonstrate what justice is to the entire community—the entire nation.

Fiss's analysis of the group disadvantaging theory is extremely attractive. He examines in minute detail the deeper structures, analytical methods, and underlying assumptions of equal protection doctrine under the antidiscrimination principle and allows us to scrutinize them carefully and closely. He demonstrates that the application of the accepted equal protection doctrine under the antidiscrimination principle is not objective nor easily applied but rather requires difficult value judgments in every aspect. He compares the antidiscrimination doctrine and his

---

[15] The doctrine has clearly gone in this direction. *See, e.g.*, Parents Involved in Cmty. Schs. v. Seattle Sch. Dist. No. 1, 127 S. Ct. 2738 (2007).

[16] Fiss, *supra* note 1, at 154.

[17] *Id.*

group disadvantaging theory with respect to several elements, including the former's greater congeniality to judges and, even more importantly, their normative bases. Perhaps the most significant point he makes in support of his theory, however, is that under the antidiscrimination principle the existing equal protection doctrine, despite the textual reference to "persons," is inevitably based on certain ideas about groups, such as their identity, social status, and other characteristics. This article is path breaking particularly because Fiss so boldly insists that political morality and legal reasoning must recognize the existence of social groups and take the group status of individuals into account in describing harms. This article, particularly because of its emphasis on groups, significantly contributes to an understanding of the theory and practice of equal protection—what it is and what it could be.

Fiss's group disadvantaging theory, therefore, has had a tremendous impact on the scholarly literature.[18] The article has been cited nearly 1,000 times.[19] It has been the subject of two symposia.[20] Many well-regarded legal academics have seized and elaborated on his group disadvantaging principle.[21]

---

[18] Fiss wrote the article mid-way between two of the Supreme Court's most important decisions on affirmative action, DeFunis v. Odegaard, 416 U.S. 312 (1974), and Regents of the Univ. of Cal. v. Bakke, 438 U.S. 265 (1978). One major purpose of the article was to intervene in the debate unleashed by *DeFunis* about the constitutionality of affirmative action for African-Americans. Nevertheless, the article is usually cited for Fiss's argument that the Equal Protection Clause is not meant simply to protect individuals but is instead intended to recognize the existence and importance of groups.

[19] According to the Web of Science, it has been cited 153 times, and according to Lexis, it has been cited 820 times, for a total of 973.

[20] Symposium, *Fiss's Way: The Scholarship of Owen Fiss*, 58 U. MIAMI L. REV. 9 (2003); Symposium, *The Origins and Fate of Antisubordination Theory*, ISSUES IN LEGAL SCHOLARSHIP, Aug. 2002, http://www.bepress.com/ils/iss2/.

[21] This principle has been variously called the antisubordination principle, the antisubjugation principle, the equal citizenship principle, and the anticaste principle. *See, e.g.,* DERRICK BELL, AND WE ARE NOT SAVED: THE ELUSIVE QUEST FOR RACIAL JUSTICE (1987); KENNETH L. KARST, BELONGING TO AMERICA: EQUAL CITIZENSHIP AND THE CONSTITUTION (1989); CATHERINE A. MCKINNON, FEMINISM UNMODIFIED: DISCOURSES ON LIFE AND LAW 32-45 (1987); CATHERINE A. MCKINNON, SEXUAL HARASSMENT OF WORKING WOMEN 117 (1979) (arguing that courts should inquire "whether the policy or practice integrally contributes to the maintenance of an underclass or a deprived position because of gender status"); LAURENCE H. TRIBE, AMERICAN CONSTITUTIONAL LAW, § 16-21, at 1043-52 (1978); Jack Balkin, *The Constitution of Status*, 106 YALE L.J. 2313 (1997); Charles R. Lawrence III, *The Id, the Ego, and Equal Protection: Reckoning with Unconscious Racism*, 39 STAN. L. REV. 317, 319 (1987); Reva B. Siegel, *Why Equal Protection No Longer Protects*, 49 STAN. L. REV. 1111 (1997); Reva B. Siegel, *Equality Talk: Antisubordination and Anticlassification Values in Constitutional Struggles over Brown*, 117 HARV. L. REV. 1470 (2004).

Despite the many positive contributions of the article,[22] Fiss's vision of equal protection has also engendered severe criticism. The perceived wisdom is that Fiss's group-oriented analysis is of academic interest only because the Supreme Court has, at every turn, rejected his theory and instead adopted a contrary and inconsistent theory of equality[23]—the antidiscrimination principle. Other critics contend that Fiss overstates the extent to which the antidiscrimination theory leads to a formal conception of equality that has characterized the Supreme Court's view of equality for the past four decades.[24] Still other critics contend that Fiss did not go far enough and should have linked his group oriented analysis to social welfare rights.[25] Finally, some critics claim that he failed to develop an understanding of the moral point of law, of constitutionalism and equal protection which would have supported an antisubordination interpretation of the Equal Protection Clause.[26]

Perhaps the most serious objections concern his definition of groups,[27] his understanding of how groups work in American society, and his failure to provide a more coherent account of status and status harm.[28] Nevertheless, no one, not even his harshest critics, denies that Fiss's emphasis on groups—his group disadvantaging theory—is a pathbreaking

---

[22] *See, e.g.*, Kenneth Karst, *Sources of Status-Harm and Group Disadvantage in Private Behavior*, Issues in Legal Scholarship, Aug. 2002, http://www.bepress.com/ils/iss2/art4/.

[23] A relatively few scholars, however, argue that the scope of group disadvantaging or antisubordination and the antidiscrimination (anticlassification) principles overlap, that their application shifts over time in response to social struggle, and that the antisubordination values have shaped the historical development of antidiscrimination understandings. Jack M. Balkin & Reva B. Sigel, *The American Civil Rights Tradition: Anticlassification or Antisubordination*, 58 U. Miami L. Rev. 9, 10 (2003).

[24] Michael C. Dorf, *A Partial Defense of an Anti-Discrimination Principle*, Issues in Legal Scholarship, Aug. 2002, http://www.bepress.com/ils/iss2/art2/.

[25] Mark Tushnet, *The Return of the Repressed: Groups, Social Welfare Rights, and the Equal Protection Clause*, Issues in Legal Scholarship, Aug. 2002, http://www.bepress.com/ils/iss2/art.7/.

[26] Robin West, *Groups, Equal Protection and Law*, Issues in Legal Scholarship, Aug. 2002, http://www.bepress.com/ils/iss2/art8/.

[27] It is important to remember, however, that when Fiss created this theory about groups he was working in uncharted territory.

[28] Peter H. Schuck, *Groups in a Diverse, Dynamic, Competitive, and Liberal Society: Comments on Owen Fiss's "Groups and the Equal Protection Clause,"* Issues in Legal Scholarship, Aug. 2002, http://www.bepress.com/ils/iss2/art15/; Richard Thompson Ford, *Unnatural Groups: A Reaction to Owen Fiss's "Groups and the Equal Protection Clause,"* Issues in Legal Scholarship, Aug, 2002, http://www.bepress.com/ils/iss2/art12/; Iris Marion Young, *Status Inequality and Social Groups*, Issues in Legal Scholarship, Aug. 2002, http://www.bepress.com/ils/iss2/art9/.

article.[29] Indeed, it stands as a barrier against the Supreme Court's formal equality jurisprudence and as a theory that, if employed, will successfully address structural discrimination.

---

[29] Fiss responded to these critiques and other criticisms with a very strong defense of his position. Owen Fiss, *Another Equality*, Issues in Legal Scholarship, Jan. 2004, http://www.bepress.com/ils/iss2/art20.

GROUPS AND THE EQUAL PROTECTION CLAUSE[*]

This is an essay about the structure and limitations of the antidiscrimination principle, the principle that controls the interpretation of the Equal Protection Clause. To understand the importance of that principle in constitutional adjudication a distinction must first be drawn between two different modes of interpretation.

Under one mode the constitutional text is taken pure—the primary decisional touchstone is the actual language of the Constitution. The text of the Constitution is viewed as providing an intelligible rule of decision and that text, rather than any gloss, is the primary referent; at most, disagreement may arise as to how much weight should be given to one or two words and what the words mean. This is a plausible—arguable, though far from persuasive—approach to the Free Speech Clause. It is the approach associated with Justice Black.

The second mode of constitutional interpretation deemphasizes the text. Primary reliance is instead placed on a set of principles—which I call *mediating* because they "stand between" the courts and the Constitution—to give meaning and content to an ideal embodied in the text. These principles are offered as a paraphrase of the particular textual provision, but in truth the relationship is much more fundamental. They give the provision its only meaning as a guide for decision. So much so, that over time one often loses sight of the artificial status of these principles—they are not "part of" the Constitution, but instead only a judicial gloss, open to revaluation and redefinition in a way that the text of the Constitution is not.

The Equal Protection Clause has generally been viewed in this second way. The words—no state shall "deny to any person within its jurisdiction the equal protection of the laws"—do not state an intelligible rule of decision. In that sense the text has no meaning. The Clause contains

* Owen M. Fiss, *Groups and the Equal Protection Clause*, 5 PHIL. & PUB. AFF. 107 (1976). This article uses the footnote numbers and citation form of this particular publication.

the word "equal" and thereby gives constitutional status to the ideal of equality, but that ideal is capable of a wide range of meanings. This ambiguity has created the need for a mediating principle, and the one chosen by courts and commentators is the antidiscrimination principle. When asked what the Equal Protection Clause means, an informed lawyer—even one committed to Justice Black's textual approach to the First Amendment—does not repeat the words of the Clause—a denial of equal protection. Instead, he is likely to respond that the Clause prohibits discrimination.

One purpose of this essay is simply to underscore the fact that the antidiscrimination principle is not the Equal Protection Clause, that it is nothing more than a mediating principle. I want to bring to an end the identification of the Clause with the antidiscrimination principle. But I also have larger ambitions. I want to suggest that the antidiscrimination principle embodies a very limited conception of equality, one that is highly individualistic and confined to assessing the rationality of means. I also want to outline another mediating principle—the group-disadvantaging principle—one that has as good, if not better, claim to represent the ideal of equality, one that takes a fuller account of social reality, and one that more clearly focuses the issues that must be decided in equal protection cases.

I. The Structure of the Antidiscrimination Principle

The construction of the antidiscrimination principle proceeds in three steps. The first is to reduce the ideal of equality to the principle of equal treatment—similar things should be treated similarly. The second step is to take account of the fact that even the just state must make distinctions, must treat some things differently from others; for example, even the most noncontroversial criminal statute distinguishes between people on the basis of their conduct. Recognition of the inevitability and indeed the justice of some line-drawing makes the central task of equal protection theory one of determining which lines or distinctions are permissible. Not all discriminations can be prohibited; the word "to discriminate," once divested of its emotional connotation, simply means to distinguish or to draw a line. The mediating principle of the Equal Protection Clause therefore must be one that prohibits only "arbitrary"[1] discrimination.

---

[1] Sometimes the word "invidious" is used interchangeably with "arbitrary" to describe the universe of impermissible discriminations, though with little attention to the special connotations of the word "invidious"—"tending to cause ill will, animosity, or resentment." Professor Karst, in a valuable article, reveals a sensitivity to the difference between the two

The Clause does not itself tell us which distinctions are arbitrary, and as the third step in this process a general method is posited for determining the rationality and thus the permissibility of the lines drawn. The method chosen by the Supreme Court, and the one that generally goes under the rubric of the antidiscrimination principle, has two facets: (a) the identity of the discrimination is determined by the criterion upon which it is based, and (b) the discrimination is arbitrary if the criterion upon which it is based is unrelated to the state purpose.

To illustrate this method of determining whether a discrimination is arbitrary, let us suppose the state wishes to pick the best employees or students for a limited number of openings. That process inevitably involves choices. The state must discriminate. Assume also that the choice is made on the basis of performance on a written test designed to pick the most productive workers or the most brilliant students. The state would then be making an academic discrimination. Presumably it would not be arbitrary since the criterion is related to the state purpose. This would be true even if it turned out that the only applicants selected happened to be white. But suppose the criterion for selection is color: the state grants the position to whites and denies it to blacks, on the basis of their color. That would make the discrimination a racial one and arbitrary because the criterion is not related to the state purpose of selecting the most brilliant students or most productive employees.

In this example, the racial criterion has been deemed arbitrary because it is not related to the state purpose. But Tussman and tenBroek, in their now classic article of the late 1940s,[2] pointed out that unrelatedness is

---

terms. "Invidious Discrimination: Justice Douglas and the Return of the 'Natural-Law–Due Process Formula'," 16 U.C.L.A. L. Rev. 716, 732-34 (1969). He, however, uses the term "invidious discrimination" in a conclusory sense, devoid of descriptive meaning. The term is used "to describe the Court's ultimate conclusion on the question of a violation of equal protection." Ibid., p. 740 fn. 110.

[2] "The Equal Protection of the Laws," 37 Calif. L. Rev. 341 (1949) (hereafter cited as Tussman and tenBroek). Tussman and tenBroek saw three principles, not one, governing the application of the Equal Protection Clause. The one I am describing under the rubric of the antidiscrimination principle was called the "reasonable classification" principle. They also spoke of a principle opposing "discriminatory legislation" and a third guarantee, one of "substantive equal protection." By the latter they meant that certain "rights" (analogous to those that were previously protected by the doctrine of "substantive due process") were to be protected by the Equal Protection Clause; these rights could not be interfered with even though the interference was even-handed. They sought to explain Shelley v. Kraemer on the basis of this principle—the enforcement of a racially restrictive covenant was not a form of unequal treatment, but rather an interference with the "right" of a willing seller to sell to a willing buyer. They sought to justify the use of the Equal Protection Clause as "a sanctuary" for these "rights," not because they have any connection to equality, but because, in their words,

not a dichotomous quality. In most cases it is not a question of whether the criterion and end are related or unrelated, but a question of how well they are related. A criterion may be deemed arbitrary even if it is related to the purpose, but only poorly so. Tussman and tenBroek explained that, given the purpose, a criterion could be ill-suited in two different ways: it could be over-inclusive (it picked out more persons than it should) or underinclusive (it excluded persons that it should not). These evils can be described, to use the jargon of contemporary commentators, as ill-fit.[3]

This is the core idea—the foundational concept—of the antidiscrimination principle, one of means-end rationality. But it must also be recognized that the principle contemplates a series of additional inquiries that yield a superstructure. First, the principle requires that the court identify the underlying criterion. This means that a distinction must be drawn between the stated criterion and the *real* criterion. If the challenge is to a statute in all its applications, then the stated criterion may be taken at face value. But if the challenge is to the statute as applied, or to administrative action, then there is no reason why the stated criterion should be treated as the real criterion. The administrator may say he is selecting students on the basis of academic performance, when in fact he is ignoring their test scores, and making his decision on the basis of race.

---

the Clause "was placed in our Constitution as the culmination of the greatest humanitarian movement in our history." Ibid., p. 364. This doctrine has received little formal recognition by the Court in the past twenty-five years. At most, strands of this doctrine are reflected in the fundamental-right trigger of the strict scrutiny branch of the antidiscrimination principle; in that instance the "right" is used to determine the appropriate degree of fit. On the other hand, what Tussman and tenBroek referred to as the ban on "discriminatory legislation," is completely integrated within what I call the antidiscrimination principle. For Tussman and tenBroek the ban on "discriminatory legislation" was a "criticism of legislative purpose," a "demand for purity of motive." Ibid., pp. 357, 358. Certain legislative purposes, such as the subordination of blacks, were denied to the state altogether, and thus it was irrelevant that the fit might have been perfect between the criterion (or classification) and the (forbidden) purpose. They were not especially clear as to which purposes were forbidden—they spoke in terms of "bias," "prejudice," "hostility," and "antagonism." They also recognized that the word "discrimination" could also be used in the sense that it is being used here (that is, as a term to describe the reasonable classification doctrine), but they failed to integrate the two senses of the word. Ibid., p. 358 fn. 35.

[3] Tussman and tenBroek did not use the term "ill-fit." They did, however, make the points about over- and underinclusiveness (words they actually used and introduced into legal discourse) by the use of diagrams: P is the universe of person that *should* be selected given the purpose, and C is the universe of person actually selected by the criterion. The diagram where P is a subset of C is used by them to represent overinclusiveness and the diagram where C is a subset of P is used to represent underinclusiveness. The term "fit" is suggested by these diagrams, and perhaps for that reason is used by the contemporary commentators, such as, Ely, "The Constitutionality of Reverse Racial Discrimination," 41 U. CHI. L. REV. 723, 727 fn. 26 (1974) (hereafter cited as Ely), and is now part of ordinary constitutional parlance.

Second, the court must identify the state's purpose and determine whether it is legitimate. For example, suppose the state's purpose is to subordinate blacks rather than to choose the best students or employees. Then the color black would be well-suited for determining who should be excluded from the state colleges or jobs, and under a test consisting exclusively of means-end rationality, this use of the racial criterion would be permissible. The Equal Protection Clause would thereby be transformed into a minor protection against state carelessness, permitting intervention only when it was plain that the state did not know how best to achieve its ends.[4] Accordingly, it seemed necessary to go beyond the concept of ill-fit, and the anti-discrimination principle has been modified so as to require that the state purpose against which the criterion is to be measured be legitimate (or permissible).

This account of the inquiry into purpose suggests two steps: first, identifying the state purpose and second, determining whether the purpose is legitimate. But if the court need not take the state's professed purpose as that against which the criterion is to be measured, then the two steps collapse into one. The court fixes the state's purpose by the process of imagination: only legitimate purposes would be imagined, and the judge's mind would scan the universe of legitimate purposes until he identified the legitimate state purpose that was best served by the criterion, the one that left the smallest margins of over- and underinclusiveness. The universe of imaginable purposes would not contain those purposes disavowed by the state, and the disavowal could occur implicitly, for example, it could be implied by the overall statutory framework of the state.[5]

Some have argued that the criterion should be measured against the *stated* purpose. Such a restriction might enhance the invalidating power of the Equal Protection Clause, for it was always assumed—perhaps out of simple fairness—that the process of imagination would yield the best purpose, the one most favorable to the state. This restriction would also reduce judicial maneuverability. And some have further hypothesized that a stated-purpose requirement would invigorate the political process—for "it would encourage the airing and critique of those reasons [justifying the legislative means] in the state's political process."[6] This hypothesis

---

[4] See generally, Note, "Legislative Purpose, Rationality, and Equal Protection," 82 YALE L. J. 123 (1972).

[5] See, for example, Eisenstadt v. Baird, 405 U.S. 438 (1972).

[6] Gunther, "Foreword: In Search of Evolving Doctrine on a Changing Court: A Model for a Newer Equal Protection," 86 HARV. L. REV. 1, 47 (1972) (hereafter cited as Gunther). See also Greenawalt, "Judicial Scrutiny of 'Benign' Racial Preference in Law School Admissions," 75 COLUM. L. REV. 559, 600 (1975) (hereafter cited as Greenawalt).

seems to me to posit a somewhat naive conception of the state political process and what might invigorate it. But more importantly, the restriction is inconsistent with judicial practice in other areas (such as determining whether legislation is authorized by the enumerated powers), and it would be hard to apply. The state rarely identifies its purpose with any degree of precision, and the restriction would be virtually meaningless if, as one proponent of this idea has suggested, "A state court's or Attorney General office's description of purpose should be acceptable."[7] For these reasons, the stated-purpose requirement has not taken root, and probably should not be viewed as an important or permanent feature of the antidiscrimination principle.

A third set of auxiliary concepts is responsive to two facts—that the critical inquiry of ill-suitedness, as modulated by Tussman and tenBroek, is one of degree and that some margin of over- and underinclusiveness can always be discovered. Standards must therefore be set for determining how poor the relationship must be between criterion and purpose before it is deemed arbitrary—or to use the jargon of the contemporary commentators, how tight a fit must there be? The doctrines of "suspect classification" and "fundamental right" seek to answer this question. They are essentially standards for determining the requisite degree of fit. In contrast to the more permissive standard called "mere rational relationship" or "minimum scrutiny," which tolerates broad margins of over- and underinclusiveness, these doctrines trigger a strict scrutiny, one that demands a tight fit. If the criterion is "suspect" (the exemplar being race) or the "right" affected "fundamental" (the exemplar being the right to vote)[8] there has to be a very tight fit—any degree of avoidable over-inclusiveness or underinclusiveness would be deemed "too much."[9]

---

[7] Gunther, P. 47.

[8] See, for example, Carrington v. Rash, 380 U.S. 89 (1965) (denying the right to vote to those serving in the armed forces). As originally conceived, the "fundamental right" did not have to be of constitutional stature. The constitutional status of the right to vote is shrouded in controversy, but strict scrutiny seems also to have been applied to laws restricting rights clearly of nonconstitutional stature, such as the right to procreate. Skinner v. Oklahoma, 316 U.S. 535 (1952). In 1973, a majority of the Supreme Court said the right had to be of constitutional stature—though in order to pay respects to precedent—they acknowledged that the constitutional right may be an *implicit* one. San Antonio Ind. School District v. Rodriguez, 411 U.S. 1 (1973). It might also be noted that both triggers of strict scrutiny—suspect classification and fundamental right—might be present at the same time (for example, a state denying some ethnic group the right to procreate). The operative significance of this double trigger is not clear. One trigger alone may be sufficient to result in the invalidation of the law, and in that instance the second one would be superfluous—merely frosting on the cake.

[9] In these cases it is often difficult to describe the discrimination as "arbitrary" within the ordinary meaning of that word. But one loses sight of the need to make that judgment.

The use of the term "avoidable" gives the state an out: ill-fit would be accepted if there is no closer-fitting way of satisfying its purpose. Assuming a legitimate purpose and no better alternative, the discriminatory criterion, however "suspect," would seem necessary, and so acceptable under the Equal Protection Clause.

The strict-scrutiny branch of the antidiscrimination principle has necessitated the establishment of methods for determining which criteria are "suspect" and which rights are "fundamental." It has also required, as the fourth feature of the superstructure, the introduction of defensive doctrines—those that allow for the validation of laws and practices that would otherwise seem invalid. There is no analytic reason why these defensive doctrines cannot be applied in the minimum-scrutiny context (and on some occasions they have been); the point is simply that there is less need for them there. In the minimum-scrutiny context, the impulse toward validation could easily be accommodated in the judgment that the margins of over- and underinclusiveness are not "excessive." In the strict-scrutiny context, on the other hand, that method of avoidance is not available since, by definition, any margin of over- or underinclusiveness is "excessive."

One defensive doctrine permits the state to take one step at a time. It is a defense aimed at excusing underinclusiveness. For example, assume there is a literacy requirement for voting at time-1. Later, at time-2, the state decides to pass a law establishing that the completion of the sixth grade in a school where subjects are taught primarily in English or Spanish (including schools in Puerto Rico or Mexico) is sufficient proof of literacy. An individual who completed the sixth grade in France (or Poland) complains that the change wrought by the new law is underinclusive—given the purpose of the state, there is no reason why he should not be included. The state might defend on the ground that it is simply taking one step at a time, and the defense has been allowed.[10]

Such a defense obviously has the capacity for completely undermining the complaint of underinclusiveness—each instance of underinclusiveness might be explained as an instance in which the legislature chose to take

---

The concept of arbitrariness enters only in the establishment of the general method, as a foundational concept, and other factors account for the additional tiers. For an awareness of how the suspect-classification branch of the antidiscrimination principle causes this departure from the rationality test, see Justice Harlan's dissent in Harper v. Virginia Bd. of Elections, 383 U.S. 663, 682 n. 3 (1966).

[10] See Katzenbach v. Morgan, 384 U.S. 641 (1966) (involving American-flag schools). In Williamson v. Lee Optical Co., 348 U.S. 483, 489 (1955), the Court said, "The reform may take one step at a time, addressing itself to the phase of the problem which seems most acute to the legislative mind."

one step at a time. Tussman and tenBroek, fully aware of this risk, sought to limit the defense by drawing a distinction between the reasons that explained why the state took only one step at a time. If the reach of the law was confined because of *administrative* considerations (for example, additional complications would be introduced) as opposed to *political* considerations (for example, the sponsors could not muster enough votes for extending the law to others), then the one-step-at-a-time defense was allowable. The Supreme Court, on the other hand, has on at least one occasion sought to use the concept of "reform" as the limiting one: the state is allowed to take one step at a time on when the law is a "reform" measure—a law that improves (rather than worsens) the status quo.

Another defensive doctrine requires the court to rank the legitimate purposes of the state—to make a distinction between ordinary and special state purposes. Hence, the concept of "a compelling state interest": the achievement of such an interest or purpose is so important that it excuses imperfect means. This doctrine seems to have its roots in the *Japanese Relocation Cases*, where the Supreme Court permitted the use of a racial or national-origin criterion (clearly a suspect one) for determining who should be relocated and otherwise confined.[11] The state purpose-self-preservation of the nation in time of war—was deemed to be of sufficient importance to excuse the overinclusiveness (not all Japanese were security risks) and underinclusiveness (those of German origin might be as much of a security risk).

This appeal to a compelling state interest must be carefully delineated. In the *Japanese Relocation Cases*, the concept was used defensively, to excuse what would otherwise be impermissible, and there was no doubt that the evil to be excused was ill-fit—over- and underinclusiveness. It was not part of a general balancing test. A minor debate has broken out recently, however, as to whether the exclusive focus must remain on ill-fit, or whether there can be, in a case where there is admittedly a perfect fit between means and ends, a "weighing of ends"—a balancing of the harm to the individuals subjected to the law and the good to be achieved.[12] Professor Brest poses the issue in his hypothetical: "How should a court

---

[11] Korematsu v. United States, 323 U.S. 214 (1944) (relocation); see also Hirabayashi v. United States, 320 U.S. 81 (1943) (curfew).

[12] Compare, for example, Ely, p. 727 fn. 26 ("I have argued that, rhetoric to the contrary notwithstanding, special scrutiny in the suspect classification context has in fact consisted not in weighing ends but rather in insisting that the classification in issue fit a constitutionally permissible state goal with greater precision than any available alternative.") with Greenawalt, p. 565 fn. 41 ("It is clear, however, that in some suspect classification cases, the Court has weighed ends, even though it has not been explicit about what it is doing.").

treat a school principal's decision, based solely on aesthetics, to have black and white students sit on opposite sides of the stage at the graduation ceremony?"[13]

There is little doubt in my mind as to how a court would or should decide the case: the practice is a violation of the Equal Protection Clause. But that is not the issue. The issue is whether it is possible to get to that result (or get there as easily as one should) from the antidiscrimination principle—taken as the mediating principle of the Equal Protection Clause. I think not. If the court finds a state purpose that does not allow the slightest degree of over- or underinclusiveness, as is indeed suggested by Professor Brest's hypothetical, then the statute or practice would be valid under the antidiscrimination principle. This would be true even though the criterion is "suspect," for example, race. It would not be permissible, within the structure of the antidiscrimination principle, to decide the question by "balancing" or "weighing" the harm done by the state practice (for example, blacks are stigmatized) against the (noncompelling) interests to be served by the state practice (for example, aesthetic satisfaction). The antidiscrimination principle—as I understand it, as Tussman and tenBroek designed it, and as the Supreme Court has generally used it—is a theory about ill-fit, not about the balance of advantage.[14]

---

[13] *Processes of Constitutional Decisionmaking* (Boston, 1975), p. 489. The oddity of the example is important: it is testimony of how far one must go to find a situation in which complaint of ill-fit could not be made, and thus it reveals the potential reach of the antidiscrimination principle, even as a means focused tool. It is always possible to find ill-fit. I might also add that the example is meant only to reveal the structure of the antidiscrimination principle and it can fulfill that purpose even if it is an unlikely case.

[14] I realize it is difficult to document this assertion (or perhaps any assertion about a so-called mediating principle). The meaning of the word "discrimination" as gleaned from ordinary usage or the dictionaries is hardly decisive. The word merely requires that a distinction be involved in the analysis—perhaps be the trigger of scrutiny. It does not set the limit or terms of scrutiny. Nor is there an authoritative (official) text to which I can point and say, here is the full and definitive statement of the antidiscrimination principle. Even if there were, one might contend (as those who take opposite sides in the issue do) that the rhetoric is not decisive—what is important is not what the courts say, but what they do. But let me say by way of defense that it is important to be clear about what is at stake—I am only trying to construct a prototype for purposes of analysis and exposition. I will ultimately contend that this prototype is too limited, and seek to supplement it. Of course, it might be contended that my conception of the antidiscrimination principle is too narrow and that the supplemental principle could be viewed as only a slight modification of what I call the antidiscrimination principle, for example, that it might be called "antidiscrimination principle 2." The force of that contention depends on the degree of resemblance—whether the supplemental principle is a close relative of the antidiscrimination principle or rather the member of a new family altogether. To decide that issue it is important to understand the intellectual roots of what might be deemed the primary version of the antidiscrimination principle, and there is no dispute that the version focusing on means—the one that conceives of the evil as ill-fit and does not weigh

II. The Appeal of the Antidiscrimination Principle

Antidiscrimination has been the predominant interpretation of the Equal Protection Clause. The examples I have given are cast primarily in terms of race, but the principle also controls cases that do not involve race. It is the general interpretation of the Equal Protection Clause; and indeed it is viewed as having preemptive effect—if the state statute or practice passes the means-end test, then it does not violate the Clause. There have been exceptions, but they have been criticized precisely because they were departures from the principle. It was the substantive character of the one-man, one-vote standard of *Reynolds v. Sims*[15] that prompted Justice Harlan's strong dissent. The standard criticism of that decision invokes the antidiscrimination principle, which would have allowed distinctions among voters if, for example, those differences in treatment were related to legitimate interests, such as preserving the integrity of government subdivisions.

Why, it might fairly be asked, has the antidiscrimination principle been given this position of preeminence? The Equal Protection Clause may need some mediating principle, but why this one? An answer couched in terms of text and history does not suffice. The antidiscrimination principle is not compelled or even suggested by the language of the Clause. That language stands in sharp contrast to that of the Fifteenth Amendment, which does speak in terms of discrimination—the right to vote shall not be denied on account of race. Nor is the antidiscrimination interpretation securely rooted in the legislative history of the Clause. The debates preceding the adoption of the Equal Protection Clause, as best I have been able to determine, do not justify this choice.[16] Nor is there

---

ends—is the primary one. At the very most commentators such as Brest or Greenawalt argue that the principle should be extended far enough to embrace a weighing of ends, and concede that it is predominantly expressive of a conception of means-end rationality.

[15] 377 U.S. 533, 615-624 (1964). See also Justice Harlan's dissent in Harper v. Virginia Bd. of Elections, 383 U.S. 663, 682 (1966).

[16] The materials which have been examined, including the debates on the Fourteenth Amendment itself, are not revealing, and obviously not decisive on an intended mediating principle. See, for example, H. Flack, *The Adoption of the Fourteenth Amendment* (Gloucester, Mass., 1908); Frank & Munro, "The Original Understanding of 'Equal Protection of the Laws,'" 50 COLUM. L. REV. 131 (1950); J. James, *The Framing of the Fourteenth Amendment* (1956); J. tenBroek, *Equal Under Law* (New York, 1965). In all fairness I should report that tenBroek's research led him to conclude that "equal" was of secondary importance to "protection" in the Fourteenth Amendment. He wrote, "It was because the protection of the laws was denied to some men that the word 'equal' was used. The word 'full' would have done as well." tenBroek, p. 237. I have not examined the history of all the civil rights debates during the Thirty-ninth Congress. As secondary sources on these debates, see C. Fairman,

any reason to believe that antidiscrimination was chosen by the Court as *the* interpretation because of some special view of the legislative history. Yet, even with history and text aside, it is important to note that the predominance of the antidiscrimination principle can in large part be traced to considerations that are particularly appealing to a court.

First, the antidiscrimination principle embodies a conception of equality that roughly corresponds to the conception of equality governing the judicial process. When we speak of "equal justice" we have in mind a norm prohibiting the adjudicator from taking into account certain irrelevant characteristics of the litigants—their race, wealth, and so on. That is the message conveyed by the blindfold on the icon of justice. The antidiscrimination principle also invokes the metaphor of blindness—as in "color blindness."[17] The overarching obligation is to treat similar persons similarly, declaring certain individual characteristics—such as color—irrelevant.

It is natural for the Justices to seize upon the ideal of their craft in setting norms to govern others. Their craft sets limits to their horizons, it influences their choice among the many meanings of equality. This limit on vision may have been reinforced by the fact that some of the early equal protection cases challenged exclusionary conduct occurring in the course of the judicial process.[18] Moreover, the words "protection of the laws" in the Clause may have led the Justices to think primarily of the Administration of justice, and the concept of equality that governs judicial activity in general (equal justice). At some point in history the word "equal" shifts its location so as to deemphasize the word "protection"—it becomes understood that the Clause guarantees "the protection of

---

Oliver Wendell Holmes Devise History of The Supreme Court, Volume VI, Reconstruction and Reunion 1864-1888, part one (New York, 1971), pp. 1117-1300; Bickel, "The Original Understanding and the Segregation Decision," 69 HARV. L. REV. 1 (1955); and Casper, "Jones v. Mayer: Clio, Bemused and Confused Muse," 1968 SUP. CT. REV. 89. But the provisions of the Civil Rights Act of 1866 which are still with us, 42 U.S.C. 1981 and 1982, do not speak in terms of discrimination. Instead, they say all persons "shall have the same right . . . as is enjoyed by white citizens. . . ."

[17] This metaphor first surfaced in Justice Harlan's dissent in Plessy v. Ferguson, 163 U.S. 537, 559 (1896) ("our Constitution is color-blind"). The metaphor was suggested by the attorney for the blacks, Albion W. Tourgee, and he—clever lawyer that he must have been—understood why this metaphor would be appealing to a judge. Page 19 of Tourgee's brief in *Plessy* reads: "Justice is pictured blind and her daughter, the Law, ought at least to be color-blind."

[18] For example, Strauder v. West Virginia, 100 U.S. 303 (1880); Virginia v. Rives, 100 U.S. 313 (1880) (both involve the exclusion of blacks from the jury).

equal laws," rather than just the "equal protection of the laws"; but the implications of the original version still linger.[19]

Second, the antidiscrimination principle seems to further another supposed norm of the craft—value neutrality—that the judges not substitute their preferences for those of the people. The antidiscrimination principle seems to respond to an aspiration for a "mechanical jurisprudence"—to use Roscoe Pound's phrase—by making the predicate of intervention appear technocratic. The antidiscrimination principle seems to ask no more of the judiciary than that it engage in what might at first seem to be the near mathematical task of determining whether there is, in Tussman and tenBroek's terms, "overinclusiveness" or "underinclusiveness," or, in the terms of the contemporary commentators, whether there is the right "fit" between means and ends. The terms used have an attractively quantitative ring. They make the task of judicial judgment appear to involve as little discretion as when a salesman advises a customer whether a pair of shoes fit. Moreover, under the antidiscrimination principle, whatever judgment there is would seem to be one about means, not ends, thereby insulating judges from the charge of substituting their judgments for that of the legislature. The court could invalidate state action without passing on the merit or importance of the end—a task, it might be argued, that is especially committed to the more representative branches of government.[20]

The belief that the countermajoritarian objection to judicial review can be avoided by a "mechanical jurisprudence" is false. The entitlement of the judiciary to intervene is no less controversial because only the means are being attacked. They too have been chosen by the people. And there is, in any event, nothing mechanical about the antidiscrimination principle. The promise of value neutrality is only an illusion. On the explicit level, the court must determine whether the state end is legitimate, which classifications are suspect, which rights are fundamental, which legitimate state interests are compelling, and whether the occasion is a proper one for invoking the one-step-at-a-time defense. On the implicit level, the preferences of the judge enter the judicial process when he formulates the imaginable state purposes and chooses among them, and also

---

[19] Tussman and tenBroek, p. 342.

[20] See Gunther, pp. 21, 23, 28, 43, who echoes the sentiment expressed in Justice Jackson's concurrence in Railway Express Agency v. New York, 336 U.S. 106, 111-13 (1949). Professor Gunther makes the argument as part of his plea to abandon the fundamental-right branch of the strict-scrutiny inquiry, and thus to make the antidiscrimination principle more focused on means.

when he decides whether the criterion is sufficiently ill-suited to warrant invalidation—whether the right degree of fit is present. In contrast to the case of shoes, the concept of fit here has no quantitative content. It only sounds quantitative—as do the words "how much" when used to describe the intensity of affection.

A third explanation for the predominance of the antidiscrimination principle may be found in another supposed ideal of the law—objectivity. In this instance the aspiration is for rules with three characteristics: (a) the rules can be stated with some sharpness or certainty; (b) they are not heavily dependent on factual inquiries or judgments of degree; and (c) they are not time-bound. Rules of this sort are thought to be more "manageable"[21] and to conform to some abstract view about the necessary attributes of "legal rules"—a view likely to be shared by those seeking a "mechanical jurisprudence" and value-neutrality. I once again doubt the validity of the supposed ideal of objectivity,[22] but it cannot be denied that the antidiscrimination principle makes some contribution toward the satisfaction of this ideal, perhaps to a greater degree than toward the ideal of value-neutrality. With the possible exception of the inquiries necessary to identify the true criterion, an inquiry that need be taken only when administrative action is being challenged, the antidiscrimination principle is not especially fact-oriented. More often than not, over- and underinclusiveness is established, not by a presentation of evidence, but rather by the process of imagination—imagining whether, given the state purpose, other persons might be included within the coverage of the statute or whether people who were included might properly have been excluded. Little turns on the actual numbers involved. Moreover, although uncertainty and gradations of degree may be introduced by certain of the critical judgments required by the principle, for example, judgments about which purposes are legitimate and what is the requisite degree of fit, it is entirely possible that these judgments could be made with a high degree of generality. Once the Supreme Court spoke to an issue—for example, once the Court declared a certain criterion (such as race) to be suspect—a flat rule would emerge (no racial discrimination) that could easily be applied by the lower courts. Indeed, when the antidiscrimination principle was adopted by the legislative branch, and made the central regulatory device of the Civil Rights Acts of 1964 and 1968, it was expressed in a form that satisfied the objectivist ideal. The

---

[21] Gunther, p. 24.

[22] Fiss, "The Jurisprudence of Busing," 39 *Law & Contemp. Prob.* 194 (1975).

statutes specified the criteria (such as race, sex, religion, and national origin) that could not be the basis of discrimination.[23]

Fourth, the appeal of the antidiscrimination principle may derive from the fact that it appears highly individualistic. The method for determining the permissibility of classifications does not rely, so Tussman and tenBroek proclaim, on the concept of a "natural class" (where "natural" refers not to the biological origins of the class, but rather to the fact that it is not formally created by the law in question). They acknowledge that a judgment about the arbitrariness of a classification might conceivably depend on whether it "coincides with" social groupings deemed appropriate; in that instance, the central inquiry in an equal protection case would be "whether, in defining a class, the legislature has carved the universe at a natural joint."[24] Tussman and tenBroek sought to avoid that inquiry, an inquiry they declared to be "fruitless," and did so by making the permissibility of the classification turn exclusively on the relation of means to end. Hence, the antidiscrimination principle would seem individualistic in a negative sense—it is not in any way dependent on a recognition of social classes or groups. Indeed, that is why means-end rationality is such an attractive concept: it avoids the need of making any statement about the basic societal units.

To some degree this appearance is misleading. The foundational concept—means-end rationality—is individualistic. It is not dependent on the recognition of social groups. On the other hand, elements of groupism appear as one moves up the superstructure. For one thing, the recognition and protection of social groups may be required to determine which state purposes are legitimate, or even to rank state purposes to apply the compelling state-interest doctrine. The paradigm of a state purpose that is illegitimate is couched in terms of a group: "The desire to keep blacks in a position of subordination is an illegitimate state purpose." And the standard of illegitimacy is constructed by attributing what might be viewed as a group-oriented purpose to the Equal Protection Clause—to

---

[23] Some statutes make exceptions for certain criteria: under the Civil Rights Act of 1968, religion is a permissible criterion for allocating housing owned by a religious society, and under the Civil Rights Act of 1964 discrimination on the basis of sex is permitted in employment when sex is a "bona fide occupational criterion." Moreover, the courts have permitted the remedial use of a criterion that seemed to be flatly forbidden (for example, color-conscious employment is often decreed to correct the effects of past discrimination)—a judicial improvisation that has been ratified by Congress in the course of reenactments (Equal Employment Opportunity Act of 1972). From this perspective, despite the striking difference in language, the civil rights statutes have been treated as mini-equal protection clauses.

[24] Tussman and tenBroek, p. 346.

protect blacks from hostile state action.[25] Admittedly the paradigm of a "compelling state interest" is not often expressed in group terms. That doctrine emerged in the *Japanese Relocation Cases* of the 1940s and there the state interest deemed "compelling" was "self-preservation of a nation at a time of war." But, as Justice Brennan recently perceived, the concept of a compelling state interest might be stretched to embrace the protection of certain groups. In the context of a statute that embodied a classification favoring women, he wrote: "I agree that, in providing a special benefit for a needy segment of society long the victim of purposeful discrimination and neglect, the statute serves the compelling state interest of achieving equality for such groups."[26]

The suspect-classification doctrine also affords some recognition to the role or importance of social groups or natural classes. This is apparent from the original and classic statement of the doctrine by Justice Black: "It should be noted, to begin with, that all legal restrictions which curtail the civil rights of a single racial group are immediately suspect."[27] Tussman and tenBroek, intent on keeping groups out of their account of the Equal Protection Clause, quoted this passage of Justice Black but were then careful to add that "suspect classification" should not be thought of as coextensive with a "single racial group." The obvious next question is whether there are any "suspect classifications" that do not identify a natural class or social group. To this, they simply replied, "[A]n attempt at an exhaustive listing of suspect classifications would be pointless. It suffices to say that this is of necessity a rather loose category."[28] In the last twenty-five years, the category has been kept "loose"; but the important fact to note is that almost all of the serious candidates for the status of suspect classification are those that coincide with what might be conceived of as natural classes—for example, blacks, Chicanos, women, and maybe the poor. Moreover, although Tussman and tenBroek did not even try to explain why certain classifications were suspect, it is not at

---

[25] I think this might—to be somewhat cynical—explain why Tussman and tenBroek tried to talk in terms of two different principles—that of "reasonable classification" and that of "discriminatory legislation"—even though they perceived the interconnections between the principles and the fact that they might be embraced with one principle—what I have called the antidiscrimination principle.

[26] Kahn v. Shevin, 416 U.S. 351, 358-59 (1974) (dissenting opinion, joined by Justice Marshall). I suspect that group recognition might also enter through deciding when to honor the one-step-at-a-time defense. See *Katzenbach v. Morgan*, referred to fn. 10 above, another opinion written by Justice Brennan.

[27] Korematsu v. United States, 323 U.S. 214, 216 (1944).

[28] Tussman and tenBroek, p. 356.

all clear to me that an adequate explanation can be given that does not recognize the role and importance of social groups.

Some might explain the suspectness of race, to use the exemplar of a suspect classification, in terms of the special history of the Equal Protection Clause.[29] But that explanation does not altogether avoid the reference to groups, for it may be contended that the Clause was not intended to ban the racial classification but rather to protect blacks—as a group—from hostile state action. And in any event, that explanation might be too confining. It anchors the category of suspect classification in historical fact, without room for the kind of generality expected of constitutional doctrines, a generality that might be sufficient to embrace new situations (for example, the demand of women that sex be treated as a suspect classification).[30] Others might seek to explain the suspectness of race solely on the grounds of immutability.[31] That would avoid the reference to groups, but would be an inadequate explanation for it would also render suspect such classifications as "height," "good hearing," "good eyesight," or "intelligence"—a result the antidiscrimination theorist would no doubt deny. A final explanation for the suspectness of race that might avoid the reference to groups, and that indeed does have a connection with the foundational concept of means-end rationality, asserts that race is "generally . . . irrelevant to any legitimate public purpose."[32] This would make the individualism of the antidiscrimination strategy pure. But I fail to understand how a claim about general practices

---

[29] In his dissent in Harper v. Virginia Bd. of Elections, 383 U.S. 663, 682, fn. 3 (1966), Justice Harlan argued that "insofar as that clause may embody a particular value in addition to rationality, the historical origins of the Civil War Amendments might attribute to racial equality this special status."

[30] See Getman, The Emerging Constitutional Principle of Sexual Equality, 1972 SUP. CT. REV. 157.

[31] See, for example, Frontiero v. Richardson, 411 U.S. 677, 686 (1973).

[32] "Developments in the Law–Equal Protection," 82 HARV. L. REV. 1065, 1108 (1969). In response to this explanation, Professor Ely argues, "The fact that a characteristic is irrelevant in almost all legal contexts (as most characteristics are) need not imply that there is anything wrong in seizing upon it in the rare context where it does make a difference." Id. at n.39. But this response seems to confuse the suspect-classification doctrine with the forbidden-classification doctrine—an absolute ban on all racial classification. This is seen most clearly by noting that Ely's fn. 39 refers to that portion of the Tussman and tenBroek article that eschews the forbidden-classification doctrine (for the reason he articulates) not to the portion of their article that deals with the suspect classification doctrine. It should be noted that Professor Ely's explanation for the suspectness of race, the we-they theory discussed below, is a theory cast in group terms—it seeks to explain legislative motivation in terms of group membership.

(race is generally unrelated) can yield a special standard about the degree of fit (or relatedness) to be required—and that is precisely the function of the suspect-classification doctrine—to trigger strict scrutiny, making any avoidable over- or underinclusiveness impermissible.

Once again, what we are left with is an illusion—that the antidiscrimination principle need not depend on the recognition of "natural classes." This illusion of individualism can be maintained only by ignoring or failing to justify some of the key elements of the antidiscrimination strategy—elements that might be deemed part of the superstructure, but are nonetheless essential for they have made us willing to live with that strategy.

Wholly apart from this question of whether all the elements of the antidiscrimination principle—the superstructure as well as the foundation—are explicable on individualistic premises, it should be noted that the antidiscrimination principle furthers the ideal of individualism more subtly by making classification the focus of the Equal Protection Clause. Classification is the triggering mechanism and the object of inquiry. To be sure, not all classifications are prohibited, only those that are imprecise. Yet the demand for greater and greater precision in classification has the inevitable effect of disqualifying one classification after another, and that demand is consistent with, and indeed furthers the ideal of treating people as "individuals"—recognizing each person's unique position in time and space, his unique combination of talent, ability and character, and his particular conduct. The pervasiveness of this ideal in society cannot be denied, nor is it likely that judges would be insensitive to it.

The tie between individualism and the antidiscrimination principle may also stem from the fact that it yields a highly individualized conception of rights. Under the antidiscrimination principle, the constitutional flaw inheres in the structure of the statute or the conduct of the administrator, not in its impact on any group or class. Any individual who happens to be burdened by a statute or practice, or any individual excluded from the benefits, can complain of the wrong. True, other persons—namely all those within the legal classification—can make a similar complaint; and in a sense the individual is making the claim as part of a group or class (the legal class). But, the individual's entitlement to relief is not dependent on the interests or desires of others similarly subject to or excluded from the statute or practice.

Such an individualized conception of rights coincides with one strong view of what we mean by a "constitutional right"—the vindication turns on the judgment of the tribunal, not upon the views or action of third parties. Institutional considerations also make the individualized conception of rights appealing. The Equal Protection Clause is primarily enforced through litigation, and it is especially difficult to fit the vindication of group rights into the mold of the law suit. There is no way of making certain that the plaintiff is the appropriate representative of the group, and even more, there is no mechanism for resolving intraclass conflicts—differences among the members of a group as to what is in their best interest.[33]

Finally, under the antidiscrimination principle, equal protection rights are not only individualized, but also universalized and this is another source of its appeal. Everyone is protected. There may be a limitation on the laws brought within its sweep—they must contain a discrimination or classification. But once a distinction among persons is made by a state statute or practice, that measure can be tested by anyone who happens to be burdened by it. Even the suspect-classification doctrine can be construed in universalistic terms—any racial classification, whether black, yellow, or white, is suspect. In contrast, a mediating principle that is, for example, built on the concept of social groups might not be so universal in scope, since it is conceivable that some individual adversely affected by the state might not be a member of one of the protected groups.

The universalizing tendency of the antidiscrimination principle no doubt accounts for its popular appeal—no person seems to be given more protection than another. This universalizing tendency also appeals to a court. It relieves the judiciary of the burden of deciding who will receive the protection (in the jurisdictional sense) of a constitutional provision and then explaining why some are left out. It also creates a strategic advantage for the court—it enables the court to use the Equal Protection Clause to fill some of the gaps created by the (temporary?) retirement of substantive due process. The antidiscrimination principle can be used just as comfortably to challenge a statute that draws a distinction between opticians and optometrists or one that draws a distinction between filled

---

[33] Such differences frequently arise and they are not in any way resolved by the class action device. That procedural device (viewed from the plaintiff's side) only legitimizes the concept of the self-appointed representative, and then seeks to erect safeguards—such as notice—to limit, as far as possible the risk of abuse arising from this power of self-appointment. But the factors that tend to legitimize the mechanism of self-appointment also tend to undermine the effectiveness of the safeguards—each individual stands to gain so little. When the stakes are small it does not make sense for an individual to start a law suit, and for the very same reason it does not make sense for the individual to respond to the notice in order to scrutinize the adequacy of his self-appointed representative. And without such a response, there is no reliable way of judging the adequacy of representation. There is an adversarial void—neither the defendant nor the self-appointed representative has an interest in challenging the adequacy. Indeed, from the defendants' perspective the best representative is an inadequate one (at least if adequacy is judged from the perspective of effectiveness).

milk and margarine as it can be used to challenge a statute that draws a distinction between whites and blacks.[34] The result may be different, but that is not due to any fundamental shift of theory, but only to a difference in the degree of fit required.

III. The Limitations of the Antidiscrimination Principle

The appeal of the antidiscrimination principle may be unfounded. The ideals served by the principle may not have any intrinsic merit, or the connection between those ideals and the principle may be nothing more than an illusion. As we have seen, the antidiscrimination principle may be criticized on this level. But I believe the criticism runs deeper. The antidiscrimination principle has structural limitations that prevent it from adequately resolving or even addressing certain central claims of equality now being advanced. For these claims the antidiscrimination principle either provides no framework of analysis or, even worse, provides the wrong one. Conceivably, the principle might be adjusted by making certain structural modifications; and indeed, on occasion, over the last twenty-five years, that has occurred, though on an ad hoc and incremental basis, and at the expense of severing the principle from its theoretical foundations and widening the gap between the principle and the ideals it is supposed to serve.

The Permissibility of Preferential Treatment

One shortcoming of the antidiscrimination principle relates to the problem of preferential treatment for blacks. This is a difficult issue, but the antidiscrimination principle makes it more difficult than it is: the permissibility of preferential treatment is tied to the permissibility of hostile treatment against blacks. The antidiscrimination principle does not formally acknowledge social groups, such as blacks; nor does it offer any special dispensation for conduct that benefits a disadvantaged group. It only knows criteria or classifications; and the color black is as much a racial criterion as the color white. The regime it introduces is

---

[34] See, for example, Williamson v. Lee Optical Co., 348 U.S. 483 (1955). It is striking that Tussman and tenBroek built their "reasonable classification" principle (which I call the antidiscrimination principle) almost entirely out of the business regulation cases—the traditional province of substantive due process. This can be explained in part by the fact that at least up until 1949, this was the principal use of the Equal Protection Clause. Their formulation was bound by the prior practice, just as mine is bound by the intervening twenty-five years' experience—where the Clause was principally used as a means of protecting the racial minority.

a symmetrical one of "color blindness," making the criterion of color, any color, presumptively impermissible. Reverse discrimination, so the argument is made, is a form of discrimination and is equally arbitrary since it is based on race.

The defense of preferential treatment under the antidiscrimination regime begins with the search for a purpose that the racial criterion (the color black) would fit perfectly. This is not an easy undertaking. To illustrate the difficulty, let us assume that the policy at issue is one preferring blacks for admission to law school.[35] The first impulse is to identify the purpose as one of increasing the number of black lawyers. Surely if that is the purpose, there is a perfect fit between criterion and purpose—no margins of over- or underinclusiveness. But what appears at first to be a purpose seems to be nothing more than a restatement of the practice. Why does the state want to increase the number of black lawyers? The answer to this question yields what may more properly be deemed a purpose.

An answer cast in terms of the self-interest of the class or in terms of the preferences of those in power (for example, they happen to like blacks) would not be adequate. These answers would not yield a legitimate state purpose. But a number of purposes would be served by the preferential treatment that could be deemed permissible. Here are some examples: to elevate the status of a perpetual underclass by giving certain members of the group positions of power and prestige (on the theory that the elevation of the group will enhance the self-image and aspirations of all members of the group); to insulate the minority from future hostile action by strategically placing members of the group in positions of power; to diversify the student body intellectually and culturally and thereby enrich the educational experience of all; or, finally, to atone for past wrongs to the group. The difficulty with each of these purposes is, however, that once the perspective shifts from groups to individuals, as the antidiscrimination principle requires, the margins of under- and/or overinclusiveness become apparent and indeed pronounced. The fit between criterion (black) and purpose is not perfect—perhaps just as imperfect as the fit between the criterion and purpose when the action is hostile. The overinclusiveness stems from the fact that there are blacks who are not entitled to the preferential treatment if any of these were the state purpose (the common example is the upper class black, who arguably did not suffer past discrimination and/or independently of the

---

[35] DeFunis v. Odegaard, 416 U.S. 312 (1974). See also two symposia, "DeFunis: The Road Not Taken," 60 VA. L. REV. 917 (1974), and "DeFunis Symposium," 75 COLUM. L. REV. 483 (1975).

preferential admission to the law school, would be a "success"). The underinclusiveness stems from the fact that there are other persons who are not black and who are nevertheless as entitled to preferential treatment as blacks if the state purpose is what I have imagined (for example, Chicanos, Orientals, the poor).

The next move in the defense of preferential treatment under the antidiscrimination principle is to discover ways of tolerating these margins of ill-fit. The defense of the overinclusion is likely to be couched in terms of administrative convenience.[36] True, not all blacks are entitled to the preferential treatment, but it would be exceedingly difficult and costly to try to pick out those not deserving the preferential treatment, and the costs would not be worth the gains. Administrative convenience may also be used to justify the underinclusion, particularly as it relates to the poor. It would be difficult, so the argument runs, to pick out those nonblacks who have the same social or economic status as blacks and thus, under the stipulated purposes, are as deserving of preferential treatment as blacks. Blackness is an easy criterion to work with, and although there may be mistakes, they are small compared to the costs inherent in the use of alternative criteria ("poor" or "low socioeconomic status"). The difficulty with this administrative convenience argument is that it is standard practice to reject such a defense when whites rather than blacks are the preferred race. Why should this defense be accepted in one context and not another?

Professor Ely's we-they analysis (see fn. 3) might be thought to be responsive to this dilemma. He argues that when the dominant group (whites) use the racial criterion for conferring benefits on the minority (preferential treatment for blacks), there is less reason to be suspicious than when they use the racial criterion for conferring benefits on their own class (preferential treatment for whites). When benefits are conferred by one class upon its own members, the risk is high that the arguments about administrative convenience are a sham: it is like voting oneself a pay raise. The risk is high that you would believe any argument in favor of the decision, irrespective of the merits. But when a sacrifice is involved, so the argument continues, as when members of one group (we) confer a benefit on another group (they) at its own (our) expense, then there is less reason to be suspicious of the arguments used to defend that action.

I have some difficulty with the psychological model upon which the we-they analysis rests. It is incomplete. The only motivational factor

---

[36] See Nickel, "Preferential Policies in Hiring and Admissions: A Jurisprudential Approach," 75 Colum. L. Rev. 534, 550-53 (1975).

reflected is self-interest (elaborated in terms of group membership). But, of course, as seems particularly true in the case of preferential admission of blacks to law school, there may be other motivational factors that make arguments about administrative convenience especially suspect. The body making the decision may tend to overvalue arguments about administrative convenience out of a feeling of guilt or fear (for example, of disruption in the university) and there may be little to check those impulses since the costs of the preferential policy are primarily borne by "others" (not the professors or administrators who decide upon the admission policy but by some of the rejected nonblack applicants—not the superstars, but rather by those who are at the end of the meritocratic queue).[37]

The principal difficulty with this we-they analysis is not, however, the incompleteness of the psychological model; for it is conceivable this could be corrected. Rather the principal difficulty stems from what this model (or perhaps any model focusing on the psychology of the discriminators) yields. As Professor Ely acknowledges, the we-they analysis can only provide grounds for (asymmetrical) suspicion, and yet that does not seem sufficient.[38] For even if suspicion turns out to be wrong, and the argument of administrative convenience is determined to have merit, to be sincere and well-founded, the argument would still be rejected as a justification for ill-fit when preferential treatment is being conferred on whites.

For example, imagine it is the 1940s, the state electorate is predominantly white and the state legislature directs the law school to adopt a preferential admission policy in favor of whites.[39] Assume also that this

---

[37] Burt, "Helping Suspect Groups Disappear" (unpublished manuscript, 1975); Greenawalt, pp. 573-74.

[38] I think Ely went wrong in reading the suspect-classification doctrine too weakly. When the Supreme Court and commentators, such as Tussman and tenBroek, spoke of suspect classification, they were trying to express a substantive, not just an evidentiary judgment—that in the generality of cases certain kinds of classification will be invalid. The suspect-classification doctrine was simply a way of avoiding a flat no-exception per se rule—a doctrine of forbidden classifications (no racial classifications at all). When it rejected the forbidden-classification doctrine, the Court may have been looking ahead to the problem of preferential treatment and for that reason rejected the forbidden-classification doctrine. But the discussion of this issue in Tussman and tenBroek, and the fact that the doctrine originates in the *Japanese Relocation Cases*, leads me to other explanations: a forbidden-classification doctrine would be hard to reconcile with the generality of the language of the Equal Protection Clause; and it would have tied the hands of the legislators and administrators too much, precluding the use of the classification in even extraordinary instances—such as those involving the relocation of the Japanese.

[39] See Sweatt v. Painter, 339 U.S. 629 (1950).

policy is justified on the ground that whites are better prepared academically (given the dual school system) and that the state wishes to have the most brilliant persons as members of the bar. Color is used because of administrative convenience. Under the we-they analysis, there is reason to be suspicious about this explanation of the use of race; the policy in effect serves the class interest of whites and it is likely that the white legislators (or administrators) will undervalue the costs to the blacks of an imprecise fit and mistakenly believe only the "negative myths" about blacks. But it would seem to me that even if that suspicion were refuted, even if it were (somehow) demonstrated that the argument about administrative convenience was sincere and well-founded and in some sense accurate, the result would still be unacceptable under the Equal Protection Clause. Those who are committed to the antidiscrimination principle can reach this result only by insisting that the arguments of administrative convenience are no defense to ill-fit, even assuming that they are sincere and well-founded. It is that move, above all, that plays into the hands of those who wish to attack preferential treatment in favor of blacks: why, they will ask, should administrative convenience be allowed to justify ill-fit when the state action is beneficial to the minority but not when it is hostile to the minority?

The we-they analysis cannot resolve this dilemma because it is only an evidentiary, and not a substantive, approach. There are, however, two other strategies employed within the context of the antidiscrimination principle to justify preferential treatment, and these do seem more substantive. One such strategy shifts the definition of the harm—classifications should not be judged in terms of the means-end relationship (fit), but rather in terms of whether they stigmatize.[40] An exclusionary classification aimed at blacks stigmatizes them in a way that preferential treatment does not stigmatize whites; administrative convenience cannot justify or offset the stigmatizing harm caused by the exclusionary policy, and the nonstigmatizing preferential policy does not call for a justification (or if it calls for one, it need be only a weak one, for which administrative convenience will suffice). I am willing to assume that the preferential policy does not stigmatize the rejected applicants,[41] and yet this strategy still seems unsatisfactory. It moves beyond the structure of

---

[40] See Brest, "Palmer v. Thompson: An Approach to the Problem of Unconstitutional Legislative Motive," 1971 SUP. CT. REV. 95, 116 fn. 109; and Brest, *Processes of Constitutional Decisionmaking* (Boston, 1975), p. 481. See also Greenawalt, p. 566.

[41] Fiss, "School Desegregation: The Uncertain Path of the Law," 4 *Philosophy & Public Affairs* 3, 13 (1974). Some have argued that a preferential admissions policy stigmatizes the blacks admitted under it. See Burt, fn. 37 above.

the antidiscrimination principle in that (a) the evil becomes stigma rather than ill-fit, and (b) it contemplates a weighing of ends—a judgment as to whether the state interest is of sufficient importance to offset the harm. A connection with the original antidiscrimination principle remains: the trigger remains the same—classification. But that seems to be a trivial connection. The tie with the foundational concept—means-end rationality—is severed. And once this step is taken, it is hard to confine the modification. It is difficult to explain why classification should be the only trigger for the Equal Protection Clause and, even if it is, why that Clause should be concerned only with stigmatic harm (or why stigmatic harm alone is capable of overriding a defense of administrative convenience). The rejected white applicant may not be stigmatized, but he is being harmed in other ways; and there is nothing in the theory underlying the antidiscrimination principle that suggests why nonstigmatic harm should be given a subordinate (or weaker) status. And if it is not given that subordinate status, then we are back to the same dilemma of symmetry: why reject administrative convenience in one context and not in the other?

The final move in defense of preferential treatment under the antidiscrimination principle is to invoke one or both of the standard defenses. The charge of underinclusiveness might be defended on the one-step-at-a-time theory—this time the law school helps blacks, next time Chicanos, and so on. This would be considered a "reform" measure, while the exclusionary policy would only be a "regression." The defense of compelling state interest may also be deployed: the purposes served by the preferential admission program are especially desirable or important, while those served by the exclusionary one (having the bar consist of the academically superior) are ordinary.[42] The up-shot of both defenses is that the ill-fit (the over- and underinclusiveness) is excused in one case (the preference for blacks) but not in the other (the exclusion of blacks).

The problem with both these defensive moves is that they are devoid of any theoretical foundations. In the ultimate analysis, they are resolution by fiat; for the antidiscrimination principle does not supply any basis or standards for determining what is "reform" and what is "regression," what is an "ordinary" state purpose, and what is a "special" one. These

---

[42] Greenawalt, pp. 574-79, distinguishes between a "compelling interest" and a "substantial interest." He argues, "Because benign racial classifications are less 'suspect,' however, a 'substantial' public interest should be enough to support them." Karst and Horowitz, on the other hand, contend that racial classifications "must be tested against the exacting standard of the 'compelling state interest' formula." "Affirmative Action and Equal Protection," 60 VA. L. REV. 955, 965 (1974).

distinctions can only be made if the court has some notion of what is "good" or "desirable," only if the court identifies certain substantive ends as those to be favored under the Equal Protection Clause. As an intellectual feat this may be possible but not within the confines of the antidiscrimination principle. That principle disclaims any reliance on substantive ends.[43] Indeed that is thought to be a primary source of its appeal.

In my judgment, the preferential and exclusionary policies should be viewed quite differently under the Equal Protection Clause. Indeed, it would be one of the strangest and cruelest ironies to interpret that Clause in such a way that linked—in some tight, inextricable fashion—the judgments about the preferential and exclusionary policies. This dilemma can only be avoided if the applicable mediating principle of the Clause is clearly and explicitly asymmetrical, one that talks about substantive ends, and not fit, and one that recognizes the existence and importance of groups, not just individuals. Only then will it be possible to believe that when we reject the claim against preferential treatment for blacks we are not at the same time undermining the constitutional basis for protecting them. Of course, even if the antidiscrimination principle were not the predominant interpretation of the Clause, it might still be possible to formulate a claim against preferential treatment. The element of individual unfairness to the rejected applicants inherent in preferential treatment could be considered a cost in evaluating the state action in the same way as a loss of liberty or a dignitary harm might be. The failure of the state to include other disadvantaged groups, such as the Chicanos, might also become significant. But the impenetrable barrier posed by the seemingly symmetrical antidiscrimination principle would be gone. The stakes would not be so high.

Nondiscriminatory State Action

The antidiscrimination principle has created several gaps in the coverage of the Equal Protection Clause. The principle purports to be universalistic in terms of the persons protected, and yet it turns out to be far from universalistic in terms of the state practices proscribed. The gaps in coverage arise from the fact that not all objectionable state conduct is discriminatory. Discrimination involves a choice among persons and, as I said, an antidiscrimination principle operates by prohibiting government

---

[43] It might also be noted that this disclaimer is also inconsistent with the legitimate purpose limitation.

from making that choice arbitrarily. But there are government enactments or practices where no choice is made among persons and of these it does not make sense to ask whether there is "arbitrary" discrimination. I am not complaining of the fact that the antidiscrimination principle leaves standing state conduct that should be invalidated; but rather that it provides no frame of reference for assessing certain types of state conduct and for that reason is incomplete.

This gap in part accounts for the difficulty the Supreme Court has had with some of the classic state action cases. One such case is *Shelley v. Kraemer*. The Court there invalidated a state policy of enforcing racially restrictive covenants, and although that result seems right, on an analytic level *Shelley v. Kraemer*[44] is generally deemed to be an extraordinarily difficult case—the Finnegans Wake of constitutional law.[45] The difficult question was not, in my judgment, whether the state judges who enforced the restrictive covenant were acting as representatives of the "state." True, that issue was discussed by the Court, but it hardly seemed of any moment. Rather the troublesome question arose in trying to determine whether the state's action was the kind of "action" prohibited by the Equal Protection Clause. The Clause was viewed as prohibiting (racial) discrimination, and only that. The state asserted that its policy was not in any way discriminatory—restrictive covenants would be enforced against blacks and whites alike.

The basis of the Court's rejection of this defense remains a mystery to me to this day. Only a couple of sentences in the opinion purport to be responsive. In one the Court mentions the factual assertions of plaintiffs that, by and large, these racially restrictive covenants are used against blacks, rather than whites. The Court seemed willing to assume the truthfulness of this assertion as a factual matter, but it was hesitant to conclude much from it. That seemed a sound instinct, provided the Court was confined to the antidiscrimination principle and wanted to invalidate the policy, rather than its application; as long as the state stands ready to, and in fact would, enforce a racially restrictive covenant against whites this state policy cannot itself be deemed a form of racial discrimination. The other response is the well-known passage of *Shelley v. Kraemer* declaring that the Equal Protection Clause protects individual rights.[46] But I fail to see why this is responsive to the state's

---

[44] 334 U.S. 1 (1948).

[45] Kurland, "Foreword: Equal in Origin and Equal in Title to the Legislative and Executive Branches of the Government," 78 HARV. L. REV. 143, 148 (1964).

[46] The text reads: "The rights created by the first section of the Fourteenth Amendment are, by its terms, guaranteed to the individual. The rights established are personal rights." 334

defense—there is no discrimination by the state. The more appropriate response to the state would be to reject its premise as to the kind of state action prohibited by the Clause. Why, I would ask, must the action of the state be discriminatory before it is deemed a violation of the Equal Protection Clause?

Recently, the Court was faced with another state action case that presented a similar problem and, given the faulty frame of reference, the result was not so fortuitous. In *Moose Lodge*,[47] Pennsylvania granted a liquor license to a private club that discriminated on the basis of race. The club refused to serve blacks. The liquor license did not confer monopoly power but it was of great benefit to the club and, even more importantly, it had the effect of limiting the places available in the locality for blacks to purchase liquor. Only a limited number of liquor licenses were made available in each area, and a license was required before liquor could be sold. Once again, the defense of the state was that it did not discriminate on the basis of race: the state did not exclude blacks from the Lodge, nor did it grant the license because the Lodge was discriminating on racial grounds. The state simply regarded the admission practice of the club as an irrelevance. The Court thought it had to link the state with the discriminatory refusal to serve. According to Justice Rehnquist, the black was claiming that "the refusal to serve him was 'state action' for the purposes of the Equal Protection Clause."[48] Of course, under this formulation the black could not win, and relief was in fact denied.[49]

Both the result of *Moose Lodge* and the mode of analysis seem wrong. The Equal Protection Clause does not govern the behavior of private clubs, but it does govern the conduct of the state. The state was not

---

U.S., at 22. A clever lawyer might have asserted that the discrimination was not between whites and blacks, but rather between two classes of sellers—those who sell land burdened with a restrictive covenant and those who sell unencumbered land. But if that were the challenged distinction, we have moved beyond the realm of suspect classifications and thus might have to operate under a minimum scrutiny inquiry. The Court did not seem willing to operate at that level; for them it was a racial case—a wrong to blacks. It is interesting to note that Tussman and tenBroek did not see *Shelley* v. *Kraemer* as resting on the "reasonable classification" (or antidiscrimination) principle. They did not view the case as a racial one, but rather as a matter of "substantive due process"—interference with the liberty to sell—though recognizing, given the bad taste left by that doctrine, that it might have to be called "substantive equal protection." Tussman and tenBroek, at 362; see fn. 2 above.

[47] Moose Lodge No. 107 v. Irvis, 407 U.S. 163 (1972).

[48] 407 U.S., at 165.

[49] With a nod toward *Shelley* v. *Kraemer*, the Court prohibited the state from directing the club to comply with the national Supreme Lodge rules, which embodied the racial policy. The local was allowed to make up its own mind.

discriminating, racially or otherwise, but it was engaging in conduct—the conferral of liquor licenses (without regard to admission policies)—and that action could be evaluated in terms of the Equal Protection Clause. Moose Lodge may be free to discriminate, but that does not make it correct for the state to confer a scarce franchise on the club, thereby foreclosing opportunities to blacks. It was the premise of the Court that the only kind of action denied the state is discriminatory action that prevented it from focusing on this foreclosure of opportunities to blacks.

In the state action cases such as *Shelley* v. *Kraemer* and *Moose Lodge* there were clearly acts of discrimination—the restrictive covenant itself or the refusal of the club to serve blacks. Those discriminatory acts were not performed by the state, and the Court saw the question as whether the discriminatory acts could be *imputed* to the state.[50] In another group of cases, also put beyond the Equal Protection Clause by the antidiscrimination interpretation, there was no clear act of discrimination, racial or otherwise, that could easily be imputed to the state. The acts in question clearly belonged to the state, but they were not discriminatory. The antidiscrimination principle left the Court even more at sea. Here I have in mind the on-off decisions of government—the decision whether or not to have a public facility, such as a swimming pool[51] or a public housing project.[52]

The principal challenge to these decisions focused attention on the basis for the decision—why did the town close the swimming pools? Why did the town refuse to build a public housing project? These questions *seem* similar to the inquiry required by an antidiscrimination principle, but that appearance is misleading. The kind of decision most amenable to an antidiscrimination analysis is one choosing among persons, a state decision, for example, about who shall be admitted to the swimming pool or the public housing project. With decisions of that sort, the why-question asks for an identification of the *criterion* of selection: why were these individuals and not others allowed into the swimming pool or the housing project? Answer: because of their race. Once identified,

---

[50] I think this imputation occurs in the Proposition 14 case, Reitman v. Mulkey, 387 U.S. 369 (1967). The Court thought it had to impute the discrimination (the refusal to sell) to the state, and it tried to create the linkage by saying that Proposition 14 had the effect of "encouraging" the discrimination. This conceptualization probably prevented the Court from relying on the rationale linked to Charles Black's name, "Foreword: 'State Action,' Equal Protection and California's Proposition 14," 81 HARV. L. REV. 69 (1967) (an additional obstacle was created for blacks in their effort to obtain protective legislation).

[51] Palmer v. Thompson, 403 U.S. 217 (1971).

[52] James v. Valtierra, 402 U.S. 137 (1971).

the criterion of selection could be judged under the antidiscrimination principle in terms of its relatedness to the state purpose. With an on-off decision, such as a decision whether or not to provide a public service, the why-question asks, not for the criterion, but for the *motive* or *purpose* itself: why did the town close the swimming pool? Answer: in order to save money or to prevent integration. Why did the town refuse to build a public housing project? Answer: in order to save money or in order to limit the number of poor persons in the community. Accordingly, in this context there is no criterion of selection that can be evaluated for its relatedness.[53] Guided by the antidiscrimination principle, and that alone, one hardly knows where to begin in analyzing these governmental decisions, and I think that accounts for the difficulty the Court has experienced with them. One might conclude that these decisions are not invalid, or that relief should not be provided because it is impossible to fashion an appropriate judicial remedy. But the difficulty with the antidiscrimination interpretation is that it puts these on-off decisions beyond purview of the Equal Protection Clause.

The Problem of Facially Innocent Criteria

The classic state action cases and those cases involving on-off decisions reveal the inability of the antidiscrimination principle to deal adequately with state conduct that does not discriminate among persons. Another problem area arises from state conduct that does in fact discriminate among persons, but not on the basis of a suspect criterion. The discrimination is based on a criterion that seems innocent on its face and yet nonetheless has the effect of disadvantaging blacks (or other minorities). For example, when the state purports to choose employees or college students on the basis of performance on standardized tests, and it turns out that the only persons admitted or hired are white.

As originally conceived—both by Tussman and tenBroek and by the Supreme Court in the important formative period of the 1940s and 1950s—the antidiscrimination principle promised to evolve a small, finite

---

[53] In some situations, it may be able to reformulate the on-off decision as a choice among various public activities: why did the town decide to close the swimming pool rather than stop the buses. That why-question does yield a criterion of selection, but a different type of one—not an individual trait (such as race or performance on a test), but rather communal goals (to promote full employment). And it is the former type of criterion of selection that permits a court to ask the foundational question of the antidiscrimination principle—one of over-and underinclusiveness of persons. The reader should consult Professor Brest's article on *Palmer v. Thompson* (see fn. 40 above), for he views the motivational analysis as a much closer relative of the antidiscrimination analysis than I would.

list of suspect criteria, such as race, religion, national origin, wealth, sex. These would be presumptively impermissible. The great bulk of other criteria may ultimately be deemed arbitrary in some particular instances because of ill-fit, but they would be presumptively valid. For these criteria—which I call *facially innocent*—the mere rational-relation test would suffice, and the probability would be very high that the statute or administrative action incorporating or utilizing such criteria would be sustained.

In some instances the presumption of validity may be dissolved, and the contrary presumption created, through the use of the concept of the *real* criterion. The plaintiffs can charge cheating: while the state says that it is selecting on the basis of an innocent criterion (such as performance on a written test), in truth the selection is being made on the basis of a suspect criterion (race). The substantiation of this charge confronts the plaintiffs with enormous evidentiary burdens. No one can be expected to admit to charges of cheating, and rarely is the result so striking (for example, the twenty-eight-sided voting district of *Gomillion* v. *Lightfoot*[54] or no blacks on the work force) as to permit only one inference—discrimination on the basis of a suspect criterion. But if the charge could be substantiated (perhaps with an assist from the reallocation of the burdens of proofs when the criterion had almost the same effect as a suspect one), then there would be no problem of using the strict-scrutiny branch of the antidiscrimination principle: the real criterion, as opposed to the stated criterion, is a suspect one, and there the court should insist upon a very tight fit between purpose and criterion. The troublesome cases arise, however, when the charge of cheating cannot be substantiated, where, for example, the court finds that in truth the jobs were allocated or students selected on the basis of academic performance. What then?

One possible response is, of course, to apply the mere rational-relation test and validate the practice: there is certainly some connection between the state's purposes and these criteria. The fit may not be perfect, but perfection is not required. But the courts have balked. They have been troubled by the fact that the practice is particularly injurious to a disadvantaged group and for that reason have scrutinized state conduct with the greatest of care. The judicial inclination is all toward invalidation.[55]

---

[54] 364 U.S. 339 (1960).

[55] See, for example, Lau v. Nichols, 414 U.S. 563 (1974); Keyes v. School Dist. No. I, Denver, Colo., 413 U.S. 189 (1973); Swann v. Charlotte-Mecklenburg Board of Education, 402 U.S. 1 (1971); Griggs v. Duke Power Co., 401 U.S. 424 (1971); Gaston County v. United States, 395 U.S. 285 (1969). Some of these cases, such as *Griggs*, involve civil rights statutes. The language and legislative history of those statutes generally restrain rather than encour-

This impulse seems correct as a matter of substantive justice, and yet it is difficult to reconcile treatment of the facially innocent criteria with the original, modest conception of the antidiscrimination principle.

One response—that which emerged most clearly during the mid-1960s phase of the Warren Court[56]—was to postulate a second trigger for strict scrutiny—impingement of a fundamental right. This, of course, constituted a radical modification of the antidiscrimination principle, for it introduced a ranking of ends or interests, and it meant that the anti-discrimination principle could no longer be justified exclusively in terms of means-end rationality. The pretense of value-neutrality could not be easily maintained. That is why Tussman and tenBroek did not anticipate the doctrine,[57] and why Professor Gunther, who wrote in the early days of the Burger Court, and who appears committed to returning the Equal Protection Clause to its former glory as a means-focused inquiry, disavows the fundamental-right trigger of the strict-scrutiny inquiry.[58] But even if this modification of the antidiscrimination principle were accepted, and ends were ranked and weighed, the problem of justifying the judicial treatment of facially innocent criteria that especially disadvantaged blacks could not be solved. Admittedly in some instances, the criteria in fact invalidated impinged on what might be considered a fundamental interest; the literacy test for voting might be such an instance.[59] On the other hand, the striking fact is that the Supreme Court has afforded strict scrutiny to facially innocent criteria that do not impinge on fundamental interests—for example, test scores as a criterion for jobs[60] and residence

---

age the judicial inclination. The Court may have been responding to the fact that legislative revision is easier when a statute is being construed, though my impression is that civil rights statutes soon become minimum guarantees not open to the ordinary legislative processes of revision, and thus have the same degree of permanence as a constitution.

[56] See Note, "Developments in the Law–Equal Protection," 82 HARV. L. REV. 1065, 1120, 1127 (1969), which was written at the peak of the fundamental-right development, codified the development and was thereby instrumental in legitimating it.

[57] See fn. 2 above.

[58] Gunther, p. 24. Professor Gunther retains the suspect classification branch of the traditional equal protection analysis.

[59] Gaston County v. United States, 395 U.S. 285 (1969). In that case, however, the Court did not seek to explain its decisions in terms of a fundamental interest, and this is not surprising since the opinion was written by Justice Harlan. See fn. 8 above.

[60] Griggs v. Duke Power Co., 401 U.S. 424 (1971). Although that case involved a statutory discrimination claim (Title VII of the Civil Rights Act of 1964), recent cases illustrate use of the same principle outside the statutory context, e.g. Bridgeport Guardians, Inc. v. Bridgeport Civil Serv. Comm'n., 482 F. 2d 1333 (2d Cir. 1973), cert. denied 421 U.S. 991 (1975); Carter v. Gallagher, 452 F. 2d 315, 327 (8th Cir. 1972), cert. denied, 406 U.S. 950 (1972).

as a criterion for assignment to schools.[61] Although "jobs" and "schools" might in some view be deemed fundamental, certainly as important as the right to procreate, one of the first rights deemed "fundamental," this extension of the fundamental-right test would make what might first have seemed to be an exception much greater than the rule.

A second, and seemingly more modest way of rationalizing the judicial treatment of facially innocent criteria, is to introduce the concept of past discrimination. Strict scrutiny should be given, so the argument runs, to state conduct that perpetuates the effects of earlier conduct (it might be state or private) that was based on the use of a suspect classification. Conduct that perpetuates the effects of past (suspect-criterion) discrimination is as presumptively invalid as the present use of suspect criteria. An objective civil service test is presumptively impermissible whenever it perpetuates the past discrimination of the dual school system (the dual school system put the blacks at a competitive disadvantage and the test perpetuates that disadvantage). The use of geographic proximity is an impermissible criterion of school assignment whenever it perpetuates the past discrimination of the dual school system. The racial assignments of that school system led to the present residential segregation and account for the location and size of the school buildings, and both of these factors in turn explain why the use of geographic proximity as a criterion of assignment results in segregated patterns of school attendance today.

A ban on "the perpetuation of past arbitrary discrimination" looks like a close cousin of the ban on "arbitrary discrimination." But this tie can only be maintained at great expense to important institutional values—those that cluster around the ideal of objectivity, an ideal the antidiscrimination principle is supposed to serve. A true inquiry into past discrimination necessitates evidentiary judgments that are likely to strain the judicial system—consume scarce resources and yield unsatisfying results. It would require the courts to construct causal connections that span significant periods of time, periods greater than those permitted under any general statute of limitations (a common device used to prevent the judiciary from undertaking inquiries where the evidence is likely to be stale, fragmentary, and generally unreliable). The difficulties of these backward-looking inquiries are compounded because the court must invariably deal with aggregate behavior, not just a single transaction; it must determine the causal explanation for the residential patterns of an entire community, or the skill levels of all the black applicants.

---

[61] Keyes v. School Dist. No. 1, Denver, Colo., 413 U.S. 189 (1973). But see Milliken v. Bradley, 418 U.S. 717 (1974).

There are techniques for reducing these strains. The court can create presumptions to limit the evidentiary inquiries or dispense with the need for a showing of identity between victim and beneficiary, or between past perpetrator and present cost-bearer. But these techniques have their own costs. The use of presumptions involves the court in fictionalizing and thereby impairing its credibility. And, more importantly, once the connections between victim and beneficiary and between past perpetrator and present cost-bearer are severed, we have ceased talking about the perpetuation of past discrimination in any individualized sense. The past discrimination that we are talking about is of a more global character— for example, that the group were slaves for one century and subject to Jim Crow laws for another. The ethical significance of this global past discrimination cannot be denied; it gives the group an identity and might explain why we are especially concerned with its welfare. But at the same time it should be understood that once we start talking of global past discrimination, the link between the proposed anti-past-discrimination principle and the original antidiscrimination principle becomes highly attenuated. We have embarked on another journey altogether, one that is decidedly not individualistic—and, as a result, one important source of appeal of the antidiscrimination principle is lost.

The third move designed to deal with the problem of facially innocent criteria—the introduction of the concept of de facto discrimination (or discriminatory effect)—does not focus on the past. Instead it shifts the trigger for strict scrutiny from the *criterion* of selection to the *result* of the selection process, and the result is stated in terms of a *group* rather than an individual. What triggers the strict scrutiny is not the criterion of selection itself, but rather the result—the fact that a minority group has been especially hurt. (This special hurt is sometimes described as a "differential impact.")

This concept of de facto discrimination also involves a basic modification of the antidiscrimination principle. The trigger is no longer classification, but rather group-impact. This modification deeply threatens two goals allegedly served by the antidiscrimination principle—objectivity and individualism.[62] Of course, even with group-impact as the trigger,

---

[62] And that is why Professor Goodman, upon becoming aware of this fact, believes he has discovered the decisive argument against a theory of de facto discrimination: "These and countless other de facto discriminations would be disallowed by a rule condemning, or requiring special justification for, all state action disproportionately harmful to members of minority groups. The objection to such a rule is not solely one of practicality, but also one of principle. It is the individual, not the group, to whom the equal protection of laws is guaranteed. See "De Facto School Segregation: A Constitutional and Empirical Analysis," 60 CALIF. L. REV.

it is still possible to ask the ultimate question of the antidiscrimination principle—are there (excessive) margins of over- and underinclusiveness? But the modification does reveal the basic poverty of antidiscrimination theory. It makes me acutely aware of the failure to explain (a) why this finite list of criteria deemed suspect should ever trigger the demand for stricter scrutiny and (b) why scrutiny should be confined to determining the fit of the criterion and purpose. The concern with the result reveals to me that what is ultimately at issue is the welfare of certain disadvantaged groups, not just the use of a criterion, and if that is at issue, there is no reason why the judicial intervention on behalf of that group should be limited to an inquiry as to the degree of fit between a criterion and a purpose.

IV. The Group-Disadvantaging Principle

The Shift from Classification to Class: Integrating the Concept of a Disadvantaged Group into the Law

In attempting to formulate another theory of equal protection, I have viewed the Clause primarily, but not exclusively, as a protection for blacks. In part, this perspective stems from the original intent—the fact that the Clause was viewed as a means of safeguarding blacks from hostile state action. The Equal Protection Clause (following the circumlocution of the slave-clauses in the antebellum Constitution)[63] uses the word "person," rather than "blacks." The generality of the word chosen to describe those protected enables other groups to invoke its protection; and I am willing to admit that was also probably intended. But this generality of coverage does not preclude a theory of primary reference—that blacks were the

---

275, 300-301 (1972). Goodman's fn. 102 does not elaborate, but only refers the reader to the mystifying sentence of *Shelley v. Kraemer* quoted above in fn. 46.

[63] At least three clauses in the Constitution refer to slaves without using the word "slave," though the circumlocution in fact is so transparent as to be mystifying. The Slave Trade Clause provides, "The Migration or Importation of such Persons as any of the States now existing shall think proper to admit, shall not be prohibited by the Congress prior to the Year one thousand eight hundred and eight, but a Tax or duty may be imposed on such Importation, not exceeding ten dollars for each Person." (Article I, section 9, clause I). See also Article I, section 2, clause 3 ("three-fifths of all other Persons") and Article IV, section 2, clause 3 ("Person held to Service or Labour"). The issue of circumlocution was debated in the original convention in connection with the Slave Trade Clause, some arguing that the generality of the word "persons" would have unintended effects—impliedly creating national power over immigration. For the discussion during the Constitutional Convention see Farrand, 2 Records of the Federal Convention 415 & fn. 8 (1937).

intended primary beneficiaries, that it was a concern for their welfare that prompted the Clause.

It is not only original intent that explains my starting point. It is also the way the courts have used the Clause. The most intense degree of protection has in fact been given to blacks; they have received a degree of protection that no other group has received. They are the wards of the Equal Protection Clause, and any new theory formulated should reflect this practice. I am also willing to speculate that, as a matter of psychological fact, race provides the paradigm for judicial decision. I suspect that in those cases in which a claim of strict scrutiny has been or reasonably could have been made, it is common-place for a judge to reason about an equal protection case by thinking about the meaning of the Clause in the racial context and by comparing the case before him to a comparable one in the racial area. Moreover, the limitations or inadequacies of the antidiscrimination principle surface most sharply when it is used to evaluate state practices affecting blacks.

Starting from this perspective, a distinctively racial one, it strikes me as odd to build a general interpretation of the Equal Protection Clause, as Tussman and tenBroek did, on the rejection of the idea that there are natural classes, that is, groups that have an identity and existence wholly apart from the challenged state statute or practice. There are natural classes, or social groups, in American society and blacks are such a group. Blacks are viewed as a group; they view themselves as a group; their identity is in large part determined by membership in the group; their social status is linked to the status of the group; and much of our action, institutional and personal, is based on these perspectives.

I use the term "group" to refer to a social group, and for me, a social group is more than a collection of individuals, all of whom, to use a polar example, happen to arrive at the same street corner at the same moment. A social group, as I use the term, has two other characteristics. (1) It is an *entity* (though not one that has a physical body). This means that the group has a distinct existence apart from its members, and also that it has an identity. It makes sense to talk about the group (at various points of time) and know that you are talking about the same group. You can talk about the group without reference to the particular individuals who happen to be its members at any one moment. (2) There is also a condition of *interdependence*. The identity and well-being of the members of the group and the identity and well-being of the group are linked. Members of the group identify themselves—explain who they are—by reference to their membership in the group; and their well-being or status is in part determined by the well-being or status of the group. That is why the free blacks of the antebellum period—the Dred Scotts—were not really free, and could never be so long as the institution of Negro slavery still existed.[64] Similarly, the well-being and status of the group is determined by reference to the well-being and status of the members of the group. The emancipation of one slave—the presence of one Frederick Douglass—may not substantially alter the well-being or status of the group; but if there were enough Frederick Douglasses, or if most blacks had his status, then surely the status of blacks as a social group would be altered. That is why the free black posed such a threat to the institution of slavery. Moreover, the identity and existence of the group as a discrete entity is in part determined by whether individuals identify themselves by membership in the group. If enough individuals cease to identify themselves in terms of their membership in a particular group (as occurs in the process of assimilation), then the very identity and separate existence of the group—as a distinct entity—will come to an end.

I would be the first to admit that working with the concept of a group is problematic, much more so than working with the concept of an individual or criterion.[65] It is "messy." For example, in some instances, it may be exceedingly difficult to determine whether particular individuals are members of the group; or whether a particular collection of persons constitutes a social group. I will also admit that my definition of a social group, and in particular the condition of interdependence, compounds

---

[64] On the plight of the free blacks, see I. Berlin, *Slaves Without Masters: The Free Negro in the Antebellum South* (New York, 1974); J. Franklin, *From Slavery to Freedom*, 3d ed. (New York, 1967); Dred Scott v. Sandford, 60 U.S. (19 How.) 393 (1857).

[65] For a sensitive discussion of all the difficulties of working with the concept of groups, see B. Bittker, *The Case for Black Reparations* (New York, 1973), particularly Chapters 8, 9, and 10. It should be noted that the peculiar remedial context of that discussion—the payment of money—accentuates the difficulties; some of these difficulties may be modulated in the injunctive context, where less turns on individual errors of classification. For an earlier legal literature on groupism, see Reisman, "Democracy and Defamation: Control of Group Libel," 42 Colum. L. Rev. 727 (1942); Pekelis, "Full Equality in a Free Society: A Program for Jewish Action," in *Law and Social Action*, ed. M. Konvitz (Ithaca, N.Y., 1950), pp. 187, 218. The comparative literature includes Marc Galanter's work on India, "Equality and 'Protective Discrimination' in India," 16 Rutgers L. Rev. 421 (1962) and "The Problem of Group Membership: Some Reflections on the Judicial View of Indian Society," 4 *J. of the Indian L. Institute* 331 (1962). For a discussion of the role of groups in John Rawls' work, *A Theory of Justice*, see R. Nozick, *Anarchy, State, and Utopia* (New York, 1974), p. 190; Van Dyke, "Justice as Fairness: For Groups?" 6g *Am. Pol. Sci. Rev.* 607 (1975). And for the recent sociological and psychological literature see R. Dahrendorf, *Class and Class Conflict in Industrial Society* (Stanford, Calif., 1959); M. Gordon, *Assimilation in American Life* (New York, 1964); *Ethnicity*, ed. N. Glazer and D. Moynihan (Cambridge, Mass., 1975); R. Sennett and J. Cobb, *The Hidden Injuries of Class* (New York, 1972).

rather than reduces, these classificatory disputes. But these disputes do not demonstrate the illegitimacy of this category of social entity nor deny the validity or importance of the idea. They only blur the edges. Similarly, the present reality of the social groups should not be obscured by a commitment to the ideal of a "classless society" or the individualistic ethic—the ideal of treating people as individuals rather than as members of groups. Even if the Equal Protection Clause is viewed as the means for furthering or achieving these individualistic ideals (and I am not sure why it should be), there is no reason why the Clause—as an instrument for bringing about the "good society"—must be construed as though it is itself governed by that ideal or why it should be assumed that the "good society" had been achieved in 1868, or is so now.

The conception of blacks as a social group is only the first step in constructing a mediating principle. We must also realize they are a very special type of social group. They have two other characteristics as a group that are critical in understanding the function and reach of the Equal Protection Clause. One is that blacks are very badly off, probably our worst-off class (in terms of material well-being second only to the American Indians), and in addition they have occupied the lowest rung for several centuries. In a sense, they are America's perpetual underclass. It is both of these characteristics—the relative position of the group and the duration of the position—that make efforts to improve the status of the group defensible. This redistribution may be rooted in a theory of compensation—blacks as a group were *put* in that position by others and the redistributive measures are *owed* to the group as a form of compensation. The debt would be viewed as owed by society, once again viewed as a collectivity.[66] But a redistributive strategy need not rest on this idea of compensation, it need not be backward looking (though past discrimination might be relevant for *explaining* the identity and status of blacks as a social group). The redistributive strategy could give expression to an ethical view against caste, one that would make it undesirable for any social group to occupy a position of subordination for any extended period of time.[67] What, it might be asked, is the justification for that

---

[66] See generally Bayles, "Reparations to Wronged Groups," 33 *Analysis* 177 (1973); Cowan, "Inverse Discrimination," 33 *Analysis* 10 (1972); Shiner, "Individuals, Groups and Inverse Discrimination," 33 *Analysis* 182 (1973); Taylor, "Reverse Discrimination and Compensatory Justice," 33 *Analysis* 185 (1973); Sher, "Justifying Reverse Discrimination in Employment," 4 *Philosophy & Public Affairs* 159 (1975).

[67] The critical temporal issue is one of duration, not whether the subordination has taken place in the past or in the future. The past has only an evidentiary relevance; it enables us to make judgments about how long the group will occupy the position of subordination. If the group has occupied the position of subordination for the last two centuries, certainly it

vision? I am not certain whether it is appropriate to ask this question, to push the inquiry a step further and search for the justification of that ethic; visions about how society should be structured may be as irreducible as visions about how individuals should be treated—for example, with dignity. But if this second order inquiry is appropriate, a variety of justifications can be offered and they need not incorporate the notion of compensation. Changes in the hierarchical structure of society—the elimination of caste—might be justified as a means of (a) preserving social peace; (b) maintaining the community as a community, that is, as one cohesive whole; or (c) permitting the fullest development of the individual members of the subordinated group who otherwise might look upon the low status of the group as placing a ceiling on their aspirations and achievements.

It is not just the socioeconomic status of blacks as a group that explains their special position in equal protection theory. It is also their political status. The power of blacks in the political arena is severely limited. For the last two centuries the political power of this group was circumscribed in most direct fashion—disenfranchisement. The electoral strength of blacks was not equal to their numbers. That has changed following the massive enfranchisement of the Voting Rights Act of 1965, but structural limitations on the political power of blacks still persist.[68] These limitations arise from three different sources, which can act either alternatively or cumulatively and which, in any event, are all interrelated. One source of weakness is their numbers, the fact that they are a numerical minority; the second is their economic status, their position as the perpetual underclass; and the third is that, as a "discrete and insular" minority, they are the object of "prejudice"—that is, the subject of fear, hatred, and distaste that make it particularly difficult for them to form coalitions with others (such as the white poor) and that make

---

is likely they will occupy that position for a long time in the future unless remedial steps are taken. On the other hand, if we were somehow assured that notwithstanding past history the subordination will end tomorrow, there would be no occasion for redistributive strategy on this group's behalf. Similarly, if we are told that today a period of perpetual subordination is about to begin for another group, we should be as concerned with the status of that group as we are with the blacks.

[68] For the time being, I put to one side the problems of dilution (districting that divides the group) or submersion (including the group in a larger universe through the technique of multi-member districts) since I do not have a full sense of either the prevalence of these practices or their constitutionality. See Witcomb v. Chavis, 403 U.S. 124 (1971); White v. Regester, 412 U.S. 755 (1973); Richmond v. United States, 422 U.S. 358 (1975); United Jewish Organizations of Williamsburgh v. Wilson, 510 F.2d 512 (2d Cir. 1975), cert. granted, CCH Sup. Ct. Bull. (Nov. 11, 1975) (No. 75-104, 1975 Term).

it advantageous for the dominant political parties to hurt them—to use them as a scapegoat.[69]

Recently, in some localities, such as large cities, the weakness of the group derived from their number has been eliminated; indeed in certain of these localities blacks may no longer be in the minority. The blacks may have a majority of a city council, or there may even be a black mayor. It would be wrong, however, to generalize from these situations. They are the exception, not the rule, and therefore should not control the formulation of a general theory of the Equal Protection Clause. Moreover, these black-dominated political agencies—the black city council or the black mayor—must be placed in context. One facet of their context is the white domination of those extra-political agencies such as the banks, factories, and police, that severely circumscribe the power of the formal political agencies. Another facet is the persistent white domination of the national political agencies, such as the Congress and presidency, agencies that have become the critical loci of political power in American society.

Hence, despite recent demographic shifts in several large cities, I think it appropriate to view blacks as a group that is relatively powerless in the political arena and in my judgment that political status of the group justifies a special judicial solicitude on their behalf. When the product of a political process is a law that hurts blacks, the usual countermajoritarian objection to judicial invalidation—the objection that denies those "nine men" the right to substitute their view for that of "the people"—has little force. For the judiciary could be viewed as amplifying the voice of the powerless minority; the judiciary is attempting to rectify the injustice of the political process as a method of adjusting competing claims. The need for this rectification turns on whether the law is deemed one that harms blacks—a judgment that is admittedly hard to make when the perspective becomes a group one, for that requires the aggregation of interests and viewpoints, many of which are in conflict. It is important to emphasize, however, that the need for this rectification does not turn on whether the law embodies a classification, racial or otherwise; it is sufficient if the state law simply has the *effect* of hurting blacks. Nor should the rectification, once triggered by a harmful law, be confined to

---

[69] The quoted words are from Justice Stone's fn. 4 in United States v. Carolene Prods. Co., 304 U.S. 144, 152-53 (1938), which in part reads: "Nor need we enquire . . . whether prejudice against discrete and insular minorities may be a special condition, which tends seriously to curtail the operation of those political processes ordinarily to be relied upon to protect minorities, and which may call for a correspondingly more searching judicial inquiry." For a stimulating and illuminating discussion of the footnote, see Ball, "Judicial Protection of Powerless Minorities," 59 IOWA L. REV. 1059 (1974).

questions of fit—the judicial responsibility is more extensive than simply one of guarding against the risk of imprecise classifications by the political agencies. The relative powerlessness of blacks also requires that the judiciary strictly scrutinize the choice of ends; for it is just as likely that the interests of blacks as a group will not be adequately taken into account in choosing ends or goals. Maximizing goals such as reducing transportation costs (a goal that might account for the neighborhood-school plan) or having the most brilliant law students (a goal that might account for requiring a 650 on the LSAT) are constitutionally permissible goals in the sense that there is no substantive constitutional provision (or implied purpose lying behind some provision) that deny them to the state. On the other hand, these maximizing goals are obviously not in any sense constitutionally compelled goals and there is a chance—a most substantial one—that they would not be chosen as *the* goals (without any modification) if the interests of the blacks as a group were adequately taken into account—if the goal-choosers paid sufficient attention to the special needs, desires, and views of this powerless group.

The injustice of the political process must be corrected, and perhaps as a last resort, that task falls to the judiciary. But this claim does not yield any basis for specifying what the corrected process would look like, or what the court should say when it amplifies the voice of the powerless minority. A just political process would be one in which blacks would have "more" of a voice than they in fact do, but not necessarily one in which they would "win." In a sense there is a remedial lacuna; a pure process claim cannot determine substantive outcomes. (At the very most, it could yield those substantive outcomes that would tend to enhance the position of this group in the political process—such as favoring an increase in the numbers of black lawyers given the pivotal role lawyers play in the political process or favoring electoral districting that enhances the power of blacks as a group.) But this processual theory focusing on the relative powerlessness of blacks in the political arena need not stand alone. The substantive standards can be supplied by the other critical characteristics of this social group—perpetual subordination. The political status of the group justifies the institutional allocations—our willingness to allow those "nine men" to substitute their judgment (about ends as well as means) for that of "the people." The socioeconomic position of the group supplies an additional reason for the judicial activism and also determines the content of the intervention—improvement of the status of that group.

I would therefore argue that blacks should be viewed as having three characteristics that are relevant in the formulation of equal protection theory: (a) they are a social group; (b) the group has been in a position of perpetual subordination; and (c) the political power of the group is severely circumscribed. Blacks are what might be called a specially disadvantaged group, and I would view the Equal Protection Clause as a protection for such groups. Blacks are the prototype of the protected group, but they are not the only group entitled to protection. There are other social groups, even as I have used the term, and if these groups have the same characteristics as blacks—perpetual subordination and circumscribed political power—they should be considered specially disadvantaged and receive the same degree of protection. What the Equal Protection Clause protects is specially disadvantaged groups, not just blacks. A concern for equal treatment and the word "person" appearing in the Clause permit and probably require this generality of coverage.

Some of these specially disadvantaged groups can be defined in terms of characteristics that do not have biological roots and that are not immutable; the Clause might protect certain language groups and aliens. Moreover, in passing upon a claim to be considered a specially disadvantaged group, the court may treat one of the characteristics entitling blacks to that status as a sufficient but not a necessary condition; indeed the court may even develop variable standards of protection[70]—it may tolerate disadvantaging practices that would not be tolerated if the group was a "pure" specially disadvantaged group. Jews or women might be entitled to less protection than American Indians, though nonetheless entitled to some protection. Finally, these judicial judgments may be time-bound. Through the process of assimilation the group may cease to exist, or even if the group continues to retain its identity, its socioeconomic and political positions may so improve so as to bring to an end its status as specially disadvantaged.[71]

All this means that the courts will have some leeway in identifying the groups protected by the Equal Protection Clause. I think, however, it would be a mistake to use this flexibility to extend the protection to what might be considered artificial classes, those created by a classification

---

[70] Compare Justice Marshall's variable approach in San Antonio Ind. School Dist. v. Rodriguez, 411 U.S. 1, 70 (1973).

[71] Talcott Parsons commented on the changing status of Chinese and Japanese in the United States in "Some Theoretical Considerations on the Nature and Trends of Change of Ethnicity," in *Ethnicity*, ed. N. Glazer and D. Moynihan (Cambridge, Mass., 1975), pp. 73-74. On the claim that the socioeconomic status of blacks has changed, see Wattenberg & Scammon, "Black Progress and Liberal Rhetoric," 55 *Commentary* 35 (1973) and "Letters, An Exchange on Black Progress: Ben J. Wattenberg and Richard M. Scammon and Critics," 56 *Commentary* 20 (1973).

or criterion embodied in a state practice or statute, for example, those classes created by tax categories (those having incomes between $27,000 and $30,000, or between $8,000 and $10,000) or licensing statutes (the manufacturers of filled milk).[72] By definition those classes do not have an independent social identity and existence, or if they do, the condition of interdependence is lacking. It is difficult, if not impossible, to make an assessment of their socioeconomic status or of their political power (other than that they have just lost a legislative battle). And, if this is true, neither redistribution nor stringent judicial intervention on their behalf can be justified. It is not that such arguments are unpersuasive, but that they are almost unintelligible. Thus, in only one sense should the group-disadvantaging strategy be viewed as conducive to "more equality": it will get more for fewer. It will get more for the specially disadvantaged groups but will not provide any protection for artificial classes, those solely created by statute or a state practice. Of course, this loss may be more formal than real. Artificial classes constitute part of the universe that the antidiscrimination principle *purports* to protect, but in truth almost never does protect given the permissibility of the minimum-scrutiny inquiry.

The Nature of the Prohibited Action

The Concept of a Group-Disadvantaging Practice. Some state laws or practices may just be a mistake—they make all groups and all persons worse off, and equally so. These do not seem to be the concern of a constitutional provision cast in terms of equality. Equality is a relativistic idea. The concern should be with those laws or practices that particularly hurt a disadvantaged group. Such laws might enhance the welfare of society (or the better-off classes), or leave it the same; what is critical, however, is that the state law or practice aggravates (or perpetuates?) the

---

[72] What about those with income under $4,000? To some extent Justice Powell addresses this issue in his opinion in San Antonio Ind. School District v. Rodriguez, 411 U.S. 1 (1973) and he there employs a concept of social group similar to the one articulated in this essay. See also Michelman, "Forward: On Protecting the Poor Through the Fourteenth Amendment," 83 HARV. L. REV. 7 (1969), suggesting the inappropriateness of using an antidiscrimination theory in this context, and attempting to shift the mode of analysis (which may take the courts beyond the Equal Protection Clause) to "just wants" and "minimum needs." For further development of this theme, see also Michelman, "In Pursuit of Constitutional Welfare Rights: One view of Rawls' Theory of Justice," 121 U. PA. L. REV. 962 (1973). On the increasing saliency of primordial rather than economic (or "class") categories, see Bell, "Ethnicity and Social Change," in *Ethnicity,* ed. N. Glazer and D. Moynihan (Cambridge, Mass., 1975), p. 141.

subordinate position of a specially disadvantaged group. This is what the Equal Protection Clause prohibits.

Implicit in this formulation of the prohibition of the Equal Protection Clause is a view that certain state practices may be harmful to the members of a specially disadvantaged group, and yet not impair or threaten or aggravate the status or position of the group. For example, it is conceivable that a sales tax is harmful to blacks, and yet, due to several factors—such as the diffuseness of the impact[73] and the nature of the deprivation—it need not be viewed as a practice that aggravates the subordinate status of blacks as a group. What is needed in order to bring a state practice within the equal protection ban is a theory of status-harm, one that shows how the challenged practice has this effect on the status of the group.

It is from this perspective—one of a proscription against status-harm—that discriminatory state action should be viewed. Such action is one form of state conduct that impairs the status of a specially disadvantaged group. The Equal Protection Clause prohibits the state, for example, from using race as the criterion of admission to a swimming pool or a public housing project because that practice tends to aggravate the subordinate position of blacks by excluding them from a state facility. The same is true for the dual school system—the practice of assigning students to schools (or other public facilities) on the basis of race in order to segregate them. Once again, this state action is prohibited by the Equal Protection Clause because it aggravates the subordinate position of blacks, not because the classification is "unrelated" or only "poorly related" to a (permissible) state purpose.

I acknowledge that in these examples the state action may also be viewed as "arbitrary discrimination." Yet it is important to emphasize that "arbitrary discrimination" is the species, not the genus. Discrimination, arbitrary or otherwise, is only one form—one form among many—of conduct that disadvantages a group. There may be group-disadvantaging conduct that is not discriminatory. This would be true of state conduct that seemed beyond the reach of the Equal Protection Clause under the antidiscrimination principle because it embodied no discrimination, racial or otherwise; for example, the state policies of enforcing all racially restrictive covenants, allocating the scarce supply of liquor licenses without regard to whether the recipients will serve blacks, closing a municipal swimming pool or other public facilities in order to avoid integration, and refusing to build a public housing project

---

[73] Goodman, fn. 62 above, p. 306.

in order to limit the number of poor blacks in the community. Similarly, conduct that did discriminate but on the basis of criteria innocent on their face, such as performance on a standardized test for employment or college admission, or geographic proximity for student assignment, could be evaluated from the perspective of whether it had the effect of impairing the status of a specially disadvantaged group. There would be no need to attempt to force them into the "arbitrary discrimination" pigeonhole. The need, instead, would be to formulate a theory that linked the practice and the status of the group. To be sure, such a theory may be highly problematic; for it might well require something more than a statistical showing that by and large the practice hurts blacks more than any other group (the differential impact). To take one central example, in the context of determining whether it is permissible to use performance on a standardized test as an employment criterion, a full theory of status-harm might have to include an assessment of (a) the status (determined on several scales such as income and prestige) of the job itself (professor vs. street cleaner), (b) the public visibility of the position (a judge vs. a chemist), (c) the diffuseness of the exclusionary impact (whether blacks are the predominant group excluded), and (d) the strength of the reasons justifying the use of the criterion (how accurate a test was it and how significant were the differences).

Admittedly, racially discriminatory conduct need not be viewed from this perspective—as a species of the genus of group-disadvantaging conduct. It could be viewed as the member of another genus, that of unfair treatment: what is wrong, it may be argued, with using race as the criterion for admission to a swimming pool or a public housing project is that it is a form of unfair treatment—an individual is being judged (for the purpose of allocating the scarce resource) on the basis of an irrelevant characteristic. The problem, however, is one of double membership: arbitrary discrimination is a member of the genus of unfair treatment as well as that of group-disadvantaging conduct. Double membership is possible because of an area of overlap of the two genuses (unfair treatment and group-disadvantaging conduct), though to be sure, the genuses are not coextensive, nor is one embraced by the other.

This analytic distinction between the two genuses is important. It preserves the possibility that conduct may be unfair and yet not a group-disadvantaging practice. Preferential treatment in favor of one of the specially disadvantaged groups would be an instance of such conduct. The white applicant who is rejected because of the preference for blacks may have been treated unfairly—may claim that he is being treated unfairly because he is being judged on the basis of an inappropriate criterion (not being black) and because the costs of a social policy are being localized on him.[74] The individual unfairness to the rejected nondisadvantaged applicant is relevant in assessing the justification of the state's refusal to institute the practice of preferential treatment; it might be relevant in fashioning a remedy, or it might even give rise to the violation of another constitutional provision, such as the Due Process Clause. But I do wish to deny that unfair treatment—such as being judged on the basis of an inappropriate criterion—is the domain of the Equal Protection Clause—even though such unfair treatment may be viewed from the individual perspective as a form of unequal treatment. As a protection for specially disadvantaged groups, the Equal Protection Clause should be viewed as a prohibition against group-disadvantaging practices, not unfair treatment.

Even if the claim of individual unfairness is put to one side, and the Equal Protection Clause is viewed as a protection for specially disadvantaged groups, a state policy of preferential treatment for blacks may be nonetheless constitutionally vulnerable. For one thing, it remains to be seen whether this policy in fact improves the position of the disadvantaged group. A preferential law-school admission program for blacks, to take a familiar example, may be justified on the ground that it gives positions of power, prestige, and influence to members of the racial group, positions that they would not otherwise attain in the immediate future, and that the acquisition of those positions will be an advantage to both the individual blacks admitted and, more importantly, to the group. The theory is that an increase in the number of black lawyers will disperse members of the racial group through the higher economic and social strata, raise aspirations of all members of the group, and create a self-generating protective device for the group—providing some members of the group with the power and leverage needed to protect the group from hostile attacks in the future. The status of the group will be improved. This is the theory, but, of course, these assertions of group-benefit are not totally free from doubt; indeed, some might raise the claim of counter-productivity—a regime of preferential treatment casts doubt upon the ability of all members of the group for it gives expression to the belief that the group would not succeed on its own.

If the court truly believed that a state policy—even if called "benign"—impaired the status of blacks then the policy would be invalid. But I doubt whether anyone believes that preferential admissions to law schools for

---

[74] For elaboration of this point see my article, "School Desegregation: The Uncertain Path of the Law," 4 *Philosophy & Public Affairs* 3, 7-11 (1974).

blacks impairs the status of the group; those who argue that the policy is counterproductive today do so for the more limited purpose of casting doubt on the truth of the assertions supporting the policy. They wish to make the factual assertions on behalf of the policy open to controversy. And if that is so, it is important to delineate the role of the court in such a dispute. The dispute is simply over the constitutional permissibility of the preferential policy, and from that perspective the question for the court is whether there is *some rational basis* for legislators and administrators believing that a preferential policy would benefit the group. The appropriate standard for viewing a policy that appears to the court to benefit a specially disadvantaged group should be a rational-basis standard. The judicial activism authorized by the Equal Protection Clause is, under the group-disadvantaging principle, asymmetrical.

Another possible objection to a preferential admission policy under the group-disadvantaging principle seeks to expand the universe of beneficiaries—the relevant group preferred should not be blacks, but rather the poor. The resolution of this objection might be thought to call for a judicial inquiry into what are the "true" groups in American society today—an inquiry into what group identifications are the most important to the individual, either on a psychological, political, economic, or sociological level, or which ones should be encouraged.[75] However, once again, I believe that the judicial inquiry should be a much more modest one. The court should ask whether there is any rational basis for the legislator or administrator choosing the group delineation that it did. There would be little doubt that an antipoverty strategy—an admission policy preferring the poor—would be constitutionally permissible. But that is not the issue. This particular objection to preferential treatment for blacks—the one that demands the preferred group be the poor rather than blacks—seeks to make an antipoverty strategy the only constitutionally permissible redistributive strategy. It is this constitutional strait jacket that I find is troubling and without basis in the Equal Protection Clause.

The fact that some individual blacks may identify themselves in terms of their economic position ("poor") does not deny—at least today—the reality of the racial identification—that these individuals also identify themselves as blacks or that blacks are a social group. To acknowledge the multiplicity of group identifications is not to embrace a reductionism that denies the reality of some of the groups. Nor can the reductionism be justified on the ground that the preferential policy seeks to improve the socioeconomic status of blacks. The focus on blacks (as opposed

---

[75] Bell, fn. 72 above.

to persons who happen to have the same economic status) should be viewed as a matter of legislative or administrative prerogative—a question of setting priorities. The plight of the poor may be bad, but, so the legislator or administrator should be allowed to say, not as bad as that of the blacks.[76] Such a judgment about the urgency of the situation of blacks may be rooted in two considerations. The first is the caste quality of the blacks' low status—the fact that blacks have occupied the lowest socioeconomic rung in America for at least two centuries and will continue to do so unless redistributive measures are instituted. True, we may have always had and perhaps will always have people called "the poor," but that is to confuse a stratum with the occupant of a stratum. The second consideration is that blacks face disabilities not encountered by the poor (even conceived of as a group). These disabilities manifest themselves in all spheres of life—economic, social, and political—and derive from the fact that the individuals are members of the racial group. These are disabilities that do not saddle persons who are poor. Indeed, in order to elevate themselves, the white poor have incentives to disassociate themselves from the blacks and to accentuate the racial distinction. They have incentives to make blackness the lowest status, for of necessity it is a status into which they cannot fall.[77]

Similarly, there are reasons—good ones, though not necessarily compelling—for the legislators or administrators to treat blacks as a single group without trying to sort out the "rich blacks," without trying to fractionate the group. One reason is administrative convenience—the likely number of rich blacks are so few, and the costs of the mechanisms needed to identify them are so high, that the sorting is not worth the effort. Under the antidiscrimination principle, the central evil was one of loose fit and all arguments of administrative convenience were suspect; but under the group-disadvantaging principle, imprecision is not itself a constitutional vice. Imprecision can be tolerated when the state law or practice seeks to improve the position of a disadvantaged group and is in fact related to that end. Moreover, wholly apart from considerations of administrative convenience, the decision not to exclude the rich black (even once identified) can be justified. The argument is not that rich blacks as individuals are as "entitled" (in the compensatory sense) to as much of an assist as persons who are poor (though that may entirely be possible, for even though these individuals are rich, they are still black

---

[76] See the penetrating article of Duncan, "Inheritance of Poverty or Inheritance of Race?" in *On Understanding Poverty: Perspectives from the Social Sciences,* ed. Moynihan (New York, 1968).

[77] Parsons, fn. 71 above, p. 77.

and being black may have been as severe a disadvantage in our society as being poor, if not greater). Rather, the claim is that the preference of the rich blacks may be justified in terms of improving the position of the group. Even if the blacks preferred happen to be rich, a benefit abounds to the group as a whole. Members of that group have obtained these positions of power, prestige, and influence that they otherwise might not have and to that extent the status of that group is improved. On the other hand, it is not clear that preferring a poor person confers a benefit on the poor conceived as a group—the preferred individual merely leaves the group; and even if there were group benefits entailed in a preference for the poor, certainly legislators or administrators are entitled to rank the improvement of blacks as a group as a social goal of first importance, more important than elevating the poor conceived of as a social group.

Finally, the preferential admission program for blacks (or any other single disadvantaged group) may be thought vulnerable because of its impact on other disadvantaged groups, whether they be American Indians, Chicanos, or perhaps even the poor, the poor black, or the poor black women (if these latter categories can be considered discrete disadvantaged social groups). The adverse impact on these groups arises in a two-step fashion and is ultimately traceable to the fact of scarcity: starting with a fixed number of openings, the preference for blacks lessens the number of places available to the members of these other groups. What is given to one group cannot be given to another.

There are several lines of response to this particular objection. One might argue, for example, that the nonpreferred group is not as badly off as the preferred group (for example, Chicanos are not as badly off as blacks). Another might emphasize the indirect quality of the exclusion (exclusion occurs because blacks are preferred and the places are limited), a factor that has an important bearing on the question whether the preferential treatment gives rise to a status-harm to the nonpreferred disadvantaged group. Preferring blacks may limit the number of places open to other disadvantaged groups, but it is not clear that it impairs their status. Finally, the objection might be answered by invoking the standard defense to underinclusion—one step at a time. Under the antidiscrimination principle, this defense was troubling because it seemed to threaten the claim of underinclusiveness; the defense could be raised to every instance of underinclusiveness. With the group-disadvantaging principle, no particular importance is attached to the claim of underinclusiveness itself, and thus the defense is less threatening; and in any event, it is conceivable that substantive standards could be developed to limit the defense and to thereby maintain as much pressure on the political agencies to remain responsive to the demands of all specially disadvantaged groups.

Having identified these possible lines of defense to this particular objection to preferential treatment for blacks, I do not want to obscure its force. The harm to other disadvantaged groups that arises from the fact of scarcity would be a significant point of constitutional vulnerability for a restricted preferential policy. It invokes the prohibition against group-disadvantaging practices and in responding to this objection, unlike the others, no help can be derived from the asymmetrical quality of judicial activism. The claim is that specially disadvantaged groups are being hurt, and the group-disadvantaging principle requires the court to be particularly attentive to such claims. But perhaps it is correct that a *restricted* preferential policy should be constitutionally vulnerable; and that it should be vulnerable precisely for this reason—because of its impact on other disadvantaged groups rather than because of its impact on the dominant group—the rejected white males. This is more than a purely analytic point, for it indicates what must be done to save the policy constitutionally—extend it to those specially disadvantaged groups that are as entitled to the preferential treatment as blacks.

The Accommodation of Considerations of Total Welfare. The overriding concern is with the status of the specially disadvantaged groups, and any state practice which aggravates their subordinate position would be presumptively invalid. There is, however, an element of restraint, and that arises from the fact that certain group-disadvantaging practices further interests of the polity as a whole, some of which are material (for example, increased productivity) and others nonmaterial (for instance, increased individual liberty). There must be some accommodation of other such competing interests. I doubt, for example, whether the Equal Protection Clause should be construed so stringently as to deny the state the right to insist upon certain minimum levels of proficiency or competence for its employees or students, even if such insistence were to aggravate (or at least perpetuate) the subordinate position of blacks. The problem, of course, is that if too large a role is allowed these considerations of total welfare, the protectionist edge of the Equal Protection Clause would be severely dulled: the state could always defend against an equal protection claim on the ground that, even though a disadvantaged group is especially harmed, total welfare is being maximized.

Two analytic tools must be introduced in order to avoid this dilemma. The first is the concept of a nonallowable interest. An example would be the interest of whites to keep blacks in a subordinate position. That interest should be given no weight in determining whether the group-disadvantaging practice is justified. In that sense it has no normative weight, although account of it might have to be taken out of sheer necessity. It *should* not be taken into consideration, but it might *have to be* because the court has no choice. For example, the resistance to the busing decree may be so intense as to be expressed in open rebellion, and in that case the court might have to proceed more slowly.[78] Resistance is an obstacle to be reckoned with, though there are limits to what can be done.

The concept of a nonallowable interest corresponds roughly to the concept of an illegitimate state purpose under the antidiscrimination principle. The difference relates not so much to the content of what is allowed or illegitimate; rather the standard for legitimacy or allowability is directly anchored in the governing principle. The antidiscrimination principle talks in terms of fit, in terms of over- and underinclusiveness, and such a principle can provide no standard for determining the legitimacy of state purposes; the antidiscrimination principle had to go beyond itself, and in that sense is incomplete, not in itself fully intelligible. The group-disadvantaging principle, on the other hand, does itself provide a standard of legitimacy or allowability. Interests should not be allowed when they would effectively give the dominant group a veto power over the elevation of the specially disadvantaged group. Such a veto would be inconsistent with what I perceive to be the very purpose of the Equal Protection Clause and with the notion of a constitutional restraint.

The second analytic tool that must be introduced to prevent the weighing process from degenerating into no-protection is the concept of a compelling benefit. This concept structures the relationship between the harm to the group's status and the benefit to the polity. If some compelling benefit is to be obtained by the practice or statute, either because of the importance of the interest served or the size of the benefit, the practice will be permitted, notwithstanding the status-harm to the specially disadvantaged group. The required benefit is linked to the harm: the more severe the disadvantage, the more compelling the benefit must be. But in linking the two, it is important to emphasize that the harm caused the disadvantaged class by the practice need not be greater than the benefit to the polity. That is why, in thinking of the Equal Protection Clause as a redistributional device, the balancing metaphor seems inapt: relief would be granted even if the harm to the group were less than the benefit to society. The more appropriate metaphor would be one that conceives of

[78] See Hart v. Community School Board No. 21, 383 F. Supp. 699 (E.D.N.Y. 1974); Cooper v. Aaron, 358 U.S. 1, 16-17 (1958); Buchanan v. Warley, 245 U.S. 60, 81 (1917).

the status-harm to the disadvantaged group as the trigger of the remedial effort with the legitimate interests of the polity serving as the restraining force. The restraint starts once the benefit is greater than the harm, but only when it reached a certain quantity and intensity—denoted by the term "compelling"—would the remedial effort be brought to a halt.

In the first instance the concept of compelling benefit will require the court to ask if there are alternative ways available to society for furthering its interests, and whether these alternatives are less harmful to the disadvantaged group. If so, the practice will be invalidated, for the state practice is not, in the ordinary meaning of that word, compelled. If, however, there are no alternatives that are less disadvantaging, then the court must move to a second order inquiry: it must gauge the status-harm to the disadvantaged group and the benefit to society and, in the final analysis, determine whether the benefit is of a compelling quality.

It might be noted that the first step of this inquiry is similar to that required by the strict-scrutiny branch of the antidiscrimination principle: strict scrutiny requires a search for better alternatives. But the difference is four-fold. First, we have an explanation for the strictness of the scrutiny, and one that is contained within the principle—the scrutiny is stringent because the status of an already subordinated group is being threatened. Under the antidiscrimination principle, the strictness of the scrutiny depends on a judgment about which interests are fundamental and which criteria are suspect; and although it might be possible to explain and justify those choices, the explanation would take the court far beyond the foundational concept of the antidiscrimination principle—means-end rationality—and thus transform the antidiscrimination principle so as to make it inconsistent with the ideals it is supposed to serve. Second, the action that triggers the inquiry differs. Under the group-disadvantaging principle, it is harm to a specially disadvantaged group, not the use of a criterion (somehow) deemed "suspect" or impingement on an interest deemed "fundamental." Third, there is a difference in the standard of what is a "better" alternative. Under the group-disadvantaging principle the alternative is judged not in terms of fit (reduction of under- and over-inclusiveness) but rather in terms of its status-harm to the disadvantaged group. Fourth, the inquiry goes on to a second level if there is no better alternative. Under the antidiscrimination principle, the inquiry stops once it is determined there is no closer fitting or more precise criterion; the statute or practice is validated. But under the group-disadvantaging principle, even if the judge determines there is no less harmful way of satisfying the purpose, he must still gauge the harm to the group and the benefit to society. He must determine whether the benefit to society is so important or so great as to make the status-harm to the specially disadvantaged group tolerable—an inquiry that has no meaning under the antidiscrimination principle, and one that is inconsistent with the assurance that the principle exclusively rests on the modest conception of means-end rationality.

The State Action Requirement. I identified the state action requirement of the Fourteenth Amendment as one of the persistent sources of difficulty with the antidiscrimination principle. The problem to me, seemed to me to stem not so much from the "state" component, but from the "action" component, or more specifically, from the requirement that the "action" be a form of forbidden "discrimination." This artificial conception of the requisite "action" prevented the courts from tracing the effects of the state law or practice on the status of various disadvantaged groups in society, such as the blacks. Under the group-disadvantaging principle, however, this artificial limitation is eliminated.

In removing this limitation I do not mean to suggest an abandonment of the traditional view that the prohibition of the Equal Protection Clause applies only to the conduct—the laws and practices—of the state. Due account has been taken of this view. It is the state that is prohibited from aggravating the subordinate position of specially disadvantaged groups. There is a state action requirement. The most troublesome question that is likely to arise is whether state "inaction" shall be treated as "action." Should the failure of the state to *initiate* redistributive measures on behalf of specially disadvantaged groups—to counteract the inequalities imposed by private activity—be viewed as a practice that aggravates the position of subordination and thus as a violation of the Equal Protection Clause? As a purely analytic matter, it is possible to answer that question in the affirmative. But, on the other hand, there are three factors that argue for a negative answer, for preserving the distinction between action and inaction.

One is a concern for the text. Professor Black has argued that the words "denial" and "protection" suggest to him an affirmative obligation, an obligation to throw a life preserver.[79] On the other hand, without the distinction between action and inaction, the words "state" and "laws" in the Clause would become superfluous. The line between individual action and governmental action would be obliterated; the Clause would oblige the state to enact laws counteracting private group-disadvantaging practices and thus, in that sense, private action would be covered by the Clause.

---

[79] Black, fn. 50 above, p. 73.

The conception of constitutional prohibitions as restraints on the use of governmental power is a second factor that suggests that the distinction between action and inaction be preserved. This negative conception has historical roots. I suspect that this is probably how the framers viewed their task in drafting the first section of the Fourteenth Amendment (in contrast to those provisions of the Constitution establishing the structure of government). I also think the negative conception would be the one most consistent with the goal—of some undeniable validity—to minimize intervention by the judiciary (the agency primarily entrusted to enforce the Equal Protection Clause). If inaction were viewed as action, the intervention by the judiciary would be enormously increased, if not endless. This degree of intervention might be at odds with our democratic traditions, even tempered by a concern for minority rights, and it might push the judiciary beyond the limits of its competence. There is some awkwardness in having the judiciary act as the primary redistributive agency, in large part because it does not set its own agenda and thus cannot rationally order its priorities: should it be bread rather than housing?[80] A court must depend on the choices set by the litigators and I suspect that the resulting pattern of decision would tend to over emphasize those redistributive measures connected to the criminal process (for example, providing free transcripts on appeal). The criminal defendant always has the incentive to litigate, and society facilitates that proclivity by subsidizing litigation costs.

The problems of fashioning an appropriate remedy also bear on the action/inaction issue. Of course, even if the state action limitation is taken seriously, and the distinction between action and inaction preserved, acute remedial problems can arise. It is these factors, above all, that might persuade a court not to intervene when, for example, a town decides to close the swimming pool or to close its public schools in order to avoid integration. I have little doubt that such action disadvantages blacks, and yet the difficulty of fashioning an effective decree may be so great as to lead the court to deny injunctive (though perhaps not declaratory) relief. These negative decisions of the state come very close to no decision (the pure state inaction category), but once the line is crossed, and the court moves from action to inaction, these problems of fashioning an effective remedy are compounded.[81] The court would have to imagine a universe

---

[80] See Winter, "Poverty, Economic Equality and the Equal Protection Clause," 1972 *Sup. Ct. Rev.* 41, 88.

[81] It is hard to know on which side of the line to place a decision not to enter a field all together, for example, not to build public housing. See James v. Valtierra, 402 U.S. 137 (1971).

of possible measures that might be taken (by the legislature) on behalf of the disadvantaged group, make a choice among the permissible ones, compel its enactment, and then police the police.[82] This is not an impossible task but it is exceedingly treacherous, and perhaps further reason for limiting the group-disadvantaging principle to actions of the state.

V. The Choice of Principle

In many situations it will not make a great deal of difference whether the court operates under the antidiscrimination principle or the group-disadvantaging one. An example of such a situation—which I would like to call "first-order"—would be one in which the state excludes blacks from public institutions. In these first-order situations, which were the focus of judicial attention up to the late 1940s, and the following decade or two, the same result is likely to flow from either principle. I would still prefer the group-disadvantaging principle on the ground of frankness—it more accurately captures the intellectual process that should go on in the mind of the judge. It is nevertheless hard to believe much turns on the choice of principle.

Today, however, we find ourselves beyond these first-order situations. A new situation arises when the court is confronted with challenges to nondiscriminatory state action (such as conferring liquor licenses without regard to admission practices or closing public facilities) and with challenges to the state use of facially innocent criteria (such as test performance for allocating jobs or college places). With these second-order situations, there is more than frankness to recommend the group-disadvantaging principle. I believe this principle will frame matters in such a way as to expose the real issues and thus be more likely to lead to the correct decision—invalidation of those state practices that aggravate the subordinate position of the specially disadvantaged groups. It is, of course, possible that under the antidiscrimination principle a court willing to stretch and strain could reach the same result as it would under the group-disadvantaging principle; but that seems either to be a fortuity, or to require such a modification of the antidiscrimination principle— as evidenced by the "past discrimination," "de facto discrimination," or "fundamental right" offshoots—as to deprive the principle of any intel-

---

[82] In addition to enjoining the legislature and compelling the enactment of an ameliorative measure, a court could act negatively. For example, instead of ordering the state legislature to enact a law prohibiting operators of public accommodations from refusing to serve individuals because of their race, it could overturn the trespass convictions of those who were not served because of their race.

lectual coherence and transform it into something it was never intended to be. In these situations, the group-disadvantaging principle should be preferred because it has a degree of coherence and completeness that can never be achieved with the antidiscrimination principle.

There is, to be sure, a third-order situation—as exemplified by state preferential treatment of blacks. In this instance more turns on the choice of principle than frankness, increased likelihood of the right result, or formal elegance. With these third-order problems there is a genuine conflict of principles. The antidiscrimination principle, with its individualistic, means-focused, and symmetrical character, would tend toward prohibiting such preferential treatment; the group-disadvantaging principle, on the other hand, would tend toward permitting it (and indeed might even provide the foundation for the fourth-order claim that may lie around the corner—that of requiring the preferential treatment). I believe this conflict should be resolved in favor of the group-disadvantaging principle but conceivably that this preference need not be one that has preemptive effect (all the way back down the scale). The antidiscrimination principle has coexisted with at least one other equal protection principle, the numerical-equality-of-persons principle of *Reynolds v. Sims*; and, similarly, the group-disadvantaging principle can coexist with other principles.[83] If that be so, then the group-disadvantaging principle can be viewed as a supplemental one: the use of the principle becomes more important as one moves from the first order to the second and then on to the third; and when one arrives at the third order, a hierarchy of the principles must be constructed; and when there is a conflict of principles, the principle of first priority takes precedence. I would argue that in this hierarchy the

---

[83] If the group-disadvantaging principle did have a preemptive effect (all the way down the scale), it would knock-out the antidiscrimination principle as it now exists, that is, with its elaborate superstructure. It might, nevertheless, be possible to find a place in the Constitution—either in the Equal Protection Clause or perhaps more appropriately in the Due Process Clause—for a stripped-down version of the antidiscrimination principle—that is, simply a guarantee of means-end rationality. A law that bore no relation (or very little relation to) an end would be thought "arbitrary." (It might even be possible to append to this basic guarantee of means-end rationality a requirement that the end be constitutionally permissible, though the standard of permissibility would derive from other provisions, such as the First Amendment, rather than the Equal Protection Clause itself—now viewed as a protection for specially disadvantaged groups.) This basic guarantee of means-end rationality would sometimes enable a court to invalidate a state law that, for example, curtailed in a strikingly underinclusive way the speaking privilege of some particular individual or individuals who are not members of a disadvantaged group. The court could reach that result under a means-end test without passing on the general validity of the particular end chosen (for example, to prevent incitement), as it might have to if exclusive reliance were placed on a substantive constitutional provision (such as the First Amendment).

group-disadvantaging principle should be the one of first priority, should be placed ahead of the antidiscrimination principle. But I would be the first to acknowledge that this choice is not an easy one.

Part of the difficulty of making the choice stems from the fact that the usual material of judicial decisions—legislative history and text—provides no guidance. History indicates that the Clause was extended to protect blacks. But it does not tell us whether blacks were to be viewed as a group or as individuals, nor does it say much about the intensity or degree of protection that is to be afforded. Similarly the text does little more than give the ideal of equality constitutional status and circumscribe it with a state action requirement. It is hard to believe that the use of the word "person" was intended to foreclose the recognition of the importance and status of groups. In essence, the text clothes the court with the authority to give specific meaning to the ideal of equality—to choose among the various subgoals contained within the ideal. A judge must become a natural lawyer out of default. The ethical issue is whether the position of perpetual subordination is going to be brought to an end for our disadvantaged groups, and if so, at what speed and at what cost.

The antidiscrimination principle roughly corresponds to the lay concept of equal treatment, and some might argue that the antidiscrimination principle should be given priority (and perhaps pre-emptive effect) because equal treatment is a more widely accepted goal of personal and social action (or more in accord with traditional American values, such as individualism). But this argument seems wrong, even if the informal Gallup Poll came out as imagined. It is not the job of the oracle to tell people—whether it be persons on the street or critical moralists—what they already believe.

For one thing, the public morality may be only an echo: the concept of equal treatment may be the more widely accepted subgoal of the ideal of equality because it more nearly accords with the concept of equality previously propounded by the Supreme Court and because it is the one embodied in the law. The Equal Protection Clause provides the Court with a textual platform from which it can make pronouncements as to the meaning of equality; it shapes the ideal. There pronouncements are viewed as authoritative, part of the "law," and play an important—though by no means decisive—role in shaping popular morality.[84] Law

---

[84] The impact of Brown v. Board of Education on popular morality, especially of those growing up in the 1950s and 1960s, is ample testimony of this phenomenon. So is the wait in the spring of 1974 for the Supreme Court's decision in DeFunis. More seemed to be at stake than a directive against the University of Washington Law School, or for that matter all other state schools. People looked to the Court for some guidance in the solution of an intractable

is a determinant, not just an instrument, of equality. Of course, this relationship between law (viewed as pronouncement rather than directive) and popular morality does not deny the existence of the latter; an echo is still a sound. But it does mean that the group-disadvantaging principle may also be widely accepted once it too is propounded to be the chosen strategy of the Supreme Court, once the judiciary says that this principle and the concept of equal status has an important claim to the constitutional ideal of equality.

Moreover, deference to the prevailing popular morality seems particularly inappropriate when what is being construed is a constitutional protection for minorities. Our commitment to democracy might dictate a reference to the people for the adoption and amendment of the Constitution, but once those processes are complete, a second reference to the electorate to elaborate the content of the ideal embodied in the Constitution seems inconsistent with the very idea of a constitutional restraint. This is particularly true of one that was in large part intended to protect a racial minority. All constitutional restraints are to be countermajoritarian, and this one particularly so.

It might be contended that the priority between the two principles should be set, not on the basis of text, history, or a rough sense of popular morality, but rather on the basis of certain institutional values—which strategy would best further the ideals of the craft. As we have seen, the predominance of the antidiscrimination strategy could in part be explained in terms of its supposed institutional advantages, objectivity and value-neutrality. Supposedly, judges will not be called on to make judgments about ends. The lines that emerge will be sharp. The decisions of the courts will not be heavily steeped in factual inquiries. In contrast, under the group-disadvantaging interpretation, the courts must deal with highly speculative entities, social groups. Subtle factual inquiries are required as to the contours and status of the group and the impact of a challenged practice on the group. Invariably value judgments would have to be made as to the costs and benefits of the practice to the disadvantaged group and to the polity.

I am willing to assume that the group-disadvantaging strategy will strain the resources, the imagination and even the patience of the judiciary. From the perspective of "mechanical jurisprudence" the group-disadvantaging principle offers no advantages. But I doubt whether these institutional considerations ought to be the bases for the choice between

---

moral problem, and this guidance was supposed to emerge from the Court's decision on the meaning of the Equal Protection Clause.

principles. For one thing, as we saw, this image of what judicial life will be under the antidiscrimination principle—no value judgments, sharp lines and no factual judgments—is largely illusory. The court must make determinations about whether the purpose served by the classification is "legitimate," which classifications are "suspect," what rights are "fundamental," what purposes are special or ordinary, whether it is permissible to take one step at a time, and whether the "fit" is sufficient. The quantitative ring to the terms "fit," "overinclusion," and "underinclusion" is decidedly an illusion. Moreover, once the antidiscrimination strategy is modified to embrace "the perpetuation of past discriminations" or "de facto discrimination," as I believe it must, the factual inquiries become overwhelming and the value judgments used (for example, in determining which effects of past discrimination are to be eliminated) become commonplace.

In any event, even if it can (somehow) be demonstrated that the antidiscrimination principle is more conducive to the traditional ideals of the craft, it still remains to be seen why these ideals—the ideals of "mechanical jurisprudence"—should be preserved at all[85] or at least at the expense of substantive results deemed just. It is understandable why judges will choose that strategy most in accord with the ideal of their craft but that hardly makes it just, nor, for the self-conscious judge, inevitable. The redistributive aims served by the group-disadvantaging principle—the elevation of at least one group that has spent two centuries in this country in a position of subordination—may simply override these supposed institutional advantages.

Finally, even if these institutional arguments provide a basis for preferring the antidiscrimination principle, it must be remembered that at best they dictate a choice of the judicial strategy. These arguments cannot be used by all. A sharp line should be drawn between the principles governing the judicial process and those that govern nonjudicial processes, some legislative, some private. This is one sense in which law and morals should be separated. For the institutional considerations have little relevance for those who do not act as judges, but nonetheless must struggle with the task of giving meaning to the ideal of equality—for example, citizens deciding upon admissions policies to a law school and legislators acting under Section 5 of the Fourteenth Amendment. Nor should these institutional considerations be allowed to operate subsilentio in nonjudicial spheres, a danger created when the citizenry gives excessive deference to the judicial pronouncement as to the meaning of equality—when sight

---

[85] This view is elaborated in the article referred to in fn. 22 above.

is lost of the reason for the choice of strategy, and the citizenry defers to judicial pronouncement as to the meaning of "equality" simply because it is "The Law," or even worse, "The Constitution."

The roots of such excessive deference are deep. It may reflect the psychological need for an authoritative agency to decide questions of individual morality. The need becomes particularly acute when, as is true here, the ethical questions become more difficult, the arguments on each side more balanced, and when it is not just a conflict between liberty and equality, but in essence a conflict between two important senses of equality—equal treatment and equal status. Moreover, when what is demanded is a nationwide morality, one that could subordinate the morality of a particular region, as has been true in racial matters, the Supreme Court is particularly well positioned to perform the function of such an authoritative decision-making agency. The impact of judicial pronouncement on positive morality may also be traced to the strategic position of lawyers in our society, as managers of important nonlegal institutions and as formulators of opinion. The Court is "their" institution and they are bound to look to it in formulating their conception of equality.[86]

But whatever the reasons for this deference, and regardless of how understandable it might be, what strikes me as important is that we should become increasingly aware of the role of judicial pronouncement in translating the ideal of equality, the nature of the choices the courts have made, and the explanation for the choices. We should become aware of the fact that the antidiscrimination principle is not inevitable and, indeed, that its predominance may be traceable to institutional values that have little relevance for individual morality or legislative policy. At best they explain the choice of judicial strategy. This increased consciousness does not necessarily mean that the group-disadvantaging principle must be adopted as a matter of individual morality or legislative policy. Indeed considerations that might have given little weight in determining what should be the correct interpretation of the Equal Protection Clause—such as the consideration of individual fairness—may play a larger role in determining what is right for a citizen or legislator. Old dilemmas may appear in new guises.

---

[86] Indeed a person committed to the Court as a legal institution—because of constitutional structure or results in particular cases—might be willing or even desirous to have the Court's sphere of influence broadened as a means of buttressing or fortifying its legal position.

II

THE FORMS OF JUSTICE[1]

Simultaneously with his work on equality, Fiss began to write about the role of the judiciary in the civil rights revolution and in the excesses of the modern bureaucratic state. As a professor at the University of Chicago Law School, his teaching and writing interests began with an attempt to understand his experiences in his clerkships and in the Civil Rights Division of the Department of Justice by teaching a course in equity. Fiss, however, did not teach a traditional equity course. While he explored the role of the injunction in many different but traditional contexts, such as in commercial litigation, labor, nuisance and antitrust, the heart of the course dealt with the use of injunctive relief in the civil rights cases of the 1960s. By 1972, Owen Fiss had culled and edited the materials into a casebook entitled *Injunctions*, published by the Foundation Press.

He did not stop there, however. He continued to deepen his exploration of the civil rights revolution and the injunction. In 1974, Owen Fiss moved to Yale. That same year, he delivered a series of lectures—The Addison C. Harris lectures—at Indiana University. In 1978, these lectures were published in a book entitled *The Civil Rights Injunction*. Other articles followed, such as *Dombrowski*, published in 1977 in the Yale Law Journal, and then the second article in this book—*The Forms of Justice*—which appeared in the foreword to the Supreme Court issue of the 1979 Harvard Law Review.

During the decade in which Owen Fiss developed his views on remedies and the role of the judiciary, the injunction became increasingly important and took on a new status. In Fiss's view, and indeed in the real world itself, the role of the injunction reached new levels of impact and import. Not only did the scope of school desegregation remedies become broader and more ambitious, but injunctions became the tools

---

[1] Owen M. Fiss, *The Supreme Court, 1978 Term—Foreword: The Forms of Justice*, 93 HARV. L. REV. 1 (1979).

to reform the modern bureaucratic state and its institutional structure. The injunction moved from desegregating public schools to reforming and restructuring a wide range of state institutions, such as state prisons and mental institutions.

During the same period, however, the Supreme Court began a counterattack on the structural civil rights injunction. This attack was led by then Associate Justice William Rehnquist, at that time a recent Nixon appointee to the Court. Rehnquist had a huge impact on reversing the Warren Court's revolution. Indeed, he authored the decision that can be taken as the turning point in the battle and which assured victory for those opposed to the structural injunction. In *Rizzo v. Goode*,[2] the Court reversed lower court orders that attempted to stop the Philadelphia police department's abuses against African-Americans. The suit charged a pattern of police abuse of minorities in Philadelphia and sought structural reform. This included an internal disciplinary system to reduce the likelihood of these abuses. Lawyers for the plaintiffs modeled the suit on the then standard school desegregation case initiated in *Brown*. These structural reform cases and the school desegregation cases, of course, had almost always been brought in federal courts. Rehnquist's opinion dismissed *Rizzo* because the remedy sought required a federal court to oversee and restructure the operation of a state institution. Rehnquist's opinion was an overt attack on *Brown* and subsequent civil rights cases and on the use of the civil rights injunction. It denied the principle implicit in those hard fought cases that federal courts are the guardians of federal constitutional rights.

The Forms of Justice can be seen, on one level, as a response to this counterattack. For forty years, Owen Fiss has fought and stood for justice and for the belief that justice is the end goal and, of course, the most significant purpose of constitutional adjudication. He has always championed the same idea of justice—what he refers to as the group disadvantaging principle or the antisubordination doctrine—group justice. The defining moment of his intellectual life, and that which shaped his values, was the Second Reconstruction—the Civil Rights Movement of the 1960s. This was, of course, a struggle for group justice. Moreover, it was both a legal and political struggle. To Fiss, the demand for group justice was a legal claim because the purpose of law, as he has reminded us for decades, is to do justice.

---

[2] Rizzo v. Goode, 423 U.S. 362 (1976).

In his earlier writings, particularly in *The Forms of Justice* and *Groups and the Equal Protection Clause,*[3] constitutional adjudication and the importance of the judicial role in that process was his frame of reference for achieving justice. By 1979, Owen Fiss generalizes the vision of the federal judge as a hero from the civil rights cases of the 1960s and early 1970s to the issues presented by the modern bureaucratic state.

In *The Forms of Justice*, he attacks the false premises of the "craft" or perceived methodology of law and argues that the role of the judge is nothing less than securing justice. He moves from the Equal Protection Clause and its special solicitude for African- Americans, seen primarily in his work *Groups and the Equal Protection Clause*, to the broader injustices of the modern bureaucratic state. Owen Fiss makes an impressive argument that judges, particularly federal judges, must save the citizenry—all of us—not just a particular historically disadvantaged group, from the moral failings of the bureaucratic state.

Indeed, the article introduces a model of adjudication called structural reform. The model is, of course, influenced by the school desegregation cases and the then more recent prison litigation. To Fiss, in order to be able to attack the moral and practical failings of the modern bureaucratic state, the judge must escape from the idea that dispute resolution is the only correct model of adjudication. The role of judges is not to resolve individual disputes but rather to "give concrete meaning and application to our constitutional values."[4] Their job is to do this by searching for "what is true, right, or just."[5] As Fiss puts it:

> Structural reform is premised on the notion that the quality of our social life is affected in important ways by the operation of large-scale organizations, not just by individuals acting either beyond or within these organizations. It is also premised on the belief that our constitutional values cannot be fully secured without effectuating basic changes in the structures of these organizations. The structural suit is one in which a judge, confronting a state bureaucracy over values of constitutional dimension, undertakes to restructure the organization to eliminate a threat to those values posed by the present institutional arrangements.

---

[3] Owen M. Fiss, *Groups and the Equal Protection Clause*, 5 PHIL. & PUB. AFF. 107 (1976).

[4] Fiss, *supra* note 1, at 9.

[5] *Id.*

The injunction is the means by which these reconstructive directives are transmitted.[6]

The article provides a history of structural reform. With its roots in the Warren Court era and the decision in *Brown v. Board of Education*,[7] the effort to translate the rule of *Brown* required courts "to radically transform the status quo, in effect to reconstruct social reality."[8] Desegregation revised familiar conceptions of "party structure, required new norms governing judicial behavior and called for a redefinition of the relationship between rights and remedies."[9] The lessons of *Brown* and school desegregation soon influenced other contexts, including the protection of persons and their property from police abuses, the assurances of due process in the administration of welfare, the equalization of expenditures in state educational systems, and, of course, the requirement of fair and humane treatment of prisoners and mental patients. Therefore, structural reform, in addition to public schools, challenged the policies of prisons, mental hospitals, and housing authorities.

Ironically, by the mid-to-late 1970s, structural reform began to lose favor with the Supreme Court in school desegregation cases, but not necessarily in other contexts. Fiss attempts to elucidate the importance of structural reform and urges us to reconsider it as a mainstay form of adjudication. As Fiss sees it, the state bureaucracy's vehicles of repression are more numerous and complex than intentional racial prejudice. They are intertwined in every aspect of the modern state, including its very social structure. Moreover, not only minorities but all citizens are potential victims of these institutional structures. These institutions are among the most public and important in the life blood of our communities. They include schools, prisons, hospitals, and other large-scale bureaucracies.

Structural reform attempts to give meaning to constitutional values in the operation of these large-scale organizations. However, structural reform is often harshly criticized, particularly because it vests so much power in judges.[10] Fiss, of course, has a completely different view. The

---

[6] *Id.* at 2.

[7] Brown v. Bd. of Educ., 347 U.S. 483 (1954).

[8] Fiss, *supra* note 1, at 2.

[9] *Id.* at 3.

[10] One of the main criticisms of structural reform, which is represented in the work of members of the Supreme Court as well as that of members of the academy, is an objection in the name of the "federalist principles." For example, in *Missouri v. Jenkins III*, 515 U.S. 70, 124 (1995), Justice Thomas deplores the disregard for the principle of limited judicial authority and the fact that the courts have "unprecedented authority to shape a remedy in

role of the judge is not to be criticized but to be honored. Indeed, to Fiss, the judge's role must be large and even heroic. The judge must make the institutional structure of the state bureaucracy an expression of justice. While *Carolene Products* footnote four[11] and its theory of legislative failure are the blueprint for ordering the relationship between the judiciary and other government agencies, its limited application beyond the scope of racial justice can help explain some of the backlash against structural reform. The point of footnote four is that unless the legislative process is inadequate the courts should defer to the Legislative Branch. However, in those cases in which the legislative action is likely to result in laws promoting differential and adverse treatment based on membership in a minority group, a heightened judicial scrutiny test applies, requiring the Legislative Branch to provide a stronger justification for such laws. The tacit presumption behind this requirement is that all persons are entitled to equal treatment and that, unless courts step in, minority groups will be unconstitutionally discriminated against and thus disadvantaged.

---

equity." Moreover, he argues that there is no constitutional support for such broad judicial power and he thus seeks to eliminate structural reform injunctions on the ground that they adversely affect the balance of power between federal and state governments. *Id.* at 126. Another argument against increased judicial authority is one based on the separation of powers principle. Critics who endorse this argument, such as John Yoo, argue that federal courts lack any inherent authority to exercise equitable remedies and "even with congressional approval, certain exercises of the remedial power lie outside the judiciary's Article III powers." John Yoo, *Recognizing the Limits of Judicial Remedies: Who Measures the Chancellor's Foot? The Inherent Remedial Authority of the Federal Courts*, 84 CAL. L. REV. 1121, 1141 (1996). In addition to the separation of powers and federalism objections to the remedial power of the courts, there are also some functional objections to it. According to Yoo and other critics, courts are structurally incapable of addressing and remedying complex problems, particularly those that involve multiple relationships and require courts to weigh policies and analyze costs and benefits. In this view, legislatures are much better suited for such tasks and therefore they should be the ones developing solutions to social problems. *Id.* at 1137-38. Myriam Gilles argues that the demise of structural reform resulted from the fear of judicial activism and from the argument that judges—in employing structural reform injunctions—might impose their own views and values on the institutions and on the community. By doing so they are "playing God." Myriam Gilles, *An Autopsy of the Structural Reform Injunction: Oops . . . It's Still Moving!*, 58 U. MIAMI L. REV. 143, 161-62 (2003).

[11] U.S. v. Carolene Prods. Co., 304 U.S. 144 (1958). This famous footnote distinguishes cases warranting deference from those in which greater judicial scrutiny might be appropriate. Justice Stone's "political process" rationale in footnote four suggests that judicial intervention is more appropriate the less political processes may be trusted to even out winners and losers over time. On this view, judicial interventions help to reinforce democracy by clearing the channels of political change and preventing entrenched advantage or disadvantage in the political process. For an especially influential elaboration of the "political process" argument for heightened judicial scrutiny in some areas but not others depending on whether it corrects political market failure see JOHN HART ELY, DEMOCRACY AND DISTRUST (1980).

Footnote four, however, becomes increasingly unclear in explaining and justifying the judicial role vis-à-vis state bureaucracies like public housing authorities, the welfare department, the police, the state university, taxing authorities, and health maintenance organizations.

The theory underlying footnote four and the legislative failure theory that it espouses is radically incomplete in these broader institutional contexts. There are two sources of this incompleteness: "First, the footnote gives no account of the judicial function . . . it never explains why legislative failure is to be corrected by judicial action. Second, the footnote never justifies its major normative premise, the one positing the supremacy of the majoritarian branches even when constitutional values are at stake."[12]

The theory of legislative failure identifies occasions for a strong independent use of judicial power. However, it does not tell us what should be done with that power. Fiss, on the other hand, does have a strong position on what the judge must do. In Fiss's view, the function of a judge is to give meaning and application to our constitutional values independent of political preferences. As he sees it:

> The right of the judge to speak, and the obligation of others . . . (like governmental agencies) . . . to listen, depends not on the judge's personal attributes, nor even on the context of his message, but on the quality of his process—on his ability to be distant and detached from the immediate contestants and from the body politic, yet fully attentive to grievances, and responsive in terms that transcend preferences and that are sufficient to support a judgment deemed 'constitutional.'[13]

Criticism of structural reform also stems from the observation that it involves a departure from some ideal form of lawsuit. The vision of the ideal is, of course, the dispute-resolution model. The article goes on to compare the structural reform suit to that of the ideal form and then argues that the dispute-resolution model does not have an exclusive claim on the concept of adjudication.[14] Furthermore, Fiss argues that the structural reform model more adequately describes the social function of courts. According to Fiss, courts exist to give meaning to our public

---

[12] Fiss, *supra* note 1, at 8-9.

[13] *Id.* at 16.

[14] See, e.g., Owen Fiss, *The Social and Political Foundations of Adjudication*, 6 LAW & HUM. BEHAV. 121 (1982), for a detailed comparison between the two models.

values, not to resolve disputes. In a structural suit a judge performs this function by reorganizing the institution to meet the requirements of our constitutional values.[15]

Fiss then questions whether dispute resolution is the ideal against which structural reform is to be judged. He concludes that the dispute resolution model strictly honors the right of each affected individual to participate in the process, and thus stresses the importance of the individual. This leaves the individual without institutional support that is often necessary to realize the true self because it ignores institutional failures readily addressed by the structural reform model. The structural reform model reconstructs the party structure of a suit, making it less individualistic and more group oriented. The remedy, in turn, emphasizes protection of the rights of the individuals that comprise the group.

While structural reform more closely represents the ideal of constitutional adjudication by giving meaning to public values, in the remedial phase it tests the boundaries of the Judicial Branch. "The desire to be efficacious leads the judge to attempt the remarkable feat of reconstructing a state bureaucracy . . . and that ambition in turn forces the judge to abandon his position of independence and to enter the world of politics."[16]

To understand the cause of this dilemma we must understand the relationship between rights and remedies. But Fiss first asks us to abandon the "tailoring principle"—that which insists that the remedy must fit the violation. This principle gives us an incomplete notion of remedy because it looks back to identify discrete incidents as the object of the remedy. Since the point of the structural remedy is not to eliminate a violation, but rather to remove the threat posed by an organization to constitutional values, the tailoring principle falls short.

Fiss suggests looking at the structural remedy in instrumental terms. Instrumentally, the remedy exists for and is determined by the finite purpose of protecting the constitutional value threatened. Moreover, the remedy actually chosen is one among many ways of achieving that purpose. It incorporates considerations that might not be rooted in any direct and obvious way in the constitutional value that occasions the intervention. The remedy is shaped most critically by considerations of fairness and strategy. The article identifies a weakness in instrumentalism, namely the problem that arises "from an absence of a conceptual

---

[15] Some of Fiss's arguments are similar to those expressed by Abram Chayes, in one of the most influential legal articles ever published. Abram Chayes, *The Role of the Judge in Public Law Litigation*, 89 HARV. L. REV. 1281 (1976).

[16] Fiss, *supra* note 1, at 46.

connection between the processes that give courts their special competency and instrumental judgments."[17] The rightful place of the court is in giving meaning to constitutional values. But the task of determining the meaning of those values is quite different from fashioning the most effective strategy for actualizing those values—for eliminating the threat posed to those values by the particular state bureaucracy.

Why then should we entrust the remedial task to judges? The answer, according to Fiss: "If the judge's function is to give meaning to our public values, and the remedy must be understood as an integral part of that process, then we can understand—and indeed appreciate—the judge's involvement in reforming the state bureaucracy."[18] Fiss defines a right as "a particularized and authoritative declaration of meaning. It can exist without a remedy—the right to racial equality . . . can exist even if the court gave no relief. . . . A remedy, on the other hand, is an effort of the court to give meaning to a public value in practice. A remedy is more specific, more concrete . . . it constitutes the actualization of the right."[19] The declaration of the public value, the right, and the actualization of that right are tightly connected. Separating the two functions by allowing an administrative agency the task of actualization would compromise the entire process, simply because there is a "risk that the remedy might distort the right, and leave us with something less than the true meaning of the constitutional value."[20] Both functions "must be entrusted to the same agency to preserve the integrity of the meaning-giving enterprise itself."[21]

Much of Fiss's essay is concerned with tracing the procedural implications of his vision of the judicial role and defending it against what he perceives as the incomplete tradition of the judicial method or craft. In place of the traditional virtues of judicial method or craft and because of the weaknesses of the "tailoring principle"—the idea that the remedy must fit the violation—Fiss appeals to other virtues of the judicial function. These are, of course, independence and dialogue. The judge is independent of the parties and of politics. He must determine the meaning of constitutional values only after a long, complex process of hearing many different viewpoints and then he must offer public reasons as

[17] *Id.* at 51.

[18] *Id.* at 53.

[19] *Id.* at 52.

[20] *Id.* at 53.

[21] *Id.*

justification for his conclusions. This process of discourse provides the ground of judicial legitimacy.

Although the entire process should be committed to one agency—the courts—Fiss argues that there is the risk that judges may disturb the balance of powers between its sister branches of government and, in the process of actualization, partake in political or policy-making functions. However, a judge's activity is constrained by limits deriving from the will of the people. That is, judges realize that the practical success of the remedy vitally depends on public preferences. Thus, no judge is likely to institute a remedy that would compromise or push that boundary. The unfortunate result is that, while actualization requires a judge to maximize the remedy in order to realize and articulate the public values completely, judges are loathe to bargain against people's preferences or to promote a controversial stance. Thus, because of this factor, judges will strive to lessen the gap between declaration and actualization and tailor the right to fit the remedy.

Fiss urges us to recognize and understand these weaknesses in structural reform, but to continue to favor structural reform in spite of them. The article warns against "turn[ing] back in despair, renounce[ing] the adjudicative enterprise altogether."[22] Fiss proposes that we live with the judicial dilemma in an effort to learn from and apply the lessons derived from the Warren Court—an extraordinary period in this history of the American judiciary. We must, then, accept in the spirit of advocating structural reform, that judges will always straddle two worlds—the world of public value and the world of subjective preference.

By 1979, Fiss is increasingly fighting and writing against the judicial grain. The ambitions of Justice Brennan, which Fiss is clearly attempting to preserve, have been defeated in a Supreme Court led by Justice Rehnquist. Brennan, the heroic judge of the structural injunction, is in a box from which he cannot escape. If he is true to his role of doing justice, he becomes a dissenter without effect. If he compromises this vision, he risks compromising with justice.

Even within the confines of this dilemma, or perhaps because of it, the article has had a tremendous impact, being cited at least 783 times in the literature.[23] It has been criticized by many scholars and yet, thirty years later, it retains its relevance. Indeed, it is clear that Fiss's ideas

---

[22] *Id.* at 57.

[23] A LexisNexis terms and connectors search for "Owen M. Fiss" and "The Forms of Justice" generates 783 results from sources including American and Canadian law reviews; American Bar Association Journals; federal court cases; and state court cases combined. The Web of Science states that it has been cited 276 times. It is possible, of course, to claim, adding

remain timeless. He established a paradigm that is still frequently cited today, both to illustrate the way the legal system works, and as a point of comparison for any new theories of the forms of litigation and the role of the judiciary.

Nevertheless, since its publication in 1979, critics have questioned almost every aspect of Fiss's essay:[24] the perhaps over-exalted role of the

---

the two figures together, that the article has been cited a total of 1,059 times. However, the two bases of information probably cite some of the same sources.

[24] Fiss's insistence that courts serve as active participants in restructuring institutions is perhaps the most frequent source of complaint and critique by scholars. Robert Bone, for example, argues that although Fiss's theories may work well for creating and implementing public values, the same system cannot be applied to "purely private disputes." Robert Bone, *Rethinking the "Day in Court" Ideal and Nonparty Preclusion*, 67 N.Y.U. L. REV. 193, 201 (1992). However, not everyone agrees with Bone. In response to Bone's argument, Phoebe Haddon argues:

> Of course it can be argued persuasively that not every dispute for which private individuals seek resolution has significant public dimensions. I agree with Fiss, however, that this is indicative of the fact that we have misused the resources of the courts and that we should explore the alternatives for resolving disputes which do not have a public significance.

Phoebe A. Haddon, *Rethinking the Jury*, 3 WM. & MARY BILL RTS. J. 29 (1994).

Critics also argue that Lon Fuller's individual participation theory—that the individual affected by a dispute must take part in its adjudication—should not be completely undone because it leaves the individual with nothing to stand on in a private dispute. While arguing that outcome determinative adjudication creates problems with accuracy and procedural justice, Laurence Solum questions Fiss's representative participation model. Individuals represent themselves not because in Fissian terms, "they are the best or most efficient representative of their own interests" but because "they are human persons, who act on their own behalves, define their own interests, and speak for themselves." Lawrence Solum, *Procedural Justice*, 78 S. CAL. L. REV. 181, 302-03 (2004). Robert Fallon Jr. perhaps best summarizes the concern academics have with Fiss's insistence on the structural suit. In Fallon's view, the problem is not merely that Fiss persists in undermining the dispute resolution theory, it is that he offers no discussion on private-rights suits. "Fiss argues that the special-functions approach [the structural suit], to use my terminology, should be preferred. He offers no suggestion as to how cases reflecting a contrary position might be distinguished. Operating at a remove from interpretivist argument, Fiss urges major reforms. Prudentialism appears to have no place in his vision." Robert Fallon Jr., *Marbury and the Constitutional Mind: A Bicentennial Essay on the Wages of Doctrinal Tension*, 91 CAL. L. REV. 1, 44-45 (2003).

As Fallon points out, Fiss is interested in major reforms, and academics who share his belief that structural reform should be a main task of the court rely on *The Forms of Justice* in developing their arguments. Susan Sturm, for example, agrees with Fiss's structural reform approach as that best suited to handling prison, school and housing cases. Her main critique is that Fiss's strict requirement of judicial purity and independence keeps him from offering a viable solution to the problem of creating remedies. As she puts it:

> Given his recognition of the inadequacy of the liability norm as the determinant of the terms of structural injunctions, Fiss is confronted with the issue of how the

judge,[25] the appropriateness (propriety?) of the structural reform suit to different types of cases, and the rights-remedies dilemma. None of the critics, however, question the importance of the issues Fiss addresses or the impact his theories have had on the adjudication process.

---

judge is to develop an appropriate remedy. On this issue, however, Fiss' vision is blocked by the liability model of judicial process. Fiss fails to extend his insights concerning the substantive relationship of right and remedy in public law litigation to the processes of remedial formulation in these cases.

Susan Sturm, *A Normative Theory of Public Law Remedies*, 79 GEO. L.J. 1357, 1369 (1991).

Sturm is not alone in her criticism. Paul Gerwitz makes almost the identical argument, pointing to how Fiss tangles himself in his austere expectations of the judge in his role as independent-minded reformer. Gerwitz claims that, having isolated and legitimated the pure rights-declaring function, Fiss then tries to leverage in the impure remedy-supplying function like a tied-in product. But to Gerwitz, given Fiss's own premises of legitimacy, the tie-in, the 'unity of functions' as Fiss calls it, is hard to defend. If legitimacy is undercut when judges behave adaptively and compromise with social realities, then this behavior undercuts legitimacy at whatever 'stage' it occurs. The problem cannot be solved by the bifurcation of rights and remedies. Paul Gerwitz, *Remedies and Resistance*, 92 YALE L.J. 585, 628-29 (1983).

[25] Sanford Levinson, for example, mocks Fiss for putting so much faith in the judicial system by pointing to Fiss's criticism of the Rehnquist Court. He posits the following, "Will Professor Fiss argue that the interpretive community has been taken over by a false pope, a usurper, against whom the truly faithful must rally?" Sanford Levinson, *Law as Literature*, 60 TEX. L. REV. 373, 399 (1981-82).

THE FORMS OF JUSTICE*

The Constitution establishes the structure of government. It creates the agencies of government, describes their functions, and determines their relationships. The Constitution also identifies the values that will inform and limit this governmental structure. The values that we find in our Constitution—liberty, equality, due process, freedom of speech, no establishment of religion, property, no impairments of the obligation of contract, security of the person, no cruel and unusual punishment—are ambiguous. They are capable of a great number of different meanings. They often conflict. There is a need—a constitutional need—to give them specific meaning, to give them operational content, and, where there is a conflict, to set priorities.

All of us, both as individuals and institutional actors, play a role in this process. In modern society, where the state is all-pervasive, these values determine the quality of our social existence—they truly belong to the public—and as a consequence, the range of voices that give meaning to these values is as broad as the public itself. The legislative and Executive Branches of government, as well as private institutions, have a voice; so should the courts. Judges have no monopoly on the task of giving meaning to the public values of the Constitution, but neither is there reason for them to be silent. They too can make a contribution to the public debate and inquiry.

Adjudication is the social process by which judges give meaning to our public values. Structural reform—the subject of this essay—is one type of adjudication, distinguished by the constitutional character of the public values, and even more importantly, by the fact that it involves an encounter between the judiciary and the state bureaucracies. The judge tries to give meaning to our constitutional values in the operation of these organizations. Structural reform truly acknowledges the bureaucratic character of the modern state, adapting traditional procedural forms

---

* Owen M. Fiss, The Supreme Court, 1978—Foreword: The Forms of Justice, 93 HARV L. REV. 1 (1979). This article uses the footnote numbers and citation form of this particular publication.

to the new social reality, and in the years ahead promises to become a central—maybe the central—mode of constitutional adjudication.

Structural reform is premised on the notion that the quality of our social life is affected in important ways by the operation of large-scale organizations, not just by individuals acting either beyond or within these organizations. It is also premised on the belief that our constitutional values cannot be fully secured without effectuating basic changes in the structures of these organizations. The structural suit is one in which a judge, confronting a state bureaucracy over values of constitutional dimension, undertakes to restructure the organization to eliminate a threat to those values posed by the present institutional arrangements. The injunction is the means by which these reconstructive directives are transmitted.

As a genre of constitutional litigation, structural reform has its roots in the Warren Court era and the extraordinary effort to translate the rule of *Brown v. Board of Education*[1] into practice. This effort required the courts to radically transform the status quo, in effect to reconstruct social reality. The courts had to overcome the most intense resistance, and, even more problematically, they had to penetrate and restructure large-scale organizations, public school systems. The imagery was rural and individualistic—the black child walking into an all-white school—but the reality, especially by the mid-1960's, as the focus shifted to the urban centers and the nation at large, was decidedly bureaucratic.

Brown was said to require nothing less than the transformation of "dual school systems" into "unitary, nonracial school systems," and that entailed thoroughgoing organizational reform. It required new procedures for the assignment of students; new criteria for the construction of schools; reassignment of faculty; revision of the transportation systems to accommodate new routes and new distances; reallocation of resources among schools and among new activities; curriculum modification; increased appropriations; revision of interscholastic sports schedules; new information systems for monitoring the performance of the organization; and more.[2] In time it was understood that desegregation was a total transformational process in which the judge undertook the reconstruction of an ongoing social institution. Desegregation required a revision of familiar conceptions about party structure, new norms governing

---

[1] 347 U.S. 483 (1954).

[2] *See, e.g.,* Lee v. Macon County Bd. of Educ., 267 F. Supp. 458 (M.D. Ala. 1967) (per curiam) (three-judge court), *aff'd per curiam sub nom.* Wallace v. United States, 389 U.S. 215 (1967); United States v. Jefferson County Bd. of Educ., 372 F.2d 836 (5th Cir.1966), *aff'd per curiam*, 380 F.2d 385 (5th Cir.) (en banc), *cert. denied*, 389 U.S. 840 (1967).

judicial behavior, and new ways of looking at the relationship between rights and remedies.

No one had a road map at the outset. No one had a clear vision of all that would be involved in trying to eradicate the caste system embedded in a state bureaucracy, or how the attempt would transform the mode of adjudication. The second *Brown* decision[3] was far from such a vision: it was but a recognition of the magnitude of the task and an attempt to buy time. It delegated the reconstructive task to the lower federal judges. They, in turn, discovered what the task required and adjusted traditional procedural forms to meet the felt necessities. Legitimacy was equated with need, and, in that sense, procedure became dependent upon substance. It was the overriding commitment to racial equality that motivated the procedural innovation and that was seen as the justification for the departures from tradition.

At critical junctures—*Cooper v. Aaron*,[4] the faculty desegregation cases of the mid-1960's,[5] and *Green v. County School Board*[6]—the Warren Court stepped in. The Justices emphasized their continuous commitment to *Brown* and acknowledged the comprehensiveness of the reform required: the dual school system would have to be eradicated "root and branch."[7] The process continued and, in time, the lessons of school desegregation were transferred to other contexts: to protect the security of the person and home from police abuses, to realize the ideal of humane treatment in prisons and mental hospitals, to ensure procedural due process in the welfare Administration, and to equalize expenditures in state educational systems. In that way school desegregation became a vitally important occasion for procedural innovations that transcended the substantive claim, for the emergence of a whole new conception of adjudication, one that was particularly suited to cope with a new unit of constitutional law—the state bureaucracy.

Today we are at a new phase in the evolutionary process. The change did not occur in 1969, immediately upon the ascension of Warren Burger to the Chief Justiceship. In fact, during the first few years, in cases like

---

[3] Board v. Board of Educ., 349 U.S. 294 (1955).

[4] 358 U.S. 1 (1958).

[5] United States v. Montgomery County Bd. of Educ., 395 U.S. 225 (1969); Bradley v. School Bd., 382 U.S. 103 (1965) (per curiam).

[6] 391 U.S. 430 (1968).

[7] *Id.* at 438.

Swann[8] and *Keyes*,[9] the Supreme Court strongly supported the emergent model of adjudication; in the early 1970's structural reform continued to occur in the lower courts at a brisk pace and with a broad reach, including more and more state bureaucracies. By the mid- and late-1970's, however, a new position had formed on the Supreme Court; a strong bloc of Justices, sometimes obtaining support from the center of the Court, sought to reverse the processes that were still afoot in the lower courts. The major assault occurred, ironically enough, in the school desegregation cases of the mid-1970's—the *Detroit* metropolitan case,[10] the *Pasadena* case,[11] and the *Dayton* case.[12] In other cases, in racial areas and elsewhere, the pattern has been mixed: in a police case the Burger Court was sharply critical of structural reform;[13] in a prison case it was strongly supportive;[14] and so on and so on.[15] In most the Court was deeply divided; even when structural reform survived, there was usually a high-pitched dissent.

---

[8] Swann v. Charlotte-Mecklenburg Bd. of Educ., 402 U.S. 1, 15-16 (1971). *See also* Wright v. Council of Emporia, 407 U.S. 451 (1972); Davis v. Board of School Comm'rs, 402 U.S. 33 (1971).

[9] Keyes v. School Dist. No. 1, 413 U.S. 189 (1973).

[10] Milliken v. Bradley, 418 U.S. 717 (1974).

[11] Pasadena City Bd. of Educ. v. Spangler, 427 U.S. 424 (1976).

[12] Dayton Bd. of Educ. v. Brinkman, 433 U.S. 406 (1977).

[13] Rizzo v. Goode, 423 U.S. 362 (1976). This case involved the Philadelphia police department, and, with a touch of bravado, the Department of Justice recently filed, in the name of the United States, a similar suit against the Philadelphia police department. N.Y. Times, Aug. 13, 1979, at A1, col. 2. The change from private to government plaintiff may avoid some of the difficulties of the first suit, such as those pertaining to the majority's view of the "case or controversy" requirement or the dictates of "Our Federalism," *see* Fiss, *Dombrowski*, 86 YALE L.J. 1103, 1154-60 (1977), but it may cause some difficulties of its own, *see* Estelle v. Justice, 426 U.S. 925 (1976) (Rehnquist, J., dissenting from denial of certiorari).

[14] Hutto v. Finney, 437 U.S. 678 (1978). On other occasions, the Court has been more ambivalent towards judicial review of prison conditions. *Compare* Bounds v. Smith, 430 U.S. 817 (1977) (obligation to provide law libraries or legal assistance); Wolff v. McDonnell, 418 U.S. 539 (1974) (minimum standards required for disciplinary proceedings); *and* Procunier v. Martinez, 416 U.S. 396 (1974) (mail censorship regulations invalidated), *with* Jones v. North Carolina Prisoners' Labor Union, 433 U.S. 119 (1977) (regulations prohibiting prisoners from soliciting other inmates to join union sustained); Meachum v. Fano, 427 U.S. 215 (1976) (no right to factfinding hearing when prisoner is transferred); *and* Pell v. Procunier, 417 U.S. 817 (1974) (prohibition on press and other media interviews upheld).

[15] *See* Hills v. Gautreaux, 425 U.S. 284 (1976) (public housing); Gerstein v. Pugh, 420 U.S. 103 (1975) (pretrial detention); Spomer v. Littleton, 414 U.S. 514 (1974) (prosecutor's office); O'Shea v. Littleton, 414 U.S. 488 (1974) (state court system); Gilligan v. Morgan, 413 U.S. 1 (1973) (National Guard).

The Burger Court counterassault—sniping is probably a more accurate description—has not sealed the door on structural reform—indeed, just this past Term two broad desegregation plans squeaked by, one involving Columbus,[16] and the other involving a return of the *Dayton* case[17]—but it has changed our vision. In the midst of the Warren Court era, the procedural innovations implicit in structural reform were almost invisible. Each step was small and incremental; each seemed unquestionably correct. Now that is past. We have a clearer understanding of the 1960's. The counterassault has brought into focus the changes in adjudication that occurred during those times and, even more importantly, it has called them into question. We have been forced, as perhaps we should, to examine the legitimacy of those changes. That is why the academy is today filled with talk about procedure.[18] That is why we believe we are at a historic moment, a turning point in the history of procedure—not because we are in the midst of an intellectual revolution, but because we are in the midst of a counterrevolution; not because we are at the verge of a new discovery, but because the discovery of an earlier era is now in jeopardy.

I. Adjudication and Public Values

As a type of adjudication, structural reform is in large part distinguished by the effort to give meaning to constitutional values in the operation of large-scale organizations. This organizational aspiration has important consequences for the form of adjudication, raising new and distinct problems of legitimacy. But much of the criticism of structural reform, and what I wish to begin with, focuses on that characteristic common to all forms of injunctive litigation: the fact that so much power is vested in judges.

The great and modern charter for ordering the relation between judges and other agencies of government is footnote four of *Carolene*

---

[16] Columbus Bd. of Educ. v. Penick, 99 S.Ct. 2941 (1979).

[17] Dayton Bd. of Educ. v. Brinkman, 99 S.Ct. 2971 (1979). Prison reform did not fare that well. *See* Bell v. Wolfish, 99 S.Ct. 1861 (1979) (various regulations affecting pretrial detainees sustained).

[18] My colleague Robert Cover and I have sought to capture the academic flurry in our new book, THE STRUCTURE OF PROCEDURE (1979). Following the completion of that book in January of this year, at least three issues of major law journals appeared which were devoted to procedure: *Dispute Resolution*, 88 YALE L.J. 905 (1979); 78 COLUM. L. REV. 707 (1978) (issue containing three Articles and one student-written Special Project on procedure) (received in February 1979); PRIVATE ALTERNATIVES TO THE JUDICIAL PROCESS, 8 J. LEGAL STUD. 231 (1979).

Products.[19] The greatness derives not from its own internal coherence, or any theoretical insight, but from its historical position. The footnote codified the hard fought victory of the Progressives and seemed to provide a framework for the judicial activism that was about to transpire. The Progressives, and their 1930's successors, the New Dealers, fought their battles in the legislature, and the footnote reflected the terms of their victory: it posited the supremacy of the legislature. The role of the courts, even on constitutional questions, was defined in terms of "legislative failure": the courts should defer to the legislative branch, the footnote proclaimed, unless there is some reason for assuming that the processes of the legislature are inadequate. The footnote identified two instances of legislative failure: abridgment of the right to vote and victimization of a discrete and insular minority, a group disabled from forming coalitions and thus from effectively participating in majoritarian politics.

Although *Carolene Products* involved a challenge to a statute, it has been taken, as perhaps it was intended, to be a more general statement on the role of courts in our political system. The theory of legislative failure should be understood as a general presumption in favor of majoritarianism: the legislature should be seen as standing for those agencies of government, whether they be the chief executive of the polity, or the local school board, or director of corrections, that are more perfectly tied to majoritarian politics than are the courts. *Carolene Products* and the theory of legislative failure thus have important implications for structural reform; they provide a basis, invoked with increasing frequency these days, for criticizing the strong judicial role implicit in that mode of adjudication.

Structural reform arose in a context that did not test the limits of the theory of legislative failure. The early school desegregation cases, concentrated as they were in the South, could be conceptualized as a compounded type of legislative failure. The normal presumption in favor of majoritarianism clearly did not control. The group being victimized was a discrete and insular minority, indeed it was the paradigmatic discrete and insular minority; the group was also denied formal participation in the majoritarian process—at the time of *Brown*, blacks were disenfranchised. It should be recognized, however, as a first attempt to assess the theory of legislative failure, and to understand its implications, that the politics of race are different today, and, as a consequence, *Carolene Products* and its

---

[19] United States v. Carolene Prods. Co., 304 U.S. 144, 152 n.4 (1938). For a new and highly suggestive commentary on the footnote, see R. Cover, The Origins of Judicial Activism in the Protection of Minorities (1979) (unpublished manuscript on file at the Yale Law School Library and the *Harvard Law Review*).

commitment to majoritarianism pose significant challenges to structural reform even when it seeks to secure the value of racial equality.

The disenfranchisement of blacks has been brought to an end. In some communities throughout the nation, particularly the large cities, blacks represent a sizeable portion of the electorate. On a national level blacks represent a numerical minority, but that circumstance alone would not entitle us to assume the legislative process has failed. The footnote does not entitle any group to have a voice that exceeds its numbers—quite the contrary. Account must also be taken of the fact that blacks are now in a position to form coalitions. They are no longer insular, and their discreteness, their cohesiveness, may in fact give them a certain edge in forming coalitions, especially compared with other groups of their size. True, poverty, or more precisely the absence of large concentrations of wealth in the black community, stands as a barrier to effective political participation of that group. But poverty was not identified by footnote four as a category of legislative failure, and for good reason. The absence of wealth is so pervasive a handicap, it is experienced by so many groups in society, even the majority itself, that to recognize it as a category of legislative failure would stand the theory of the *Carolene Products* footnote on its head—it would undermine the premise of majoritarianism itself.

I might also add that it seems increasingly important, especially as we look to the 1980's, for structural reform to move beyond the bounds of racial justice; and in these new domains the usefulness of footnote four in explaining and justifying the judicial role is also unclear. Structural reform aimed at total institutions—prisons and mental hospitals—may be understood in terms of legislative failure, or more aptly, legislative neglect. These institutions are intended to remove people from the body politic[20] and judicial intervention might be seen as the catalyst of majoritarianism rather than its enemy. Similarly, few of the other state bureaucracies—the public housing authority, the welfare department—might be seen as posing threats to distinct subgroups that are politically powerless. But when the focus shifts, as I believe it must, to the broad-based bureaucracies that typify the modern state—the police, the state university, the taxing authorities, the health maintenance organizations, the state owned industries, and so forth—the theory of footnote four is of little use. The victim of these organizations is the citizenry itself.

With respect to these broad-based organizations, majoritarianism and judicial intervention might seem reconcilable on the theory that

---

[20] *See* M. FOUCAULT, DISCIPLINE AND PUNISH (1977); E. GOFFMAN, ASYLUMS 3-124 (1961).

bureaucratization causes unique distortions of the legislative process; bureaucrats have special incentives and means for insulating their practices from public scrutiny.[21] But such an approach would expand footnote four far beyond its original scope, and, given the large role of these broad-based state bureaucracies in our social life today, it would undermine the premise of legislative supremacy itself. The commitment to majoritarianism would be a sham. Alternatively, the emphasis may be on egalitarian values, and the threat posed to those values by these broad-based organizations; but it seems to me that the relevant subgroup invoking the claim of equality against these organizations—women, the aged, or the lower and middle classes—is not likely to be one that is disadvantaged in terms of majoritarian politics. Footnote four can be twisted and turned, and expanded,[22] to accommodate these groups and their claims, but only at a price: incoherence. Such an accommodation would require us virtually to assume that whichever group happens to lose the political struggle or fails to command the attention of the legislature or executive is—by that fact alone—a discrete and insular minority.

It is not just a question of usefulness—it now seems clearer than ever that footnote four and the theory of legislative failure that it announces is radically incomplete. The incompleteness derives from two sources. First, the footnote gives no account of the judicial function even in the acknowledged cases of legislative failure. It never explains why legislative failure is to be corrected by judicial action. Second, the footnote never justifies its major normative premise, the one positing the supremacy of the majoritarian branches even when constitutional values are at stake. At the root of both failings is, I believe, a denial of the special character of our constitutional values.

The theory of legislative failure identifies *occasions* for a strong independent use of judicial power, but it does not prescribe what should be done with that power. If there is an abridgement of the right to vote, the judicial function may be clear enough: restore the vote. Majoritarianism is thereby perfected. But there is no simple way of understanding

---

[21] *See generally* W. Niskanen, Bureaucracy and Representative Government (1971); Niskanen, *Bureaucrats and Politicians*, 18 J.L. & Econ. 617 (1975); Margolis, *Comment*, 18 J.L. & Econ. 645 (1975); *see also* G. Allison, Essence of Decision (1971).

[22] Professor Ely's we-they theory was intended to explain the asymmetry of the theory of legislative failure in the racial area and why strict scrutiny is appropriate for measures to help blacks but not for those that hurt them; but it may have applicability beyond that sphere. *See* Ely, *The Constitutionality of Reverse Racial Discrimination*, 41 U. Chi. L. Rev. 723 (1974). For my critique of the theory, see *Groups and the Equal Protection Clause*, 5 Philosophy & Pub. Aff. 107 (1976), *reprinted in* Equality and Preferential Treatment 84 (M. Cohen, T. Nagel & T. Scanlon eds. 1977) [hereinafter cited as *Groups*].

the judicial function when failure arises from other causes, say, from the fact that a discrete and insular minority is being victimized. In such a situation the legislative decision may not be entitled to any presumption of correctness, at least as it affects that group, but the task still remains of determining, as an affirmative matter, what the group is entitled to, either by way of process rights or substantive rights.[23] Even if the legislative resolution is not entitled to a presumption of correctness, there is no reason for assuming that the opposite resolution would prevail if the legislative process were working perfectly; there is no reason for assuming that the discrete and insular group would win rather than lose. Nor would it make much sense in terms of the ideals of the craft to view the judge as a representative of, or as a spokesman for, the otherwise voiceless minority. The judge is not to speak for the minority or otherwise amplify its voice. The task of the judge is to give meaning to constitutional values, and he does that by working with the constitutional text, history, and social ideals. He searches for what is true, right, or just.[24] He does not become a participant in interest group politics.

The function of a judge is to give concrete meaning and application to our constitutional values. Once we perceive this to be the judicial function in cases of admitted legislative failure, then we are led to wonder why the performance of this function is conditioned upon legislative failure in the first place. What is the connection between constitutional values and legislative failure? If the legislative process promised to get us closer to the meaning of our constitutional values, then the theory of legislative failure would be responsive to this puzzlement. But just the opposite seems true. Legislatures are entirely of a different order. They are not ideologically committed or institutionally suited to search for the meaning of constitutional values, but instead see their primary function in terms of registering the actual, occurrent preferences of the people—what they want and what they believe should be done. Indeed, the preferred status of legislatures under footnote four is largely derived from this conception of their function. The theory of legislative failure, much like the theory of market failure,[25] ultimately rests on a view that declares supreme the people's preferences.

---

[23] *Groups, supra* note 22, at 131. *See also* Sandalow, *Judicial Protection of Minorities,* 75 MICH. L. REV. 1162, 1184 (1977).

[24] *See* Dworkin, *No Right Answer?,* in LAW, MORALITY AND SOCIETY 58 (P. Hacker & J. Raz eds. 1977); R. DWORKIN, TAKING RIGHTS SERIOUSLY (1977).

[25] At one point, the theory of market failure, much like the theory of legislative failure, was monolithic in its prescription in cases of failure (market failure inexorably led to government regulation), though today it has a broader, more pluralistic vision. *See* O. WILLIAMSON,

How might such a view be reconciled with the very idea of a Constitution? There is, to be certain, another part of footnote four, one that I have not yet described. It concerns not legislative failure, but textual specificity—highly specific prohibitions of the Constitution. The free speech clause is the example.[26] Footnote four is prepared to recognize these provisions as a limitation on legislative supremacy; they stand as a qualification of the view that postulates the supremacy of the people's preferences. It is assumed that these prohibitions are small in number. The more important point to note, however, is that with respect to these textually-specific prohibitions, footnote four does not condition judicial intervention upon legislative failure, but instead looks to the courts as the primary interpretative agency. Here the judicial function is to "apply" these provisions, or to put the same point somewhat differently, the judicial function is to give the values implicit in these provisions their operative meaning.

This view of the judicial role in the domain of the textually-specific, plus an understanding of the judicial function in cases of legislative failure, is sufficient to call into question the theory of legislative failure itself. They imply a view of the judicial function that is not easily cabined. They suggest that in fact courts are not default institutions, that their rightful place does not turn on the failure of another institution, whether it be the legislature or the executive. They suggest that courts be seen as a coordinate source of government power with their own sphere of influence, one that is defined in terms that unify both the *occasion* and *function* of the exercise of power. The judicial role is limited by the existence of constitutional values, and the function of courts is to give meaning to those values.

The values that lie at the heart of most structural litigation today— equality, due process, liberty, security of the person, no cruel and unusual

---

MARKETS AND HIERARCHIES (1975); Coase, *Discussion*, 54 AM. ECON. REV. 194 (1964) (Papers & Proceedings); Coase, *The Problem of Social Cost*, 3 J.L. & ECON. 1 (1960). I am grateful to Judith Lachman for first drawing attention to the parallelism in the intellectual structures of the theories of market and legislative failure.

[26] The example is inferred from the citations, Stromberg v. California, 283 U.S. 359 (1931), and Lovell v. City of Griffin, 303 U.S. 444 (1938), two early Hughes Court decisions heralding a new era for free speech. In discussing the theory of specificity the footnote speaks of the entire Bill of Rights, giving us a further insight into what that Court actually meant by textual specificity. The entire discussion of this branch of *Carolene Products* reads: "There may be narrower scope for operation of the presumption of constitutionality when legislation appears on its face to be within a specific prohibition of the Constitution, such as those of the first ten amendments, which are deemed equally specific when held to be embraced within the Fourteenth." 304 U.S. at 152 n.4. Then followed the citation to *Stromberg* and *Lovell*.

punishment—are not embodied in textually-specific prohibitions; the equal protection clause—no state shall deny any person equal protection of the laws—is as specific as the free speech clause—Congress shall pass no law abridging the freedom of speech—but neither is very specific. They simply contain public values that must be given concrete meaning and harmonized with the general structure of the Constitution. The same is probably true of all the other provisions of the Constitution (*e.g.,* the commerce clause) that have been central to constitutional litigation for almost two centuries. The absence of textual specificity does not make the values any less real, nor any less important. The values embodied in such non-textually-specific prohibitions as the equal protection and due process clauses are central to our constitutional order. They give our society an identity and inner coherence—its distinctive public morality. The absence of a textually-specific prohibition does not deny the importance of these values, but only makes the meaning-giving enterprise more arduous: less reliance can be placed on text.

Of course, the further one moves from text, the greater the risk of abuse; it is easier for judges, even unwittingly, to enact into law their own preferences in the name of having discovered the true meaning, say, of equality or liberty. It was just this risk, elaborated by the Legal Realists, that haunted the Progressives, and that helped sell the theory of legislative failure as the principle governing the interpretation of those values not embodied in textually-specific prohibitions—better the preferences of the people than the preferences of the judges.[27] But the Progressives never explained why one set of preferences was a more appropriate basis for a constitutional judgment than the other; both seem inappropriate. Nor did they explain why the risk of abuse, any more than the risk of mistake, was itself a sufficient basis for denying the intelligibility of the meaning-giving enterprise altogether. The judges of *Brown* may have, as the critics of the Right and Left keep reminding us, enacted into law their own preferences, peculiarly reflecting their privileged social position; but it is also possible, indeed, I would say, it is eminently probable, that these judges had given a true account of the constitutional value of equality. The judges involved in contemporary prison litigation may have enacted into law their own preferences, peculiarly reflecting their social background, their squeamishness, when they proscribed the use of tor-

---

[27] In the case of the textually-specific prohibitions, it would seem that the preferences of the Framers, rather than that of the people or judges, would control. The authors of *Carolene Products* seemed prepared to respect the preferences of that particular social group, and yet some Progressives appeared intent on discrediting those preferences, *see, e.g.,* C. BEARD, AN ECONOMIC INTERPRETATION OF THE CONSTITUTION OF THE UNITED STATES (1913).

ture in all its varieties—the teeterboard, the Tucker telephone, the strap, the failure to provide medical care, the heavy use of armed, mounted, and undisciplined trusties to supervise field labor, and the housing of anywhere from 85 to 150 inmates in a single dormitory room, leaving the weak and attractive to spend each night terrorized by the "creepers" and "crawlers";[28] but it is also possible, indeed, I would say eminently probable, that these judges had given a true account of the constitutional ban on cruel and unusual punishment.

This conception of the judicial function, which sees the judge as trying to give meaning to our constitutional values, expects a lot from judges—maybe too much. The expectation is not founded on a belief in their moral expertise, or on a denial of their humanity. Judges are most assuredly people. They are lawyers, but in terms of personal character-istics they are no different from successful businessmen or politicians. Their capacity to make a special contribution to our social life derives not from any personal traits or knowledge, but from the definition of the office in which they find themselves and through which they exercise power. That office is structured by both ideological and institutional fac-tors that enable and perhaps even force the judge to be objective—not to express his preferences or personal beliefs, or those of the citizenry, as to what is right or just, but constantly to strive for the true meaning of the constitutional value.[29] Two aspects of the judicial office give it this special cast: one is the judge's obligation to participate in a dialogue, and the second is his independence.

The judge is entitled to exercise power only after he has participated in a dialogue about the meaning of the public values. It is a dialogue with very special qualities: (a) Judges are not in control of their agenda, but are compelled to confront grievances or claims they would otherwise prefer

---

[28] These examples are all taken from a single, but protracted case involving the Arkansas prison system, recently sustained in some particulars by the Supreme Court in Hutto v. Finney, 437 U.S. 678 (1978). See Talley v. Stephens, 247 F. Supp. 683 (E.D. Ark. 1965); Jackson v. Bishop, 268 F. Supp. 804 (E.D. Ark. 1967), vacated, 404 F.2d 571 (8th Cir. 1968); Courtney v. Bishop, 409 F.2d 1185 (8th Cir. 1969); Holt v. Sarver, 300 F. Supp. 825 (E.D. Ark. 1969); Holt v. Sarver, 309 F. Supp. 362 (E.D. Ark. 1970), aff'd, 442 F.2d 304 (8th Cir.1971); Holt v. Hutto, 363 F. Supp. 194 (E.D. Ark. 1973), aff'd in part and reversed in part sub nom. Finney v. Arkansas Bd. of Correction, 505 F.2d 194 (8th Cir.1974); Finney v. Hutto, 410 F. Supp. 251 (E.D. Ark. 1976), aff'd, 548 F.2d 743 (8th Cir.1977). See also B. JACKSON, KILLING TIME (1977); M. HARRIS & D. SPILLER, AFTER DECISION (1976).

[29] In understanding the role of the objective perspective in adjudication I have been particularly helped by two essays of Thomas Nagel dealing with objectivity in ethics: Subjec-tive and Objective, in MORTAL QUESTIONS 196 (1979); and The Limits of Objectivity (1979) (Tanner Lecture at Oxford University) (on file at the Harvard Law Review).

to ignore. (b) Judges do not have full control over whom they must listen to. They are bound by rules requiring them to listen to a broad range of persons or spokesmen. (c) Judges are compelled to speak back, to respond to the grievance or the claim, and to assume individual responsibility for that response. (d) Judges must also justify their decisions.

The obligation to justify a decision has given rise to never-ending debates as to the proper sources of judicial decisions—text, intentions of the Framers, general structure of the Constitution, ethics, the good of the nation, etc.[30] For the notion of justification, as opposed to explanation, implies that the reasons supporting a decision be "good" reasons, and this in turn requires norms or rules for determining what counts as a "good" reason. My intention is not to participate in the debate about the rules for justification, but to stress two facts that all seem to agree on as to what might count as a "good" reason. The first is that the reason cannot consist of a preference, be it a preference of the contestants, of the body politic, or of the judge. The statement "I prefer" or "we prefer" in the context of a judicial, rather than a legislative decision, merely constitutes an explanation, not a justification.[31] Second, the reason must somehow transcend the personal, transient beliefs of the judge or the body politic as to what is right or just or what should be done. Something more is required to transform these personal beliefs into values that are worthy of the status "constitutional" and all that it implies—binding on society as a whole, entitled to endure, not forever but long enough to give our public morality an inner coherence, and largely to be enforced by courts.

The judge is required to listen and to speak, and to speak in certain ways. He is also required to be independent. This means, for one thing, that he not identify with or in any way be connected to the particular contestants. He must be impartial, distant, and detached from the contestants, thereby increasing the likelihood that his decision will not be an expression of the self-interest (or preferences) of the contestants, which is the antithesis of the right or just decision. The norm of impartiality also requires that the judge be independent from politics, in this instance understood as the process of expressing the preferences of the people. The judge must not view his job as one of registering those preferences. Independence is clearly the norm in the federal system with its promise of life tenure, but is present also in those state systems in which judges are elected. The judge might be vulnerable to the body politic when he

---

[30] *See* Wellington, *Common Law Rules and Constitutional Double Standards: Some Notes on Adjudication,* 83 YALE L.J. 221 (1973).

[31] *See* Wechsler, *Toward Neutral Principles of Constitutional Law,* 73 HARV. L. REV. 1 (1959).

stands for election, but that does not determine how he should define his job, or how the body politic should use its power.

The task of a judge, then, should be seen as giving meaning to our public values and adjudication as the process through which that meaning is revealed or elaborated. The question still remains of determining the relationship between the courts and the other agencies of government, for structural reform places the courts in the position of issuing directives to other agencies of government. The judiciary's essential function is to give meaning to our constitutional values, but many of these other agencies can perform that function in addition to that of registering the preferences of the people. The legislature or the school board or the warden of a prison is entitled to express the preferences of the citizenry, a function not entrusted to the courts, but these agencies can also strive to give meaning to equality, or to work out the complicated relationship between liberty and equality, or to decide whether the punishment meted out is cruel and unusual. The existing practices in and of themselves cannot be taken as a reflection of the considered judgment of another branch of government on the meaning of a constitutional value, particularly since we are dealing with bureaucracies, in which policy is often determined by internal power plays and default.[32] On the other hand, there can be genuine conflicts. Situations—school desegregation is probably a good example—will arise where the courts and other agencies of government will come to the opposite conclusion as to the meaning of a constitutional value, and the need will arise to work out the relationship between the branches.

To simply postulate the supremacy of the more majoritarian branches, the legislative or the executive, as the promoters of footnote four do,[33] is no answer, for, as we saw, the people's preferences are not the standard, and there is no discernible connection between majoritarianism and the meaning of a constitutional value. Courts may have their difficulties in giving a constitutional value its correct meaning, but so would the other branches. History is as filled with legislative and executive mistakes as it is filled with judicial ones. Admittedly, adjudication will have its class and professional biases, because so much power is entrusted to lawyers, but the legislative and executive processes will have their own biases— wealth, dynasty, charisma. It is not clear which set of biases will cause the greatest departure from the truth.

---

[32] M. CROZIER, THE BUREAUCRATIC PHENOMENON 187-98 (1964).

[33] Ely, *The Supreme Court, 1977 Term—Foreword: On Discovering Fundamental Values*, 92 HARV. L. REV. 5 (1978); Ely, *Toward a Representation-Reinforcing Mode of Judicial Review*, 37 MD. L. REV. 451 (1978).

One may be tempted to invoke the democratic ideal to resolve this conflict, and yet it is far from dispositive. There are many places at which the people bind the adjudicatory process, even in the federal system; they elect the officers who appoint the judges, they can pass statutes controlling procedural matters, and they even have the power to overrule a constitutional judgment by amending the Constitution. Of course, it is hard to amend the Constitution, harder than it is to revise the work of common law judges through the passage of statutes, but democracy is not a fixed rule that always prefers a simple majority, as opposed to a special majority, any more than it deifies the subjective preference. Democracy, as an ideal of our constitutional system, allows a role for both subjective preference and public value, and the special majority requirement of the amendment process may well be seen as a way of preserving the delicate balance between those two domains in our political life.

I suspect that the relationship between the branches in the constitutional domain—in giving meaning to the non-textually-specific values, as well as others—is a more pluralistic or dialectical relationship than footnote four permits: all can strive to give meaning to constitutional values.[34] The theory of structural reform, no more than any other form of constitutional litigation, does not require that courts have the *only* word or even the *last* word, but that they be allowed to speak and to do so with some authority. Process is the measure of that authority. The right of the judge to speak, and the obligation of others to listen, depends not on the judge's personal attributes, nor even on the content of his message, but on the quality of his process—on his ability to be distant and detached from the immediate contestants and from the body politic, yet fully attentive to grievances, and responsive in terms that transcend preferences and that are sufficient to support a judgment deemed "constitutional." There may be other processes or methods for giving meaning to constitutional values, though what they might be is not clear to me, but the process I have just described—the core of adjudication—is the only one open to the judge. This process is a limitation on his legitimacy, and even more importantly, it has a close conceptual connection—not just a contingent or instrumental one—to the very act of giving meaning to a constitutional value. We impute function largely on the basis of process and at the same time function shapes process. Others may search for the true meaning of

---

[34] The concept of dialogue lies at the heart of the work of two of my colleagues. *See* R. BURT, TAKING CARE OF STRANGERS (1979); B. Ackerman, Social Justice in the Liberal State (1979) (unpublished manuscript on file at the Yale Law School Library and the *Harvard Law Review*).

our constitutional values, but when they do, they will have to mimic—if they can—the process of the judge.

In the 1960's, the courts played a central role in our social life because they saw that the ideal of equality was inconsistent with the caste system implied by Jim Crow laws. In the decade that followed, they struggled to give meaning to a broader range of constitutional values, and perceived the threat to those values in a wide variety of contexts—the barbarisms of total institutions, the abuses of the police, the indignities of welfare systems. Today we have doubts about the role of courts and, just as we are rediscovering the market, we are quickly resurrecting footnote four and the claim of legislative supremacy. This development cannot be wholly explained in terms of increasing doubts as to the competency of courts; for without a belief in the conceptual connection between function and process, without a belief in the capacity of courts to give meaning to our constitutional values, even the subscribers to *Carolene Products* are at a loss to explain the judicial function in cases of legislative failure or why the void left by legislative failure should be filled by the courts. In my judgment, the resurgence of *Carolene Products* does not stem from doubts about the special capacity of courts and their processes to move us closer to a correct understanding of our constitutional values, but from the frail quality of our substantive vision. We have lost our confidence in the existence of the values that underlie the litigation of the 1960's, or, for that matter, in the existence of any public values. All is preference. That seems to be the crucial issue, not the issue of relative institutional competence. Only once we reassert our belief in the existence of public values, that values such as equality, liberty, due process, no cruel and unusual punishment, security of the person, or free speech can have a true and important meaning, that must be articulated and implemented—yes, discovered—will the role of the courts in our political system become meaningful, or for that matter even intelligible.

II. Form and Function

At the core of structural reform is the judge, and his effort to give meaning to our public values. This allocation of power raises questions of legitimacy common to all types of adjudication, but the structural mode raises new and distinct issues of legitimacy as well. These issues arise from the organizational setting of the structural suit, from the fact that the judge is responding to a threat posed to our constitutional values by a large-scale organization. He seeks to remove the threat by restructuring the organization, and that ambition has important implications for the *form* of the lawsuit.

The structural mode is most often attacked on the ground that it involves a departure from some ideal form. This criticism obviously presupposes a prototypical or "model" lawsuit, an ideal form, against which all lawsuits will be measured. The usual standard of comparison, the dispute-resolution model, is triadic and highly individualistic: a lawsuit is visualized—with the help of the icon of justice holding the scales of justice—as a conflict between two individuals, one called plaintiff and the other defendant, with a third standing between the two parties, as a passive umpire, to observe and decide who is right, who is wrong, and to declare that the right be done. From this perspective, structural reform surely is a transformation; it looks breathtakingly different.[35] It is important, though, to be clear about the specific terms of the formal transformation before wondering whether the dispute-resolution model can properly be considered an ideal.

A. The Transformation

1. The Focus of the Suit: Incident of Wrongdoing v. Social Condition.—The dispute-resolution model presupposes a social world that is essentially harmonious. A set of norms confers rights and duties upon individuals. Individuals make arrangements within those norms, but sometimes incidents occur that disturb the harmony; for example, the farmer may not honor his promise to sell the cow. The aggrieved individual then turns to the courts, either to implement or enforce one of the norms, or, possibly, to fill out the meaning of the norm. The focus of the evidentiary inquiry will be the incident, or in the language of pleading rules, the "transaction" or "occurrence."[36]

---

[35] Two of the most spectacular instances of the transformation are Judge Henley's decade-long struggle with the Arkansas prison system, *see* note 28 *supra*, and Judge Weinstein's attempt to reorganize the Mark Twain School in Coney Island, *see* Hart v. Community School Bd., 383 F. Supp. 699, *supplemented,* 383 F. Supp. 769 (E.D.N.Y. 1974) (remedial order), *aff'd,* 512 F.2d 37 (2d Cir.1975). *See also* Fishman, *The Limits of Remedial Power: Hart v. Community School Board* 21, in LIMITS OF JUSTICE 115 (H. Kalodner & J. Fishman eds. 1978); Berger, *Away from the Court House and Into the Field: The Odyssey of a Special Master,* 78 COLUM. L. REV. 707 (1978); Rosenbaum & Presser, *Voluntary Racial Integration in a Magnet School,* 86 SCH. REV. 156 (1978); Oelsner, *New York's Best Public Schools Defy Racial Stereo-typing,* N.Y. Times, Jan. 23, 1978, at B1, col. 1. For a theoretical analysis of the case, see R. Katzmann, Judicial Intervention: Changing the Processes and Policies of Public Bureaucracies (1979) (unpublished manuscript on file at the Yale Law School Library and the *Harvard Law Review*).

[36] *The Role of the Judge in Public Law Litigation,* 89 HARV. L. REV. 1281, 1290 (1976).

In contrast, the focus of structural reform is not upon particular incidents or transactions, but rather upon the conditions of social life and the role that large-scale organizations play in determining those conditions. What is critical is not the black child turned away at the door of the white school, or the individual act of police brutality. These incidents may have triggered the lawsuit. They may also be of evidentiary significance: evidence of a "pattern or practice"[37] of racism or lawlessness. But the ultimate subject matter of the lawsuit or focus of the judicial inquiry is not these incidents, these particularized and discrete events, but rather a social condition that threatens important constitutional values and the organizational dynamic that creates and perpetuates that condition.

2. *Party Structure: The Plaintiff.*—The concept of a plaintiff consists of three distinct analytic components: (a) victim; (b) spokesman; and (c) beneficiary. The individual who claims that a contract has been breached is the victim of the wrongdoing. He is also the one to gain, primarily, or maybe even exclusively, from the action of the court. And there is every reason to assume he is a highly competent spokesman, in the same sense that there is every reason to assume that an individual is the best judge of his self-interest. The ethic of the market is transferred to the courtroom. In structural reform, the unity implicit in the concept of party disintegrates, the components become separate, and the exclusively individualistic perspective shifts to one that includes social groups and institutional advocates.

The victim of a structural suit is not an individual, but a group. In some instances the group is defined in terms of an institution: the inmates of the prison or welfare recipients. Or the victim may consist of a group that has an identity beyond the institution: in a school desegregation case, for example, the victims are not the pupils, but probably a larger social group, blacks.[38] In either instance, it is important to stress two features of the group. First, it exists independently of the lawsuit; it is not simply a legal construct. Wholly apart from the lawsuit, individuals can define themselves in terms of their membership in the group, and that group can have its own internal politics, struggles for power, and

---

[37] The "pattern or practice" concept plays a pervasive role in structural litigation. Sometimes it is used as an evidentiary requirement, as a necessary predicate for structural relief (only a series of acts that amount to a "pattern or practice" will justify so thoroughgoing relief); sometimes it is used as a technique for marshalling the resources of the Executive Branch (the Department of Justice should sue only when there is a "pattern or practice" of discrimination); sometimes it is even used as a basis for inferring intent. *See generally* International Bhd. of Teamsters v. United States, 431 U.S. 324 (1977).

[38] *See generally Groups, supra* note 22; *see also* Note, *Antidiscrimination Class Actions Under the Federal Rules: The Transformation of Rule 23(b)(2)*, 88 YALE L.J. 868 (1979).

conflicts.[39] Secondly, the group is not simply an aggregation or collection of identifiable individuals. We understand the plight of the inmates of an institution subjected to inhuman conditions without knowing, or, in the case of future inmates, without even being *able* to know, who they are in any particularized sense. The group exists, has an identity, and can be harmed, even though all the individuals are not yet in being and not every single member is threatened by the organization.

Once we take the group perspective on the victim, it also becomes clear that the spokesman need not—indeed cannot—be the victim. A group needs people to speak on its behalf. An individual member of the victim group can be a spokesman, but there is no reason why individual membership should be required, or for that matter even preferred. An individual must be a minor hero to stand up and challenge the status quo: imagine the courage and fortitude required to be the spokesman in a school desegregation suit, or even worse, one challenging the Administration of a total institution, such as a prison. Individuals are in such a vulnerable position, so much at risk, that it is a cruelty to insist, as some of the Justices have done on occasion,[40] that the spokesman be the individual member of the group, for example, brutalized by the prison guards. Institutional advocates, some governmental (the Department of Justice), others private (the NAACP or the ACLU), are often needed to play a key role as spokesmen for the victim group.[41] Such spokesmen may even be preferred. They may introduce their own biases, but on the whole they are likely to present a fuller picture of the law or facts than would the individual victim.

The relation between the victim and the spokesman in the structural context is entirely instrumental; it is not a relationship of identity. As an affirmative matter this means that the court must determine whether the interests of the victim group are adequately represented. This inquiry is not without parallel in the dispute-resolution context, though there individuals rather than groups or interests are being represented. In either context, it is an extremely difficult inquiry. At the same time,

---

[39] *See* Bell, *Serving Two Masters: Integration Ideals and Client Interests in School Desegregation Litigation,* 85 YALE L.J. 470 (1976); *cf.* Yeazell, *Group Litigation and Social Context: Toward a History of the Class Action,* 77 COLUM. L. REV. 866 (1977) (describing the origins of class action suits in terms of more cohesive social groups).

[40] *See, e.g.,* Estelle v. Justice, 426 U.S. 925 (1976) (Rehnquist, J., dissenting from denial of certiorari); Rizzo v. Goode, 423 U.S. 362 (1976).

[41] *See generally* Galanter, *Why the "Haves" Come Out Ahead: Speculations on the Limits of Legal Change,* 9 LAW & SOC'Y REV. 95 (1974); Stone, *Should Trees Have Standing?—Toward Legal Rights for Natural Objects,* 45 S. CAL. L. REV. 450 (1972).

the instrumental character of the relationship between spokesman and victim group, the separation of the two, means that certain technical qualifications for the victim—that he be subject to a risk of future harm,[42] or that he be subject to irreparable injury[43]—need not be satisfied by the spokesman. For the structural suit it is sufficient if these requirements are satisfied by the victim group. What the court must ask of the spokesman is whether he is an adequate representative, and, as difficult a question as that may be, technical requirements such as irreparability or the risk of future harm do not have any important bearing on that question. They do not make the question any easier: they are neither necessary nor sufficient conditions of adequacy.

The instrumental connection between spokesman and victim is also conducive to a view that tolerates, or even invites, a multiplicity of spokesmen. In the dispute-resolution model, where the victim is an individual, and that victim is identified with the spokesman, the typical party structure is bipolar: a single plaintiff vied against a single defendant. In a structural lawsuit the typical pattern is to find a great number of spokesmen, each perhaps representing different views as to what is in the interest of the victim group. Moreover, it would be wrong to assume that the relationship between all those on the plaintiff side is equally antagonistic to all those on the defendant's: the physical image of the antagonism is not binary, but an array grouped around a single issue. One spokesman for the victim group may want two-way busing; another, more sensitive to "white flight" or more insistent on "quality education," may want a magnet school; and, in fact, some of those speaking for the defendants may also favor the magnet school or some mild form of busing.[44] The

---

[42] A contrary attitude was expressed by the Supreme Court in Rizzo v. Goode, 423 U.S. 362 (1976), *see* note 13 *supra*. On the other hand, in considering related problems of mootness, the Burger Court has been more equivocal. *Compare* Franks v. Bowman Transp. Co., 424 U.S. 747, 752-57 (1976) (a statutorily-based employment discrimination case); Gerstein v. Pugh, 420 U.S. 103, 110 n.11 (1975); *and* Sosna v. Iowa, 419 U.S. 393, 397-403 (1975), *with* Kremens v. Bartley, 431 U.S. 119 (1977), *and* Board of School Comm'rs v. Jacobs, 420 U.S. 128 (1975). Equally confusing has been the attempt to square the traditional standing requirements with the dictates of the structural suit. *Compare, e.g.,* Warth v. Seldin, 422 U.S. 490 (1975), *with* Village of Arlington Heights v. Metropolitan Hous. Dev. Corp., 429 U.S. 252 (1977). On the topic of standing, and more generally on the relations between public values and adjudication, see the inspiring book by Joseph Vining, LEGAL IDENTITY (1978).

[43] Once again the Burger Court has been highly divided on this issue. See Allee v. Medrano, 416 U.S. 802 (1974); O'Shea v. Littleton, 414 U.S. 488 (1974). I discuss these cases in detail in Dombrowski, 86 YALE L.J. 1103, 1148-60 (1977).

[44] Conflicts of this nature were acutely present in the Coney Island case, Hart v. Community School Bd., 383 F. Supp. 699, *supplemented*, 383 F. Supp. 769 (E.D.N.Y. 1974) (remedial order), *aff'd*, 512 F.2d 37 (2d Cir. 1975), and also in the famed Norwalk Core school

multiplicity of spokesmen does not create these differences. They exist in the real world, and the court must hear from all before it can decide what the ideal of racial equality requires.

Paralleling this separation between victim and spokesman, the structural mode of litigation also contemplates a distinction between the victim and the group who will benefit from the remedy. In a suit for breach of contract, the remedy is aimed at making the victim whole, whether the remedy be damages or specific performance. In the structural context, however, the victims and the beneficiaries need not be coextensive. Though the beneficiary of structural relief is necessarily also a group, it could have a different membership and a different contour than the victim group. Consider, for example, a police brutality case.[45] Let us assume that the concern is with lawless conduct by the police directed at members of racial minorities in the city. The court believes an internal disciplinary procedure should be established within the police department to lessen the threat to constitutional values. The court could make that machinery available only to members of the victim group, say blacks and Chicanos, but it need not. The court may decide that such a limitation would be both inefficient and counterproductive—indeed might even raise its own problems of fairness and constitutionality (reverse discrimination)—and for that reason the court may extend the protection of the decree to a much larger group—all the city.[46]

The separability of victim and beneficiary derives in part from the group nature of the victim since, at best, the limits of that group can only be approximated. More fundamentally, it derives from the instrumental nature of the remedy.[47] The whole judicial enterprise, as is true of any exercise of governmental power, is constrained by considerations of efficacy and fairness, and, in the context of structural reform, these factors may lead the court to structure the beneficiary class so that it is not coextensive with the victim group. There is no reason why the shape of the benefited class is to be determined by one factor and one factor alone, namely, a guess as to the approximate shape of the victim group.

---

litigation, Norwalk Core v. Norwalk Bd. of Educ., 298 F. Supp. 203 (D.Conn. 1968), aff'd, 423 F.2d 121 (2d Cir. 1970).

[45] Rizzo v. Goode, 423 U.S. 362 (1976).

[46] Having reached that conclusion, the Court may now redefine the victim group so that it is coextensive with the beneficiary—the victim of police brutality is all the people of the city, not just the racial minority—but that post hoc redefinition does not seem useful or necessary.

[47] See pp. 47-50 infra.

3. Party Structure: The Defendant.—As might be imagined, the disaggregation of roles that I have just discussed on the plaintiff's side is repeated on the defendant's. The defendant envisioned in the dispute-resolution model is expected to perform three different functions: (a) spokesman; (b) wrongdoer; and (c) addressee (or the person who must provide the remedy). The dispute-resolution model assumes that all three functions are unified, or put another way, combined in the same individual, for example, the farmer who refuses to perform his contract. In the structural context, the functions are separated, and even more significantly, one function, that of the wrongdoer, virtually disappears.

The concept of wrongdoer is highly individualistic. It presupposes personal qualities: the capacity to have an intention and to choose. Paradigmatically, a wrongdoer is one who intentionally inflicts harm in violation of an established norm. In the structural context, there may be individual wrongdoers, the police officer who hits the citizen, the principal who turns away the black child at the schoolhouse door, the prison guard who abuses the inmate; they are not, however, the target of the suit. The focus is on a social condition, not incidents of wrongdoing, and also on the bureaucratic dynamics that produce that condition. In a sense, a structural suit is an in rem proceeding where the res is the state bureaucracy.[48] The costs and burdens of reformation are placed on the organization, not because it has "done wrong," in either a literal or metaphorical sense, for it has neither an intention nor a will,[49] but because reform is needed to remove a threat to constitutional values posed by the operation of the organization.

---

[48] *See* Holt v. Sarver, 309 F. Supp. 362, 365 (E.D. Ark. 1970), *aff'd,* 442 F.2d 304 (8th Cir. 1971) ("This case, unlike earlier cases . . . which have involved specific practices and abuses alleged to have been practiced upon Arkansas convicts, amounts to an attack on the System itself."); Talley v. Stephens, 247 F. Supp. 683, 691 (E.D. Ark. 1965) ("The Court does not think that it should bring this opinion to a close without stating that nothing said herein should be construed as a claim that the respondent personally is an evil, brutal, or cruel man or that he personally approves of all long standing practices of the penitentiary system.").

[49] Washington v. Davis, 426 U.S. 229 (1976), makes the intent to segregate a necessary condition of an equal protection violation, and as such might be regarded as another assault—this time in the substantive domain—on the idea of structural reform. The Court did not come to grips with the theoretical problems created by the use of the concept of "intent" in an organizational setting, such as the problem of aggregation (whose intent shall count as the intent of the organization?), nor has the Court even defined what intent should mean in such a context. These issues are explored in my address before the Second Circuit Judicial Conference in September 1976, on the inappropriateness of the intent test in equal protection cases, *Equality in Education,* 74 F.R.D. 276, 278 (1977), and in Seth Kreimer's brilliant Note, *Reading the Mind of the School Board: Segregative Intent and the De Facto/De Jure Distinction,* 86 YALE L.J. 317 (1976).

From the perspective of certain remedies, such as damage judgments and criminal sanctions, this conclusion may seem startling. Those remedies are retrospective in the sense that a necessary condition for each is a past wrong; they require some evaluative judgment as to the wrongfulness of the defendant's conduct in terms of preexisting norms. But the remedy at issue in a structural case is the injunction, and it does not require a judgment about wrongdoing, future or past. The structural suit seeks to eradicate an ongoing threat to our constitutional values and the injunction can serve as the formal mechanism by which the court issues directives as to how that is to be accomplished. It speaks to the future. The prospective quality of the injunction, plus the fact that it fuses power in the judge, explains the preeminence of the injunction in structural reform.[50] Only at later stages of structural reform, after many cycles of supplemental relief, when the directives have become very specific, do criminal sanctions or even damage judgments become available (in an independent proceeding or as part of the contempt process).[51] Then the wrongdoing largely consists of disobedience of judicial orders.

In the course of the reconstructive process, the judge must ultimately penetrate the institutional facade, take the lid off the so-called black box, in order to locate critical operatives within the institution to whom the reconstructive directives must be issued. These directives seem addressed to individuals, often to avoid eleventh amendment problems,[52] but in truth they are addressed to bureaucratic offices, not to the persons who happen to occupy those offices at any single point of time.[53] These directives are not predicated on the view that the present or even the prior occupants

---

[50] *See generally* O. Fiss, The Civil Rights Injunction (1978). Other factors, such as the insensitivity of state bureaucracies to market incentives and the decentralized system of initiation, might also help explain the preeminence of the injunction in structural reform. It should be noted that some other remedies (*e.g.*, declaratory judgments, conditional habeas corpus) have many of the same qualities as the injunction, for example, its prospectivity, and could be expected to be found in structural suits. *See, e.g.*, Bell v. Wolfish, 99 S.Ct. 1861, 1867 n.6 (1979) (saving the question whether conditional habeas could be used as the injunction in altering the conditions of pretrial detention).

[51] For an attempt to address the problems of harmonizing the criminal law with bureaucratic reality, see Note, *Decisionmaking Models and the Control of Corporate Crime*, 85 Yale L.J. 1091 (1976).

[52] *See Ex parte* Young, 209 U.S. 123, 159-60 (1908). At one point, the personalization of the defendant may have reflected a desire to avoid the special problems of 42 U.S.C. § 1983 (1976), *see* City of Kenosha v. Bruno, 412 U.S. 507 (1973), but those needs have been removed, *see* Monell v. Department of Social Servs., 436 U.S. 658 (1978).

[53] *Compare, e.g.,* Spomer v. Littleton, 414 U.S. 514 (1974), *with* Lankford v. Gelston, 364 F.2d 197, 205 n.9 (4th Cir. 1966), *and* Lucy v. Adams, 224 F. Supp. 79 (N.D. Ala. 1963), *aff'd sub nom.* McCorvey v. Lucy, 328 F.2d 892 (5th Cir. 1964) (per curiam).

of the office are guilty of wrongdoing, in the individualistic sense, but rather that the judicially prescribed action—with all its attendant burdens, financial and other—is necessary to eliminate the threat that the institution as a whole poses to constitutional values.[54]

4. *The Posture of the Judge.*—The dispute-resolution model envisions a passive role for the judge. He is to stand as umpire or observer between the two disputants, relying on all their initiatives for the presentation of the facts and the law and the articulation of the possible remedies. The judge's task is simply to declare which one is right. The appropriateness of such a passive pose is questioned by many factors not the least of which is inequalities in the distribution of resources, whether it be wealth or talent. These inequalities give the judge every reason to assume a more active role in the litigation, to make certain that he is fully informed and that a just result will be reached, not one determined by the distribution of resources in the natural lottery or in the market. These concerns are present in structural litigation, and indeed may intensify when the organization has a clientele that predominantly comes from the lower economic classes, as is true with a prison or a welfare agency. But structural litigation introduces other, quite distinct reasons for abandoning a purely passive judicial posture. They stem from the special character of the parties. Exclusive reliance on their initiatives becomes even more untenable.

As noted earlier, the named plaintiff and his lawyer speak not just for themselves, but also for a group, for example, the present and future users of the institution. There is no basis for assuming they are adequate representatives of the group, for they simply elect themselves to that position. Similarly, there is no reason to assume that the named defendant and his lawyer are adequate representatives of the organization's interests. Here it is not a matter of self-election, but election by an adversary.

The spokesmen for the state bureaucracy usually have a formal connection to the organization; the superintendent of schools may be appointed by a school board, which in turn is duly elected; the warden of the prison may be appointed by the Governor, and his lawyer, the Attorney General, may be elected. The existence of these formal connections, however, should not obscure the fact that the initial choice as to who shall speak or represent the organization *in this proceeding* is made by forces standing in an antagonistic relationship to it, the named plaintiff and his lawyer, the adversaries. The risk is ever present that they may choose an inappropriate officer, or have a too narrow conception of the

---

[54] *See* p. 49 *infra.*

institutional framework that accounts for the condition. The plaintiff, for example, may see the segregated schools as the responsibility of the school board alone, when in truth both housing and school policies are implicated.[55]

The presence of an improper representative on either side of the lawsuit may have consequences that far transcend the interests of the participants. The court may be led into error. The named plaintiff may also wittingly or unwittingly compromise the interests of the victim group in a way that cannot easily be rectified in subsequent proceedings. The defendant, it must also be remembered, speaks not just for himself in any personalized sense, but for all occupants of the office, past and future; all the other offices within the hierarchy of the institution; and all those who stand outside the institution but who are nonetheless directly affected by any reorganization of the institution, including the taxpayers who finance it and those who depend on the institution to provide some vital service.

Starting from this perspective, it seems almost absurd to rely exclusively on the initiatives of those persons or agencies who happened to be named plaintiff and defendant. The judge must assume some affirmative responsibility to assure adequate representation, but what form might that action take? It would seem foolish for the judge to assume a representational role himself; indeed, it would compromise the very ideal of impartiality, which is so important a predicate for judicial legitimacy. The more appropriate response, and the one typically employed in the structural context is for the judge—often acting on his own—to construct a broader representational framework. This might be done in a number of ways that are consistent with the commitment to impartiality.

First, a notice can be sent to many of those who are purportedly represented in the litigation. The notice would explain the litigation, and invite a contest to the fullness and adequacy of the representation. Even here, it should be noted, the judge cannot rely exclusively on the named parties to insist on notice or to formulate its content. On the one hand, extensive notice requirements might compound the adversary's costs of continuing the litigation,[56] while on the other hand, neither party has much of an incentive to make certain that his adversary is the best representative. Second, the judge may invite certain organizations or agencies to participate in the lawsuit, as an amicus or as a party, or as a

---

[55] See Hart v. Community School Bd., 383 F. Supp. 699, *supplemented*, 383 F. Supp. 769 (E.D.N.Y. 1974) (remedial order), *aff'd*, 512 F.2d 37 (2d Cir. 1975).

[56] See Eisen v. Carlisle & Jacquelin, 417 U.S. 156 (1974).

hybrid—the litigating amicus. Of course, ever mindful of the conditions of his legitimacy, the judge should not limit the invitation to those who would say what he wants to hear, nor has that been the practice. The concept of a litigating amicus first took root in school cases where trial judges invited the United States to participate; the intent was to obtain the Executive's commitment to enforce the decree, and also to broaden the representational structure.[57] More recently, this practice has been transferred to the context of total institutions, prisons and mental hospitals, where it is even more urgently required, given the relative absence of private institutional advocates and the distortion likely to flow from exclusive reliance on complaints from individual victims.[58] Third, the trial courts have sometimes found it necessary, perhaps when they could no longer rely on the Executive or private institutional advocates, to create their own agencies, such as special masters, to correct any representational inadequacies. The special master is an institution with many roles, as we will see, but one of them is representational.[59] He sometimes acts as a party, presenting the viewpoints about liability and remedy not otherwise likely to be expressed by the participants in the lawsuit.

5. *The Remedial Phase.*—The focus in the dispute-resolution model is the incident, the transaction or occurrence, and the remedial phase is largely episodic. The remedy is designed to correct or prevent a discrete event, and the judicial function usually exhausts itself when judgment is announced and the amount of damages calculated or the decree aimed at some discrete event is issued. Under these assumptions, the lawsuit has, as Abram Chayes expressed it at a workshop at Yale this past year, an Aristotelian's dramatic unity, a beginning, a middle, and an end. In some cases involving a recalcitrant defendant, there may be more to the

---

[57] *See* Lee v. Macon County Bd. of Educ., 221 F. Supp. 297 (M.D. Ala. 1963); O. Fiss, INJUNCTIONS 618-19, 626-28 (1972); note 2 *supra*.

[58] In a dissent from denial of certiorari, three Justices objected to the United States having party status. Estelle v. Justice, 426 U.S. 925 (1976) (Rehnquist, J., with whom Burger, C.J., and Powell, J., join, dissenting from denial of certiorari) (intervenor). *See also* United States v. Solomon, 563 F.2d 1121 (4th Cir. 1977) (plaintiff). Bills have been introduced to remove any doubts about the authority of the United States as a litigant. *See* H.R. 9400, 95th Cong., 2d Sess. (1978) ("An Act To Authorize Actions for Redress In Cases Involving Deprivations of Rights of Institutionalized Persons Secured or Protected by the Constitution or Laws of the United States"), *reprinted in Civil Rights for Institutionalized Persons: Hearings Before the House Comm. on the Judiciary*, 95th Cong., 1st Sess. 286-88 (1977). *See also* note 13 *supra*.

[59] *See* G. Aronow, The Special Master in School Desegregation Cases: The Evolution of Roles in the Reformation of Public Institutions Through Litigation (1979) (unpublished manuscript on file at the Yale Law School Library and the *Harvard Law Review*) (excerpts are reprinted in R. COVER & O. FISS, *supra* note 18, at 370).

remedial phase—for example, seizure and sale of assets or a contempt proceeding.[60] But these struggles with the recalcitrant defendant are the exception, and in any event they are not considered an integral part of the first proceeding. They often involve a collateral proceeding handled by different personnel, the sheriff or a master, to enforce the remedy given in the initial proceeding.

The remedial phase in structural litigation is far from episodic. It has a beginning, maybe a middle, but no end—well, almost no end. It involves a long, continuous relationship between the judge and the institution; it is concerned not with the enforcement of a remedy already given, but with the giving or shaping of the remedy itself. The task is not to declare who is right or who is wrong, not to calculate the amount of damages or to formulate a decree designed to stop some discrete act. The task is to remove the condition that threatens the constitutional values. In some instances, where deinstitutionalization is conceivable, as in the mental health field, closing the institution may be a viable option.[61] For the most part, in cases involving schools, prisons, welfare agencies, police departments, and housing authorities, for example, that option is not available. Then the remedy involves the court in nothing less than the reorganization of an ongoing institution, so as to remove the threat it poses to constitutional values. The court's jurisdiction will last as long as the threat persists.

Limitations on our knowledge about organizational behavior, coupled with the capacity of organizations to adapt to the interventions by reestablishing preexisting power relationships, invariably result in a series of interventions—cycle after cycle of supplemental relief. A long term supervisory relationship develops between the judge and the institution, for performance must be monitored, and new strategies devised for making certain that the operation of the organization is kept within constitutional bounds.[62] The judge may even create new agencies—once again the special master—to assist in these tasks. In doing so, he reflects either doubts about the capacity of the existing parties to discharge these tasks or an awareness of the magnitude of these tasks.

---

[60] See Eisenberg & Yeazell, *The Ordinary and the Extraordinary in Institutional Litigation* (1979) (forthcoming in the *Harvard Law Review*).

[61] See, e.g., Halderman v. Pennhurst State School & Hosp., 446 F. Supp. 1295 (E.D. Pa. 1977) (appeal pending); New York State Ass'n for Retarded Children v. Carey, 393 F. Supp. 715 (E.D.N.Y. 1975) (consent decree) (unpublished decree ordered a gradual phase-out of Willowbrook) (on file at the Yale Law School Library and the *Harvard Law Review*).

[62] O. FISS, *supra* note 50, at 31.

B. The Significance of the Transformation

Assume that the structural lawsuit has the formal features I have just described and also that it can be sharply differentiated from the dispute-resolution model in these particulars. The two lawsuits do not look alike. Gone is the triad, the icon of Justice holding two balances, and in its place a whole series of metaphors are offered to describe the structural suit. Some, emphasizing the distinctive party structure, speak of town meetings,[63] others, emphasizing the posture of the judge, speak of management or the creation of a new administrative agency. Of course, these metaphors decide nothing; they merely express a feeling that something is different. The question still remains as to the significance of the distinctive form of the structural suit. Differences do not provoke doubts as to legitimacy unless a normative priority can be established for the dispute-resolution model; and that seems to me precisely where the standard critique of structural reform fails.

The ultimate issue is whether dispute resolution, particularly in the individualistic sense just described, has a prior or exclusive claim on the concept of "adjudication"; I might begin, however, by expressing my doubt as to whether it has any claim—any significant claim—on the central adjudicatory institution, courts. I doubt whether dispute resolution is an adequate description of the social function of courts. To my mind courts exist to give meaning to our public values, not to resolve disputes. Constitutional adjudication is the most vivid manifestation of this function, but it also seems true of most civil and criminal cases, certainly now and perhaps for most of our history as well.[64]

Most accounts of the judicial function begin with the same story: two people in the state of nature are squabbling over a piece of property, they come to an impasse, and, rather than resorting to force, turn to a third party, a stranger, for a decision. Courts are but an institutionalization of the stranger. This story, much like the story of the social contract, operates in the ill-defined land between the normative and descriptive. It does not purport to be an accurate portrayal of social history, of how courts actually came into being, but nevertheless is supposed to capture or express the underlying "social logic" of courts, even though no attempt is

---

[63] For a sympathetic use of the town meeting metaphor, using it as a predicate for expanding the possibilities of intervention, see Yeazell, *Intervention and the Idea of Litigation: A Commentary on the Los Angeles School Case*, 25 U.C.L.A. L. REV. 244 (1977).

[64] *See, e.g.*, Posner, *A Theory of Negligence*, 1 J. LEGAL STUD. 29 (1972); G. CALABRESI, THE COSTS OF ACCIDENTS (1970).

made to reconcile this story with the underlying social reality.[65] It seems to me, however, that once full account is taken of the role of courts in modern society, in ordinary criminal, constitutional, and statutory cases (*e.g.*, antitrust, environmental, or securities law), and perhaps also in the traditional common law cases, it becomes clear that the familiar story fundamentally misleads. It does not capture the "social logic" of courts, and might well be replaced by another story: the sovereign sends out his officers throughout the realm to speak the law and to see that it is obeyed.

Disputation has a pervasive role in litigation. Disputes may arise as to the meaning of a public value or as to the existence of a norm, and thus provide the *occasions* for judicial intervention. Also, courts may rely on the antagonistic relationship between various individuals or agencies for the presentation of the law and facts. The judge hopes that the desire of each to win provides a motivating force. Disputation can thus be viewed as a *mode of judicial operation*. I will also concede that the judge's decision may bring an end to the dispute; dispute resolution may be one *consequence* of the judicial decision. But as pervasive a role as disputation may play in litigation, it is equally important to recognize that the *function* of the judge—a statement of social purpose and a definition of role—is not to resolve disputes, but to give the proper meaning to our public values. Typically, he does this by enforcing and thus safeguarding the integrity of the existing public norms or by supplying new norms. These norms may protect the fruits of one's bargains or labors; they may regulate the use of automobiles or determine responsibility for compensation; they may preserve the integrity of markets by curbing fraud or monopolization; or they may impose limits on the use of state power. In the structural suit, the judge reorganizes the institution as a way of discharging this very same function.

Of course, some disputes may not threaten or otherwise implicate a public value. All the disputants may, for example, acknowledge the norms and confine their dispute to the interpretation of the words of the contract or the price of a bumper. Such disputes may wind their way into court, and judges may spend time on these purely private disputes—private because only the interests and behavior of the immediate parties to the dispute are at issue. That seems, however, an extravagant use of public resources, and thus it seems quite appropriate for those disputes to be handled not by courts, but by arbitrators (though courts may have to

---

[65] Shapiro, *Courts*, in 5 HANDBOOK OF POLITICAL SCIENCE 321-71 (F. Greenstein & N. Polsby eds. 1975).

act as background institutions enforcing or maybe even creating obligations to arbitrate).[66] Arbitration is like adjudication in that it too seeks the right, the just, the true judgment.[67] There is, however, an important difference in the two processes arising from the nature of the decisional agency—one private, the other public. Arbitrators are paid for by the parties; chosen by the parties; and enjoined by a set of practices (such as a reluctance to write opinions or generate precedents) that localizes or privatizes the decision.[68] The function of the arbitrator is to resolve a dispute. The function of the judge, on the other hand, must be understood in wholly different terms: he is a public officer; paid for by public funds; chosen not by the parties but by the public or its representatives; and empowered by the political agencies to enforce and create society-wide norms, and perhaps even to restructure institutions, as a way, I suggest, of giving meaning to our public values.

I may have overstated the position, and have drawn too sharp a distinction between arbitration and adjudication. I may have a too grandiose view of what people expect from judges as opposed to arbitrators. But it must be remembered that wholly apart from the question of whether dispute resolution has *any* claim on judicial resources, the question still remains whether it has a normatively *prior* claim on the office of the judge. The ultimate issue is whether dispute resolution is the ideal against which structural reform is to be judged. How might that priority be established? Three different tacks have been taken—one is instrumental, another is historical, and the third is axiomatic.

The instrumental critique, most strongly suggested by David Horowitz in a recent book, *The Courts and Social Policy*,[69] emphasizes the high risk of error in structural reform as opposed to dispute resolution. The argument is that the judge should be limited to doing what he does best—dispute resolution. Under the instrumental critique, dispute resolution becomes the ideal simply because it is what courts can do best.

---

[66] *See* Landes & Posner, *Adjudication as a Private Good*, 8 J. LEGAL STUD. 235 (1979). When a court acts as a background institution, it is giving expression to the public value favoring the peaceful resolution of disputes, which is quite different from resolving the dispute itself.

[67] Mediation is also a dispute-resolution process, but distinguished from arbitration or adjudication by its subjective quality: the correct result is defined as that which the parties accept. *See generally* M. GOLDING, PHILOSOPHY OF LAW 106-25 (1975); Eisenberg, *Private Ordering Through Negotiation: Dispute-Settlement and Rulemaking*, 89 HARV. L. REV. 637 (1976).

[68] *See* Getman, *Labor Arbitration and Dispute Resolution*, 88 YALE L.J. 916, 920-22 (1979) (describing the incipient departures from this established practice).

[69] D. HOROWITZ, THE COURTS AND SOCIAL POLICY 264 (1977).

Some of the empirical premises underlying this position seem plausible enough. The task of structural reform is fraught with danger, not just in defining the rights, but also in implementing them within the operation of the state bureaucracy. It may also be true—note I only say "may"—that the risk of judicial error in dispute resolution is not nearly as great as it is in structural reform: in many instances there is virtually nothing to the remedial phase in dispute resolution, simply declaring whether plaintiff or defendant wins, nothing to compare to the difficulties inherent in the reorganization of an ongoing social institution, a public school system, a welfare department, or worse yet, an institution we know the least about, a prison. All of this may be safely conceded without, I am certain, accepting the normative conclusion that idealizes dispute resolution.

In the first place it is not clear why any social institution should be devoted to one and only one task, even the one it does best. Traditional separation of powers doctrine assumes a differentiation of judicial power from that of the executive and legislative branches, but it does not require that the differentiation be along *formal* as opposed to *functional* lines, nor does it require that any branch be devoted to one function alone. (Legislators, for example, spend considerable time on constituent services.) Each of the three great divisions of powers may have several different functions. The performance of one function may interfere with another, failures in one domain impair its capacity to perform in others, but there is no reason to believe that the relationship between the structural and dispute-resolution modes of discharging the judicial function is one of interference, that involvement in the structural litigation will compromise the judiciary's capacity to resolve disputes. The functions may well be independent, or maybe even complementary.[70]

Furthermore, even if a choice must be made between the two functions, the instrumental critique assumes too narrow a criterion of choice in insisting that we preserve that function the institution performs best. Success rate is important in evaluating institutions, but two further factors must be introduced into the analysis: the value of a successful performance, and the success rate of alternative institutions performing comparable tasks. On either criterion, structural reform fares quite well.

The hypothesized low success rate of structural reform is amply compensated by the promise of greater social returns. If the choice be between resolving a dispute between two individuals, such as a dispute between a citizen and a policeman over some alleged incident of wrongdoing, or on the other hand, trying to eradicate conditions of lawlessness through

---

[70] Though each may have its own problem. *See* p. 202-03 *infra*.

a reorganization of the police department, the claim that the first is more likely to be "successful" clearly does not make it the more socially worthwhile enterprise, in terms of either the breadth of the corrective action or its durability. Success may come more rarely or less perfectly in a structural case, but a structural success, even if it is only partial, may well dwarf all the successes of dispute resolution; it may greatly reduce the need for dispute resolution by eliminating the conditions that give rise to incidents of wrongdoing; and it may even compensate for all its own failures.

The instrumental critique might have more appeal if it were clear that there were alternative institutions that could better perform this worthwhile but perilous activity. But just the opposite is true. Dispute resolution might be diverted to arbitration, but obviously such a diversion is not available for structural reform. It is among the most public of all forms of adjudication, involving constitutional values and the state bureaucracies. Some have suggested administrative agencies as the alternative, on the theory that these agencies might have some special expertise in the reorganization of ongoing social institutions not otherwise available to courts. But this suggestion also seems without basis. Before explaining why, let me emphasize that my intent is not to deny a role for administrative agencies in the constitutional domain, in the effort to give meaning to our constitutional values through structural reform, but only to suggest that their claim of special competency is not so strong as to altogether oust the courts, to justify transferring structural reform from the courts to administrative agencies, leaving the courts to do nothing more than resolve disputes. The instrumental critique must make a claim as strong as that in order to idealize dispute resolution as the judicial function and to accuse courts of acting illegitimately whenever they undertake structural reform.

The claim for diversion is largely predicated on the view that these administrative agencies possess some expert knowledge, and yet I for one fail to see the evidence to support that position. The instrumental critic in essence makes a comparative argument, one about the superiority of administrative agencies, but only attempts to document one-half of that argument. He typically points to "failures" of the courts, but never considers the "failures" of the administrative agencies, of which there are many. The literature is filled with the evidence of administrative failures,[71] and

---

[71] *See, e.g.*, J. FREEDMAN, CRISIS AND LEGITIMACY (1978); J. GETMAN, S. GOLDBERG & J. HERMAN, UNION REPRESENTATION ELECTIONS (1976). *See also* R. RABIN, PERSPECTIVES ON THE ADMINISTRATIVE PROCESS (1979). The myth of expertise is not confined to administrative agencies, *see, e.g.*, Morse, *Crazy Behavior, Morals and Science: An Analysis of Mental Health*

teaches us to be wary of the claim of administrative expertise, also voiced at earlier times by the Progressives. Admittedly, structural reform is a perilous and arduous activity, but the problem is largely one of knowledge, knowing how large-scale organizations operate, not the distribution of that knowledge among various agencies. I doubt whether there is some special body of knowledge relevant for such a remedial undertaking, but even if there were, it still remains to be seen why it could not be made available to the judge, either through expert witnesses, or through auxiliary structures such as special masters. The evidentiary process of the administrative agency has long promised to be more open, broader, and freewheeling than that available to the judiciary, but it is not clear to me that this promise has ever been fulfilled, that such a liberated process would be consistent with rudimentary notions of due process, or even that such a process is needed for structural reform. The focus of a structural suit is necessarily broad, concerned with social conditions and organizational dynamics, not discrete and particularized incidents of wrongdoing; but the judicial process is capable of that breadth. Some might, I realize, emphasize the insight that comes from accumulated experience, rather than a body of knowledge that could be communicated to a decisionmaker; yet it is hard to see how this reformulation of the claim of expertise advances the cause. Some judges have been engaged in the reconstructive enterprise over a long period of time, say a decade, and though, as we will see,[72] this involvement creates its own problems, it probably dwarfs all the experience presently possessed by administrative agencies on how to reconstruct ongoing social institutions.

The argument for diversion to administrative agencies thus seems to rest on exaggerated claims of expertise, a recurrence of a myth of Progressivism, but even more fundamentally it reflects a misunderstanding of why courts are involved in the first place. Courts are not entrusted with the reconstructive task on the theory that they possess some expertise (either in the form of knowledge or experience) on how best to perform that task. In the domain of instrumentalism, of means-end rationality, courts have no special claim to competency. Their special competency lies elsewhere, in the domain of constitutional values, a special kind of substantive rationality, and that expertise is derived from the special quality of the judicial process—dialogue and independence. The reconstructive endeavor, calling for instrumental judgments, should be seen

---

Law, 51 S. CAL. L. REV. 527 (1978), nor even to the law, see, e.g., J. HABERMAS, Technology and Science as "Ideology," in TOWARD A RATIONAL SOCIETY 81 (1970); I. ILLICH, TOWARD A HISTORY OF NEEDS (1977).

[72] See p. 202-03 infra.

(for reasons to be elaborated later[73]) as but a necessary incident of that meaning-giving enterprise, as an attempt by the judge to give meaning to constitutional values in practical reality. Thus, even if one were to assume, as the instrumental critique would have us do, that administrative agencies possess an expertise in the domain of instrumental rationality, the diversion argument would still be deeply problematic because administrative agencies lack any special competency in this particular domain of substantive rationality. They lack the independence that is so essential for giving expression to our constitutional values.

The specialized jurisdictions of administrative agencies may lend support to the claim of expertise, but it also poses a threat to the independence of the agency: the regulators become too closely identified with the regulated.[74] More fundamentally, administrative agencies are, as the Progressives well-realized, more tied to majoritarian politics than are courts, both because of ideology (they are sometimes allowed to make their judgments on the basis of the preferences of the body politic) and institutional arrangements (appointment for short terms, subject to removal when Administrations change). The so-called independent regulatory agencies of the federal system might be seen as standing somewhere between the courts, on the one hand, and Congress and the Executive, on the other, but surely their relationship to the majoritarian branches is close enough as to make us wary of any claim, such as that embodied in the instrumental critique, that would make them the exclusive or even the primary agencies for giving meaning to our constitutional values. The truth of this assertion would be, I venture to say, conceded in most contexts. It seems no less true—maybe even more so—when the threat to those values is posed by the bureaucracies of the modern state and when structural reform is needed to remove that threat.

A second method for establishing the priority of the dispute-resolution model is historical—dispute resolution is "traditional," and structural reform "new." Support for this position comes from Abram Chayes, who in an important, recent article[75] identified a mode of adjudication

---

[73] See p. 201-03 infra.

[74] The dynamics of cooptation in the administrative field may be especially tied to the linkage of specialized jurisdiction and short term appointments (the administrator develops an expertise that has a limited market). As such, the loss of independence of the regulator from the regulatee may be more severe in the administrative domain than in the judicial, and less curable.

[75] Chayes, The Role of the Judge in Public Law Litigation, 89 HARV. L. REV. 1281 (1976). For a parallel and important account of contemporary civil litigation, see Scott, Two Models of the Civil Process, 27 STAN. L. REV. 937 (1975).

that is quite similar to the structural one (though he attributes its formal characteristics to the "public" character of the rights, while I see them more linked to the organizational setting—all rights enforced by courts are public). He celebrates the "new" model, but, rather than centrally dealing with the questions of legitimacy, he emphasizes the positivistic or descriptive dimensions of his enterprise. He presents himself as a "biologist" describing the "evolution" of a "new" form of adjudication, which will, he adds secondarily, legitimate itself by winning the assent of the people, provided it is given chance to work.

I have my doubts as to whether the historical claim is wholly accurate as a purely descriptive matter. To my mind, what has evolved has been the *form* of adjudication, but not the *function*. The function of adjudication, whether in the nineteenth century or twentieth century, torts or criminal law, contract or antitrust, *McCulloch v. Maryland*[76] or *Brown v. Board of Education*,[77] has not been to resolve disputes between individuals, but rather to give meaning to our public values. What has changed is social structure, the emergence of a society dominated by the operation of large-scale organizations, and it is these changes in social structure that account for the changes over time in adjudicatory *forms*. Such changes should hardly be a cause for concern. What would, in fact, provoke a genuine crisis of legitimacy would be to insist on procedural modes shaped in a different social setting, to assume that adjudicatory forms created centuries ago should control today.

But, even assuming for a moment that the dispute-resolution model has a claim to historical priority, it remains to be seen what that has to do with legitimacy, which is essentially a normative judgment. One response to this puzzlement may try to link dispute resolution with the "case or controversy" requirement of article III, but this claim is without foundation. There is nothing in the text of article III—in the rather incidental use of the words "cases" or "controversies"—that constitutionally constricts the federal courts to dispute resolution. The late eighteenth century was the heyday for the common law, and, though that litigation may inform the construction of the words "cases" and "controversies," the function of courts under the common law was paradigmatically not dispute resolution, but to give meaning to public values through the enforcement and creation of public norms, such as those embodied in the criminal law and the rules regarding property, contracts, and torts.[78] The

---

[76] 17 U.S. (4 Wheat.) 316 (1819).

[77] 347 U.S. 483 (1954).

[78] *See* M. Horwitz, The Transformation Of American Law, 1780-1860, at 1-30 (1977). *See also* note 64 *supra*.

courts created our law. They were the central lawmaking institutions. The judicial function implied by contemporary constitutional litigation, of which structural reform is part, is continuous with and maybe even identical to that of the common law. The issues have changed, and so has the social setting; that has required a change in the form of adjudication, though not its function.

Alternatively, it may be thought that the historical critique derives its normative power not from article III, but from the application of a theory that sees the people's "consent" as the basis of legitimacy.[79] This argument equates "implied consent" with "actual consent," interprets the people's acceptance of the status quo as implying a consent to the existing institutional arrangements, and then locates the dispute-resolution model—but not the structural one—in the status quo. Such an argument might seem capable of transforming a historical priority into a normative priority, but in truth the argument fails, on a number of grounds.

First, one can wonder about this interpretation of the status quo, which reads dispute resolution in and structural reform out. Some historians, for example, Eisenberg and Yeazell, find antecedents for contemporary institutional litigation in the nineteenth century equity and receivership cases or the antitrust and bankruptcy cases of the early twentieth century.[80] Indeed, following this line of thought one might also argue that the very existence of the structural mode in constitutional litigation for the past decade or so is sufficient to place it within the status quo—it, too, implicitly has received the people's consent.

A second response, primarily exemplified by Chayes,[81] is to table the question of legitimacy, to suggest that it has arisen prematurely. Assent by the people need not be given prospectively, in the way that might be suggested by the social contract metaphor: all the people come together at one historic moment and decide whether they wish to have a particular social institution. Consent can also be *earned*. But that takes time and thus structural reform should be given a chance to operate—a so-called trial run (assuming the past decade has not been sufficient). If it survives, it will then be given the same claim to legitimacy as the so-called traditional model: the institution will have legitimated itself.

---

[79] The most ambitious attempt to relate consent theory to courts is Shapiro, *supra* note 65. As might be expected, it ultimately rests on the story, discussed p. 29 *supra*, that links dispute settlement and the evolution of courts.

[80] Eisenberg & Yeazell, *supra* note 60. *See also* O. FISS, *supra* note 57, at 325-414; Chayes, *supra* note 75, at 1303.

[81] Chayes, *supra* note 75, at 1313-16.

A third response—and the one that seems most appealing to me—is to question consent theory itself. In part, the problem with the theory is one of ambiguity. What is it that one consents to when one "accepts" the status quo in adjudication? Is it the form? Or the function? Or is it the substantive results? Consent theory fails to answer these questions, or even to suggest a procedure for working toward answers, and as a consequence transforms the historical argument into an endorsement of the status quo. It might well work a colossal collapse of "is" and "ought." Beyond that, however, one can question the very premise upon which this critique of structural reform rests—the identification of consent with legitimacy. Institutions can seek their justifications in domains other than consent, even in a democracy.

A democratic political system is one ultimately dependent upon the consent of the people, but each and every institution need not be founded on consent. Consent goes to the system, not the particular institution; it operates on the whole rather than each part. The legitimacy of particular institutions, such as courts, depends not on the consent—implied or otherwise—of the people, but rather on their *competence,* on the special contribution they make to the quality of our social life.[82] Legitimacy depends on the capacity of the institution to perform a function within the political system and its willingness to respect the limitations on that function. Legitimacy does not depend on popular approval of the institution's performance, and even less on popular approval of the processes through which that performance is rendered. It is the legitimacy of the political system as a whole that depends on the people's approval, and that is the source of its democratic character.

The people have the power to express their disapproval of how courts are discharging their function. Presumably, they can pass statutes to curb procedural innovations, or they can adopt constitutional amendments for overturning particular outcomes. Some might argue that the failure of the people to exercise this power is "implied approval" of all that the courts are doing today, but such an argument would be mistaken (this is surely a situation when inaction is not tantamount to action), and more importantly, it is unnecessary. The existence of the power of the people to express disapproval should be understood as the means by which institutions such as courts can be integrated into a system ultimately founded on the people's consent. Some institutions—the legislature, the school board, the police chief—may have a tighter, more direct connection to

---

[82] This way of looking at the matter was first suggested by G. Zweifach, Institutional Reform and Paradigms of the Judiciary (1979) (unpublished manuscript on file at the Yale Law School Library and the *Harvard Law Review*).

consent: particular incumbents serve at the pleasure of the people. To insist upon a similar consensual connection for the judiciary would, however, impair its independence and thus destroy its capacity to discharge its constitutional function within our political system.

For these reasons it seems impossible to ground the historical critique either on article III or on consent theory, and thus it, like the instrumental critique, fails to give dispute-resolution a normative priority. There is one further strategy to be considered, the one I called axiomatic. It postulates some formal attribute of a social process as a morally necessary attribute, on the basis of which the structural and dispute-resolution modes are to be evaluated. As it turns out, that attribute—individual participation, present in dispute resolution, absent in the structural mode—also implicates consent theory and shares many of its difficulties. It places adjudication on a moral plane with two other activities exalted by consent theory, voting and bargaining, and then tries to construct an ideal form of adjudication that preserves this connection with consensual activity, now in a highly individualized form, though it still fails to explain why consent is the touchstone of legitimacy of all institutions.

The most sustained effort to build a case for dispute resolution on the basis of moral axioms is Lon Fuller's essay, *The Forms and Limits of Adjudication*.[83] This essay was written in the late 1950's, shortly before the heyday of structural reform. It was published in 1978, shortly after Professor Fuller's death, but was not updated to account, either as a descriptive or normative matter, for the intervening twenty years, the civil rights era.[84] It is as though the period never occurred—an erasure of some portion of the history of procedure. The essay is nevertheless important for our purposes, for it seems largely motivated by a desire to establish the limits of adjudication, and the one limit Fuller in fact develops is clearly at war with the notion of structural reform. Borrowing an idea of Michael Polanyi, interestingly enough also introduced in the 1950's,[85] Fuller insists that courts cannot perform "polycentric" tasks.

Fuller does not give any single, straightforward definition of polycentrism. It seems to refer to a type of dispute or problem which is many centered, much like, he says, a spider web, in the sense that a resolution

---

[83] 92 HARV. L. REV. 353 (1978).

[84] During this 20-year period the essay did not lie dormant: it was used in Professor Fuller's courses at Harvard, it received a wide "underground" circulation in mimeographed form, it was widely cited, and portions appeared in two articles by Fuller: *Adjudication and the Rule of Law*, 54 PROC. AM. SOC'Y INT'L L. 1 (1960), and *Collective Bargaining and the Arbitrator*, 1963 WIS. L. REV. 3.

[85] M. POLANYI, THE LOGIC OF LIBERTY (1951).

of a polycentric dispute would necessarily have broad and never-ending repercussions. These disputes are to Fuller inappropriate for adjudication. Fuller explains why through an analysis of a series of examples. One example, appearing near the end of the essay, seems, remarkably enough, to address the problem of structural reform:

> The suggestion that polycentric problems are often solved by a kind of "managerial intuition" should not be taken to imply that it is an invariable characteristic of polycentric problems that they resist rational solution. There are rational principles for building bridges of structural steel. But there is no rational principle which states, for example, that the angle between girder A and girder B must always be 45 degrees. This depends on the bridge as a whole. One cannot construct a bridge by conducting successive separate arguments concerning the proper angle for every pair of intersecting girders. One must deal with the whole structure.[86]

One is left to wonder why adjudication must proceed on the basis Fuller suggests—angle by angle. Certainly that is not required by rationality; reason, even that of the judge, is not binary; it need not proceed angle by angle, but can encompass whole structures. The explanation seems much more concrete, it has to do with the enormous number of people affected by whole structures—by the construction of the bridge. It is simply impossible, Fuller explains, to have everyone affected participate in the lawsuit in a meaningful way.[87]

At the core then of Fuller's conception of the limits of adjudication and his objection to having courts resolve polycentric problems is the individual's right to participate in a proceeding that might adversely affect him. This right might be preserved in a representative suit that accords with the traditional law of agency, where there is a true consensual bond between representative (agent) and principal, but it should be recognized

---

[86] Fuller, *supra* note 83, at 403.

[87] In discussing another example, wage and price controls in a socialist regime, Fuller gives a more complete explanation of the source of the problem:

> [I]t is simply impossible to afford each affected party a meaningful participation through proofs and arguments. It is a matter of capital importance to note that it is not merely a question of the huge number of possibly affected parties, significant as that aspect of the thing may be. A more fundamental point is that [each possible solution] would have a different set of repercussions and might require in each instance a redefinition of the "parties affected."

Id. at 394-95.

that this right, taken in its highly individualistic cast, is denied, indeed seriously compromised, by the kind of representation lying at the heart of a structural suit—the representation of interests by spokesmen for groups and offices rather than identifiable individuals.[88] Just imagine the kind of representation implicit in the famed Arkansas prison litigation, in which the court's conclusion—for example, that the trusty system at Cummins Farm was a form of cruel and unusual punishment—must necessarily affect a never-ending spiral of persons, officers, and interests: inmates, guards, administrators, legislators, taxpayers, indeed all the citizens of the state—present and future.[89] The reconstruction of a prison, or for that matter the reconstruction of a school system, a welfare agency, a hospital, or any bureaucracy, is as polycentric as the construction of a bridge. All require the court to deal with whole structures. The judge must be certain that the full range of interests is vigorously represented, but he need not turn his back on the constitutional claim or deny an effective remedy because each and every individual affected will not or cannot meaningfully participate in the suit.

My conception of adjudication starts from the top—the office of the judge—and works down. I place adjudication on a moral plane with legislative and executive action. I start with the conception of state power embodied in the judge, treat courts as a coordinate source of government power, and see the form of adjudication shaped by function and social setting. Fuller rejects such an approach. He starts from the bottom and works up. Fuller starts with the individual, rather than the judge. He places adjudication on a moral plane with elections and con-tracts, analyzes these two social processes in terms of how the individual participates in each, through voting and bargaining, and then seeks to distinguish adjudication from these social processes. The distinguishing feature of adjudication, naturally enough, is also cast in individualistic terms, more precisely, in terms of how the individual participates in that process as opposed to elections and contracts—through proof and rea-soned arguments. He then treats this right of the individual to participate in the proceeding—the moral equivalent of the right to vote and the right to bargain—as the master idea of adjudication. For Fuller, it explains and justifies certain formal features of adjudication, for example, party structure and the passivity of the judge. It also sets limits on adjudica-tion. The right of individual participation is violated only at a distinct

---

[88] *But cf.* Eisenberg, *Participation, Responsiveness, and the Consultative Process: An Essay for Lon Fuller*, 92 HARV. L. REV. 410, 427 (1978).

[89] Holt v. Sarver, 309 F. Supp. 362, 373-76 (E.D. Ark. 1970), *aff'd*, 442 F.2d 304 (8th Cir. 1971). *See also* note 28 *supra*.

moral risk—the process is deemed not a form of adjudication, or at best a mixed or hybrid form of adjudication, "parasitic" upon the ideal.

At various points Fuller speaks as though he is being merely descriptive. What distinguishes adjudication from other social processes, he says, is the "institutional commitment" of adjudication to a particular mode of individual participation. On a purely descriptive level there is not much to his claim. It is not supported by a presentation of the evidence and it is contradicted by a great deal of the reality or experience that we would consider to be adjudication. Moreover, a purely descriptive account could never yield the normative judgments implicit in his conclusion as to what might constitute "parasitic" adjudication. Fuller's essay should be recognized for what it is: a postulation that the standard for judging the legitimacy of a process that purports to be adjudication is the affected individual's right to participate. I say "postulation," for although much of the essay tightly celebrates the role of reason in human affairs, and sees the important connection between reason and adjudication, there is no explanation of why reason requires the kind of individual participation that Fuller insists upon. In structural reform reason enters the process, not through the arguments of each and every individual affected, but through the arguments of the spokesmen for all the interests represented and through the decision of the judge. Reason is used to give meaning to our constitutional values.

How might an axiom such as Fuller's, proclaiming the sacredness of the individual right of participation, be judged? I realize that it may not be appropriate to demand justification of an axiom, for it is offered as a starting point, a proposition that you cannot look behind. Yet there must be more that can be said about it. Acceptance of an axiom must turn on something more than a momentary flash of intuition. In my judgment, the axiom can be assessed in terms of its consequences and its underlying social vision. An axiom might at first glance seem attractive enough, but its appeal may decline radically once its full implications are understood.

In assessing the consequences of the individual participation axiom it should first be understood that the issue is not whether there should be social processes that can further the participatory right—whether dispute resolution should exist—but whether a form of adjudication that violates that right—structural reform—is legitimate (or permissible). Fuller treats the participation axiom as a necessary condition, and that is the source of the problem. As a necessary condition, the axiom would render structural reform illegitimate, true enough, but more importantly, it would render illegitimate almost all adjudication—both of the common law and the constitutional variety—in which the courts were creating public norms. It would reduce courts to the function of norm enforcement, and reduce adjudication to a high-class (but subsidized) form of arbitration. It is no mere happenstance that Fuller spent a great deal of his professional life as an arbitrator; throughout the essay he refers to the judge as an "arbiter."

Virtually all public norm creation is polycentric. It affects as many people as structural reform, and equally impairs the capacity of each of the affected individuals to participate in the process. More often than not, there is a myriad of possible rules or solutions that could be formulated in each case. Consider the fellow-servant rule, the stop-look-and-listen doctrine, strict liability, the consideration requirement, the rules respecting offer and acceptance, the norms of the Marshall Court regarding the commerce clause, those of the Warren Court regarding free speech, racial equality, civil and criminal procedure. The list could go on and on. It would probably include all judge-made law, and the doctrine of precedent itself. The list surely includes many "mistakes" or "wrong decisions," but that is not the issue: the issue is whether all these acts of norm creation represent a misuse of the judicial power, an incorrect appropriation of the concept of "adjudication." This is a conclusion that most of us—or maybe even all of us—would reject and yet it is a conclusion that would seem to follow from Fuller's axiom.

It should also be recognized that this axiom—like the liberty-of-contract doctrine of an earlier age—would be but a formal triumph of individualism. The axiom seems to celebrate the individual, but would leave the individual at the mercy of large aggregations of power—in *Lochner*,[90] the corporation; here, the state bureaucracies. Deprived of the opportunity to use the courts to protect himself, to have the full use of these centers of government power that stand apart from the state bureaucracies, the individual is thrown back to those social processes that are supposed to respect his participatory right—dispute resolution, voting, and bargaining. Each of these processes has important roles to play in our social life, but it is hard to believe that any of them enhance the *real* or *effective*—as opposed to the formal—power of those individuals who are abused by the large-scale organizations of the modern state, the school system, the hospital, the welfare department, or, even worse, the prison.

---

[90] Lochner v. New York, 198 U.S. 45 (1905); *see* W. Duker, Mr. Justice Rufus W. Peckham: The Police Power and the Individual in a Changing World (1979) (unpublished manuscript on file at the Yale Law School Library and the *Harvard Law Review*); Pound, *Liberty of Contract*, 18 YALE L. J. 454 (1909).

In truth, the individual participation axiom is rooted in a world that no longer exists. It is rooted in a horizontal world, in which people related to one another on individual terms and on terms of approximate equality. It is rooted in a world that viewed the law of contracts as The Law—not so incidentally, Fuller's substantive field of law. Our world, however, is a vertical one; the market has been replaced by the hierarchy, the individual entrepreneur by the bureau.[91] In this social setting, what is needed to protect the individual is the establishment of power centers equal in strength and equal in resources to the dominant social actors; what is needed is countervailing power. A conception of adjudication that strictly honors the right of each affected individual to participate in the process seems to proclaim the importance of the individual, but actually leaves the individual without the institutional support necessary to realize his true self. In fact, the individual participation axiom would do little more than throw down an impassable bar—polycentrism—to the one social process that has emerged with promise for preserving our constitutional values and the ideal of individualism in the face of the modern bureaucratic state—structural reform.[92]

III. The Problem of Remedy

Dispute resolution, either as a statement of form or function, does not represent the ideal for adjudication, and thus the departures from that model of adjudication entailed in structural reform do not in and of themselves deprive that mode of adjudication of its legitimacy. The function of adjudication is to give meaning to public values, not merely to resolve disputes. Structural reform is faithful to that function, and adapts the traditional form of the lawsuit to the changing social reality—the dominance of our social life by bureaucratic organizations. A question of legitimacy might still persist, however, because, wholly apart from any comparisons to the dispute-resolution model, the entitlement of courts to speak the law—to give meaning to our constitutional values—is limited. It is limited, as I suggested at the outset, by the judge's willingness and ability to adhere to a process that typifies the judicial branch and consti-tutes the foundation of its competence—dialogue and independence.

---

[91] See generally M. Weber, The Theory Of Social And Economic Organization 329-41 (T. Parsons ed. 1947); O. Williamson, supra note 25.

[92] This model of adjudication has a relevance even beyond the state bureaucracy; it may be used to safeguard public values from the threats posed by the so-called private bureaucracies, such as the corporation or union. See, e.g., Stone, Controlling Corporate Misconduct, 49 Pub. Interest 55 (1977); Note, Monitors: A New Equitable Remedy?, 70 Yale L.J. 103 (1960).

Structural reform does not pose any distinct threats to the dialogic quality of this process—the obligation of the judge to confront grievances he would otherwise prefer to ignore, to listen to the broadest possible range of persons and interests, to assume individual responsibility for the decision, and to justify the decision in terms of the norms of the constitutional system. The transformation of party structure inherent in the structural suit stretches the notion of a dialogue, but to fault the structural suit on that ground is to overread a metaphor, to think that it refers to a conversation between two. The term "dialogue" is simply meant to suggest a rationalistic or communicative process in which the judge listens and speaks back. That process is no less possible in the multiparty context, though the visual imagery shifts from a triad to an array. It just requires a little skill and imagination.

Admittedly, the capacity or even the willingness of judges to engage in this communicative process, to listen to all grievances and to painstakingly justify their decisions, is far from secure. Like an art, it always seems in peril. But the principal threats to this capacity—impatience, self-righteousness, judicial burnout—have nothing to do with structural reform; or to put the same point somewhat differently, these threats to the integrity of the judicial process can be fought in ways that leave the structural suit untouched as a distinctive mode of constitutional litigation. Some of the critics of structural reform also voice the recurrent gripe that judges are overworked.[93] Though overwork might well threaten the integrity of the communicative process that lies at the core of adjudication, it is far from clear why the remedy should lie in the elimination of the structural suit. Each one is complex and difficult, but at the same time it may engage the judge in his most worthy and important function. A more sensible response to the claim of overwork may be to divert to other institutions the simpler, less complex cases (individual citizen versus individual policeman, inmate versus guard); they may represent a considerable burden taken as an aggregate. It may also be necessary to increase the social resources committed to the judicial branch. We cannot expect any agency of government to discharge its function adequately when it is forced to operate on a commitment of resources that reflect the needs

---

[93] This claim has its counterpart in earlier times, though then it was primarily used as part of a criticism of the activism of the newly formed Warren Court, *see, e.g.*, Hart, *The Supreme Court, 1958 Term—Foreword: The Time Chart of the Justices*, 73 HARV. L. REV. 84 (1959); for a spirited reply *see* Arnold, *Professor Hart's Theology*, 73 Harv. L. Rev. 1298 (1960). The claim of overwork often appears as the rock bottom defense of a Supreme Court practice that seems very much in tension with the competency-giving process, the failure of the Court to explain its choice of cases. *See* Gunther, *The Subtle Vices of the "Passive Virtues"—A Comment on Principle and Expediency in Judicial Review*, 64 COLUM. L. REV. 1 (1964).

of an earlier age. It would of course be a sad irony, indeed it would seriously jeopardize his legitimacy, if these resources were used to convert each judge into a minibureaucracy. The dialogue that has so far typified the judicial branch, and that underlies its claim of special competency, envisions individual responsibility for the decision and its justification. The judge must be the one who listens and speaks back.

Though these matters cannot be easily dismissed, my concern is not with the dialogic quality of the competency-giving process, but rather with the ideal of independence and the threat posed to that ideal by the remedy. The remedy expresses the judge's desire to give a meaning to a constitutional value that is more tangible, more fullblooded than a mere declaration of what is right. This desire to be efficacious is manifest in all forms of adjudication, and creates similar dilemmas for the judge, but in structural reform it takes on a special urgency and largely gives this form of constitutional litigation its special cast. The desire to be efficacious leads the judge to attempt the remarkable feat of reconstructing a state bureaucracy, say, transforming a dual school system into a unitary one, and that ambition in turn forces the judge to abandon his position of independence and to enter the world of politics.

A. The New Formalism

To understand the roots of the dilemma it is necessary to understand the complicated relationship between rights and remedies. To do that we must first free ourselves from the hold of what has become known as the tailoring principle—the insistence that the remedy must fit the violation.

At first it seemed that the tailoring principle was of unquestionable validity; indeed, it might be tautological. The problem seemed not to be the principle itself but the definition of the violation—the Court had defined the violation too narrowly. The principle was quietly introduced in *Swann*[94] but was first applied in a case in which the Burger Court upset a metropolitan desegregation plan,[95] a result that might be traced to an exceedingly narrow view of the equal protection viola-

---

[94] 402 U.S. 1, 15-16 (1971). In fact, *Swann* sustained the most untailored remedy imaginable, and the very invocation of the tailoring principle suggested a broad conception of the violation. *See* Fiss, *The Charlotte-Mecklenburg Case—Its Significance for Northern School Desegregation*, 38 U. CHI. L. REV. 697 (1971).

[95] Milliken v. Bradley, 418 U.S. 717 (1974). *See also* Milliken v. Bradley, 433 U.S. 267, 281-82 (1977); Dayton Bd. of Educ. v. Brinkman, 433 U.S. 406 (1977); Pasadena City Bd. of Educ. v. Spangler, 427 U.S. 424 (1976).

tion, namely, that it consisted of incidents of wrong-doing—past acts of discrimination—rather than a social condition—the segregated pattern of student attendance.[96] I now believe the problem is deeper: the tailoring principle fundamentally misleads. It does in fact tend to support an artificial conception of "violation"—one that looks back and that sees discrete incidents as the object of the remedy—but it also errs in an even more basic way. It suggests that the relationship between remedy and violation is deductive or formal, and thereby gives us an impoverished notion of remedy.

Deduction, strictly speaking, is never possible in the law, as the authors of the tailoring principle might well concede. There are, however, certain features of the tailoring principle, particularly the concept of "fit," that suggest that the connection between violation and remedy has a highly formalistic, almost a deductive quality, with the violation serving as the premise and the remedy the conclusion: (a) the violation is viewed as the *exclusive* source of the remedy; (b) each *specific* provision of the remedy is explicable in terms of the violation; (c) it is assumed that there is a *unique* remedy, in the same way that there is a single conclusion to a syllogism; and (d) the remedy, also like the conclusion, is thought to follow from the violation with a high degree of *certainty*. In the structural context these formalistic qualities—exclusivity, a fully determined specificity, uniqueness, and certainty—are never present. The structural remedy is decidedly instrumental.

The object of the structural remedy is not to eliminate a "violation" in the sense implied by the tailoring principle, but rather to remove the threat posed by the organization to the constitutional values. The concept "violation" can be used to describe the object of the remedy only if it is understood in a prospective, dynamic, and systemic sense. It must also be understood that there are many ways of eliminating the threat (the

---

[96] This is further suggested by several post-*Milliken I* cases, particularly Washington v. Davis, 426 U.S. 229 (1976), and Dayton Bd. of Educ. v. Brinkman, 433 U.S. 406 (1977). *Washington v. Davis* made segregative intent a necessary condition for a violation, and *Dayton* limited the remedy to eliminating the "incremental segregative effect" of the wrongful conduct, 433 U.S. at 420. Looking at the problem of school desegregation from the perspective of these two cases, it seemed that the architects of *Swann* and *Keyes* had been caught in a trap of their own making, for *Swann* and *Keyes* would have us believe that the violations in those cases consisted of the incidents of past discrimination, even though they called for systemwide remedies. *See* Fiss, *School Desegregation: The Uncertain Path of the Law*, 4 PHILOSOPHY & PUB. AFF. 3 (1974), *reprinted in* EQUALITY AND PREFERENTIAL TREATMENT 155 (M. Cohen, T. Nagel & T. Scanlon eds. 1977).

violation, if you insist). Consider the well-known *Lankford* case,[97] in which the police had engaged in a massive manhunt in the black neighborhoods in Baltimore. They conducted searches of suspects without probable cause and in a manner and at a time that the court concluded was wholly unjustified. This misconduct was part of a larger pattern of abuses by the police, and the court perceived an urgent need to protect fourth amendment values. It also became apparent that this might be done in at least three different ways: (a) a decree against the police officers, either at the operative or supervisory level, prohibiting them from engaging in conduct that violated the fourth amendment; (b) a decree requiring the chief of police to establish an internal disciplinary agency that would sanction individual police officers who engaged in such misconduct; or (c) a decree establishing (subject to some minor exceptions such as one for hot pursuits) that searches for suspects be conducted only with a search warrant, not because the fourth amendment required it, but as a means of checking the abuses that occurred in this city. The court confronted with a threat to fourth amendment values must choose among these alternatives (and maybe even others), and the tailoring principle distorts the remedial process by masking this basic fact. It obscures the need for a choice, and the fact that the remedial phase of a structural suit is largely devoted to making that choice.

The tailoring principle also obscures the criteria of choice in suggesting that the violation will be the exclusive source of the remedy: it suggests that the shape of the remedy is exclusively a function of the definition of the violation. The overriding mission of the structural decree is to remove the threat posed to constitutional values by the organization, but there are additional or subsidiary considerations—largely embraced within the traditional concept of "equitable discretion"—that play a critical role in the remedial process. They guide the choice among the host of possible remedies, and shape the terms of the alternative chosen. One set of subsidiary considerations might be considered normative: they express values other than the one that occasions the intervention. For example, a school decree might be predicated on a desire to eliminate a threat to racial equality, but other values—such as respect for state autonomy,[98] evenhandedness, or a minimization of coercion—should be considered. Another set of subsidiary considerations go to efficacy. They reflect the

---

[97] Lankford v. Gelston, 364 F.2d 197 (4th Cir. 1966). For the decree actually entered on remand see O. FISS, *supra* note 57, at 116.

[98] Hutto v. Finney, 437 U.S. 678, 704 n.1 (1978) (Powell, J., concurring in part and dissenting in part).

judge's best judgment on how he might achieve his objective of removing the threat to the constitutional value most effectively.

These subsidiary considerations have, as we saw earlier, an important bearing on some facets of the party structure—the divergence between victims and beneficiaries of the decree, and also on the identity of the office or agency that bears the burden of the remedy.[99] They also give the structural decree a tentative and hesitant character. The familiar pattern is for the judge to try—sometimes in different cases and sometimes at different times in the same case—the whole range of remedial alternatives. The judge must search for the "best" remedy, but since his judgment must incorporate such open-ended considerations as effectiveness and fairness, and since the threat and constitutional value that occasions the intervention can never be defined with great precision, the particular choice of remedy can never be defended with any certitude. It must always be open to revision, even without the strong showing traditionally required for modification of a decree,[100] namely, that the first choice is causing grievous hardship. A revision is justified if the remedy is not working effectively or is unnecessarily burdensome.

These subsidiary considerations also explain the specifics usually found in the final stages of a structural injunction. The specifics range from the date and content of the reports that must be submitted to the court on performance to the duties of the various institutional operatives. For some, these specifics are baffling: how can it be that the Constitution requires a report on September 15, or showers at 110°F, or a thirty-day limitation on confinement in an isolation cell?[101] The bafflement, it seems to me, results from a failure to recognize the instrumental character of the remedy, and the important role played by considerations of efficacy and fairness in shaping that instrument. It incorrectly assumes, as the tailoring principle permits, that the violation—viewed as a reciprocal of a constitutional right—is the exclusive source of each and every term of the remedy. It assumes that the remedy fits the violation in the same way that a suit of clothing fits the body, with each nuance of the suit being traced to a twist in the body.

Specificity is not a fixed rule; there may be some distinct advantages to ambiguity as a technique of control. But when specificity is present, it can usually be traced to considerations of efficacy and sometimes to general

---

[99] See p. 161-63 supra.

[100] United States v. Swift & Co., 286 U.S. 106 (1932). See generally Note, Flexibility and Finality in Antitrust Consent Decrees, 80 HARV. L. REV. 1303 (1967).

[101] See e.g., Hutto v. Finney, 437 U.S. 678, 711-14 (1978) (Rehnquist, J., dissenting); A. COX, THE ROLE OF THE SUPREME COURT IN AMERICAN GOVERNMENT 97 (1976).

considerations of fairness (such as notice). It is these considerations that block the attribution of these specifics "back into" the Constitution. The rights these considerations give rise to might be thought of as instrumental or remedial rights rather than constitutional rights proper, but it is equally important to recognize that these instrumental or remedial rights are created by courts in discharge of their constitutional function. The Constitution does not say anything about reports, showers, or isolation cells; much less does it say anything about the date reports are due, the temperature of showers, or the maximum numbers of days that can be spent in an isolation cell. But it does say something about equality and humane treatment, and a court trying to give meaning to those values may find it both necessary and appropriate—as a way of bringing the organization within the bounds of the Constitution—to issue directives on these matters. The court may also find it necessary and appropriate to be quite specific in these directives, either as a way of minimizing the risk of evasion or as a way of helping the bureaucratic officers know what is expected of them.

B. The Dilemmas of Instrumentalism

The formalism of the tailoring principle fails to capture the true nature of the remedial process required for structural reform (and maybe for other types of relief as well). It is a pretense that must be abandoned. The structural remedy must be seen in instrumental terms. First, the remedy exists for and is determined by some finite purpose, protecting the constitutional value threatened; second, the remedy actually chosen is one among many ways of achieving that purpose; and third, the remedy incorporates considerations that might not be rooted in any direct and obvious way in the constitutional value that occasions the intervention. The remedy is shaped in part—in critical part—by considerations of fairness and strategy.

As an instrumental activity, structural reform will have its share of failures in the sense that the threat to the constitutional value may persist—so much is required to eliminate the threat and so little is known about organizational behavior. Failure is always possible with any instrumental activity; and as a mode of thought, instrumentalism as opposed to formalism derives its appeal largely from the fact that it recognizes the possibility of failure. What is worrisome about the instrumentalism implicit in structural reform is not the risk of failure itself, but the fact that the reform is being undertaken by a court. Even a "success" might raise questions of legitimacy because the legitimacy of the institution turns on criteria that are independent of result. Legitimacy is largely a point about institutional integrity.

Some might see the instrumentalism inherent in the remedial process as inconsistent with the dictates of formal justice, the requirement of treating similarly those who are similarly situated; it might even be thought to be at odds with the idea of a single, nationwide constitution. The subsidiary considerations that give so much specific content to the remedy might, for example, require a freedom-of-choice desegregation plan in one community, while, in another, a geographic assignment plan would be best. Similar differences may emerge in the reorganization of the prisons, hospitals, or welfare agencies in various communities. Such a varying remedial pattern has, in fact, emerged, but it does not seem to me to be objectionable, for there may well be differences between the various communities that justify the different treatment. Neither formal justice nor the ideal of a single, nationwide constitution requires that *all* communities be treated identically, but only that *similar* communities be treated alike. For me, the real problem arises not from the varying remedial pattern, but from an absence of a conceptual[102] connection between the processes that give courts their special competency and instrumental judgments.[103]

The rightful place of courts in our political system turns on the existence of public values and on the promise of those institutions—because they are independent and because they must engage in a special dialogue—to articulate and elaborate the true meaning of those values. The task of discovering the meaning of constitutional values such as equality, liberty, due process, or property is, however, quite different from choosing or fashioning the most effective strategy for actualizing those values, for eliminating the threat posed to those values by a state bureaucracy.[104] As I noted before, the judge has no special claim of competency on instrumental judgments, on means-end rationality, whether it be in the bureaucratic context or elsewhere; he may be no worse than others, and now and then be even better, but there is no general or systematic reason

---

[102] These themes plus the problem of uncertainty are developed more fully in another article of mine, *The Jurisprudence of Busing*, 39 LAW & CONTEMP. PROB. 194, 215-16 (1975).

[103] *See* Nagel, *Separation of Powers and the Scope of Federal Equitable Remedies*, 30 STAN L. REV. 661, 706-12 (1978).

[104] The competency-giving processes of the judge, dialogue and independence, have a conceptual connection to those subsidiary considerations that enter the remedial process but have a more normative character, *e.g.*, evenhandedness. The problem I perceive relates to strategic considerations, so important to the success of the remedy.

for believing he will be better. There is no likely connection between the core processes of adjudication, those that give the judge the special claim to competence, and the instrumental judgments necessarily entailed in fashioning the remedy. Sometimes the best strategy is laid in silence and by someone highly sensitive to the preferences of the body politic.[105] Why then do we entrust the remedial task to the judge?

Rights and remedies are but two phases of a single social process—of trying to give meaning to our public values. Rights operate in the realm of abstraction, remedies in the world of practical reality. A right is a particularized and authoritative declaration of meaning. It can exist without a remedy—the right to racial equality, to be free of Jim Crowism, can exist even if the court gave no relief (other than the mere declaration). The right would then exist as a standard of criticism, a standard for evaluating present social practices. A remedy, on the other hand, is an effort of the court to give meaning to a public value in practice. A remedy is more specific, more concrete, and more coercive than the mere declaration of right; it constitutes the actualization of the right.

If the purpose of the remedy is to actualize the declared right, then the remedy might be understood as subordinate to the right. Yet it is also important to recognize that the meaning of a public value is a function—a product or a consequence—of both declaration and actualization. Rights and remedies jointly constitute the meaning of the public value. The declared right may be one of "racial equality," but if the court adopts a "freedom-of-choice" plan as the mode of desegregation then the right actualized is the right to choose schools free of racial distinction (though subject to all the other restraints inherent in any process that relies on individual choice). A constitutional value such as equality derives its meaning from both spheres, declaration and actualization, and it is this tight connection between meaning and remedy, not just tradition,[106] that requires a unity of functions. It requires that the decision about remedy

---

[105] Perhaps this explains one of the most striking features of opinions in structural cases: the failure to discuss the remedy with any specificity at all. This silence is probably more a function of embarrassment than an absence of self-awareness of the factors that shaped the decree.

[106] Compare Professor Bickel's account of the remedial function, suggesting it is somehow tied to the duty of disposing of concrete controversies:

[T]he Court does not sit to make precatory pronouncements. It is not a synod of bishops, nor a collective poet laureate. It does not sit, Mr. Freund has remarked, "to compose for the anthologies." If it did, its effectiveness would be of an entirely different order; and if it did, we would not need to worry about accommodating its function to the theory and practice of democracy. The Court is an organ of govern-

be vested in the judge, the agency assigned the task of giving meaning to the value through declaration. A division of functions, a delegation of the task of actualization to another agency, necessarily creates the risk that the remedy might distort the right, and leave us with something less than the true meaning of the constitutional value. Both sources of meaning must be entrusted to the same agency to preserve the integrity of the meaning-giving enterprise itself.

If the judge's function is to give meaning to our public values, and the remedy must be understood as an integral part of that process, then we can understand—and indeed appreciate—the judge's involvement in reforming the state bureaucracy. It is a necessary incident of his broader social function. This is not, however, the end of the matter. Even though the meaning-giving process may require a unity of functions, the risk is always present that the performance of one function may interfere with the other. This, in fact, occurs in the structural context and constitutes the core dilemma. It is not that actualization and declaration are analytically incompatible, but rather that they are very often in tension. Actualization of the structural variety creates a network of relationships and outlook—a dynamic—that threatens the judge's independence and the integrity of the judicial enterprise as a whole.

To some extent this threat is tied to a peculiar characteristic of the structural remedy—it places the judge in an architectural relationship with the newly reconstituted state bureaucracy. A judge deeply involved in the reconstruction of a school system or prison is likely to lose much of his distance from the organization. He is likely to identify with the organization he is reconstructing, and this process of identification is likely to deepen as the enterprise of organizational reform moves through several cycles of supplemental relief, drawn out over a number of years. There is, however, a deeper and more pervasive threat to judicial independence, one that turns not on the peculiar reconstructive character of the structural remedy, but on the desire of the judge represented by the very attempt to give a remedy, any remedy—the desire to be efficacious.

Judges are not all-powerful. They can decree some results but not all. Some results depend on forces beyond their control. Judges can issue orders, and perhaps threaten the addressees of these orders—the officers within the hierarchy—with contempt. But the success of the actualization process depends on many other forces, less formal, less identifiable, and

---

ment. It is a court of law, which wields the power of government in disposing of concrete controversies.

A. BICKEL, THE LEAST DANGEROUS BRANCH 246-47 (1962) (footnote omitted).

perhaps even less reachable. The desegregation of a school system is vulnerable to "white flight," that is, the capacity of white parents to withdraw from the public school system altogether; the reforms of a police system may depend on the cooperation of the Police Benevolent Association; the reform of a total institution depends on preserving the intricate fabric of personal relationship between keepers and inmates; and the reform of the welfare bureaucracy—maybe of all state bureaucracies—may well depend on increased appropriations and increased revenues. In each of these instances, the judge may be able to devise strategies for inducing these forces into supporting the structural reform—judges are among the shrewdest persons I have known.[107] But the issue is not shrewdness, not the capacity of judges to devise strategies for dealing with these limiting forces, but rather the very need to devise these strategies and what the perception of this need does to their sense of independence. Judges realize that practical success vitally depends on the preferences, the will, of the body politic.

This perception of dependence has obvious and important implications for the remedy: no judge is likely to decree more than he thinks he has the power to accomplish. The remedy will be limited, and even more importantly it will be viewed in adaptive terms.[108] The judge will seek to anticipate the response of others, and though he may try to transcend the limits imposed by that response, he is likely to accept the reality of those limits and compromise his original objective in order to obtain as much relief as possible. He will bargain against the people's preferences. The remedy is, as we saw, a vitally important part of the meaning of the public value, and even if the remedy were all that were affected, all that were compromised, there would be reason to be concerned. But the truth of the matter is that the stakes are likely to be higher—the distortion will

---

[107] The two most spectacular instances that come to my mind are: the New Jersey school finance case, Robinson v. Cahill, 70 N.J. 155, 358 A.2d 457 (1976) (per curiam); see R. LEHNE, THE QUEST FOR JUSTICE 128-30 (1978); and the Alabama prison case, Pugh v. Locke, 406 F. Supp. 318 (M.D. Ala. 1976), aff'd as modified sub nom. Newman v. Alabama, 559 F.2d 283 (5th Cir. 1977), rev'd in part and remanded sub nom. Alabama v. Pugh, 438 U.S. 781 (1978) (per curiam) (on 11th amendment grounds); see N.Y. Times, Feb. 4, 1979, § 1, at 26, col. 1 (describing Judge Johnson's latest strategy).

[108] Compare Chayes, supra note 75, at 1298-302, who, adopting a consent theory of legitimacy, celebrates the so-called negotiated quality of the decree, to the point of exaggerating the consensual element in the remedial process. A structural suit can be settled at the remedial stage in the same sense that it can be at the liability stage, but neither type of settlement is consensual in the same way that a bilateral transaction might be.

be felt in the realm of rights, too.[109] Just as it is reasonable to assume that a judge wishes to be efficacious, it is also reasonable to assume that no judge is anxious to proclaim his impotence. He will strive to lessen the gap between declaration and actualization. He will tailor the right to fit the remedy.

Some measures might seem capable of preserving the independence of the judge, and thus of minimizing the threat to the judicial enterprise. In the early years, recourse was made to a rule of strict passivity in the remedial phase: the judge's role was simply to decide whether the existing arrangements were constitutional. If they were not, it was entirely the defendant's responsibility to propose steps that would remedy the situation. The judge was not to choose the remedy, nor even assume a responsibility for implementing it, but leave the remedial burden entirely on the defendant. If the defendant failed to discharge that responsibility, recourse could be made to the contempt power.

This rule left the judge in the awkward position of choosing between a heavy and frequent use of criminal contempt power or an endless series of declarations of what was unacceptable. It soon became clear—particularly through the New Orleans school crisis of the early 1960's[110]—that neither alternative would effectively desegregate the schools, produce results, and as a consequence the courts abandoned this posture of strict passivity. They began to participate actively in the fashioning of remedies. They made clear their expectations as to what would be acceptable and sometimes even fashioned the remedy itself.[111] In either instance, strategic considerations entered the judicial process: what the judges required was in part shaped by what was obtainable—it was better to have something—maybe a grade a year, maybe freedom of choice—rather than nothing at all.

Today, the most vivid expression of the dilemma created by the remedy is the creation of a new procedural institution, the special master. As we saw, the special master serves as an auxiliary spokesman in structural litigation; but he can also be used as an intermediate structure, standing,

---

[109] This point emerged in the course of discussions with the Friday luncheon group—Geoffrey Aronow, Deborah Ashford, Robert Katzmann, Joel Beckman, Martha Minow, Ann Wallwork, Gerson Zweifach. I am particularly grateful to the members of the group for that idea and many others that appear in this essay.

[110] Bush v. Orleans Parish School Bd., 204 F. Supp. 568, *supplemented*, 205 F. Supp. 893 (E. D. La.), *modified*, 308 F.2d 491 (5th Cir. 1962). *See also* R. CRAIN, THE POLITICS OF SCHOOL DESEGREGATION (1968).

[111] *See* cases cited note 2 *supra*. For a modern resurgence of the rule of deference, see White v. Weister, 412 U.S. 783 (1973) (reapportionment).

if you will, between the judge and the organization and also between the judge and the body politic.[112] The special master will assume the responsibility of both fashioning and implementing the relief, on the theory that he will become the architect of the newly reconstructed institution and that he, not the judge, is the one who will become principally dependent on the good will and cooperation of all those forces—the union, the legislature, the angry parents—needed to make the remedial process work. The special master is the judge's appointee, but the hope is that once the authority is infused, the judge will be able to stand in the background, return to his position of independence, judging rather than wheeling-and-dealing.[113]

The "success" of the special master in resolving the core dilemma is largely dependent on preserving the ambiguity of his status,[114] judge and non-judge, and that ambiguity is likely to disappear over time. The success may be more apparent than real. If the special master is not a judge, not an arm of the judge, then the use of a special master represents a division of functions, a denial of the very reason why we entrust the remedial enterprise to the judge in the first place. The special master would be but a new administrative agency, now created by the judge rather than the legislature or executive, appointed by the judge and subject to dismissal by the judge.[115] This administrative agency might be thought to stand a little closer to the courts than to the majoritarian branches than does the typical administrative agency, but heavy reliance on an agency that is truly independent of the court would still present many of the dangers to constitutionalism that would be entailed in a division of functions. On the other hand, if the special master is a judge, or a mere extension of the judge, the unity of functions would be preserved, but the special master could not shield the judge from the threats to his independence;

---

[112] G. Aronow, *supra* note 59; M. Starr, Accommodation and Accountability: A Strategy For Judicial Enforcement of Institutional Reform Decrees (1979) (unpublished manuscript on file at the Yale Law School Library and the *Harvard Law Review*).

[113] For a vivid account of the bargaining of the special master, and the judge's attempt to recover his distance, see Berger, *Away from the Court House and into the Field: The Odyssey of a Special Master*, 78 COLUM. L. REV. 707 (1978). *See also* Harris, *The Title VII Administrator: A Case Study in Judicial Flexibility*, 60 CORNELL L. REV. 53 (1974).

[114] *But cf.* Note, *"Mastering" Intervention in Prisons*, 88 YALE L.J. 1062, 1082-85 (1979) (suggesting that the multiplicity of roles, which may be essential to maintain this "ambiguity," may compromise the special master's legitimacy).

[115] For another way of synthesizing functions, this time using the already established administrative agencies, see Note, *Judicial Control of Systemic Inadequacies in Federal Administrative Enforcement*, 88 YALE L.J. 407 (1978).

the acts of the special master will be attributed to the judge. The original dilemma will remain.

The list of palliatives could be continued. It might include greater use of a multitude of judges[116] or the creation of a strong representational structure.[117] I am afraid, however, it would leave us in the same position—some independence restored, but still searching for a judge who is truly independent—knowing full well that as long as we want to use adjudication to reform practical reality, that aspiration can never be fully satisfied. Some solace might be found in the fact that the dilemma is not wholly the judge's making. The dilemma arises not just from the judge's desire to be efficacious, but from a desire to be efficacious in a world in which his power is limited and in which the critical social actors are recalcitrant, unyielding to his judgment as to the meaning of the Constitution. On this account, the social order as well as the judge is implicated in the making of the dilemma, but it does not make the dilemma any less genuine. Independence is a critical element in the process that legitimates the judicial function, for having us believe that judges can articulate and elaborate the meaning of our constitutional values, and yet, to fully discharge that function, to give that meaning a practical reality, judges are forced to surrender some of their independence.

At this point one might be tempted to turn back in despair, renounce the adjudicative enterprise altogether, or escape to the formalism represented by the tailoring principle. These alternatives must be resisted at all costs: they deny an important social function, the meaning-giving enterprise implicit in constitutionalism itself, or, in the case of the tailoring principle, distort the nature of an important facet of this enterprise. Alternatively, we could confine the judge to the declarations of rights, and insist that he abandon his desire to be efficacious. That would resolve the core dilemma, and yet it would require a detachment or an indifference to this world that does not seem to me either to be a virtue or a mode of behavior that is within the reach of most American judges. The desire to be efficacious need not be seen as an assertion of will, but as a willingness of the judge to assume responsibility for practical reality and its consonance with the Constitution.

The 1960's were an extraordinary period in the history of the judiciary in America, and among its many lessons, that era suggests the possibility

---

[116] Lessons may be found in the obligation to use a different judge in cases of direct contempt. See Taylor v. Hayes, 418 U.S. 488 (1974); Mayberry v. Pennsylvania, 400 U.S. 455 (1971).

[117] See George, *The Case for Multiple Advocacy in Making Foreign Policy*, 66 AM. POL. SCI. REV. 751 (1972).

of still another alternative: to live with the dilemma. The judge might be seen as forever straddling two worlds, the world of the ideal and the world of the practical, the world of the public value and the world of subjective preference, the world of the Constitution and the world of politics. He derives his legitimacy from only one, but necessarily finds himself in the other. He among all the agencies of government is in the best position to discover the true meaning of our constitutional values, but, at the same time, he is deeply constrained, indeed sometimes even compromised, by his desire—his wholly admirable desire—to give that meaning a reality.

III

FREE SPEECH AND SOCIAL STRUCTURE[1]

There are several major themes in Owen Fiss's work. As I have already discussed, in *Groups and the Equal Protection Clause*,[2] Fiss introduced his ideas about the social reality and autonomy of groups and the relationship of groups to the interpretation of the Equal Protection Clause. In Fiss's view, the Equal Protection Clause "recognizes the existence and importance of groups, not just individuals."[3]

Fiss has devoted much of his intellectual energy to the question of the judiciary's role—particularly the federal judiciary—in pursuing equality for African-Americans. One aspect of his scholarship includes his development of equality theory and its impact on doctrine. The second aspect of his scholarship, as evidenced in *The Forms of Justice*,[4] centers on the jurisprudential and remedial role of judges in the determination of public values.[5] Indeed, Fiss's equality theory is clearly influenced by his conception of the judiciary's role in determining the content of public values. His theory of democratic legitimacy requires judicial protection and elaboration of constitutional values and, of course, the elimination of slavery's legacy.

Another important strand of his scholarship concerns free speech—the First Amendment. Fiss's engagement with the First Amendment started in the late 1960s, when he began teaching at the University of Chicago Law School. It was there that Fiss had the opportunity to develop a close relationship with one of the leading—if not the leading—figures in

---

[1] Owen M. Fiss, *Free Speech and Social Structure*, 71 IOWA L. REV. 1405 (1986).

[2] Owen M. Fiss, *Groups and the Equal Protection Clause*, 5 PHIL. & PUB AFF. 107 (1976).

[3] *Id.* at 136.

[4] Owen M. Fiss, *The Supreme Court, 1978 Term—Foreword: The Forms of Justice*, 93 HARV L. REV. (1997).

[5] *See also*, OWEN M. FISS, THE CIVIL RIGHTS INJUNCTION (1978).

the field, Harry Kalven, Jr. The relationship was an extraordinary one. It was personal as well as intellectual. It was a teacher and apprentice relationship, with Kalven as the teacher and Fiss as the apprentice.[6] According to Fiss, the teacher's method of instruction was conversation. Fiss and Kalven spent an incredible amount of their time together walking around Hyde Park (the area around the University of Chicago), talking about free speech and the special attraction that Kalven felt for the First Amendment. This was one of the most amazing experiences of Fiss's life. Fiss thought of Kalven as a genius, "a completely original intelligence— probably one of the few the law has ever known."[7] The conversations led to profound insights for Fiss, and as one would expect from this kind of relationship, the wonder and attraction Kalven felt towards the First Amendment rubbed off on Fiss.

In the fall of 1974, Kalven died and left as part of his legacy a very long manuscript—over a thousand pages—on the American Constitutional experience under the First Amendment.[8] Kalven's son, Jamie Kalven, then decided to begin the monumental task of editing and readying the manuscript for publication. At this point, Fiss's life—both his scholarly and personal life—became even more complicated. Jamie Kalven was not a lawyer. He definitely needed substantive help and emotional support in working on the manuscript. Fiss volunteered to help. I believe this was a commitment made not simply because of the intellectual interest it held for Fiss, but even more significantly, because of the personal bond he felt for Harry Kalven, Jr. Incredible as it may seem, for the next fourteen years or so, Fiss worked intimately with Jamie Kalven on this monumental project.[9] The process of editing was an exhausting, excruciatingly difficult, but nevertheless energizing task.

The manuscript was, in at least two respects, somewhat of an unusual first draft. There were approximately 600 margin notes scattered throughout the manuscript. Many of the notes were long commentaries; some were as short as a question mark. Many of the notes suggested revisions or additions and often raised extremely difficult substantive concerns.

---

[6] *See* Owen M. Fiss, *Kalven's Way*, 43 U. CHI. L. REV. 1, 4 (1975).

[7] *Id.*

[8] Kalven started working on the manuscript in 1970, but the First Amendment was a career long interest for him. To Kalven, the First Amendment had a "charisma" that set it apart from other rules of law. This is, of course, the "attraction" for free speech that he bequeathed to Fiss. *See* Jamie Kalvin, *Introduction*, to HARRY KALVEN, JR., A WORTHY TRADITION xii (1988).

[9] *See id.* at xiii. This was an incredible commitment by Fiss.

The manuscript was also unusual because of its close relationship to Kalven's teaching notes and published works. The manuscript was Kalven's culmination of decades of teaching and writing about First Amendment concerns. The manuscript was surrounded by scores of articles and books, almost 1,200 pages of handwritten notes, and in addition, his extensive teaching notes, augmented by several of Kalven's 1974 students' class notes.

The process of editing was done chapter-by-chapter. It had several phases.[10] Jamie Kalven would first prepare a clean but lightly edited draft. He would then attempt to determine what Harry Kalven, Jr.'s intentions were beyond the draft. This required him to look at and follow the marginal notes, wherever they may lead. The next step was to read the draft against the relevant cases and against Harry Kalven, Jr.'s published works, and unpublished notes. It was a case of "reading him against himself."[11]

After this painstaking research, Jamie Kalven would prepare a memorandum which addressed the problems and possibilities of the previously edited draft. Once he prepared the draft of the chapter and the memorandum, he would travel from Chicago to New Haven—Fiss had moved to Yale in 1974—to discuss them with Fiss. Fiss would read the edited draft against the original, and the original and the memorandum against the draft. He would then respond to the points Jamie Kalven made in the draft and he would also make independent suggestions. After this long and intense discussion, often lasting several days, Jamie Kalven would write another draft incorporating the revisions and the additions that he and Fiss had agreed to in their discussion. Jamie Kalven would also write another memorandum which would create an agenda for another discussion with Fiss and an outline for another draft of the chapter. Fiss and Kalven went through this process at least twice for each chapter. This continued for over fourteen years.[12]

In 1986, when this project was almost completed, Fiss engaged the First Amendment itself, and began teaching and writing in the field. As he started working in this field however, he found, much to his surprise, that he felt uncomfortable with Harry Kalven, Jr.'s celebratory mood toward

---

[10] Telephone Interview with Owen M. Fiss, Sterling Professor, Yale Law School (Aug. 8, 2007).

[11] Jamie Kalvin, *Afterword*, to Harry Kalven, Jr., A Worthy Tradition 594 (1988).

[12] It is difficult to imagine many, if any, other scholars who would have devoted so much time and effort to this kind of a project, especially since Fiss was not getting a publication credit out of this incredible project.

the then prevailing body of doctrine on free speech as evidenced by the title—*The Worthy Tradition*—and contents of his book. Fiss was confused as to why he felt so different than Kalven about the First Amendment case law and its received tradition. Part of the reason, Fiss thought, had to do with the nature of their personalities. Kalven had a very upbeat personality and always saw the best in everything. The other major reason for their different perceptions about the First Amendment tradition, however, was that Kalven premised his analysis on what Fiss thought of as an outmoded paradigm—the street corner speaker. Fiss concluded that this paradigm no longer captured social reality and, therefore, was no longer the proper paradigm to understand the First Amendment.

In 1986, in *Free Speech and Social Structure*, published in the *Iowa Law Review*, Owen Fiss announced the imminent publication of Kalven's *A Worthy Tradition: Freedom of Speech in America*[13] and declared that the "Worthy Tradition" that Kalven identified "is flawed in some important respects."[14] His concerns, he wrote, "first arose in the seventies—one of the few periods when America wondered out loud whether capitalism and democracy were compatible."[15]

Fiss traced his recent concerns with the compatibility of capitalism and democracy to events around Watergate that led to the resignation of President Richard Nixon. While the precipitating event was the break-in at the Democratic National Headquarters, by the time the impeachment process had finished, it became clear how thoroughly economic power had begun to corrupt our political system. Congress responded by passing the Campaign Reform Act of 1974.[16]

A second major influence on Fiss's concern with the compatibility of capitalism and democracy came from the academy with the publication of Charles Lindblom's book *Politics and Markets*.[17] In this book, Lindblom tries to demonstrate that, contrary to classical democratic theory, politics was not an autonomous sphere of activity. Rather, it was shaped and controlled by the dominant economic interests. As a result of what he referred to as "circularity," the "grand issues"—the most important issues of economic and social structure—remained at the margins of poli-

---

[13] HARRY KALVEN, JR., A WORTHY TRADITION: FREEDOM OF SPEECH IN AMERICA (Jamie Kalven ed., 1988).

[14] Fiss, *supra* note 1, at 1406.

[15] *Id.*

[16] Federal Election Campaign Act, Amendments of 1974, Pub. L. No. 93-443, 88 Stat. 1263 (1974).

[17] CHARLES E. LINDBLOM, POLITICS AND MARKETS: THE WORLD'S POLITICAL ECONOMIC SYSTEMS (1977).

tics. Lindblom argued that because of the control exercised by corporate interests over the political agenda, voters were not able to consider the truly important issues, such as the continued viability of capitalism, the failures of market distribution, or the existing structure within which organized labor was allowed to function.

The final influence on Fiss was the then recent First Amendment decisions in which, as he puts it, "the Supreme Court was faced with a number of cases that required it to examine the relationship of political and economic power."[18] The cases included challenges to the fairness doctrine, in which the issue was whether it was permissible for a state to extend the fairness doctrine to the print media,[19] and whether the Federal Communications Commission (FCC) was required to provide critics of the Vietnam War access to television networks.[20] Other cases attacked campaign reform legislation. These cases included attacks on the Campaign Reform Act of 1974,[21] and a challenge to a Massachusetts statute limiting corporate expenditures in a referendum on the income tax.[22] Finally, political activists who sought access to private shopping centers to get their message across because they lacked funds to purchase space or time in the media turned to the courts for this purpose.[23]

These cases presented the Supreme Court with what Fiss considered to be some of the most difficult of all First Amendment issues. That meant, of course, that it was entirely reasonable within the precedents for the Supreme Court to be divided and for the Justices to see each of the cases differently. What literally surprised Fiss, however, was the pattern of decisions. Capitalism almost always won over democracy![24]

Fiss's "first inclination" was to see these decisions as "involving a conflict between liberty and equality."[25] He saw it as another part of the

---

[18] Fiss, *supra* note 1, at 1406.

[19] Miami Herald Publ'g Co. v. Tornillo, 418 U.S. 241 (1974).

[20] Columbia Broad. Sys. v. Democratic Nat'l Comm., 412 U.S. 94 (1975).

[21] Buckley v. Valeo, 424 U.S. 1 (1976).

[22] First Nat'l Bank of Boston v. Bellotti, 435 U.S. 765 (1978).

[23] Prune Yard Shopping Ctr. v. Robins, 447 U.S. 74 (1980).

[24] For example, the court struck down a statute that granted access to the print media to those who wished to present differing views (Miami Herald Publ'g Co v. Tornillo, 418 U.S. 241 (1974)); found that the FCC was not required to grant access to the electronic media for editorial advertisements (Columbia Broad. Sys. v. Democratic Nat'l Comm., 412 U.S. 94 (1975)); held that the political expenditures for the wealthy could not be limited (Buckley v. Valeo, 424 U.S. 1 (1976)); and decided that the owners of large shopping centers and malls did not have to provide access to pamphleteers (Lloyd Corp. v. Tanner, 407 U.S. 551 (1972)).

[25] Fiss, *supra* note 1, at 1407.

ongoing struggle between the Warren and Burger Courts. The decisions of the seventies, he believed, were part of the Burger Court's program "to bring an end to the egalitarian crusade of the Warren Court. The idea was that in these free speech cases, as in *Rodriguez*,[26] the Burger Court was not willing to empower the poor or less advantaged if that meant sacrificing the liberty of anyone."[27] But he concluded that, on reflection, the problem was deeper and more complicated. It was not a conflict between equality and liberty, but a conflict between two conceptions of liberty. It was a battle not just between the First Amendment and the equal protection clause, but a battle between two notions of liberty within the First Amendment itself.

One conception of liberty sees freedom of speech as protecting the individual interest in self-expression or the right of the individual to say whatever he wishes. The state is viewed as the main threat against which the individual must be protected. Another conception of liberty understands freedom of speech in broader social terms. Those who advance this conception of liberty argue that the role of the First Amendment is to protect the fullness and openness of public debate. People must have the opportunity to be aware of all the issues and arguments on both sides of any particular question. Freedom of speech is, in this view, a public right. It is an instrument of collective self-determination. While the state may interfere with public debate, one who holds this view of free speech can imagine the state acting in a way that actually furthers the robustness of public debate and thereby the cause of freedom. Stated otherwise, Fiss argues that the state can sometimes be seen as a friend of free speech, not only as an enemy.

Fiss concluded that the Court in these First Amendment cases of the 1970s, was not advancing a false conception of liberty. It was instead working within the tradition of free speech. This perception convinced him of the inadequacies—indeed serious flaws—of the tradition itself. The street corner paradigm was no longer the proper one to understand the First Amendment. In Fiss's view, a body of doctrine that did no more than protect the street corner speaker from the state (the police) would neither fulfill the values served by the First Amendment nor protect them. This realization led him to suggest a new free speech paradigm. He proposed that we shift the organizing free speech paradigm from the street corner to CBS.

---

[26] San Antonio Indep. Sch. Dist. v. Rodriguez, 411 U.S. 1 (1973).

[27] Fiss, *supra* note 1, at 1407.

By looking at free speech issues from the CBS vantage point, Fiss concluded that it would then be possible to better understand the crucial factors that were shaping the public discourse of the 1970s. These factors were, of course, the scarcity of channels of communication and the high cost of speech. Fiss argued that the CBS paradigm would allow us to see how the present lines between the state and private sphere or between the speaker and the censor had to be reformulated and redrafted.

Under the tradition celebrated by Kalven, freedom of speech amounts to a protection of autonomy. The idea is that the concept of free speech acts as a shield to protect the speaker. Moreover, in this view, the purpose of free speech is not individual self-actualization but instead the preservation of democracy. It is meant to protect the right of the people, as a people, to decide what kind of life it wishes to live. Autonomy is protected as a means of collective self-determination. Free speech is supposed to allow people to have all the relevant information so they can make informed choices about important issues. It gives people the information they need to vote intelligently. The idea behind the autonomy principle is that it will enrich public debate. Fiss claims that from the perspective of the CBS paradigm, this idea becomes highly problematic.

Fiss argues that contemporary social structure is as much an enemy of free speech as is the policeman. The First Amendment, he argues, requires a change in our attitude about the state. As he states: "We should learn to recognize the state not only as an enemy, but also as a friend of speech. . . ."[28] The duty of the state under the First Amendment is to preserve the integrity of public debate and thus to safeguard the conditions for collective self-determination. The state must act to correct the skewing of the social structure. It must even intervene by regulating the content of speech so that all voices are heard by the people. In order to serve the ultimate purpose of the First Amendment, the state will have "to restrict the speech of some elements of our society in order to enhance the relative voice of others. . . ."[29] Indeed, Fiss argues, "unless the court allows and sometimes even requires the state to do so, we as a people will never truly be free."[30]

Two of the most prominent themes that resonate in Fiss's body of scholarship are reflected in this and his other articles on the First Amendment—the importance of an activist state to a democracy and the role of the judiciary as a significant part of state activism. In several

---

[28] *Id.* at 1416.

[29] Fiss, *supra* note 1, at 1425.

[30] *Id.*

of his writings,[31] Fiss justifies the need for an activist state by discussing and analyzing the democratic value of the First Amendment guarantee of free speech and the role of the state in furthering these free speech values. Fiss's argument, however, is not limited to free speech issues, but is meant instead to illuminate the broader issue of the role of the state in general. He employs the free speech debate as an important example of the state's and the judiciary's roles in a constitutional democracy.

To Fiss, the Constitution is not a document that "distributes to future generations pieces of property in the form of rights."[32] Instead, it is a charter of governance that establishes democratic governmental institutions and sets forth in the Bill of Rights the principles and values that are to control these institutions. Freedom of speech is one of the most essential rights in a democracy. The adjudicative process is one of the major methods of transforming these rather abstract ideals, such as freedom of speech, into concrete rights. The role of the judge is to give meaning to our public values. Indeed, in Fiss's view, the adjudicative process plays an integral role in determining the quality of our social existence.

Fiss argues that the First Amendment guarantee of freedom of speech can be understood in two ways. It can be seen as a limit on state action. This is reflected, of course, in Kalven's vision of the Free Speech Tradition. In that sense, it places a value on the autonomy of the citizen. Autonomy furthers public debate by allowing the individual to say what he wishes, free from state interference. Autonomy furthers public debate, however, only when power is equally distributed in society so that all voices have an equal chance to be heard.

Freedom of speech can also be viewed as a means of achieving a larger political purpose—the production of the "uninhibited, robust, and wide-open"[33] public debate that is an essential condition for democratic government. The public debate principle, however, does not create a presumption against state interference. As under the autonomy principle, action is not judged by whether it interferes with the autonomy of some individual or institution. Instead, action is now judged by its impact on public debate.

These two views of freedom of speech should work hand-in-hand. Ensuring the autonomy of the individual should be the means of bringing

---

[31] *See, e.g.,* OWEN M. FISS, THE IRONY OF FREE SPEECH (1996); Owen M. Fiss, *The Idea of Political Freedom, in* LOOKING BACK AT LAW'S CENTURY 35 (Austin Sarat et al. eds., 2002); Owen M. Fiss, *Free Speech and Social Structure,* 71 IOWA L. REV. 1405 (1986); Owen M. Fiss, *Why the State?,* 100 HARV. L. REV. 781 (1987).

[32] Fiss, *supra* note 31, at 783.

[33] N.Y. Times Co. v. Sullivan, 376 U.S. 254, 270 (1964).

that public debate into being. It is this linkage between autonomy and democracy that accounts for the favored position of free speech in the Constitution as well as the rule against content regulation in First Amendment jurisprudence. The goal is robust public debate, and autonomy is the means to that goal.

In ancient Greece, and perhaps in early America, where the dominant social unit was the individual and power was distributed somewhat equally, this vision of autonomy might well have enhanced public debate and thus promoted democracy. "But in modern society, characterized by grossly unequal distributions of power and a limited capacity of people to learn all that they must to function effectively as citizens, this assumption appears more problematic."[34] The problem is basic. Today, public debate occurs on national television, radio, the press, and on the internet. Effective public debate no longer takes place on street corners or in coffee houses. To participate in this discussion, one must have access to these national outlets, which are owned by private individuals who respond to market forces and pay little attention to the democratic needs of the society. The question then becomes whether the market, even one that is working perfectly, is the appropriate vehicle to ensure the proper working of democracy

Fiss says it is not. He offers several reasons. Because the market privileges select groups, the opinions of those who have the capital to own a television station, newspaper, or radio station will almost certainly be aired. In addition, those groups that determine advertising budgets and those groups that respond to that advertising certainly will be favored. These groups might constitute a significant portion of the electorate, but they are not coextensive with the electorate. In Fiss's view, "[t]o be a consumer, even a sovereign one, is not to be a citizen."[35] Moreover, the market also influences the content of the speech. The newspaper or television station has to remain in business, and so it must show a profit. This profit consideration will in large part determine which shows are aired and which stories are printed. A perfectly competitive market will produce stories or shows "whose marginal cost equals marginal revenue."[36] People are more likely to watch reruns of old sitcoms and not as likely to watch documentaries or public interest shows. Showing reruns is thus a profitable and efficient use of resources. In that event, of course, commercial television will provide reruns of sitcoms. As Fiss

---

[34] Fiss, *supra* note 31, at 786.

[35] *Id.* at 787.

[36] *Id.* at 788.

makes clear, "there is no necessary, or even probabilistic, relationship between making a profit (or allocating resources efficiently) and supplying the electorate with the information they need to make free and intelligent choices about government policy, the structure of government, or the nature of society."[37]

What is needed, Fiss argues, is for the state to act as the corrective for the market. "The state must put on the agenda issues that are systematically ignored and slighted and allow us to hear voices and viewpoints that would otherwise be silenced or muffled."[38] To put it another way, the state must pass out microphones so that excluded voices may be heard. Democracy requires it.

As Fiss acknowledges, there are serious problems with this approach. The state has no monopoly on virtue. There is certainly the risk that the state might prove self-serving in this regard, selecting only the views that are consistent with the state's position. Nevertheless, as Fiss argues, there are significant checks on state power. The private media almost certainly will attempt to provide an alternative voice. It well may be, however, that the state is the only institution powerful enough and thus capable of resisting the pressures of the marketplace.

Another potential problem with Fiss's argument is the danger of circularity.[39] For example, in our constitutional history, one of the major state functions was to regulate business, but there was good reason to believe that business actually governed the state. Nevertheless, Fiss argues that this problem is overblown. It should be remembered that the state was the agent for effective social change during the Civil Rights Movement, and this experience leads Fiss to believe that the "elements of independence possessed by the state are real and substantial."[40] This independence may not be complete, but it is nonetheless sufficient to make the theory of countervailing power viable. The judiciary also has a role to play in evaluating the intervention of the state to avoid the problem of circularity. Indeed, Fiss's view relies heavily on the courts to carry the burden of ensuring rich public debate.

Even though there may be serious problems with Fiss's views, his approach has one great virtue. The state is accountable to the citizenry; the market is not. When the state fails to provide the conditions neces-

---

[37] Id.

[38] Id.

[39] See Charles E. LINDBLOM, POLITICS AND MARKETS: THE WORLD'S POLITICAL-ECONOMIC SYSTEMS 201-21 (1977).

[40] Fiss, supra note 31, at 791.

sary for democracy, the people can vote in new leaders. When the market fails, however, there is little or no recourse.

Fiss's First Amendment theories have not been accepted either by the courts or by scholars. Robert Post, for example, one of Fiss's former students and most recognized critics, criticizes such "collectivist" political speech theories for assuming that there is some proper conception of good political discourse outside of political debate itself.[41] In several of his articles, Post argues that the primary value of free speech is to protect autonomy. To Post, autonomy is vital to collective self-determination because it resolves the conflict between individual and collective autonomy. It binds the individual to the collective. Without the interplay between collective and individual autonomy, the individual is alienated from the group, thereby defeating a primary goal of democracy. The state's function is not to determine who can and cannot be part of the collective autonomy. In addition, in Post's view, the autonomy theory better explains certain aspects of First Amendment Jurisprudence than the public debate theory. For example, the public debate theory fails to address adequately the question of commercial speech. Finally, Post argues that Fiss's arguments make little sense without full acceptance of the autonomy theory. Airing every argument would not, in fact, enrich public debate, but would confuse it by giving legitimacy to every silly theory. Post argues that autonomy is the only theory that justifies giving equal opportunity to individuals to participate in public discourse. This is because by doing so, individuals are treated with equal respect and are also bound to the collective.[42]

Several years after the publication of *Free Speech and Social Structure*, Fiss himself questioned whether the CBS paradigm was already obsolete as an organizing paradigm to understand the First Amendment. The new technological revolution that was then fully underway may have made the CBS paradigm rather quaint.[43] The revolution "is nothing less than a redefinition of the way we read and write, the way we talk to and correspond with one another, how we entertain and educate ourselves, how we resolve our conflicts—how we form friendships and communities, and how we perform our role as citizens."[44] What the new First Amendment

---

[41] *See* Robert Post, Constitutional Domains: Democracy, Community, Management (1995).

[42] *See* Robert Post, *Equality and Autonomy in First Amendment Jurisprudence*, 95 Mich. L. Rev. 1517 (1997).

[43] *See* Owen M. Fiss, *In Search of a New Paradigm*, 104 Yale L. Rev. 1613 (1995).

[44] *Id.* at 1614.

paradigm that better fits present social reality may be, however, remains open to question. But as Fiss constantly reminds us, the role of the state in protecting free speech is "full of irony and contradiction."[45] The state can be conceived as "both an enemy and a friend" of speech; it can do terrible things to undermine democracy but some wonderful things to enhance it as well.[46]

---

[45] OWEN M. FISS, THE IRONY OF FREE SPEECH 83 (1996).

[46] Id.

FREE SPEECH AND SOCIAL STRUCTURE*

Freedom of speech is one of the most remarkable and celebrated aspects of American constitutional law. It helps define who we are as a nation. The principle is rooted in the text of the Constitution itself, but it has been the decisions of the Supreme Court over the last half century or so that have, in my view, nurtured that principle, given it much of its present shape, and accounts for much of its energy and sweep. These decisions have given rise to what Harry Kalven has called a Free Speech Tradition.

In speaking of a Tradition, Kalven, and before him, Llewellyn[1] and T. S. Eliot[2] (talking about the shoulders of giants), aspire to an all-embracing perspective. Everything is included—nothing is left out, not the dissents, not even the decisions overruled. Every encounter between the Court and the first amendment is included. There is, however, a shape or direction or point to the Tradition. It is not an encyclopedia or dictionary, but more in the nature of a shared understanding. Those who speak of a Free Speech Tradition try to see all the decisions and to abstract from them an understanding of what free speech means—what lies at the core and what at the periphery, what lies beyond the protection of the first amendment and what is included, where the law is headed, etc. The whole has a shape. The shape is not fixed for all time, since each new decision or opinion is included within the Tradition and thus contributes to refiguring the meaning of the whole, but the Tradition also acts as a constraining force on present and future decisions. The Tradition is the background against which every judge writes. It defines the issues; provides the resources by which the judge can confront those issues; and also creates the obstacles that must be surmounted. It orients the judge.

---

* Owen M. Fiss, Free Speech and Social Structure, 71 Iowa L. Rev. 1405 (1986). This article uses the footnote numbers and citation form of this particular publication.

[1] K. Llewellyn, The Common Law Tradition: Deciding Appeals (1960).

[2] Eliot, *Tradition and the Individual Talent*, in Selected Prose Of T.S. Eliot 37 (1975) (first published 1919).

I believe it is useful to view the free speech decisions of the Supreme Court as a Tradition, and I am also tempted to celebrate that Tradition in much the way that Kalven does. The title of his (still unpublished) manuscript is *A Worthy Tradition*.[3] But for me that is only half the story. It also seems to me that the Tradition is flawed in some important respects—so much so that it might be necessary to begin again (if that is even possible).

My concerns first arose in the seventies—one of the few periods when America wondered out loud whether capitalism and democracy were compatible. In the political world these doubts were linked to Watergate and the eventual resignation of President Richard Nixon. The precipitating event was the break-in at the Democratic National Headquarters, but by the time the impeachment process had run its course, we realized how thoroughly economic power had begun to corrupt our politics. Congress responded with the Campaign Reform Act of 1974,[4] imposing limits on contributions and expenditures and establishing a scheme for the public funding of elections. The tension between capitalism and democracy was also a special subject of concern to the academy, as evidenced by the excitement and controversy generated by the publication in 1977 of Charles Edward Lindblom's book *Politics and Markets*.[5] Lindblom tried to show that, contrary to classical democratic theory, politics was not an autonomous sphere of activity, but was indeed shaped and controlled by the dominant economic interests. As a consequence of this 'circularity,' the most important issues of economic and social structure—what Lindblom called the 'grand issues'—remained at the margins of politics. Voters were not actually considering the continued viability of capitalism, the justness of market distributions, or the structure within which organized labor was allowed to act, because, Lindblom hypothesized, of the control exercised by corporate interests over the political agenda.[6]

While academics were reading and debating Lindblom's book, and while politicians were trying to make sense of Watergate, the Supreme Court was faced with a number of cases that required it to examine the relationship of political and economic power. The Court was asked

---

[3] The manuscript is in possession of Jamie Kalven and myself, and will appear in print by 1987.

[4] Federal Election Campaign Act Amendments of 1974, Pub. L. No. 93-443, 88 Stat. 1263 (codified at 2 U.S.C. §§ 431-434, 437-439, 453, 455, 5 U.S.C. §§ 1501-1503, 26 U.S.C. §§ 2766, 6012, 9001-9012, 9031-9042 (1982)).

[5] C.E. LINDBLOM, POLITICS AND MARKETS: THE WORLD'S POLITICAL-ECONOMIC SYSTEMS (1977).

[6] *Id.* at 201-21.

whether it was permissible for a state to extend the fairness doctrine to the print media,[7] and whether the FCC was obliged to provide critics of our efforts in Vietnam access to the TV networks.[8] In another case the Campaign Reform Act of 1974 was attacked;[9] and in still another a challenge was raised to a Massachusetts statute limiting corporate expenditures in a referendum on the income tax.[10] Political activities, lacking funds to purchase space or time in the media, sought access to the shopping centers to get their message across to the public, and they also turned to the courts for this purpose.[11] Admittedly, issues of this character had been presented to the Court before, but in the seventies they arose with greater frequency and urgency, and they seemed to dominate the Court's first amendment docket.

These cases presented the Court with extremely difficult issues, perhaps the most difficult of all first amendment issues, and thus one would fairly predict divisions. One could also predict some false turns. What startled me, however, was the pattern of decisions: Capitalism almost always won. The Court decided that a statute that granted access to the print media to those who wished to present differing views was invalid; that the FCC did not have to grant access to the electronic media for editorial advertisements; that the political expenditures of the wealthy could not be curbed; and that the owners of the large shopping centers and malls that constitute the civic centers of suburban America need not provide access to pamphleteers. Democracy promises collective self-determination—a freedom to the people to decide their own fate—and presupposes a debate on public issues that is (to use Justice Brennan's now classic formula) 'uninhibited, robust, and wide-open.'[12] The free speech decisions of the seventies, however, seemed to impoverish, rather than enrich public debate and thus threatened one of the essential preconditions for an effective democracy. And they seemed to do so in a rather systematic way.

My first inclination was to see these decisions as embodying a conflict between liberty and equality—as another phase in the struggle between the Warren and Burger Courts. I saw the decisions of the seventies as part of the program of the Court largely (and now, it seems, ironically)

---

[7] Miami Herald Publishing Co. v. Tornillo, 418 U.S. 241 (1974).

[8] Columbia Broadcasting Sys. v. Democratic Nat'l Comm., 412 U.S. 94 (1973).

[9] Buckley v. Valeo, 424 U.S. 1 (1976).

[10] First Nat'l Bank of Boston v. Bellotti, 435 U.S. 765 (1978).

[11] Lloyd Corp. v. Tanner, 407 U.S. 551 (1972).

[12] New York Times Co. v. Sullivan, 376 U.S. 254, 270 (1964).

constituted by Nixon to establish a new priority for liberty and to bring an end to the egalitarian crusade of the Warren Court. The idea was that in these free speech cases, as in *Rodriguez*,[13] the Burger Court was not willing to empower the poor or less advantaged if that meant sacrificing the liberty of anyone. On reflection, however, the problem seemed deeper and more complicated. I saw that at issue was not simply a conflict between equality and liberty, but also and more importantly, a conflict between two conceptions of liberty. The battle being fought was not just Liberty v. Equality, but Liberty v. Liberty, or to put the point another way, not just between the first amendment and the equal protection clause, but a battle *within* the first amendment itself. I also came to understand that the Court was not advancing an idiosyncratic or perverted conception of liberty, but was in fact working well within the Free Speech Tradition. The Court was not crudely substituting entrepreneurial liberty (or property) for political liberty;[14] the rich or owners of capital in fact won, but only because they had advanced claims of political liberty that easily fit within the received Tradition. Money is speech—just as much as picketing is.

In time I became convinced that the difficulties the Court encountered in the free speech cases of the seventies could ultimately be traced to inadequacies in the Free Speech Tradition itself. The problem was the Tradition not the Court. The Tradition did not *compel* the results—as though any body of precedent could. Arguably, there was room for a nimble and determined craftsman working within the Tradition to come out differently in one or two of these cases, or maybe in all of them. But, on balance, it seemed that the Tradition oriented the Justices in the wrong direction and provided ample basis for those who formed the majority to claim, quite genuinely, that they were protecting free speech when, in fact, they were doing something of a different, far more ambiguous, character. This meant that criticism would have to be directed not simply at the Burger Court but at something larger: at a powerfully entrenched, but finally inadequate body of doctrine.

I

For the most part, the Free Speech Tradition can be understood as a protection of the street corner speaker. An individual mounts a soapbox on a corner in some large city, starts to criticize governmental policy, and

---

[13] San Antonio Indep. School Dist. v. Rodriguez, 411 U.S. 1 (1973).

[14] *But see* Dorsen & Gora, *Free Speech, Property, and the Burger Court: Old Values, New Balances*, 1982 SUP. CT. REV. 195.

then is arrested for breach of the peace. In this setting the first amendment is conceived of as a shield, as a means of protecting the individual speaker from being silenced by the state.

First amendment litigation first began to occupy the Supreme Court's attention during World War I, a time when the constitutional shield was rather weak. The street corner speaker could be arrested on the slightest provocation. Those early decisions were openly criticized, most notably in the dissents of Brandeis and Holmes, but that criticism—eloquent and at times heroic—stayed within the established framework and sought only to expand the frontiers of freedom incrementally; it sought to place more restrictions on the policeman and to give more and more protection to the street corner speaker. In this incremental quality, the criticism took on the character of the progressive movement in general, and also shared its fate. The progressive critique achieved its first successes during the thirties, at the hands of the Hughes Court, but its final vindication awaited the Warren Court: It was only then that the shield around the speaker became worthy of a democracy.

What largely emerged from this historical process is a rule against content regulation—it now stands as the cornerstone of the Free Speech Tradition. The policeman cannot arrest the speaker just because he does not like what is being said. Time, place, and manner regulations are permitted—the speaker must not stand in the middle of the roadway—but the intervention must not be based on the content of the speech, or a desire to favor one set of ideas over another. To be sure, the Court has allowed the policeman to intervene in certain circumstances on the basis of content, as when the speaker is about to incite a mob. But even then the Court has sought to make certain that the policeman intervenes only at the last possible moment, that is, before the mob is unleashed. In fact, for most of this century first amendment scholarship has largely consisted of a debate over the clear and present danger test, and the so-called incitement test, in an effort to find a verbal formula that best identifies the last possible moment.[15] The common assumption of all those who participated in that debate—finally made explicit in the 1969 decision of *Brandenburg v. Ohio*,[16] perhaps the culmination of these debates and in many respects the final utterance of the Warren Court on this subject—is that the policeman should not step in when the speaker

---

[15] *See, e.g.*, Gunther, *Learned Hand and the Origins of Modern First Amendment Doctrine: Some Fragments of History*, 27 STAN. L. REV. 719 (1975); Kalven, *Professor Ernst Freund and* Debs v. United States, 40 U. CHI. L. REV. 235 (1973).

[16] 395 U.S. 444 (1969).

is only engaged in the general expression of ideas, however unpopular those ideas may be.[17]

I would be the first to acknowledge that there has been something noble and inspiring about the fifty year journey from *Schenck*[18] in 1919 to *Brandenburg* in 1969. A body of doctrine that fully protects the street corner speaker is of course an accomplishment of some note; the battles to secure that protection were hard fought and their outcome was far from certain. *Brandenburg* is one of the blessings of our liberty. The problem, however, is that today there are no street corners, and the doctrinal edifice that seems to someone like Kalven so glorious when we have the street corner speaker in mind is largely unresponsive to the conditions of modern society.

Under the Tradition extolled by Kalven, the freedom of speech guaranteed by the first amendment amounts to a protection of autonomy—it is the shield around the speaker. The theory that animates this protection, and that inspired Kalven,[19] and before him Meiklejohn,[20] and that now dominates the field,[21] casts the underlying purpose of the first amendment in social or political terms: The purpose of free speech is not individual self-actualization, but rather the preservation of democracy, and the right of a people, as a people, to decide what kind of life it wishes to live. Autonomy is protected not because of its intrinsic value, as a Kantian might insist, but rather as a means or instrument of collective self-determination. We allow people to speak so others can vote. Speech allows people to vote intelligently and freely, aware of all the options and in possession of all the relevant information.

The crucial assumption in this theory is that the protection of autonomy will produce a public debate that will be, to use the talismanic phrase once again, 'uninhibited, robust, and wide-open.' The Tradition assumes that by leaving individuals alone, free from the menacing arm of the policeman, a full and fair consideration of all the issues will emerge. The premise is that autonomy will lead to rich public debate. From the

---

[17] *Id.* at 447-49.

[18] Schenck v. United States, 249 U.S. 47 (1919).

[19] Kalven, *The New York Times Case: A Note on 'The Central Meaning of the First Amendment'*, 1964 SUP. CT. REV. 191.

[20] *See* Meiklejohn, *The First Amendment is an Absolute*, 1961 SUP. CT. REV. 245; *see also* Brennan, *The Supreme Court and the Meiklejohn Interpretation of the First Amendment*, 79 HARV. L. REV. 1 (1965).

[21] *See, e.g.*, Bollinger, *Free Speech and Intellectual Values*, 92 YALE L.J. 438 (1983). The breadth of the support is indicated by adherents as diverse as Kalven and Bork. *See* Bork, *Neutral Principles and Some First Amendment Problems*, 47 IND. L.J. 1 (1971).

perspective of the street corner, that assumption might seem plausible enough. But when our perspective shifts, as I insist it must, from the street corner to, say, CBS, this assumption becomes highly problematic. Autonomy and rich public debate—the two free speech values—might diverge and become antagonistic.[22] Under CBS, autonomy may be *insufficient* to insure a rich public debate. Oddly enough, it might even become *destructive* of that goal.

Some acknowledge the shift of paradigms, and the obsolescence of the street corner, but would nonetheless view CBS as a forum—and electronic street corner.[23] They would demand access to the network as though it were but another forum and insist that the right of access should not follow the incidence of ownership. This view moves us closer to a true understanding of the problem of free speech in modern society, for it reveals how the freedom to speak depends on the resources at one's disposal, and it reminds us that more is required these days than a soapbox, a good voice, and the talent to hold an audience. On the other hand, this view is incomplete: It ignores the fact that CBS is not only a forum, but also a speaker, and thus understates the challenge that is posed to the received Tradition by the shift in paradigms. For me CBS is a speaker and in that capacity renders the Tradition most problematic. As speaker, CBS can claim the protection of autonomy held out by the Tradition, and yet the exercise of that autonomy might not enrich, but rather impoverish, public debate and thus frustrate the democratic aspirations of the Tradition.

In thinking of CBS as a speaker, and claiming for it the benefit of the Tradition, I assume that the autonomy protected by the Tradition need not be confined to individuals. It can extend to institutions. Autonomy is not valued by Meiklejohn and his follows because of what it does for a person's development (self-actualization), but rather because of the contribution it makes to our political life, and that contribution can be made either by individuals or organizations. The NAACP, the Nazi Party, CBS, and the First National Bank of Boston are as entitled to the autonomy guaranteed by the Tradition as is an individual, and no useful purpose would be served by reducing this idea of institutional autonomy

---

[22] On the two free speech values, see Justice Brennan's remarks in *Address*, 32 RUTGERS L. REV. 173 (1979). For an opinion informed by this perspective, see Richmond Newspapers v. Virginia, 448 U.S. 555, 584-89 (1980) (Brennan, J., concurring in judgment). *See also* Blum, *The Divisible First Amendment: A Critical Functionalist Approach to Freedom of Speech and Electoral Campaign Spending*, 58 N.Y.U. L. REV. 1273 (1983).

[23] *See, e.g.,* J. BARRON, FREEDOM OF THE PRESS FOR WHOM? THE RIGHT OF ACCESS TO MASS MEDIA (1973).

to the autonomy of the various individuals who (at any one point of time) manage or work within the organization.

Implicit in this commitment to protecting institutional autonomy is the understanding that organizations have viewpoints and that these viewpoints are no less worthy of first amendment protection than those of individuals. An organization's viewpoint is not reducible to the views of any single individual, but is instead the product of a complex interaction between individual personalities, internal organizational structures, the environment in which the organization operates, etc. The viewpoint of an organization such as CBS or First National Bank of Boston might not have as sharp a profile as that of the NAACP or Nazi Party (that is probably one reason why we think of a network as a forum), but that viewpoint is nonetheless real, pervasive, and communicated almost endlessly. It is not confined to the announced 'Editorial Message,' but extends to the broadcast of *Love Boat* as well. In the ordinary show or commercial a view of the world is projected, which in turn tends to define and order our options and choices.

From this perspective, the protection of CBS's autonomy through the no-content-regulation rule appears as a good. The freedom of CBS to say what it wishes can enrich public debate (understood generously) and thus contribute to the fulfillment of the democratic aspirations of the first amendment. The trouble, however, is that it can work out the other way too, for when CBS adds something to public debate, something is also taken away. What is said determines what is not said. The decision to fill a prime hour of television with *Love Boat* necessarily entails a decision not to broadcast a critique of Reagan's foreign policy or a documentary on one of Lindblom's 'grand issues' during the same hour. We can thus see that the key to fulfilling the ultimate purposes of the first amendment is not autonomy, which has a most uncertain or double-edged relationship to public debate, but rather the actual effect of a broadcast: On the whole does it enrich public debate? Speech is protected when (and only when) it does, and precisely because it does, not because it is an exercise of autonomy. In fact, autonomy adds nothing and if need be, might have to be sacrificed, to make certain that public debate is sufficiently rich to permit true collective self-determination. What the phrase 'the freedom of speech' in the first amendment refers to is a social state of affairs, not the action of an individual or institution.

The risk posed to freedom of speech by autonomy is not confined to situations when it is exercised by CBS, or by the other media, but occurs whenever speech takes place under conditions of scarcity, that is, whenever the opportunity for communication is limited. In such situations one utterance will necessarily displace another. With the street corner, the element of scarcity tends to be masked; when we think of the street corner we ordinarily assume that every speaker will have his or her turn, and that the attention of the audience is virtually unlimited. Indeed, that is why it is such an appealing story. But in politics, scarcity is the rule rather than the exception. The opportunities for speech tend to be limited, either by the time or space available for communicating or by our capacity to digest or process information. This is clear and obvious in the case of the mass media, which play a decisive role in determining which issues are debated, and how, but it is true in other contexts as well. In a referendum or election, for example, there is every reason to be concerned with the advertising campaign mounted by the rich or powerful, because the resources at their disposal enable them to fill all the available space for public discourse with their message. Playing Muzak on the public address system of a shopping mall fills the minds of those who congregate there. Or consider the purchase of books by a library, or the design of a school curriculum. The decision to acquire one book or to include one course necessarily entails the exclusion of another.

Of course, if one has some clear view of what should be included in the public debate, as does a Marcuse,[24] one has a basis for determining whether the public debate that will result from the exercise of autonomy will permit true collective self-determination. Such a substantive baseline makes life easier but it is not essential. Even without it there is every reason to be concerned with the quality of public discourse under a regime of autonomy. For the protection of autonomy will result in a debate that bears the imprint of those forces that dominate the social structure. In the world of Thomas Jefferson, made up of individuals who stand equal to one another, this might not be a matter of great concern, for it can be said that the social structure, as well as the formal political process, is itself democratic. But today we have every reason to be concerned, for we live in a world farther removed from the democracy Jefferson contemplated than it is from the world of the street corner speaker.

The fear I have about the distortion of public debate under a regime of autonomy is not in any way tied to capitalism. It arises whenever social power is distributed unequally: Capitalism just happens to be one among many social systems that distribute power unequally. I also think it wrong, even in a capitalist context, to reduce social power to economic power, and to attribute the skew of public debate wholly to economic factors; bureaucratic structures, personalities, social cleavages, and cultural norms all have a role to play in shaping the character of

---

[24] Marcuse, *Repressive Tolerance*, in A CRITIQUE OF PURE TOLERANCE 81 (1969).

public debate. But I think it fair to say that in a capitalist society, the protection of autonomy will on the whole produce a public debate that is dominated by those who are economically powerful. The market—even one that operates smoothly and efficiently—does not assure that all relevant views will be heard, but only those that are advocated by the rich, by those who can borrow from others, or by those who can put together a product that will attract sufficient advertisers or subscribers to sustain the enterprise.

CBS is not a monopoly, and competes with a few other networks (and less powerful media) for the public's attention. The fact that CBS's managers are (to some indeterminate degree) governed by market considerations does not in any way lessen the risk that the protection of autonomy—staying the hand of the policeman—will not produce the kind of debate presupposed by democratic theory. The market is itself a structure of constraint that tends to channel, guide and shape how that autonomy will be exercised. From the perspective of a free and open debate, the choice between *Love Boat* and *Fantasy Island* is trivial. In this respect, CBS and the rest of the broadcast media illustrate, by example, not exception, the condition of all media in a capitalist society. True, CBS and the other networks operate under a license from the government or under conditions of spectrum scarcity. But the dangers I speak of are not confined to such cases, for distortions of public debate arise from social, rather than legal or technical factors.

Individuals might be 'free' to start a newspaper in a way that they are not 'free' to start a TV station, because in the latter case they need both capital and government approval, while for the newspaper they need only capital. But that fact will not close the gap between autonomy and public debate; it will not guarantee that under autonomy principles the public will hear all that it must. Licensing may distort the market in some special way, but even the market dreamt of by economists will leave its imprint on public debate, not only on issues that directly affect the continued existence of the market, but on a much wider range of issues (though with such issues it is often difficult to predict the shape and direction of the skew). No wonder we tend to identify the Free Speech Tradition with the protection of 'the marketplace of ideas.'[25]

---

[25] The metaphor stems from Holmes's famous dissent in Abrams v. United States, 250 U.S. 616, 630 (1919). (Holmes, J., dissenting) ("But when men have realized that time has upset many fighting faiths, they may come to believe even more than they believe the very foundations of their own conduct that the ultimate good desired is better reached by free trade in ideas—that the best test of truth is the power of the thought to get itself accepted in the competition of the market . . . ."). The actual phrase "marketplace of ideas" is, oddly

II

Classical liberalism presupposes a sharp dichotomy between state and citizen. It teaches us to be wary of the state and equates liberty with limited government. The Free Speech Tradition builds on this view of the world when it reduces free speech to autonomy and defines autonomy to mean the absence of government interference. Liberalism's distrust of the state is represented by the antagonism between the policeman and soapbox orator and by the assumption that the policeman is the enemy of speech. Under the received Tradition, free speech becomes one strand—perhaps the only left[26]—of a more general plea for limited government. Its appeal has been greatly enhanced by our historical commitment to liberalism.

Nothing I have said is meant to destroy the distinction presupposed by classical liberalism between state and citizen, or between the public and private. Rather, in asking that we shift our focus from the street corner to CBS, I mean to suggest that we are not dealing with hermetically sealed spheres. CBS is neither a state actor nor a private citizen but something of both. CBS is privately owned and its employees do not receive their checks directly from the state treasury. It is also true, however, that CBS's central property—the license—has been created and conferred by the government. It gives CBS the right to exclude others from its segment of the airwaves. In addition, CBS draws upon advantages conferred by the state in a more general way, through, for example, the laws of incorporation and taxation. CBS can also be said to perform a public function: education. CBS is thus a composite of the public and private. The same is true of the print media, as it is of all corporations, unions, universities, and political organizations. Today the social world is largely constituted by entities that partake of both the public and private.

A shift from the street corner to CBS compels us to recognize the hybrid character of major social institutions; it begins to break down some of the dichotomies between public and private presupposed by classical liberalism. It also renders pointless the classificatory game of deciding

---

enough, Brennan's. *See* Lamont v. Postmaster General, 381 U.S. 301, 308 (1965) (Brennan, J., concurring). The deliberative element in Brennan's thinking about the first amendment can ultimately be traced to Brandeis, who is often linked to Holmes in his use of the clear and present danger test, but who in fact had no taste for the market metaphor. On the poetics of the Tradition, see the inspired essay by David Cole, *Agon at Agora: Creative Misreading in the First Amendment Tradition*, 95 YALE L.J. 857 (1986).

[26] *See* Coase, *The Market for Goods and the Market for Ideas*, 64 AM. ECON. REV. PROC. 384 (1974); Director, *The Parity of the Economic Market Place*, 7 J. LAW & ECON. 1 (1964).

whether CBS is 'really' private or 'really' public, for the shift invites a reevaluation of the stereotypical roles portrayed in the Tradition's little drama. No longer can we identify the policeman with evil and the citizen with good. The state of affairs protected by the first amendment can just as easily be threatened by a private citizen as by an agency of the state. A corporation operating on private capital can be as much a threat to the richness of public debate as a government agency, for each is subject to constraints that limit what it says or what it will allow others to say. The state has a monopoly on the legitimate use of violence, but this peculiar kind of power is not needed to curb and restrict public debate. A program manager need not arrest someone (lawfully or otherwise) to have this effect, but only choose one program over another, and although that choice is not wholly free, but constrained by the market, that does not limit the threat that it poses to the integrity of public debate. Rather, it is the source of the problem. All the so-called private media operate within the same structure of constraint, the market, which tends to restrict and confine the issues that are publicly aired.

Just as it is no longer possible to assume that the private sector is all freedom, we can no longer assume that the state is all censorship. That too is one of the lessons of the shift from the street corner orator to CBS. It reminds us that in the modern world the state can enrich as much as it constricts public debate: The state can do this, in part, through the provision of subsidies and other benefits. Here I am thinking not just of the government's role in licensing CBS, but also and more significantly of government appropriations to public television and radio, public and private universities, public libraries, and public educational systems. These institutions bring before the public issues and perspectives otherwise likely to be ignored or slighted by institutions that are privately owned and constrained by the market. They make an enormous contribution to public discourse, and should enjoy the very same privileges that we afford those institutions that rest on private capital (and, of course, should be subject to the same limitations).

We can also look beyond the provision of subsidies, and consider whether the state might enrich public debate by regulating in a manner similar to the policeman. CBS teaches that this kind of governmental action—once again based on content—might be needed to protect our freedom. The power of the media to decide what it broadcasts must be regulated because, as we saw through an understanding of the dynamic of displacement, this power always has a double edge: It subtracts from public debate at the very moment that it adds to it. Similarly, expenditures of political actors might have to be curbed to make certain all views are heard. To date we have ambivalently recognized the value of state regulation of this character on behalf of speech—we have a fairness doctrine for the broadcast media and limited campaign financing laws. But these regulatory measures are today embattled, and in any event, more, not less, is needed. There should also be laws requiring the owners of the new public arenas—the shopping centers—to allow access for political pamphleteers. A commitment to rich public debate will allow, and sometimes even require the state to act in these ways, however elemental and repressive they might at first seem. Autonomy will be sacrificed, and content regulation sometimes allowed, but only on the assumption that public debate might be enriched and our capacity for collective self-determination enhanced. The risks of this approach cannot be ignored, and at moments they seem alarming, but we can only begin to evaluate them when we weigh in the balance the hidden costs of an unrestricted regime of autonomy.

At the core of my approach is a belief that contemporary social structure is as much an enemy of free speech as is the policeman. Some might move from this premise to an attack upon the social structure itself—concentrations of power should be smashed into atoms and scattered in a way that would have pleased Jefferson. Such an approach proposes a remedy that goes directly to the source of the problem, but surely is beyond our reach, as a social or legal matter, and maybe even as an ethical matter. The first amendment does not require a revolution. It may require, however, a change in our attitude about the state. We should learn to recognize the state not only as an enemy, but also as a friend of speech; like any social actor, it has the potential to act in both capacities, and, using the enrichment of public debate as the touchstone, we must begin to discriminate between them. When the state acts to enhance the quality of public debate, we should recognize its actions as consistent with the first amendment. What is more, when on occasions it fails to, we can with confidence demand that the state so act. The duty of the state is to preserve the integrity of public debate—in much the same way as a great teacher—not to indoctrinate, not to advance the 'Truth,' but to safeguard the conditions for true and free collective self-determination. It should constantly act to correct the skew of social structure, if only to make certain that the status quo is embraced because we believe it the best, not because it is the only thing we know or are allowed to know.

A question can be raised whether the (faint-hearted) structural approach I am advocating really represents a break with the Free Speech Tradition, for some traces of a welcoming attitude toward the state can be found within the Tradition. One is *Red Lion*, which upheld the fairness doctrine and the regulation of content for a speaker such as CBS.[27] This decision does not fit into the overall structure of the Tradition taken as a whole, and never has been sufficiently rationalized. It has been something of a freak, excused, but never justified, on the ground that broadcasters are licensed by the government. It has never grown, as an adequately justified precedent might, to allow a state to impose a similar fairness obligation on newspapers or to allow the fairness doctrine and all that it implies to become obligatory rather than just permissible. It is of no small significance to me that Kalven (and a number of the other first amendment scholars working within the Tradition) signed briefs in *Red Lion* on the side of the media.[28] There is, however, one other aspect of first amendment doctrine that evinces a welcoming attitude toward the state and that is more firmly entrenched and more adequately justified. I am now referring to what Kalven called the 'heckler's veto.'[29]

This doctrine has its roots in Justice Black's dissent in *Feiner v. New York*,[30] but it is now an established part of the Tradition. It recognizes that when a mob is angered by a speaker and jeopardizes the public order by threatening the speaker, the policeman must act to preserve the opportunity of an individual to speak. The duty of the policeman is to restrain the mob. In such a situation strong action by the state is welcomed, and the doctrine of the heckler's veto might thus appear as an opening wedge for my plea for a reversal of our ordinary assumptions about the state, but one that would allow the Court to work within the Tradition. Upon closer inspection, however, this seems to me wishful thinking, and that a more radical break with the past is called for.

First, the heckler's veto does not require an abandonment of the view that free speech is autonomy, but explains that the state intervention is necessary to make the speaker's autonomy 'real' or 'effective.' The person on the soapbox should be given a *real* chance to speak. In contrast, the approach I am advocating is not concerned with the speaker's autonomy, real or effective, but with the quality of public debate. It is listener oriented. Intervention is based on a desire to enrich public debate, and though the concept of 'real' or 'effective' autonomy might

---

[27] Red Lion Broadcasting Co. v. FCC, 395 U.S. 367 (1969).

[28] Included are Archibald Cox and Herbert Wechsler (the lawyer for the *New York Times* in *New York Times Co. v. Sullivan*). See Brief for Respondents Radio Television News Directors Ass'n and Brief for Respondent Columbia Broadcasting System in Red Lion Broadcasting Co. v. FCC, 395 U.S. 367 (1969).

[29] H. KALVEN, THE NEGRO AND THE FIRST AMENDMENT 140-45 (1965).

[30] 340 U.S. 315 (1951).

be so stretched as to embrace the full range of interventions needed to enrich the public debate, the manipulative quality of such a strategy will soon become apparent once the extensiveness and pervasiveness of the intervention is acknowledged. It is also hard to see what is to be gained by such a strategy: Autonomy, in its inflated version, would remain as the key value, but note that while in the received Tradition it operated as a response to government intervention, under this strategy it would serve as a justification of such intervention. Autonomy would be saved, but be put to a different use.

Second, although the doctrine of the heckler's veto welcomes the strong arm of the law, it does so only on rare occasions, when violence is about to break out, and then only to divert the police action away from the speaker and toward the mob. The general rule is that the state should not intervene, but when it must, it should go after someone other than the speaker. In contrast, the structural approach contemplates state intervention on a much more regular and systematic basis. A prime example of such intervention is, once again, the fairness doctrine, a varied and elaborate set of regulations and institutional arrangements that have evolved over several decades. Other instances of this sort of intervention can be found in federal and state laws regulating campaign contributions and expenditures, or in the laws of some states creating access to privately owned shopping centers for political activities. These laws entail a form of state intervention that is more regular and more pervasive than that contemplated by the occasional arrest of the heckler.

Third, when the policeman arrests hecklers, no interests of any great significance seem to be jeopardized. The government is interfering with the hecklers' freedom, but they are not objects of much sympathy. Hecklers are obstructionists, who are not so much conveying an idea as preventing someone else from doing so. They are defined rather two-dimensionally, as persons who refuse to respect the rights of others. Yes, they will have their chance on the soapbox, if that is what they want, but they must wait their turn. The issue appears to be one of timing. But the laws that have divided the Supreme Court over the past decade, and that the structural approach seeks to defend, jeopardize interests that are more substantial than those represented by hecklers.

At the very least, the laws in question involve a compromise of the rights we often believe are attached to private property—the right to exclude people from the land you own, or to use the money you earn in any way that you see fit. In some cases the stakes are even greater: free speech itself. The laws in question threaten the freedom of an individual or institution to say what it wants and to do so precisely because of the content of what is being said. One branch of the fairness doctrine requires a network to cover 'public issues,' and another requires a 'balanced presentation.' In either case, a judgment is required by government agency as to what constitutes a 'public issue' and whether the presentation is 'balanced.' By necessity, attention must be paid to what is being said, and what is not being said. Similarly, laws that regulate political expenditures to prevent the rich from completely dominating debate also require some judgment as to which views should be heard. The same is true even if the state acts through affirmative strategies, such as when it grants subsidies to candidates or purchases books or sets a curriculum.

From the perspective of autonomy these dangers are especially acute, and present what is perhaps a decisive reason against intervention. However, even if we shift the perspective, and rich public debate is substituted for autonomy as the controlling first amendment value, there is good reason to be concerned, and to a greater degree than we are when the heckler is silenced. The stated purpose of the government intervention and content regulation might be to enrich debate, but it might have precisely the opposite effect. It might tend to narrow the choices and information available to the public and thus to aggravate the skew of debate caused by the social structure. In fact, there is good reason to suspect that this might be the case, for, as suggested by Lindblom's idea of circularity, the social structure is as likely to leave its imprint on government action (especially of a legislative or administrative character) as it is to leave its mark on the quality of public debate.

The presence of these dangers is sufficient to distinguish the approach I am advocating from the heckler's veto, and the general Tradition of which it is part, but a question still remains—perhaps the ultimate one— whether these dangers are sufficient to reject the structural approach altogether and turn back to the received Tradition and the protection of autonomy. Are the dangers just too great? When the government intervention threatens what might be regarded as an ordinary value, signified by the interference with property rights, then the answer seems clearly 'no.' Free speech is no luxury. Sacrifices are required, and though there are limits to the sacrifice (as Justice Jackson put it, the Constitution is no 'suicide part'[31]), free speech lies so close to the core of our constitutional structure to warrant tipping the scales in its favor. In this regard the structuralist can confidently borrow the weighted balancing process used by progressives to protect speech in the interest of autonomy. Tra-

---

[31] Terminiello v. Chicago, 337 U.S. 1, 37 (1949) (Jackson, J., dissenting) ("[I]f the Court does not temper its doctrinaire logic with a little practical wisdom, it will convert the constitutional Bill of Rights into a suicide pact").

ditionally, speech is protected even if it causes inconvenience, a conges-
tion, etc. and I see no reason why the same rule could not be applied to
further public debate—where the state appears as a friend rather than
an enemy of speech.

This perspective could help in a number of the cases that stymied the
Court in the seventies. A law creating access to a shopping center might
interfere with the property rights of the owners, and cause a loss of sales
(by keeping away those who do not like to be bothered by politics), but
those interests might have to be sacrificed in order to fulfill the democratic aspirations that underlie the first amendment. To use one of the
phrases that inspired the progressives of the fifties and sixties and that
gave the Tradition much of its vitality, freedom of speech is a 'preferred
freedom.'[32] The only difference is that under the structural approach the
enrichment of public debate is substituted for the protection of autonomy
and free speech operates as a justification rather than as a limit on state
action. The same process of weighted balancing, with the hierarchy of
values that it implies, is used, though the traditional perspective on the
relationships between the state and freedom is reversed. The notion of
'preferred freedoms' or weighted balancing is, however, of little help when
the interests sacrificed or threatened by state action are not 'ordinary'
ones, like convenience or expense, but are also grounded on the first
amendment. Then, so to speak, the first amendment appears on both
sides of the equation: The state may be seeking to enrich public debate
but might in fact be impoverishing it.

This danger is presented by the fairness doctrine and that—not the
talk about infringement of institutional autonomy—is what makes the
doctrine so problematic. The doctrine seeks to enhance public debate by
forcing the broadcasters to cover public events and to present opposing
sides of an issue; but it simultaneously restricts debate by preventing
the media from saying what it otherwise might (in response to market
pressures, or to advance the political views of the managers or financial
sponsors, etc.). The hope is that public debate will be enriched, but the
fear is that it might work in the opposite direction, either directly by forcing the networks to cover issues that are not important, or indirectly by
discouraging them from taking chances, and by undermining norms of
professional independence. Federal and state laws that restrict political
expenditures by the rich or corporations also might be counterproductive.
These laws seek to enhance the public debate by allowing the full range
of voices to be heard, by assuring that the ideas of the less wealthy are

---

[32] See McKay, *The Preference for Freedom*, 34 N.Y.U. L. REV. 1182 (1959).

also heard. But at the same time these laws might over-correct, slanting the debate in favor of one view or position, and in that way violate the democratic aspirations of the first amendment.

I do not believe that this danger of first amendment counterproductivity arises in every single instance in which the state intervenes to enhance public debate, as is evident from my discussion of the shopping center cases (I put the displacement of Musak by the songs of protest to one side). Nevertheless, believing as I do that scarcity is the rule rather than the exception in political discourse, and that in such situations one communicative act displaces another, I must acknowledge that this danger of counterproductivity is almost always present. I also acknowledge how real a danger this truly is, for as Lindblom teaches, the state is not autonomous. We turn to it because it is the only hope, the only means to correct the distorting influence of social structure on public debate, and yet there is every reason in the world to fear that the state is not as 'public' as it appears but is in fact under the control of the very same forces that dominate the social structure. Indeed, I chose CBS (rather than, say, the shopping center) as the new paradigm, and insisted that it be viewed as a speaker (rather than as a forum), in order to underscore, rather than to minimize, the problematic character of state intervention. CBS impeaches the received Tradition, but also acts as a painful reminder to the structuralist that whenever the state adds to public debate it is also taking something away. The hope against hope is that in the final analysis we will be better off than under a regime of autonomy.

The burden of guarding against the danger of first amendment counterproductivity will largely fall to the judiciary. Judges are the ultimate guardians of constitutional values, and due to institutional arrangements that govern tenure and salary and due to professional norms that insulate them from politics, they are likely to be more independent of the forces that dominate contemporary social structure (the market) than other government officials. The burden of protecting the first amendment is theirs, and under the structural approach it is likely to be an excruciating one. Judges are accustomed to weighing conflicting values, but the conflict here is especially troublesome because the values seem to be of similar import and character. We cannot casually insist that the courts allow the political agencies to experiment or to take a risk, as we do when something like productive efficiency or administrative convenience is at stake, for the evils to be suffered are qualitatively equal to the benefits to be gained. Nor can we take comfort in doctrines of deference that generally ask courts to respect the prerogatives of legislative or administrative agencies. Those agencies might be as captive to the forces that dominate social structure as is public discourse itself. And I see no more reason in this context than I do in the discrimination area[33] to revert to an approach that emphasizes the motives or 'good faith' of the state agency involved: From democracy's standpoint, what matters is not what the agency is trying to do but what it has in fact done. To assess the validity of the state intervention the reviewing court must ask, directly and unequivocally, whether the intervention in fact enriches rather than impoverishes public debate.

This is no easy question, especially when we proceed, as we must, without Marcuse's guidance as to what kind of views are to be allowed in a democracy. The democratic aspirations of the first amendment require robust debate about issues of public importance, and as such, call for process norms, betrayed as much by the imposition of particular outcomes, as by the failure to secure meaningful conditions of debate. In constructing the required norms, however, we may find help in the old notion that it is easier to identify an injustice than to explain what is justice. In the racial area,[34] we have proceeded in this negative fashion, trying to identify impermissible effects ('group disadvantaging,' 'disproportionate impact,' etc.), without a commitment to a particular end state. I suspect that is how we must proceed in the first amendment domain as well. In fact, the notions of 'drowning out,'[35] or 'domination,'[36] used by Justice White on various occasions to explain how social or economic power under a regime of autonomy might distort public debate strike me as gestures in this direction. They are, of course, only a beginning, and perhaps a small one at that, and we should have no illusion about how long and how difficult a journey lies ahead.

Realism is not, however, the same as pessimism, and in these matters I tend to be optimistic. I believe in reason and in the deliberate and incremental methods of the law: The courts are no more disabled from giving content to the enrichment of public debate idea than to any other (including autonomy). I am also sustained by my belief in the importance—no, the urgency—of the journey that the structuralist has invited us to take. Unless we stop the by now quite tiresome incantation of Brennan's formula, and begin to explain precisely what we mean when we speak of a debate that is 'uninhibited, robust, and wide-open,' and to

---

[33] See Fiss, *Inappropriateness of the Intent Test in Equal Protection Cases*, 74 F.R.D. 276 (1977) (remarks presented at the Annual Judicial Conference, Second Judicial Circuit of the United States, Sept. 11, 1976).

[34] See Fiss, *Groups and the Equal Protection Clause*, 5 PHIL. & PUB. AFF. 107 (1976).

[35] Red Lion Broadcasting Co. v. FCC, 395 U.S. 367, 387 (1969).

[36] First Nat'l Bank of Boston v. Bellotti, 435 U.S. 765, 809-12 (1978) (White, J., dissenting).

assess various interventions and strategies in light of their contribution toward that end, we will never establish the effective precondition of a true democracy.

III

I do not expect everyone to share my optimism. I can understand someone who acknowledges how social structure and the protection of autonomy might skew public debate, but believes (for some reason) that the inquiries called for by another approach are too difficult, or too dangerous. I would argue with that position, but I would understand it. It would be an acknowledgment of the tragic condition in which we live—we know what freedom requires, but find it too difficult or too dangerous to act on its behalf. But that has not been the posture of the controlling bloc of the Burger Court in the free speech cases of the seventies, and that is why I believe a reaction stronger than mere disagreement is appropriate. The Court did not, for example, present its decision to invalidate the Massachusetts law limiting corporate political expenditures as a tragedy, where, on the one hand, it acknowledged how the 'domination' that White described might interfere with first amendment values, but on the other, explained that it might be too dangerous or too difficult even to entertain the possibility of corrective measures by the state. Rather, Justice Powell announced the Court's decision as a full and triumphant vindication of first amendment values. It is this stance, above all, that I find most troubling, and that has led me to wonder whether the real source of the problem is not the Justices, but rather the Tradition.

Some of the Justices have recognized the divergence between autonomy and rich public debate, and have been prepared to honor and further the public debate value at the expense of autonomy. Now and then they are prepared to work in patient and disciplined ways to make certain that the intervention in question will actually enrich rather than impoverish public debate. At their finest moments they are attentive to questions of institutional design and the danger of first amendment counterproductivity. Here I am thinking especially of Justices White and Brennan, though even they sometimes stumble under the weight of the Tradition. The method of the prevailing majority, perhaps best typified by the work of Justice Powell but by no means confined to the first amendment were simply character entirely. For them, it is all autonomy—as though we were back on the street corner and the function of the first amendment were simply to stop the policeman. Their method *is* the Tradition.

One part of this method is to see a threat to autonomy whenever the state acts in a regulatory manner. For example, Powell feared that a law requiring access to a shopping center might compromise the free speech rights of the owners[37]—the fourteenth amendment may not enact the *Social Statics* of Mr. Herbert Spencer, but maybe the first amendment does. The autonomy of the owners will be compromised, Justice Powell argued, because there is a risk that views of the political activists will be attributed to them. Faced with the fact that the activities gained access by force of law and under conditions that provide access to all, and that in any event, the owners could protect against the risk of attribution by posting signs disclaiming support for the views espoused, Justice Powell moved his search for autonomy to an even more absurd level. He insisted that being forced to post a disclaimer might itself be a violation of the autonomy guaranteed by the first amendment.[38] (For some strange reason, Justice White joined this opinion.)

Another part of the method of the prevailing majority is to treat autonomy as a near absolute and as the only first amendment value. The enrichment of public debate would be an agreeable by-product of a regime of autonomy (they too quote the Brennan formula), but what the first amendment commands is the protection of autonomy—individual or institutional—and if that protection does not enrich public debate, or somehow distorts it, so be it. To be sure, the fairness doctrine is tolerated, but largely out of respect for precedent, or a deference to the legislative or administrative will, and is distinguished on rather fatuous grounds. The Court has made clear that the FCC is free to abandon it, and in any event, the doctrine and the regulation of content that it implies are not to be extended to the print media (and presumably other electronic media that do not require an allocation of the scarce electromagnetic spectrum). Curbs on financial contributions to candidates are permitted once again out of deference to precedent, and as a way of curbing corruption, but curbs on expenditures are invalidated as interference with the autonomy supposedly guaranteed by the first amendment. These are the decisions that gave the seventies its special character. Reflecting the full power of the received Tradition, time and time again, the Court declared: '[T]he concept that government may restrict the speech of some elements of our society in order to enhance the relative voice of others is wholly foreign to the First Amendment. . . .'[39]

---

[37] Prune Yard Shopping Center v. Robins, 447 U.S. 74, 96-101 (1980) (Powell, J., concurring in part and in the judgment).

[38] *Id.* at 99.

[39] *See, e.g.,* First Nat'l Bank of Boston v. Bellotti, 435 U.S. 765, 790-91 (1978) (quoting Buckley v. Valeo, 424 U.S. 1, 48-49 (1976)).

Autonomy is an idea that is especially geared to the state acting in a regulatory manner—it is the shield against the policeman. When the state acts affirmatively, say through the provisions of subsidies or benefits, the Tradition does not have much to say. As a result, during this same period the Burger Court has been, much to my relief, more tolerant of such state intervention, but that tolerance has been achieved at the price of coherence. The Court has no standard to guide its review. Rather than asking whether the action in question enriches debate, the Justices have tried to reformulate the issue in terms of the received Tradition. In a school library case Justice Brennan found himself obliged to cast the censorship—a transparent attempt to narrow debate—into an infringement of autonomy and a violation of the rule against content regulation.[40] This led him to make an untenable distinction between the removal and acquisition of books, and to look into the motives of the school board—a type of inquiry for which, as he demonstrated in other contexts, he has no taste whatsoever. Even then, he was unable to secure a majority.

In this case, and in others that involved the state in some capacity other than policeman, Brennan and his allies faced a high-pitched dissent by Justice Rehnquist, in which he made explicit the distinction between when the state acts as sovereign (policeman) and when it acts in other capacities (e.g., as educator, employer, financier).[41] For the latter category, Rehnquist argued for a standard that leaves the state with almost total discretion. In this regard he speaks for others, and in one case,[42] he secured a majority and wrote the prevailing opinion (which Brennan joined—a fact he later regretted[43]). It seems to me, however, that what the first amendment requires in these cases is not indifference, but a commitment on the part of the Court to do all that it can possibly do to support and encourage the state in efforts to enrich public debate, to eliminate those restrictions of its subsidy programs that would narrow and restrict public debate, and if need be, even to require the state to continue and embark on programs that enrich debate.[44] The problem of remedies and the limits on institutional competence may, in the last instance cause the Justices—even one so strong in his conception of office as Brennan—to retreat from such an ambitious undertaking, but such a

---

[40] Board of Educ. v. Pico, 457 U.S. 853 (1982).

[41] Id. at 908-10 (Rehnquist, J., dissenting).

[42] Regan v. Taxation With Representation of Washington, 461 U.S. 540 (1983).

[43] See FCC v. League of Women Voters, 468 U.S. 364, 400 (1984).

[44] See Columbia Broadcasting Sys. v. Democratic Nat'l Comm., 412 U.S. 94, 170-204 (1973) (Brennan, J., dissenting).

failure of nerve, or exercise in prudence, should be recognized for what it is: a compromise, and not a vindication of the first amendment and its deepest democratic aspirations.

When subsidies are involved, the Court allows the state to act—the Court is torn, and the opinions incoherent, but the first amendment is not viewed as a bar to state action. When confronted with regulatory measures, however, such as ceilings and limits on political expenditures, the Court sees a threat to autonomy as defined by the Tradition and reacts in a much more straightforward and much more restricted way: The state is stopped. In so reacting the Justices give expression to the Tradition, and our longstanding commitment to the tenets of classical liberalism and its plea for limited government. They also give expression to the political mood of the day, which is defined by its hostility to the activist state. Today abolition of the fairness doctrine can be passed off as just one more instance of 'deregulation.'[45] It seems to me, however, that there is much to regret in this stance of the Court and the Tradition upon which it rests.

The received Tradition presupposes a world that no longer exists and that is beyond our capacity to recall—a world in which the principal political forum is the street corner. The Tradition ignores the manifold ways that the state participates in the construction of all things social and how contemporary social structure will, if left to itself, skew public debate. It also makes the choices that we confront seem all too easy. The received Tradition takes no account of the fact that to serve the ultimate purpose of the first amendment we may sometimes find it necessary to 'restrict the speech of some elements of our society in order to enhance the relative voice of others,' and that unless the Court allows, and sometimes even requires, the state to do so, we as a people will never truly be free.

---

[45] For the current challenge to the fairness doctrine, see *In re* Inquiry into Section 73-1910 of the Commission's Rules and Regulations Concerning the General Fairness Doctrine Obligations of Broadcast Licensees, 102 F.C.C.2d 143 (1985), *review pending in the Court of Appeals for the District of Columbia sub nom.* Radio-Television News Directors Ass'n v. FCC, No. 85-1691.

IV

THE WAR AGAINST TERRORISM AND THE RULE OF LAW[1]

Owen Fiss's interest in international issues began formally in the mid-1980s, when he was invited by the Argentine government to consult about what to do with those who committed massive human rights violations during the so-called "dirty war." In 1976, the military seized power in Argentina, and in the name of trying to maintain order and stop left-wing terrorism, created a brutal dictatorship.

This reign of terror, from 1976-1983, resulted in the murder or disappearances of at least 9000 people suspected of being subversive and to the kidnapping, torture, and rape of many thousands of other people.[2] In the 1980s, in an attempt to counter their loss of support by the Argentine people, the military started and lost a war against the British to retake the Malvinas Islands. Faced with this embarrassing defeat and burdened by a deteriorating economy, the generals decided to relinquish power. They called for national elections. In doing so, they assumed that the presidency would be won by the Peronist candidate who would not interfere with their actions. To their surprise, the people of Argentina elected the Radical Party candidate, Raúl Alfonsín, as President. He immediately set out to bring justice to those responsible for the human rights abuses. In 1985, the leaders of the junta were tried before a civilian tribunal. This

---

[1] Owen M. Fiss, *The War Against Terrorism and the Rule of Law*, 26 OXFORD J. LEGAL STUD. 235 (2006).

[2] The official estimate is 8,960. *See* COMISIÓN NACIONAL SOBRE LA DESPARICIÓN DE PERSONAS, NUNCA MAS: INFORME DE LA COMISIÓN NACIONAL SOBRE LA DESPARICIÓN DE PERSONAS [NEVER AGAIN: REPORT OF THE ARGENTINE NATIONAL COMMISSION ON THE DISAPPEARED] 16 (9th ed. 1985); *Human Rights in the World: Argentina*, 31 REV. INT'L COMMISSION OF JURISTS 1 (1983) (claiming the number of disappeared to be 15,000 due to underreporting); JUAN E. CORRADI, THE FITFUL REPUBLIC: ECONOMY, SOCIETY AND POLITICS IN ARGENTINA 120 (1985) (estimating the number of disappeared to be as high as 30,000).

absorbed the nation and continues to be a major issue in Argentina. Owen Fiss, along with several other American academics, became advisors to Alfonsín's government.[3]

Through this experience, and over the course of the next two decades, Owen Fiss became intimately involved with international human rights issues and the many issues involved in the transition from authoritarianism to democracy. He has been and continues to be the leader in holding yearly conferences in Latin America with leading and emerging Latin American scholars. The seminars are primarily concerned with the issues involved in constitutionalism and democracy.

During this time, he also became interested in the Middle East. This led him to create a yearly seminar that is usually held at Yale Law School, but sometimes held in other countries, which explores human rights issues with the high court judges of many middle eastern nations.[4] In 2003, Owen helped found the Iran Human Rights Document Center. He currently serves as Chairman of the Board. The Center's function is to objectively and systematically document human rights violations committed in the Islamic Republic of Iran since the 1979 revolution.

These experiences, of course, have made Owen Fiss particularly sensitive to ensuring that the United States remains a democracy that respects and does not violate human rights. His varied interests in constitutional adjudication, democracy and human rights converge in his analysis of recent United States Supreme Court cases dealing with that court's response to the September 11, 2001 terrorist attacks.

As Fiss claims, the "War Against Terrorism,"[5] a politically inspired phrase, has no specific legal content.[6] Its function has been to mobilize American society and to legitimate the Bush Administration's unprecedented claims of unlimited and unchecked presidential power. Nevertheless, President Bush's declaration of the "War Against Terrorism" soon after September 11, 2001 marked the beginning of a serious and unique challenge to our conception of the rule of law as embodied in

---

[3] See Owen Fiss, *The Death of a Public Intellectual*, 104 YALE L. J. 1187 (1995).

[4] His friendship with Aharon Barak, the former president of the Israeli Supreme Court, increased his interest in terrorism and national security issues. See Owen Fiss, *Law Is Everywhere*, 117 YALE L. REV. 257 (2007).

[5] Indeed, Gore Vidal finds the notion of "War on Terrorism" to be completely nonsensical. In his opinion, religious zealots, not any country, caused the terrible events of September 11, 2001. And there can be no war without a country. To Vidal, the "War on Terrorism" amounts to a war on an abstract noun, which he describes as semantically stupid and practically diabolical. See, e.g., GORE VIDAL, IMPERIAL AMERICA (2004).

[6] Owen M. Fiss, *The Fragility of Law*, 54 YALE L. REP. 40 (2007).

the Constitution—a challenge that continues to this day. Indeed, Fiss's notion of the rule of law is not one that refers to statutes and regulations "that serve the state, but to the Constitution itself, which creates the public morality of the nation."[7] Fiss's vision of the rule of law includes not only the words of the Constitution, but also the principles "that are inferred from the overall structure of the Constitution."[8] In addition, it includes certain congressional enactments "that articulate the governing principles of American Society. These principles are laden with a special normative value that derive from the role they play in defining our national identity—what it means to be American."[9]

Since September 11, 2001, the Bush Administration has intentionally attacked and put in issue—indeed seriously challenged—several of these Constitutional bedrock principles and congressional enactments. The Bush Administration has claimed the legal authority and power to detain American citizens indefinitely as enemy combatants without judicial warrants, grand jury indictments or trial by jury and even without adhering to a standard of proof beyond a reasonable doubt.[10] This Administration has asserted the legal authority and power to torture "enemy combatants" in clear violation of the Constitution and of statutes and treaties prohibiting such torture.[11] It has claimed that the Administration can conduct warrantless electronic eavesdropping on untold numbers of American citizens in clear violation of the Fourth Amendment and various federal statutes.[12] The Bush Administration has also claimed the legal authority and power to detain foreign citizens indefinitely at Guantánamo Bay, Cuba, without judicial interference.[13] In addition, the Bush Administration has engaged in the highly questionable practice of

---

[7] *Id.*

[8] *Id.*

[9] *Id.* Not surprisingly, Fiss cites the Civil Rights Act of 1964 as an example. Fiss, *supra* note 6, at 40.

[10] *See, e.g.,* Brief of the United States at 30, Rumsfeld v. Padilla, 542 U.S. 426 (2004) (No. 03-1027) (discussing military's legal authority to detain enemy combatants).

[11] *See* Memorandum from Jay S. Bybee, Assistant Attorney Gen., to Alberto R. Gonzales, Counsel to the President (Aug. 1, 2002), *in* THE TORTURE PAPERS: THE ROAD TO ABU GHRAIB 218 (Karen J. Greenberg & Joshua L. Dratel eds., 2005) [August 2002 Torture Memorandum].

[12] *See* JAMES RISEN, STATE OF WAR: THE SECRET HISTORY OF THE CIA AND THE BUSH ADMINISTRATION 39-60 (2005).

[13] *See, e.g.,* Rasul v. Bush, 542 U.S. 466 (2004) (making a strong argument in favor of indefinite detention); Brief of the United States, *supra* note 10, at 42-43.

"extraordinary rendition"—the outsourcing of interrogation to foreign governments known to torture prisioners.

These unprecendented executive branch actions are an all out attack on our cherished constitutional principles, congressional enactments, and even on our national conception of democracy. Indeed, these actions are an attack on the historical struggle for freedom in our society. The Bush Administration's position on these and other issues makes executive power supreme, and even denies the ability of courts to review its actions. President Bush's position goes so far as to reject any Congressional oversight of the executive branch's conduct in these matters. Its actions and positions cannot, of course, be reconciled with our constitutional system, which is based on a theory of checks and balances. Simply put, unchecked executive authority cannot be reconciled with the text of the Constitution nor its animating principles. Indeed, in the Constitution itself, the framers accepted broad-based executive power only in a very limited category of cases and only as a last resort.

The asserted reason for the Bush Administration's approach to executive power is as a response to the tragedy of September 11, 2001. The Bush Administration claimed that its actions were necessary to protect us—to respond to the unprecedented threat to the nation's security.[14]

In *The War Against Terrorism and The Rule of Law*, Fiss analyzes the Supreme Court's first encounters with the Bush Administration's often unconstitutional conduct of this "War Against Terrorism." He argues that the Court's rulings in three case—*Rumsfeld v. Padilla*,[15] *Rasul v. Bush*,[16] and *Hamdi v. Rumsfeld*[17]—badly compromised two foundational constitutional principles. The first principle—which he refers to as the principle of freedom—denies the government the power to detain (imprison) anyone unless that person is charged with a crime and swiftly brought to trial. The second principle requires the government to adhere to the Constitution's restrictions on its power no matter where or against whom it acts. Fiss argues that while in these cases the Supreme Court should be

---

[14] The closest examples of its overly broad assertion of executive power lie in the unconstitutional, indeed illegal actions of past presidencies, specifically in the Nixon and Reagan presidencies. Both of those Administrations claimed overbroad executive power and used that claim to violate the rule of law. The Bush Administration asserts a very similar if not the same position as these two prior Administrations to justify its actions taken in the "War on Terrorism."

[15] 542 U.S. 426 (2004).

[16] 542 U.S. 466 (2004).

[17] 542 U.S. 507 (2004).

credited for not fully endorsing the Bush Administration's position, at the same time, it must be "faulted for doing less than it should have."[18]

After a detailed analysis of the opinions, Fiss concludes that the Supreme Court's main failure is "a full appreciation of the value of the Constitution—as a statement of the ideals of the nation and as the basis for the principle of freedom—and even more, a full appreciation of the fact that the whole-hearted pursuit of an ideal requires sacrifice, sometimes substantial ones."[19] Fiss makes it clear, of course, that although it is sometimes difficult for Justices—indeed for officials of any branch of government—to recognize the importance of making these sacrifices, that is their constitutional obligation. As he puts it:

> It is hard for the Justices, or for that matter anyone, to accept that we may have to risk the material well-being of the nation in order to be faithful to the Constitution and the duties it imposes. Still, it must be remembered that the issue is not just the survival of the nation—of course the United States will survive—but rather the terms of survival.[20]

All three decisions involved individuals who were imprisoned by the United States. They were held incommunicado for at least two years without access to counsel, family, or friends. The principle of freedom at issue in these cases is rooted in Article I, section 9 of the Constitution which guarantees the writ of habeas corpus.[21] Perhaps even more fundamentally, the principle of freedom is rooted in the Fifth Amendment guarantee that no person shall be deprived of liberty without due process of law.

One of the most frightening and questionable acts of the Bush Administration has been its claim of authority to suspend the Bill of Rights by detaining Jose Padilla, an American citizen, apprehended after he arrived in Chicago from Pakistan via Switzerland. The government, pursuant to the President's determination that he was an "enemy combatant" who conspired with Al Qaeda to carry out terrorist attacks in the United States, detained him without complying with the Fourth, Fifth, and Sixth Amendments. Federal agents, executing a material witness warrant issued by the

---

[18] Fiss, *supra* note 1, at 235.

[19] Fiss, *supra* note 1, at 256.

[20] *Id.*

[21] U.S. CONST. art. I, § 9, cl. 2 ("The privilege of the writ of habeas corpus shall not be suspended, unless when in cases of rebellion or invasion the public safety requires it.").

United States Court for the Southern District of New York in connection with the September 11, 2001 terrorist attacks, apprehended Padilla at Chicago's O'Hare Airport in May 2002 and accused him of planning to build and detonate a "dirty bomb" in the United States.[22] On June 2, 2004, President Bush designated him as an illegal enemy combatant. The government imprisoned Padilla for almost four years before indicting him for any crime.[23] They then transferred him to a military prison, arguing that he was not entitled to a trial in civilian courts. Finally, on January 3, 2006, he was transferred to a Miami, Florida jail to face criminal conspiracy charges. On August 16, 2007, a jury found Padilla guilty of all charges, including that he conspired to kill people in an overseas jihad and to fund and support overseas terrorism. On January 22, 2008, U.S. District Court Judge Marcia Cook sentenced Padilla to seventeen years and four months in prison.[24]

After his arrest, officials took Padilla to New York.[25] An attorney filed a petition in the Southern District of New York to meet with him. After President Bush designated Padilla as an "enemy combatant," authorities transferred Padilla to a military prison in South Carolina.[26] But the litigation over his detention and rights remained in the Second Circuit.[27] The Second Circuit ruled in Padilla's favor and held that the government did not have the authority to hold him as an "enemy combatant."[28] The Supreme Court, in an opinion by Chief Justice Rehnquist, in a 5 to 4 decision, concluded that the Second Circuit lacked jurisdiction to hear Padilla's habeas corpus petition.[29] The Court found that a person must bring a habeas petition where he or she is being detained against the person immediately responsible for the detention.[30] Padilla needed to file

---

[22] Padilla v. Rumsfeld, 352 F.3d 695, 699, 701, (2d Cir. 2003), rev'd, 542 U.S. 426 (2004).

[23] Padilla v. Hanft, 547 U.S. 1062, 1062-63, 1649-50 (2006) (noting that authorities apprehended Padilla in May 2002 and indicted him only after he filed a writ of certiorari in September 2005).

[24] Kirk Semple, Padilla Gets 17-Year Term for Role in Conspiracy, N.Y. TIMES, Jan. 23, 2008, at A14.

[25] Rumsfeld v. Padilla, 542 U.S. at 431.

[26] Id. at 432.

[27] Padilla v. Rumsfeld, 352 F.3d at 710.

[28] Id. at 724.

[29] Rumsfeld v. Padilla, 542 U.S. at 442.

[30] Id.

his habeas petition in South Carolina against the head of the military prison there.[31]

The Supreme Court thus failed to address the lawfulness of Padilla's detention in any way. Justice Stevens wrote for the four dissenters and complained that Padilla, who had already been detained for over two years, had to begin the process all over again.[32]

But there seems little doubt that five Justices on the Supreme Court voted that it was illegal to detain Padilla as an enemy combatant. In a footnote in his dissenting opinion, Justice Stevens expressly stated that he agreed with the Second Circuit that there was no legal authority to detain Padilla as an enemy combatant.[33] Following the Court's decision, Padilla's lawyers filed a new habeas petition in the South Carolina district court. That court granted Padilla's petition. Nonetheless, the Fourth Circuit, considering Padilla's subsequent habeas petition, ruled that Padilla could be held as an enemy combatant.[34] In an opinion by Judge Michael Luttig, the court held that the President possessed authority to detain Padilla as an enemy combatant pursuant to an act of Congress passed after September 11, 2001, the Authorization for Use of Military Force Joint Resolution (AUMF).[35]

As Padilla's case headed back to the Supreme Court, the government formally indicted him and the Supreme Court ultimately denied certiorari.[36] Thus, the Supreme Court never ruled on the government's authority to detain an American citizen as an enemy combatant. Surely the government indicted Padilla before it reached the Supreme Court because it counted five votes in Padilla's favor and knew, based on the earlier ruling, that it would lose in the Supreme Court. Indeed, the Fourth Circuit strongly hinted at this conclusion and objected to the government's actions.[37] Moreover, the government downgraded the charges against Padilla. The Secretary of Defense had initially charged Padilla with plans to detonate a radioactive device in the United States. The Secretary maintained that stance and supported it with affidavits from subordinates throughout

---

[31] *Id.* at 450-51.

[32] *Id.* at 455-65 (Stevens, J., dissenting).

[33] *Id.* at 464 n.8. *See also* Hamdi v. Rumsfeld, 542 U.S. 507, 554 (2004) (Scalia, J., dissenting) (emphatically arguing that an American citizen cannot be held without trial as an enemy combatant unless Congress suspends the writ of habeas corpus).

[34] Padilla v. Hanft, 423 F.3d 386, 389 (4th Cir. 2005), *cert. denied*, 1265 S.Ct. 1649 (2006).

[35] *Id.*; *see* Pub. L. No. 107-40, 115 Stat. 224 (2001).

[36] Padilla v. Hanft, 547 U.S. 1062 (denying certiorari).

[37] Padilla v. Hanft, 432 F.3d 582, 585-87 (4th Cir. 2005).

Padilla's protracted efforts to secure his freedom, which had lasted over three years and involved the Southern District of New York, the Second Circuit, the Supreme Court, the District Court for South Carolina and the Fourth Circuit. The indictment against him dropped the charge that he planned to detonate a radioactive device in the United States. It charged him with "conspiring to murder, kidnap, and maim persons in a foreign country," and providing "material support for terrorists."[38] The government defended its shift by claiming that pursuit of the original charge would have jeopardized vital intelligence sources. Many questioned the truthfulness of that claim.[39]

As Fiss makes clear in this article,[40] the Supreme Court has full authority to rule on the merits of Padilla's claim for freedom. This is so even if Padilla had filed the habeas petition in the wrong district court. The choice between New York and South Carolina district courts did not raise any issue of subject matter jurisdiction, and this decisively implies that the issue presented by the petition is within the competence of the federal judiciary. Moreover, the Supreme Court has, in the past, made exceptions to the rule requiring a person to file a habeas petition in the district in which he is confined.[41] The reason for the rule is to assign the habeas petition to the court where a hearing could be most conveniently held and also to prevent forum shopping by prisoners. As Justice Stevens bitterly complained in his dissent, the facts of Padilla's situation—the surreptitious transfer of custody of Padilla from civilian to military authorities—were sufficiently unique to create another exception to this rule.[42] In addition, no matter in which district court the case was commenced, Padilla's claim would remain the same. As Fiss concludes: "It is therefore difficult to perceive how justice was served by requiring Padilla's lawyer—after Padilla was confined incommunicado for two years—to start the proceeding afresh. . . . Given the stakes for the individual and the nation, the failure of the court even to address the merits of Padilla's claim of freedom was, pure and simple, an act of judicial cowardice."[43] Fiss's notion of the judge's role, that of doing justice, has once again been violated.

---

[38] Fiss, *supra* note 1, at 240.

[39] *Id.*

[40] *Id.* at 239.

[41] *Id.* at 238.

[42] *Padilla*, 542 U.S. at 458-64.

[43] Fiss, *supra* note 1, at 239.

Padilla's case, of course, is not the only instance where the Bush Administration claimed the power to detain an individual without judicial review. It was simply the first of the three detention cases which made its way up to the Supreme Court. The prisoner in the second terrorism case, Yaser Hamdi, is an American citizen apprehended in Afghanistan, and brought to Guantánamo Bay, Cuba.[44] Afghanistan, of course, was a zone of active combat at the time of his capture. There, authorities discovered that Hamdi was an American citizen and then took him to a military prison in South Carolina.[45] The government held Hamdi as an enemy combatant and never charged him with any crime.[46]

In *Hamdi v. Rumsfeld*,[47] the Supreme Court ruled 5 to 4, in an opinion by Justice Sandra Day O'Connor, that the government may hold an American citizen apprehended in a foreign country as an enemy combatant.[48] Hamdi, like Padilla, maintained that his confinement violated a 1971 federal statute known as the Non-Detention Act (NDA).[49] This Act is what Fiss calls a "watered down version"[50] of the principle of freedom. The statute applies only to United States citizens and it "is aimed at avoiding a repetition of the horrors arising from the detention of persons of Japanese origin"[51] during World War II. It requires only that the detention be authorized by Congress and not that the prisoners be charged with a crime. The plurality concluded that Hamdi's detention, even assuming that the NDA applied to American citizens captured on the battlefield, was authorized pursuant to another statute—the Authorization for the Use of Military Force Joint Resolution (AUMF).[52] Writing for the plurality,[53] Justice O'Connor ruled that the AUMF constituted sufficient congressional authorization to meet the requirements of the NDA and permits detaining an American citizen apprehended in a foreign

---

[44] Hamdi v. Rumsfeld, 542 U.S. 507, 510 (2004).

[45] *Id.*

[46] *Id.* Hamdi's situation is almost identical to that of John Walker Lindh, except that Lindh was indicted and pled guilty to crimes. *See generally* United States v. Lindh, 212 F. Supp. 2d 541 (D. Va. 2002) (describing factual and procedural background of Lindh's case).

[47] Hamdi v. Rumsfeld, 542 U.S. 507 (2004).

[48] *Hamdi*, 542 U.S. at 516-17.

[49] Non-Detention Act of 1971, 18 U.S.C. § 4001(a) (2006).

[50] Fiss, *supra* note 1, at 240.

[51] *Id.*

[52] *Hamdi*, 542 U.S. at 516-17.

[53] Justice O'Connor wrote for herself and three other Justices—Rehnquist, Kennedy, and Breyer.

country as an enemy combatant.[54] Justice Thomas was the fifth vote for the government on this issue and in a separate opinion he concluded that the President has inherent authority, pursuant to Article II of the Constitution, to hold Hamdi as an enemy combatant.[55]

As to the issue whether Hamdi must be afforded due process, the Court ruled 8 to 1 that indeed he was so entitled.[56] Only Justice Thomas dissented from this position.[57] Justice O'Connor concluded that Hamdi was entitled to have his habeas petition heard before a neutral decisionmaker and in this case it may mean before a federal court. She recognized that imprisoning a person is the most basic form of depriving one of his liberty.[58] Thus, she concluded that the government must provide American citizens detained as enemy combatants on foreign soil with due process. Much to the surprise of all the parties, and certainly to Owen Fiss, Justice O'Connor applied the *Mathews v. Eldridge*[59] formula to determine Hamdi's procedural rights. This formula was created in the 1970s to determine whether an individual faced with the termination of welfare or disability benefits is, as a matter of due process, entitled to a hearing and what the character of the hearing must be. The *Mathews* test instructs courts to balance the importance of the interest to the individual, the ability of additional procedures to reduce the risk of an erroneous deprivation, and the government's interest.[60] As Fiss notes, while the *Mathews* formula has not been applied in several decades to require procedural protection for welfare recipients, "it has always been assumed that if a hearing were required before benefits were terminated that hearing need not be held before a federal judge."[61] It could, for example, be held in front of a member of the state civil service. Fiss makes clear that *Hamdi* presents a completely different issue than the one decided in *Mathews*. It is not about "the fairness of a procedure to determine whether the state was correctly classifying the individual as it did, but rather whether the

---

[54] *Hamdi*, 542 U.S. at 540-42. The Non-Detention Act establishes that no American citizen shall be detained by the government except pursuant to an Act of Congress. 18 U.S.C. § 4001 (2006). The Act also states that except for military and naval institutions, the Attorney General controls the federal penal system. *Id.*

[55] *Hamdi*, 542 U.S. at 579 (Thomas, J., dissenting).

[56] *Id.* at 533-35.

[57] *Id.* at 594-99 (Thomas, J., dissenting).

[58] *Id.* at 509, 529-30 (majority opinion).

[59] Mathews v. Eldridge, 424 U.S. 319, 334-35 (1976).

[60] *Id.*

[61] Fiss, *supra* note 1, at 244.

prisoner is entitled to the substantive right to freedom guaranteed by the Constitution."[62]

To Fiss, Justice O'Connor's mistake in applying the *Mathews* test was not in "eliding property and liberty."[63] Rather, Fiss believes her mistake "was to ignore the distinction between two types of liberty—those that are guaranteed by the Constitution itself, as for example, by the First Amendment or by . . . the principle of freedom, and those liberties that people enjoy in society, but which are not constitutionally required."[64] As an example of this second liberty, the kind he calls a personal or social liberty, Fiss suggests "the liberty a parent has with the control of his or her children."[65]

As Fiss makes clear, the *Mathews* formula may be adequate for social liberties.[66] But for liberties guaranteed by the Constitution itself, as in *Hamdi*, the individual is entitled to a hearing before a federal court on his claim, not a military tribunal. Fiss argues that the Supreme Courts failure "is important but measured."[67] While the Court did not require a hearing before a federal court, it did grant the prisoner some rights. Although the *Hamdi* Court did not specify the procedures the government must follow in Hamdi's case, the Justices were explicit that Hamdi must be given a meaningful, factual hearing.[68] At a minimum, this hearing must include notice of the charges, the right to respond and the right to be represented by an attorney.[69] However, the Court suggested that hearsay evidence might be admissible and the burden of proof might fall on Hamdi.[70] Only Justice Thomas rejected the Court's conclusion that Hamdi must be given a meaningful hearing, and accepted the government's argument that the President could detain enemy combatants without any form of due process.[71]

Fiss concludes that Justice O'Connor's proposal—only four Justices agreed with it—that a hearing before a military tribunal may be an

---

[62] *Id.*

[63] *Id.*

[64] *Id.*

[65] *Id.*

[66] *Id.*

[67] *Id.* at 245.

[68] *Hamdi,* 542 U.S. at 533.

[69] *Id.* at 533, 539.

[70] *Id.* at 533-34.

[71] *Id.* at 592 (Thomas, J., dissenting).

adequate substitute for the hearing on the habeas petition in the federal district court, violates the principle of freedom. As he puts it:

> Doubts can, of course, be raised as to whether a military tribunal can ever, no matter how it is constituted, have the 'neutrality' or 'impartiality' that fair procedure requires. After all, it is an act of the military that must be judged and a military tribunal is, as the name implies, staffed by members of the military. But Justice O'Connor's proposal—and that is all it is—can be faulted on more basic grounds. She does not fully grasp the significance of the issue to be resolved by the tribunal: the narrow technical issue is, as she says, whether the government has made a mistake in classifying Hamdi as an enemy combatant, but the stakes are much greater than she allows, because the classification of Hamdi as an enemy combatant is the basis for depriving him of the freedom that the Constitution guarantees. It is the basis for allowing the government to incarcerate Hamdi without charging or convicting him of a crime. Hamdi's claim that he was not an enemy combatant should have been tried by a federal court, not simply because such a court can achieve a measure of neutrality unavailable to a military tribunal, but also and more fundamentally because under our constitutional scheme it is the federal judiciary that has the responsibility of determining whether some individual has been deprived of a constitutionally guaranteed right, like the right to freedom. Federal judges are nominated by the President and confirmed by the Senate, and under our constitutional scheme are endowed with the authority to speak for the nation on the meaning of the Constitution.[72]

Fiss's belief in the importance of the judiciary in our constitutional scheme and the obligation of the judge to do justice has again been denied. Fiss is, of course, fighting an uphill battle in convincing the Court to play the role he believes it must in our constitutional system.

Numerically, during the Bush Administration, the most significant presidential claim of authority to detain individuals without any right to judicial review involved the detention of over 600 individuals in Guantánamo Bay, Cuba Naval Base. The United States occupies this base under

---

[72] Fiss, *supra* note 1, at 243-44.

a lease[73] and treaty[74] recognizing Cuba's ultimate sovereignty but giving this country complete jurisdiction and control for so long as it does not abandon the leased areas. Since January 2002, the United States government has held over 600 people—approximately 640—as prisoners at a military facility in Guantánamo.[75] The Bush Administration has argued that there can be no judicial review of its actions with respect to aliens detained abroad.[76] Initially, the Administration argued that federal courts lacked jurisdiction to hear a writ of habeas corpus brought on behalf of the Guantánamo prisoners. However, two habeas corpus petitions filed on behalf of Guantánamo detainees reached the Supreme Court.[77] The families of twelve individuals being held at Camp X-Ray in Guantánamo filed *Al Odah v. United States*,[78] and relatives of Australian and British detainees filed *Rasul v. Bush*,[79] the title under which the Supreme Court decided both cases.[80]

The detainees filed suits under federal law challenging the legality of their detention, alleging that 1) they had never been combatants against the United States or engaged in terrorist acts; 2) they had never been charged with wrongdoing; and 3) they had not been permitted to consult counsel or been provided access to courts or other tribunals. The government moved to dismiss both cases, contending the federal courts lacked authority to hear habeas corpus petitions by those being held in Guantánamo. The District Court construed the suits as habeas petitions and dismissed them for want of jurisdiction, holding that, under *Johnson v. Eisentrager*,[81] aliens detained outside the sovereign territory of the United States may not invoke habeas relief.[82] In March 2003, the United

---

[73] Lease of Lands for Coaling and Naval Stations, U.S.-Cuba, art. III, Feb. 23, 1903, T.S. No. 418.

[74] Treaty Defining Relations with Cuba, U.S.-Cuba, art. III, May 29, 1934, 48 Stat. 1683, T.S. No. 866.

[75] The Obama Administration, or course, has reduced that number significantly in an attempt to close that prison.

[76] Brief of Respondent at 14, Rasul v. Bush, 542 U.S. 466 (2004) (Nos. 03-334, 03-343).

[77] Rasul v. Bush, 542 U.S. 466, 475 (2004).

[78] 321 F.3d 1134, 1136 (D.C. Cir. 2003).

[79] 215 F. Supp. 2d 55, 57 (D.D.C. 2002).

[80] *See Rasul*, 542 U.S. at 470-75 (describing procedural background of Al Odah and Rasul cases and how both present the same question).

[81] 339 U.S. 763 (1950).

[82] 215 F. Supp. 2d 55, 68 (D.C. 2002).

States Court of Appeals for the District of Columbia Circuit affirmed the dismissal for lack of jurisdiction and held that no court in the country could hear the petitions brought by the Guantánamo detainees.[83]

The Supreme Court reversed the District of Columbia Circuit Court and held, 6 to 3, in an opinion by Justice Stevens, that those detained in Guantánamo do have access to the federal courts through a writ of habeas corpus.[84] Although the *Rasul* Court ruled that the detainees had a right to file a habeas application in a federal district court and to require the government to respond, it failed to specify what further rights, either procedural or substantive, they had before the court. More significantly, the Court grounded the extremely limited right it did provide not in the Constitution but in the federal habeas statute. The Court left uncertain the issue of whether the prisoners had any constitutional rights that they could raise and attempt to vindicate in the habeas proceeding it allowed. As Fiss makes clear: "The Court simply granted the prisoners the right to file a piece of paper."[85]

There are several differences between *Hamdi* and *Rasul* that clearly alter the constitutional calculus. Unlike *Hamdi*, the prisoners in *Rasul* were not American citizens. Two were Australians and twelve were Kuwaitis.[86] In addition, when the Supreme Court granted certiorari, the petitioners also included two British citizens. But, due to intense diplomatic pressure, they were released after the grant of certiorari.[87] The prisoners denied they took up arms against the United States. They claimed they were in the region for personal or humanitarian reasons. The other major difference between *Hamdi* and *Rasul* is that the *Rasul* prisoners were not held in the United States but were moved from the battlefield to the Guantánamo Naval Station and imprisoned there. This, of course, becomes important for constitutional purposes only because they were not American citizens.

The *Rasul* Court did not address what type of hearing ultimately must be accorded to the prisoners in Guantánamo.[88] The case is limited to the issue of whether a federal court could hear their habeas corpus petition.[89] The Federal Habeas Statute, 28 U.S.C. § 2241, provides that

---

[83] *Al Odah*, 321 F.3d at 1141-42.

[84] *Rasul*, 542 U.S. at 483-84.

[85] Fiss, *supra* note 1, at 246.

[86] *Rasul*, 542 U.S. at 470.

[87] *Rasul*, 542 U.S. at 471 n.1.

[88] *Rasul*, 542 U.S. at 483-84.

[89] *Id.* at 470.

the district courts can only grant habeas petitions "within their respective jurisdiction."[90] The government argued that this language means that a district court can only hear habeas petitions from prisoners being held within its jurisdiction. In this case, because the prisoners were being held at Guantánamo, they were not within the jurisdiction of the federal district court in which the petition had been filed (District of Columbia). Indeed, the government's argument went even further. They argued that the prisoners were not within the jurisdiction of any district court. The Supreme Court, in an opinion by Justice Stevens, rejected this argument. He established a scheme for § 2241: prisoners being held within the jurisdiction of a district court must apply for the habeas corpus writ within the jurisdiction of that court. Prisoners held outside the jurisdiction of any district court such as the prisoners held in Guantánamo, however, may apply for a habeas corpus writ from any district court that has jurisdiction over their custodian. One of the major factors in Justice Steven's conclusion is his fear of having American citizens held at Guantánamo without any right to file a habeas writ. As he stated: "Aliens held at the base, no less than American citizens, are entitled to invoke the federal court's authority under § 2241."[91] The linkage between American citizens and aliens is appropriate as a matter of statutory construction, particularly because § 2241 does not make any distinction between citizen and non-citizens. But this linkage overlooks the fact "that the right to file a habeas petition is meaningless unless the prisoner has constitutional rights, and the constitutional rights of aliens and citizens are, under established doctrine, conceived of in quite different terms."[92]

Citizens can claim constitutional rights wherever they are held by United States officials. Under established doctrine, however, aliens have no constitutional rights if they are being held by United States officials in a foreign country. In this circumstance, they do not even have a right to a due process hearing before a neutral tribunal to determine whether they are in fact enemy combatants. If the aliens are being held in the United States, they would presumably have the right to a due process hearing to determine if they are enemy combatants. The Supreme Court found that Guantánamo is closer to the United States—in this instance closer to South Carolina—than a foreign country.

---

[90] 28 U.S.C. §§ 2241(a)(c)(3).

[91] *Rasul*, 542 U.S. at 481.

[92] Fiss, *supra* note 1, at 247.

Unlike the Court of Appeals,[93] Justice Stevens never reached the question of what constitutional rights the prisoners might have. However, as he is undoubtedly aware, in order for the district court to issue the writ under § 2241, it must not only have jurisdiction over the petition but must also decide that the detention violates the Constitution or laws of the United States. The question is, of course, whether aliens, like the prisoners in *Rasul*, who have never resided in the United States and had no other connection to it, have constitutional rights. Justice Stevens addresses this question in a footnote[94]—Footnote 15—and in a very incidental way. In that footnote he lists five allegations that, if true, would make the detention of these prisoners unconstitutional or otherwise violate the laws of the United States. These five allegations are: (1) the prisoners have not engaged either in combat or in acts of terrorism against the United States—they are not enemy combatants; (2) they have been imprisoned for more than two years; (3) they are being held in a territory subject to the long term exclusive jurisdiction of the United States; (4) without access to counsel, and (5) without being charged with a crime.

What does Footnote 15 really mean? Obviously, its meaning is not clear. Does it mean that the prisoners must first prove that they are entitled to the protection of the Constitution, laws, or treaties of the United States in order to prevail? Or, does it mean that, if the prisoners prove their factual allegations, they are entitled to prevail?

Not surprisingly, when the case returned to the trial court level, two judges in the District Court for the District of Columbia, each presiding over different proceedings, read it differently. Indeed, they issued separate and diametrically opposed opinions. One judge, Judge Leon, granted the government's motion to dismiss the habeas petitions in the two cases before him.[95] He concluded that the Supreme Court had not "concerned itself with whether the petitioners had any independent constitutional rights."[96] Moreover, he claimed that prior doctrine made it clear that the prisoners did not have any underlying constitutional rights. As he stated: "In the final analysis, the lynchpin for extending constitutional protection beyond the citizenry to aliens was and remains the alien's presence within its territorial jurisdiction."[97] If he is correct, of course, that means

---

[93] Al Odah v. United States, 321 F.3d 1134, 1141 (D.C. Cir. 2003).

[94] *Rasul*, 542 U.S. at 483 n.15.

[95] Khalid v. Bush, 355 F. Supp. 2d 311, 314 (D.D.C. 2005).

[96] *Id.* at 322.

[97] Khalid v. Bush, 355 F. Supp. 311, 321 (D.D.C. 2005) (memorandum opinion and order quoting Johnson v. Eisentrager, 339 U.S. 763, 771 (1950)).

that while the prisoners had a statutory right to file a habeas petition, the legal proceeding was a farce with no practical import.

The second district court judge (Judge Green), however, denied the government's motion to dismiss.[98] She decided that Footnote 15 gave the prisoners the same constitutional rights they would have had if they were being held in the United States. In her view, they have the same rights as Hamdi—a right to a hearing before an impartial tribunal with the assistance of counsel. But Fiss finds even this reading of Footnote 15 troubling:

> First, it does no more than give the nationals of foreign countries a right to fair procedure to ascertain whether they are in fact enemy combatants—it does not afford them any of the substantive protections of the Constitution, including the right to freedom or any other rights embraced within the Bill of Rights, most notably the protection against cruel and unusual punishment. Second, this reading of footnote 15 makes location crucial—specifically the fact that the prisoners are being detained in Guantánamo, which has been under the exclusive control of the United States for more than a century. The *Rasul* prisoners are granted some protection, but those who are being held abroad—in Yemen, not to mention countries we are now occupying by force of our military power, like Iraq—could not claim protection of the Constitution.[99] Sadly, this limitation in the law would mean that the prisoners abused and tortured by the United States military authorities at Abu Ghraib . . . could make no constitutional claims against the United States.[100]

Footnote 15 ends with a citation to *United States v. Verdugo-Urquidez*,[101] the Supreme Court decision that denies the protection of the Fourth Amendment and presumably the entire Bill of Rights to aliens living abroad. In *Verdugo-Urquidez*, in an opinion by Chief Justice Rehnquist, the Court held that the Fourth Amendment does not apply to a search by United States agents of a home located in a foreign country, owned by an alien who did not reside in the United States and who did not otherwise voluntarily attach himself to our national community. That

---

[98] In re Guantánamo Bay Detainee Cases, 355 F. Supp. 2d 443 (D.D.C. 2005).

[99] Fiss, *supra* note 1, at 249-50.

[100] *Id.*

[101] United States v. Verdugo-Urquidez, 494 U.S. 259 (1990).

search would clearly be illegal if done in the United States. Fiss contrasts this view with Justice Brennan's dissenting view in *Verdugo-Urquidez*— what he refers to as the "cosmopolitan view of the Constitution."[102] Brennan's position, which Fiss clearly favors, makes actions of the United States subject to the Constitution, no matter where or against whom the United States acts.

Nevertheless, Fiss disagrees with the reasons Justice Brennan gives for his conclusions. Justice Brennan relied on what Fiss calls "the principle of mutuality."[103] As Brennan puts it: "If we expect aliens to obey our laws, aliens should expect that we will obey our Constitution when we investigate, prosecute, and punish them."[104] Fiss argues that this principle is clearly inadequate to protect the constitutional rights Brennan claims to champion.

To Fiss, a better defense of "cosmopolitanism" comes from the Warren Court era. It "identifies the nation with the Constitution and underscores the constitutive nature of that all-important law: the Constitution creates the structure of government and defines the limits of its authority."[105] Moreover,

[T]he limits on government authority can be derived from terms upon which power was conferred on the new government, from certain prohibitions on the government contained in the body of the Constitution, notably Article IV, and above all, from the amendments to the Constitution adopted in 1791 and known as the Bill of Rights. For the cosmopolitan, the Bill of Rights is conceived not as a testamentary document distributing a species of property to specific and limited classes of persons, but rather as a broad charter setting forth the norms that are to govern the operation of government. 'No person shall be deprived of life, liberty, or property without due process of law'. 'Congress shall make no law respecting the establishment of religion, or prohibiting the free exercise thereof; or abridging the freedom of speech'. 'Cruel and unusual punishment shall not be inflicted'. For the cosmopolitan, rights are not property belonging to particular people, but the concretization of these sweeping prohibitions of the Constitution.[106]

---

[102] Fiss, *supra* note 1, at 251.

[103] *Id.* at 251.

[104] *Verdugo-Urquidez*, 494 U.S. at 284 (Brennan, J., dissenting).

[105] Fiss, *supra* note 1, at 252 (citing Reid v. Covert, 354 U.S. 1 (1957)).

[106] *Id.* at 252-53.

Fiss's view of rights—as norms, not property—among other things, makes it more difficult for Justices like Rehnquist to limit the scope of the Bill of Rights as he does in *Verdugo-Urquidez*. It requires the protection of the Constitution "whenever it acts and regardless of against whom it acts."[107]

In Footnote 15 of *Rasul*, the Supreme Court cited Justice Kennedy's concurrence, not Chief Justice Rehnquist's majority opinion, in *Verdugo-Urquidez*. In this concurrence, Kennedy laid out an alternative standard, holding that the question of the Constitution's application to aliens abroad must be decided on a case-by-case basis taking into account the "conditions and considerations" that would make adherence to a particular constitutional provision "impracticable and anomalous."[108] The standard put forward in Justice Kennedy's concurrence and affirmed in Footnote 15 draws on the rationale of the *Insular Cases* line of jurisprudence, a group of cases deciding that fundamental constitutional rights always apply in territories governed by the United States.[109] Justice Kennedy's standard examines three factors: (1) the nature of the government action; (2) the nature of the relationship between the United States and the territory at issue; and (3) the nature of the particular right at issue, all taken in light of the particular facts and circumstances of the case.[110]

---

[107] *Id.* at 253.

[108] *Verdugo-Urquidez*, 494 U.S. at 277-78 (Kennedy, J., concurring) (citing Reid v. Covert, 354 U.S. at 74) (Harlan, J., concurring).

[109] Downes v. Bidwell (The *Insular Cases*), 182 U.S. 244 (1901). The *Insular Cases* is the collective epithet given to a line of cases decided after the conclusion of the Spanish-American War in 1898, when the United States began to acquire far-flung territories such as Puerto Rico, Guam, and the Philippines which were seen as alien to U.S. culture (and perhaps "unfit" for statehood). With the *Insular Cases*, it became generally accepted that full constitutional rights would only apply in incorporated territories. In the unincorporated territories, by contrast, only "fundamental" constitutional rights would apply of their own force and courts would determine on an objective basis what relationship Congress had created with the territory. *Id.* at 268. The distinction between incorporated and unincorporated territories was coined by Justice White in his important concurrence in the first of the *Insular Cases*. *Id.* at 311-12 (White, J., concurring). The distinction turns on whether a territory is destined for statehood. Unincorporated territories are not recognized "as an integral part of the United States." *Id.* at 312. Since Alaska and Hawaii became states, the United States has held no incorporated territories. The *Insular Cases* thus established a doctrine according to which the applicability of the Constitution in U.S. sovereign territories not destined for statehood was decided on a case-by-case basis, taking into account the particular provision at issue and the nature of the relationship that Congress had established with the particular territory. Nonetheless, "fundamental rights" always applied. The *Insular Cases* themselves are still good law, even though their scope and meaning is debated.

[110] *Verdugo-Urquidez*, 494 U.S. at 277 (Kennedy, J., concurring).

The meaning of the citation of Justice Kennedy's concurrence in *Verdugo-Urquidez* by Justice Stevens in Footnote 15 in *Rasul* is open to different interpretations. Fiss is similarly uncertain about this reference. He claims it may mean Justice Stevens agrees with Justice Kennedy's "constitutional cosmopolitanism" or it may have been an attempt to induce Justice Kennedy to join the majority.[111] In any event, it leaves open the possibility that in a case involving possible government abuse of alien prisoners, Justice Kennedy would conclude that the Constitution does indeed prohibit such treatment.

Fiss's arguments in the following article demonstrate that he remains a strong defender of justice. He believes passionately—and this article clearly supports his view—that the Court has once again missed achieving justice in these detention cases. However, the Supreme Court got a second chance to reconsider these issues.[112]

Other cases, however, will simply not go away. For example, the losing parties in the two district court detention cases I describe below—*Khalid v. Bush*[113] and *In re Guantánamo Detainee Cases*[114]—appealed to the District of Columbia Circuit and that court consolidated the appeals.[115] In *Al Odah v. United States*,[116] the District of Columbia Circuit Court affirmed the district court's dismissal of, among other claims, the Guantánamo habeas claims. The court found that § 2241 did not provide statutory jurisdiction to consider habeas relief for any alien, enemy or not, held at Guantánamo.[117] In *Rasul v. Bush*,[118] the Supreme Court reversed that decision. It held that the habeas statute extended to aliens at Guantánamo. Although the prisoners themselves were beyond the district court's jurisdiction, the Supreme Court held that the district court's jurisdiction over the prisoner's custodian was sufficient to provide subject-matter jurisdiction under § 2241.[119]

---

[111] Fiss, *supra* note 1, at 255.

[112] Boumediene v. Bush, 476 F.3d 981 (D.C. Cir. 2007), *cert. denied*, 127 S. Ct. 1478 (Apr. 2, 2007), *reh'g granted, cert. denial vacated, cert. granted*, 75 U.S.L.W. 3707 (U.S. June 29, 2007).

[113] 355 F. Supp. 2d 311 (D.D.C. 2005).

[114] 355 F. Supp. 2d 443 (D.D.C. 2005).

[115] Boumediene v. Bush, 476 F.3d 981 (D.C. Cir. 2007).

[116] 321 F.3d 1134 (D.C. Cir. 2003), *rev'd sub nom.* Rasul v. Bush, 542 U.S. 466 (2004).

[117] *Al Odah*, 321 F.3d at 1141.

[118] Rasul v. Bush, 542 U.S. 466 (2004).

[119] *Rasul*, 542 U.S. at 483-84.

Congress then responded to *Rasul* by passing the Detainee Treatment Act (DTA) of 2005.[120] The DTA added a subsection (e) to the habeas statute. This new provision stated that, "[e]xcept as provided in section 1005 of the [DTA], no court, justice, or judge" may exercise jurisdiction over

(1) an application for a writ of habeas corpus filed by or on behalf of an alien detained by the Department of Defense at Guantánamo Bay, Cuba; or (2) any other action against the United States or its agents relating to any aspect of the detention by the Department of Defense of an alien at Guantánamo Bay, Cuba, who (A) is currently in military custody; or (B) has been determined by the United States Court of Appeals for the District of Columbia Circuit . . . to have been properly detained as an enemy combatant.[121]

The "except as provided" referred to subsections (e)(2) and (e)(3) of section 1005 of the DTA, which provided for exclusive judicial review of Combatant Status Review Tribunal determinations and military commission decisions in the District of Columbia Circuit.[122]

The following June, the Supreme Court decided *Hamdan v. Rumsfeld*.[123] Among other things, the Court held that the DTA did not strip federal courts of jurisdiction over habeas cases pending at the time of the DTA's enactment. In reaching this conclusion, the Court pointed to a provision of the DTA stating that subsections (e)(2) and (e)(3) of section 1005 "shall apply with respect to any claim . . . that is pending on or after the date of the enactment of this Act."[124] In contrast, no provision of the DTA stated whether subsection (e)(1) applied to pending cases. Finding that Congress "chose not to so provide . . . after having been presented with the option," the Court concluded "[t]he omission [wa]s an integral part of the statutory scheme."[125]

---

[120] Pub. L. No. 109-148, 119 Stat. 2680 (2005) (DTA). The President signed it into law on December 30, 2005.

[121] Detainee Treatment Act § 1005(e)(1) (internal quotes omitted).

[122] *See* Detainee Treatment Act § 1005(e)(2), (e)(3).

[123] 548 U.S. 557 (2006). *See supra* note 49 (Introduction).

[124] Detainee Treatment Act § 1005(h).

[125] *Hamdan*, 548 U.S. at 584.

In response to *Hamdan,* Congress passed the Military Commissions Act of 2006, (MCA)[126] which the President signed into law on October 17, 2006. Section 7 of the MCA is entitled "Habeas Corpus Matters." In subsection (a), Congress again amended § 2241(e). The new amendment reads:

(1) No court, justice, or judge shall have jurisdiction to hear or consider an application for a writ of habeas corpus filed by or on behalf of an alien detained by the United States who has been determined by the United States to have been properly detained as an enemy combatant or is awaiting such determination.

(2) Except as provided in [section 1005(e)(2) and (e)(3) of the DTA], no court, justice, or judge shall have jurisdiction to hear or consider any other action against the United States or its agents relating to any aspect of the detention, transfer, treatment, trial, or conditions of confinement of an alien who is or was detained by the United States and has been determined by the United States to have been properly detained as an enemy combatant or is awaiting such determination.

Military Commissions Act § 7(a) (internal quotation marks omitted). Subsection (b) states:

The amendment made by subsection (a) shall take effect on the date of the enactment of this Act, and shall apply to *all cases, without exception, pending on or after the date of the enactment* of this Act which relate to any aspect of the detention, transfer, treatment, trial or condition of detention of [an] alien detained by the United States since September 11, 2001.

Military Commissions Act § 7(b).

In *Boumediene v. Bush,*[127] the District of Columbia Circuit Court rejected the prisoners' challenge to their detention. That court vacated the district court's decision and dismissed the cases for lack of jurisdiction. It held that the 2006 MCA's provision stripping federal district courts of jurisdiction over Guantánamo detainees' habeas corpus petitions was

---

[126] Pub. L. No. 109-366, 120 Stat. 2600 (2006).

[127] Boumediene v. Bush, 476 F.3d 981 (D.C. Cir. 2007), *cert. denied,* 127 S. Ct. 1478 (Apr. 2, 2007), *reh'g granted, cert. denial vacated, cert. granted,* 75 U.S.L.W. 3707 (U.S. June 29, 2007).

constitutional. In April 2007, the Supreme Court denied certiorari. On June 29, 2007, in a surprise move, however, the Supreme Court rescinded that order and agreed to hear those claims.[128]

On June 12, 2008 the Supreme Court issued its opinion in *Boumediene v. Bush*.[129] In an opinion by Justice Anthony M. Kennedy, the Court ruled 5 to 4 that all prisoners detained at Guantánamo Bay are constitutionally entitled to bring habeas corpus in federal court to challenge the legality of their detention.[130] The Court held that the procedures for review

---

[128] *Id.* From this point on in this section of the book, the analysis is an attempt to follow some of Fiss's ideas of what the role of the Supreme Court should be in these cases.

[129] Boumediene v. Bush, 128 S. Ct. 2229 (2008). In addition to *Boumediene*, the Supreme Court accepted another case dealing with habeas corpus. On March 25, 2008, the United States Supreme Court heard arguments on whether American citizens held by U.S. forces in Iraq may be turned over to Iraqi courts without recourse in U.S. courts. Two American civilians in military custody in Iraq are accused of aiding terrorists. The Supreme Court consolidated the two cases, *Geren v. Omar*, 482 F.3d 582 (D.C. Cir. 2007), *cert. granted*, 128 S. Ct. 741 (2007) and *Munaf v. Geren*, 479 F.3d 1 (D.C. Cir. 2007), *cert. granted*, 128 S. Ct. 741 (2007), to answer the federal court jurisdiction question: whether the federal courts can hear challenges brought by two men, both United States citizens, to the validity of their detention and proposed transfer, even though they are being held outside the U.S.. The Bush Administration's position is that the federal courts lack jurisdiction over the men because they are in the custody of the Multinational Force—Iraq. Indeed, the Deputy Assistant Attorney General who argued the case before the Supreme Court claimed that the men should be turned over to Iraq to face criminal charges, including kidnapping and harboring insurgents. The Bush Administration buttressed its position that the federal courts lack jurisdiction over the men based on the reasoning of *Hirota v. MacArthur*, 338 U.S. 197 (1948), an opinion that rejected habeas corpus petitions from Japanese prisoners who had been convicted of war crimes by an international tribunal. Linda Greenhouse, *Court Hears Arguments On Americans Held in Iraq*, N.Y. TIMES, Mar. 26, 2008, at A19. On June 12, 2008, in a unanimous decision, the Supreme Court ruled that United States citizens detained by military forces in Iraq do indeed have the right to habeas corpus review of the legality of their custody by a United States federal court. Nevertheless, the Court found that the United States courts will not stop their transfer to Iraqi custody by United States forces. Munaf v. Geren, 128 S. Ct. 2207 (2008).

[130] In one of two dissenting opinions, Justice Antonin Scalia predicted "devastating" and "disastrous consequences" from the decision. Boumediene v. Bush, 128 S. Ct. 2229, 2294 (2008). Indeed, he declared: "It will almost certainly cause more Americans to be killed." *Id.* "The Nation will live to regret what the Court has done today." *Id.* at 2307. He claimed that the decision was based not on principle "but rather on an inflated notion of judicial supremacy." *Id.* at 2302.

Chief Justice Roberts, writing in milder tones than Justice Scalia, said the decision represented "overreaching" that was "particularly egregious" and left the Court open to "charges of judicial activism." *Id.* at 2282-83 (Roberts, C.J., dissenting). He believes the decision "is not really about the detainees at all, but about control of federal policy regarding enemy combatants." *Id.* at 2279. The public will "lose a bit more control over the conduct of this Nation's foreign policy to unelected, politically unaccountable judges," he added. *Id.* at 2293.

Chief Justice Roberts and Justice Scalia, I believe, are wrong to suggest that the decision constitutes reckless judicial intervention in military matters that the Constitution reserves exclusively for Congress and the President.

of detainees' status, provided in the Detainee Treatment Act of 2005,[131] are not an adequate and effective substitute for habeas corpus. Thus, the Court declared unconstitutional Section 7 of the Military Commissions Act of 2006,[132] which, at the behest of the Bush Administration, stripped federal courts of jurisdiction to hear habeas corpus petitions from the detainees seeking to challenge their designation as enemy combatants.

In 2005, Congress and the Bush Administration had passed a shortened alternative to a habeas procedure for the detainees in the 2005 Detainee Treatment Act. This Act gave detainees access to the federal appeals court in Washington, D.C., to challenge their designation as enemy combatants, made by a military panel called a Combatant Status Review Tribunal. Under previous Supreme Court precedent, formal habeas corpus procedures are not necessarily required if Congress provides an "adequate substitute." The detainees' lawyers argued that because this process fell far short of the review provided by traditional habeas corpus, it could not be considered an adequate substitute. Justice Kennedy agreed. He found that procedure a constitutionally inadequate substitute for habeas because it failed to provide the "fundamental procedural protections of habeas corpus."[133]

Justice Kennedy stated that the Supreme Court, having decided that there was a right to habeas corpus, would ordinarily send the case back to the appeals court to reconsider "in the first instance" whether the alternative procedure was an adequate substitute. But he said the "gravity of the separation-of-powers issues raised by these cases and the fact that these detainees have been denied meaningful access to a judicial forum for a period of years render these cases exceptional"[134] and required the Justices to decide the issue for themselves rather than incur further delay. Justice Kennedy then concluded that the alternative procedures had serious flaws, primarily because they did not permit a detainee to present evidence that might clear him of blame but was either withheld from the record of the Combatant Status Review Tribunal or was discovered subsequently. The tribunals' own fact-finding process was so limited as to present a high risk of error, thus requiring full-fledged scrutiny on appeal.

This is clearly an important decision. It affects all the approximately 270 detainees remaining at Guantánamo. Nevertheless, it is a limited

---

[131] 119 Stat. 2739.

[132] 28 U.S.C.A. § 2241 (e) (Supp. 2007).

[133] *Boumediene*, 128 S. Ct. at 2277.

[134] *Id.* at 2263.

decision. It does not release a single detainee. The decision does not even guarantee a right to a hearing. Rather, it guarantees only a right to request a hearing. Courts, of course, retain considerable discretion regarding such requests. As such, the Supreme Court's opinion only begins marking a boundary against the government's otherwise boundless power to detain people indefinitely, treating Guantánamo as "a legal black hole."

The decision certainly does not meet Fiss's view of doing justice. Critics, such as Chief Justice John Roberts in dissent, have a modicum of validity to their argument that the majority opinion may cloud more things than it clarifies. Indeed, many important questions remain unresolved. Is the "complete and total" United States control of Guantánamo a limiting and solid enough criteria to prevent the habeas right from being extended to other United States facilities around the world where enemy combatants are being held? Are habeas rights the only constitutional protections available to the Guantánamo detainees? If other constitutional protections exist, what are they and how many are they? Why not all the rights afforded citizens? If so, can there be trials by military commissions which permit hearsay evidence and evidence produced by coercion?

These unanswered questions, of course, suggest some of the weaknesses of the reasoning in the opinion and demonstrate that *Boumediene* is rich in constitutional ironies.[135] In addressing the issue whether non-Americans detained outside of the United States are entitled to habeas corpus, the Court passed up an important opportunity to clarify the law and to answer some of these unresolved issues. Instead, the Court based its reasoning, weakly and incorrectly, on *Johnson v. Eisentrager*,[136] a habeas corpus case that was decided just after World War II. In so doing, the Court failed in its constitutional obligation to decide cases on a candid appraisal of the relevant facts and legal principles.

At the heart of the dispute in *Boumediene* is the Constitution's Suspension Clause which reads as follows: "The Privilege of the Writ of Habeas Corpus shall not be suspended, unless when in Cases of Rebellion or Invasion the public safety may require it."[137] Unfortunately, the text of the Suspension Clause, like many of the Bill of Rights guarantees, requires interpretation. And interpretation is, of course, the task of Supreme Court Justices. The text neglects to specify the grounds for granting habeas corpus. Moreover, historical precedent is inconclusive

---

[135] Owen Fiss, I believe, would agree with this analysis.

[136] 339 U.S. 763 (1950).

[137] U.S. CONST. art. I, § 9, cl. 2.

on the question of when it should be available to aliens held in American custody outside the United States.

The major precedent on the issue and the one relied on by the Court in *Boumediene* is *Johnson v. Eisentrager*.[138] *Eisentrager* is a World War II era case in which German civilians captured in the Pacific location of War and accused of being "enemy aliens" were tried and convicted by a military commission located in Germany. The *Eisentrager* Court stressed that the aliens in that case could not be extended the privilege of litigation in United States courts because they "at no relevant time were within any territory over which the United States is sovereign, and the scenes of their offense, their capture, their trial and their punishment were all beyond the territorial jurisdiction of any court of the United States."[139] The Court held that citizens could bring habeas corpus whether they were detained in the United States or abroad. Aliens, however, had the right only if they were detained within the United States.

In his majority opinion in *Boumediene*, Justice Kennedy argues that based on *Eisentrager* and the Court's reasoning in its other extraterritoriality opinions, at least three factors are relevant in determining the Suspension Clause's reach: (1) the detainees citizenship and status and the adequacy of the process through which that status was determined; (2) the nature of the sites where apprehension and then detention took place; and (3) the practical obstacles inherent in resolving the prisoners' entitlement to the writ. According to Justice Kennedy, applying this framework reveals first and foremost that the detainees' status is in dispute. They are not American citizens, but they deny they are enemy combatants. Although they have been afforded some process in Combatant Status Review Tribunal proceedings, there has been no *Eisentrager*-style trial by military commissions for violations of the laws of war. Second, while the sites of the detainees' apprehension and detention weigh against finding they have Suspension Clause rights, there are critical difference between *Eisentrager*'s German prison around 1950, and the Guantánamo Naval Station in 2008, given the Government's absolute and indefinite control over the naval station. Finally, although the Court is sensitive to the financial and administrative costs of holding the Suspension Clause applicable in a case of military detention abroad, these factors are not dispositive because the Government presents no credible claim that the military mission would be compromised if habeas courts had jurisdic-

---

[138] 339 U.S. 763 (1950).

[139] *Id.* at 778.

tion. The situation in *Eisentrager* was far different, given the historical context and the nature of the military's mission in Germany.

In writing the *Eisentrager* opinion, Justice Robert Jackson spoke about the practical difficulties of prosecuting enemy aliens overseas, but gave them little weight. In his majority opinion in *Boumediene*, however, Justice Kennedy has made that minor issue a key element of the case, acknowledging that the government may have to go to some trouble, and expense, to ensure that the prisoners at Guantánamo are able to challenge their detentions. It is certain that *Boumediene* did not have to rest on this somewhat inconsequential, indeed almost irrelevant, issue.

Justice Kennedy's major mistake is failing to directly confront the meaning of the Suspension Clause. Nothing in that clause distinguishes citizens from aliens. Likewise, the due process clause extends its constitutional protections to all "persons," citizens and aliens alike. If the conditions for suspending habeas corpus are the same for citizens and aliens, so too should be the conditions for applying it. Indeed, if citizens overseas are entitled to habeas corpus, so are aliens. If viewed in this way, there would be no need to decide whether or not the Guantánamo Naval Station is American Territory.

Moreover, overruling *Eisentrager* on this point would not routinely entitle everyone to habeas corpus all the time. A distinction is appropriate for enemy prisoners of war who are never granted habeas relief, either in the United States or abroad. The issue depends on whether a prisoner is or is not an enemy combatant. This analysis would allow the Court to distinguish *Eisentrager* in a more convincing and appropriate manner.

The defendants in *Eisentrager*, German war criminals, admitted being enemy combatants. The six plaintiffs in *Boumediene*, accused of plotting an attack on the American Embassy in Bosnia, claim they are not. They should be entitled to challenge both the government's definition of an enemy combatant and the factual basis of their arrest. Moreover, they should be able to do so, as Justice Kennedy's opinion stressed, under standard habeas corpus procedures that allow them to present evidence and confront witnesses, and not under the paltry procedures outlines by the 2006 Military Commissions Act.

If found to be enemy combatants, they can be held for the duration of the so-called "War on Terrorism" and interrogated in accordance with the same legal principles, domestic and international, as any other detainees. If not, they must be tried for some specific offense or released.

Boumediene, while leaving many issues open and by not going far enough, is certainly not a license to allow hardened terrorists to go free. It is instead an opinion meant to prevent Star Chamber type proceedings that result in arbitrary, and I might add in this case, extraordinarily long-term incarcerations.

Boumediene certainly suggests solutions to many of the most pressing issues raised by the Bush Administration's treatment of prisoners held in Guantánamo Bay, Cuba, and elsewhere. For example, while the Supreme Court in *Boumediene* did not directly address the validity of the military commission system, it is arguable that the military commissions as they now exist violate the Constitution. Indeed, if the detainees have habeas rights they undoubtedly have other constitutional rights. Moreover, the legal procedures at Guantánamo clearly violate some of our most fundamental legal protections. For example, commission rules allow hearsay evidence and evidence of coercion which, of course, would not be permitted by the Constitution.

Shortly after the Supreme Court decided the *Boumediene* case, lawyers for the detainees began a new attack on the military commission system at Guantánamo.[140] Indeed, lawyers for detainees began their attack by challenging their clients' designation as enemy combatants. On June 20, 2008, a federal appeals court ruled that a Chinese Muslim held by the United States military was improperly labeled as an enemy combatant by the Pentagon.[141] This is the first time that a Guantánamo Bay detainee has been given an opportunity in a civilian court to try to secure his release. The order from the United States Court of Appeals for the District of Columbia Circuit directed military officials "to release Parhat, to transfer him, or to expeditiously convene a new [military] Tribunal."[142]

In addition, the Constitutional parameters of *Boumediene* have been challenged on two fronts–by the detainees at Guantánamo and by the Bush Administration. On July 3, 2008, lawyers for detainee Salim Hamdan filed papers in federal court in Washington, D.C., seeking an injunction attacking the constitutionality of the military commission system at Guantánamo.[143] If granted, this would likely have been the death knell for the Bush Administration's military commissions at Guantánamo. (Mr. Hamdan, of course, was also the subject of the 2006 Supreme Court

---

[140] William Glaberson, *Lawyers for Detainees Plan to Use Justices' Ruling to Mount New Attacks*, N.Y. TIMES, June 14, 2008, at A14.

[141] Parhat v. Gates, 532 F.3d 834 (D.C. Cir. 2008).

[142] *Id.* at 836.

[143] Motion for Preliminary Injunction Enjoining Petitioner's Trial by Military Commission, Hamdan v. Gates, No. 04-CV-1519-JR (D.D.C. July 3, 2008); Memorandum of Law in Support of Petitioner's Motion for Preliminary Injunction, Hamdan v. Gates, No. 04-CV-1519-JR (D.D.C. July 3, 2008).

opinion, *Hamdan v. Rumsfeld*,[144] that overturned the Bush Administration's original plans and first system for military trials). In this case, Mr. Hamdan's lawyers are arguing that the *Boumediene* opinion suggests detainees have other constitutional rights–the right to equal protection of the law, the right against self-incrimination, and the right to confront witnesses against him, among other constitutional rights–which would be violated if he were tried in the military system.

On July 17, 2008, the United States Court of Appeals for the District of Columbia Circuit ruled that Mr. Hamdan's challenge to the constitutionality of the military commission trial he faces is only appealable to a civilian court after judgment is entered at his military trial.[145] On the same day, the military judge at Guantánamo rejected Mr. Hamdan's constitutional arguments, including that the charges against him were unconstitutional because they were based on a law passed after he was in custody and because the military commission law violates the Equal Protection Clause by treating foreigners differently than American citizens.[146]

The trial then took place and, on August 6, 2008, a panel of six military officers returned a split verdict. The commission acquitted Mr. Hamdan of the most serious charge—a conspiracy charge. But the panel convicted him of the charge of providing material support for terrorism. The panel rejected two specifications that would have supported a conviction for conspiracy. One asserted that Mr. Hamdan was part of the larger conspiracy with senior Al Qaeda leaders and shared responsibility for terror attacks, including the 2001 attack. The second conspiracy specification rejected by the panel claimed Mr. Hamdan was part of a conspiracy to murder Americans in Afghanistan in 2001 with shoulder-fired missiles. The panel voted to convict Mr. Hamdan on five of the eight specifications that made up the charge of providing material support for terrorism. These specifications include claims that he was a driver for Mr. Bin Laden, served as his body guard, was a member of Al Qaeda, and knew its goals. The panel could have sentenced Mr. Hamdan to anything from no imprisonment to a life term. This is the first military commission trial to be held since World War II. The case was certainly not over at this point of the proceedings. Indeed, after an appeal to a military appeals court, convicted detainees have a right to a

---

[144] 548 U.S. 557 (2006).

[145] *See*, Hamdan v. Gates, 565 F. Supp. 2d, 30 (D.C. Cir. 2008).

[146] Scott Shane & William Glaberson, *Rulings Clear Military Trial of a Detainee*, N.Y. TIMES, July 18, 2008, at A1.

civilian federal appeals court. Potentially, they may have an opportunity to present their case to the Supreme Court.[147]

On August 7, 2008, the military jury sentenced Mr. Hamdan to five and one half years (sixty-six months) in prison. Under tribunal rules, the jury imposes the sentence, not the judge. A Pentagon legal official later reviews the sentence and can reduce but not increase it. The military judge had ruled previously that Mr. Hamdan should receive five years and one month (sixty-one months) of credit for the time he has served at Guantánamo Bay since the Pentagon charged him. Thus, he would have been eligible for release in five months. However, at the time of his sentencing in August, his fate remained uncertain because the Bush Administration claimed that it could hold detainees until the end of the war on terror.[148] It was not clear that he would be released at the expiration of the five months. At the end of November 2008, the military decided to transfer him to his native Yemen, where he was to serve the remaining month of his sentence.[149] Yemen released him during the first week of January 2009.[150]

Simultaneously, as detainees' lawyers began to attack the military commissions system in federal court, the Pentagon began moving ahead with trials at Guantánamo. On June 30, 2008, prosecutors filed charges against a Saudi detainee charged as a planner of the attacks on the Navy destroyer Cole that killed seventeen sailors. Hearings were also scheduled for the week of July 7, 2008, before a military judge at Guantánamo for five detainees charged with attacks on September 11, 2001.[151]

In a related case, on December 5, 2008, the Supreme Court agreed to decide one of the most fundamental questions about the scope of executive power in terrorism cases: May the president order the indefinite detention of people living legally in the United States?[152] The case concerns Ali al-Marri, the only person on the American mainland being held as an enemy combatant. He had been held in isolation for more

---

[147] William Glaberson, *Panel Convicts Bin Laden Driver In Split Verdict*, N.Y. TIMES, Aug. 7, 2008, at A1.

[148] William Glaberson, *Panel Sentences Bin Laden Driver to a Short Term*, N.Y. TIMES, Aug. 8, 2008, at A1.

[149] Robert F. Worth, *Bin Laden Driver to be Sent to Yemen*, N.Y. TIMES, Nov. 26, 2008, *available at* 2008 WLNR 22586313.

[150] *Yemen Releases Former Bin Laden Driver from Jail*, N.Y. TIMES, Jan. 12, 2009, at A9, *available at* 2009 WLNR 581279.

[151] William Glaberson, *In 2 Cases, Potential for a Decisive Ruling on Detainee Prosecutions*, N.Y. TIMES, July 4, 2008, at A12.

[152] Al-Marri v. Pucciarelli, 534 F.3d 213 (4th Cir.), *cert. granted*, 129 S. Ct. 680 (2008).

than five years without being charged. On January 22, 2009, President Obama issued a memorandum order to review the factual and legal basis for al-Marri's continued detention and thoroughly evaluate alternative dispositions.[153] It now appears that the Justice Department has decided to move the case into a civilian criminal court. This decision should give the Obama Administration the necessary opportunity to sidestep the issue of whether the government had the legal authority to detain legal residents indefinitely without charges.[154] Indeed, that is in fact what happened. On March 6, 2009, the Supreme Court vacated the lower court ruling in the case and remanded the case to the United States Court of Appeals for the Fourth Circuit with instructions to dismiss the appeal as moot.[155] The Court decided not to hear the case after all in light of Mr. al-Marri's indictment on criminal charges in federal court. But the one paragraph Supreme Court ruling leaves open the question of whether the military detention of legal residents as enemy combatants can ever be constitutional. In addition, in the first lower court hearing on the government's evidence for holding detainees at the Guantánamo Bay detention camp, a federal judge ruled that five Algerian men had been held unlawfully for nearly seven years and ordered their release.[156] These men were among the group of plaintiffs who won the right to seek habeas corpus relief in *Boumediene*.

One other notorious case deserves mention. It involves Maher Arar, a Syrian-born Canadian with no ties to terrorism who became a victim of the Bush Administration's questionable policy of "extraordinary rendition"—the outsourcing of interrogation to foreign governments known to torture prisoners. Mr. Arar was seized by federal agents in 2002 when he attempted to change planes on his way home to Canada from a family vacation. He was held incommunicado in solitary confinement by United States officials and subjected to harsh interrogation techniques without proper access to a lawyer. He was later "rendered" to Syria, where he was imprisoned and tortured for almost a year before he was released. The Canadian government later declared it had provided erroneous information about Mr. Arar to American authorities. In 2007, the Canadian government apologized to him and agreed to pay him

---

[153] Memorandum on Review of the Detention of Ali Saleh Kahlah al-Marri (Jan. 22, 2009), 2009 WL 149623.

[154] David Johnston & Neil A. Lewis, *In Reversal, U.S. Plans to Try Queda Suspect in Civilian Court*, N.Y. TIMES, Feb. 27, 2009, at A1.

[155] Al-Marri v. Spagone, No. 08-368, 2009 WL 564940 (U.S. Mar. 6, 2009).

[156] Boumediene v. Bush, 579 F. Supp. 2d 191 (D.C. Cir. 2008).

ten million dollars. A three-judge federal appeals panel dismissed Mr. Arar's civil rights lawsuit on national security grounds and strangely on his failure to seek court review within the time period specified in our immigration laws. This decision rewarded the government's egregiously bad behavior in denying Mr. Arar's initial requests to see a lawyer, and then lying to his lawyer about his whereabouts, which obstructed his access to the courts. But the appellate court took the unusual step of deciding to schedule a rehearing *en banc* before an appeal was filed.[157] This case presents an important test to determine the federal court's role in protecting constitutional rights.

In another positive development for the rule of law, the Supreme Court has revived a lawsuit brought by four former prisoners at Guantánamo Bay against Donald H. Rumsfeld, the former Secretary of Defense, and other officials. The former prisoners, all British citizens, claim they were tortured and subjected to religious persecution. In a brief order, the justices instructed a federal appeals court to take a second look at the case in light of the Supreme Court's decision in *Boumediene* granting Guantánamo prisoners the right to challenge their detention in federal court.[158] The appeals court, the United States Court of Appeals for the District of Columbia Circuit, ruled against the men in January 2008, finding that neither the Constitution nor a federal law protecting religious freedom gave them the right to sue in American courts.[159] Pursuant to the Supreme Court's order, Rasul petitioned the Court of Appeals for the District of Columbia for an initial hearing en banc. The court denied the petition.[160]

On January 22, 2009, President Obama issued an executive order which directed government officials to take immediate steps to assure that military commission cases "are halted".[161] Nevertheless, a military judge in the case of one of the best-known terrorism suspects, Abd al-Rahim al-Nashiri, a Saudi charged as the chief planner of the attack on the Navy destroyer Cole in 2000, which killed seventeen American sailors, declined an Obama Administration request to delay an arraignment scheduled

---

[157] Arar v. Ashcroft, 532 F.3d, 157 (2d Cir. 2008), *reh'g granted*, No. 06-4216 (Aug. 12, 2008) (en banc).

[158] Rasul v. Myers, 129 S. Ct. 763 (2008).

[159] Rasul v. Myers, 512 F.3d 644 (D.C. Cir. 2008).

[160] Rasul v. Rumsfeld, Nos. 06-5209, 06-5222, 2009 WL 395238 (D.C. Cir. Feb. 13, 2009).

[161] Exec. Order No. 13,492, 74 Fed. Reg. 4897 (Jan. 27, 2009).

for February 9, 2009.[162] The decision differed from rulings by two other military judges in the war crimes system at the prison in Guantánamo Bay, Cuba, who during the week of January 22, 2009, granted requests filed by military prosecutors for four-month delays to allow the Obama Administration to study detainees' files and its legal options. This decision is clearly in conflict with President Obama's January 22, 2009 executive order that directed immediate steps to assure that military commission cases "are halted."

---

[162] William Glaberson, *Judge Refuses to Delay a Case at Guantánamo*, N.Y. Times, Jan. 30, 2009, at A21, *available at* 2009 WLNR 1784134.

The War Against Terrorism and the Rule of Law[*]

A ll the world sighed. On 28 June 2004, the Supreme Court handed down its decisions arising from the so-called 'War Against Terrorism' and they were greeted with a deep sense of relief. We had been braced for the worst of all possible outcomes—an endorsement of the Administration's position. Such a result would have betrayed the most elementary principles of American constitutionalism, and left vulnerable many of the constitutional courts around the world that had built upon American principles to make certain that their governments fought terrorism within the terms of the law. The Supreme Court must be credited with having avoided that result, and yet faulted for doing less than it should have.

The Court rendered three decisions. All three involved individuals who were imprisoned by the United States—in fact held incommunicado for two years, with no access to family, friends, or counsel. All three cases put into question a fundamental tenet of the American Constitution— what I will call the principle of freedom. This principle denies the United States the authority to imprison anyone unless that person is charged with a crime and swiftly brought to trial. This principle is rooted in Section 9 of Article I, guaranteeing the writ of habeas corpus[1]—the historic means of testing the legality of detention—and perhaps even more fundamentally, in the Fifth guarantee that no person shall be deprived of liberty without due process of law.

Over the years, the principle of freedom has been qualified to permit civil commitment proceedings, which allow the state to confine to a hospital or mental institution persons who are a threat to themselves or others. More recently, the principle has been adjusted to allow the United States to detain persons who might serve as material witnesses in

---

[*] Owen M. Fiss, *The War Against Terrorism and the Rule of Law*, 26 OXFORD J. LEGAL STUD. 235 (2006). This article uses the footnote numbers and citation form of this particular publication.

[1] U.S. Const, art. 1, § 9, cl. 2 ('The privilege of the writ of habeas corpus shall not be suspended, unless when in cases of rebellion or invasion the public safety may require it.').

a criminal prosecution or before a grand jury but who are likely to flee the jurisdiction. Presumably, such detention would be of limited duration. An even more fundamental qualification—and the one invoked by the government in these cases and recognized by international law—allows the armed forces to capture and imprison enemy combatants during ongoing hostilities.

All three cases before the Court were removed from the battlefield. One involved an American citizen—Jose Padilla—who was first arrested at O'Hare Airport in Chicago as he alighted from a plane.[2] He had arrived in Chicago from Pakistan via Switzerland. He was immediately taken to New York and then transferred to a naval brig in Charleston, South Carolina. The second case also involved an American citizen—Yaser Esam Hamdi.[3] He was first arrested in Afghanistan, taken to Guantánamo Naval Station, later transferred to a naval brig in Norfolk, Virginia, and finally, after the grant of certiorari by the Supreme Court, brought to the same naval brig in Charleston in which Padilla was being held. The third case involved a group of Australians and Kuwaitis who were first seized in Afghanistan and Pakistan and then imprisoned at Guantánamo.[4]

In all three cases, the prisoners, acting through various representatives, some self-appointed, others appointed by the trial courts, sought writs of habeas corpus to challenge the legality of their detention, and in doing so invoked the principle of freedom. The government maintained that the prisoners were enemy combatants—one was allegedly affiliated with Al Qaeda and the others were said to be soldiers of the Taliban. All the prisoners denied the government's charges and demanded a meaningful opportunity to contest the factual basis of their detention. Admittedly, if the government failed to prove that they were enemy combatants, the government might still be able to detain them. The principle of freedom is not an absolute or unconditional protection of freedom, but rather tightly identifies the circumstances under which an individual may be deprived of his or her freedom. If the prisoners were not enemy combatants then the government would have the burden of charging them with a crime. Requiring the government to proceed in this way would bring into play the protections of the Sixth Amendment that specifically govern criminal prosecutions, including a speedy trial, trial by jury, the right to cross ex-amination, proof beyond a reasonable doubt, and the right to counsel. A criminal prosecution would also fully reveal, beyond the numbing

---

[2] *Rumsfeld v. Padilla*, 542 U.S. 426 (2004).

[3] *Hamdi v. Rumsfeld*, 542 U.S. 507 (2004).

[4] *Rasul v. Bush*, 542 U.S. 466 (2004).

drumbeat of war, the gravity of what the government had in mind for these individuals—incarceration for a substantial period of time.

By the time these cases reached the Supreme Court, the government was prepared to recognize the right of the two prisoners who were American citizens—Padilla and Hamdi—to seek a writ of habeas corpus. The government sought to reduce this right, however, to a mere formality. The government insisted that there should be no evidentiary inquiry into the prisoners' claim that they were not enemy combatants; an affidavit from some official in the Administration attesting to Padilla's and Hamdi's status as enemy combatants was, according to the government, in and of itself a sufficient basis for denying the writ. The demand for unlimited power on the part of the Executive was even more extreme in the case of the Australians and Kuwaitis. The government insisted that those prisoners had no right even to apply for a writ of habeas corpus, or put differently, no federal court had jurisdiction to grant the writ. Although the Supreme Court did not embrace all these audacious and somewhat startling demands for executive power, it failed to vindicate what I have called the principle of freedom.

Padilla's habeas petition struck a note of urgency. The government held him as an enemy combatant, but the war that the government had in mind was not the kind that had been fought in Afghanistan and for which international law allows the belligerents to detain enemy combatants. Rather, it was the vast, ill-defined, and never ending 'War Against Terrorism'. Political rhetoric had been confused with a rule of law. Moreover, by the time the Supreme Court ruled on his petition in June 2004, Padilla had been imprisoned for more than two years. For most of that period he was held incommunicado, without access to family or counsel. Only after the grant of certiorari did the government allow Padilla access to counsel. The purpose of such extended isolation had long been manifest. In an affidavit filed in open court, Vice Admiral Lowell E. Jacoby, the Director of the Defense Intelligence Agency, explained that the total isolation of Padilla for such an extended period—at the time Jacoby filed the affidavit it had already been eight months—was necessary to cultivate in Padilla a complete sense of dependency on his interrogators and to convince him of the hopelessness of his situation.[5]

According to the government, Padilla was associated with Al Qaeda and was planning to engage in terrorist acts in the United States, including the detonation of a device—known as a dirty bomb—that would disperse radioactive material. The government's claim was supported

---

[5] *Padilla v. Rumsfeld*, 243 F. Supp. 2d 42, 49-50 (S.D.N.Y. 2003).

by nothing more than an affidavit of an official in the Department of Defense, which, of course, contained multiple layers of hearsay. The federal district court in New York ruled that Padilla had a right to an evidentiary hearing to contest the veracity of the affidavit, and provided him with access to counsel for that purpose. The judge did not ground the right to counsel in the Bill of Rights, either the Due Process Clause of the Fifth Amendment or the Sixth Amendment guarantee of the right to counsel in criminal prosecutions. Rather, he gave Padilla access to counsel simply as an exercise of his power to hold a hearing on Padilla's habeas petition.[6] The Court of Appeals went even further. Concluding that Padilla was being unlawfully detained, it ordered his release unless he was transferred to civilian authorities and either held as a material witness before a grand jury or charged with a crime.[7]

The Supreme Court failed to address the lawfulness of Padilla's detention in any way. The Court simply ruled that Padilla's lawyer had filed the habeas petition in the wrong district court. Padilla had been brought from Chicago to New York on a material witness warrant requiring him to testify before a grand jury. The district judge in New York who had issued the material witness warrant appointed counsel to represent Padilla before the grand jury. Padilla in fact consulted with counsel, but two days before a scheduled hearing on a motion to contest his arrest on the warrant, the Department of Defense took custody of him and transferred him to the naval brig in South Carolina—all without prior notice to Padilla's counsel. Upon learning that Padilla was in the custody of the Department, Padilla's lawyer immediately filed a habeas petition in New York in order to contest the legality of his detention, naming the Secretary of Defense as the respondent. In an opinion by Chief Justice William Rehnquist, the Supreme Court held that under the relevant statute the habeas application should have been filed in South Carolina, not New York, and that the proper defendant was not the Secretary of Defense, but rather the commander of the Charleston brig. Padilla remained imprisoned, and his lawyer was required to begin the habeas proceeding once again.

The commander of the Charleston brig is a subordinate of the Secretary of Defense and fully subject to his control and discretion. The requirement that the commander be named as the respondent to the habeas petition is of no independent significance, but rather is derived from the more general rule requiring a prisoner to bring a habeas petition

---

[6] *Padilla v. Bush*, 233 F. Supp. 2d 564, 605 (S.D.N.Y. 2002).

[7] *Padilla v. Rumsfeld*, 352 F.3d 695, 699 (2d Cir. 2003).

in the district in which he is confined. This rule allocating work among the federal district courts seeks to assign the habeas petition to the court where a hearing might be most conveniently held and also to prevent forum shopping by prisoners. On previous occasions exceptions had been made to this rule, but Chief Justice Rehnquist insisted that those exceptions were not applicable in Padilla's case. Although this might indeed be true, the Chief Justice did not explain why the Court could not create yet another exception. As the dissenters bitterly complained, the facts of Padilla's situation—the surreptitious transfer of custody from civilian to military authorities—were sufficiently unique to allow the Court to create another exception without enabling prisoners to shop for the most hospitable judge and without threatening the overall aims of Congress in distributing the responsibility for habeas writs among the district courts.

The responsibility of the Court to address the merits of Padilla's claim to freedom stands, however, independent of whether an exception should have been made to the rule for allocating habeas petitions among the district courts. The choice between the South Carolina and New York district courts did not raise any issue of subject-matter jurisdiction,[8] which necessarily implies that the issue presented by the petition is within the province or competence of the federal judiciary. As a result, the Supreme Court had full authority to rule on the merits of Padilla's claim for freedom, even if the habeas proceeding had been commenced in the wrong district court. Even more, Padilla's claim would remain the same no matter in which district court the case was commenced. It is therefore difficult to perceive how justice was served by requiring Padilla's lawyer—after Padilla had been confined incommunicado for two years—to start the proceedings afresh. Sometimes we accept the Court's forbearance as a matter of judicial statesmanship, but here my sentiments are of another sort. Given the stakes for the individual and the nation, the failure of the Court even to address the merits of Padilla's claim of freedom was, pure and simple, an act of judicial cowardice.

The institutional failure of the Court was manifest at the moment of decision. Subsequent developments only aggravated the offence. Following the Court's decision, Padilla's lawyers filed a new habeas petition in the South Carolina district court. The South Carolina district court granted Padilla's petition, but the Fourth Circuit reversed, affirming the summary power of the government to detain Padilla as an enemy com-

---

[8] As acknowledged by Justice Kennedy in his concurrence. *Padilla*, 542 U.S. at 451 (Kennedy, J., concurring).

batant. With that victory in hand, and only days before it had to respond to Padilla's petition for a writ of certiorari, the government reversed its strategy. It filed a petition in the Fourth Circuit declaring its intention to transfer Padilla from military to civilian custody and to try him on criminal charges in a district court in Florida.

This stunning turn of events occurred on 22 November 2005. On that day—almost three and a half years after his initial arrest (8 May 2002) and sixteen months after the Supreme Court declined to rule on the merits of Padilla's petition (28 June 2004)—the principle of freedom was vindicated. The government took upon itself the burden of charging Padilla with a crime, and by that act brought into play all the strictures of the Bill of Rights, including the provision guaranteeing Padilla access to counsel and a speedy trial. Of course, justice delayed is better than no justice at all, but the government never satisfactorily explained why it took this action so belatedly—only just before it would have had, for a second time, to justify its position before the Supreme Court. Could it be, as the author of the Fourth Circuit opinion denying the government's petition later charged, that the government feared a reversal by the Supreme Court?[9]

The decision of the government to downgrade the charges against Padilla was also puzzling. The Secretary of Defense had initially charged Padilla with plans to detonate a radioactive device in the United States. The Secretary maintained that stance and supported it with affidavits from subordinates throughout Padilla's protracted efforts to secure his freedom—which had lasted over three years and involved the Southern District of New York, the Second Circuit, the Supreme Court, the District Court for South Carolina, and the Fourth Circuit. The indictment against Padilla filed in November 2005 made no mention of his alleged plan to detonate a radioactive device in the United States. The charges now against him were 'conspiracy to murder, kidnap, and maim persons in a foreign country' and providing 'material support for terrorists'. Before the press, the government defended its shift on the ground that pursuit of the original charge would have jeopardized vital intelligence sources, but many in the United States questioned the truthfulness of that explanation.

---

[9] *Padilla v. Hanft*, 432 F.3d 582, 585 (4th Cir. 2005). On 4 January 2006, the Supreme Court granted the Government's application to transfer Padilla from military to civilian custody to face criminal charges, adding that it 'will consider (Padilla's) pending petition for certiorari in due course'. *Hanft v. Padilla*, 546 U.S. 1084 (2006). In response to the petition for certiorari, the government has insisted that the transfer of Padilla to civilian authority has rendered moot the question of whether he can be detained as an enemy combatant.

In his habeas petition, Padilla maintained that his confinement violated a 1971 federal statute known as the Non-Detention Act. This statute could be viewed as a watered-down version of what I have called the principle of freedom. It is aimed at avoiding a repetition of the horrors arising from the detention during World War II of persons of Japanese origin then resident in the western United States. I say watered-down because the statute applies only to citizens (the Japanese interned in World War II included non-US citizens as well as citizens) and because it required not that the prisoners be charged with a crime, but only that the detention be authorized by Congress—it appears more concerned with unilateral action by the Executive than vindicating the principle of freedom. The Act provides that 'no citizen shall be imprisoned or otherwise detained by the United States except pursuant to an Act of Congress'.[10]

In the original habeas proceeding the Second Circuit held that Padilla's confinement in fact violated the Non-Detention Act. This was a bold advance over the decision of the District Court for the Southern District of New York, which did not put the government to the burden of filing criminal charges against Padilla, required only an evidentiary hearing on the question of whether he was an enemy combatant, and allowed indefinite detention if that charge were proved. The Second Circuit ruling was still limited, however, as it only governed situations like Padilla's, where a citizen was seized in the United States. The Second Circuit specifically declined to address whether the Non-Detention Act had any force for American citizens captured on the battlefield.[11]

Yaser Hamdi—the prisoner in the second of the terrorism cases— also relied on the Non-Detention Act, but there was a crucial difference between him and Padilla. Although Padilla, much like the Japanese who were interned, was taken prisoner in the United States, Hamdi was seized in Afghanistan, which, at the time of his capture (October 2001), was a zone of active combat. Yet Justice Sandra Day O'Connor, writing for herself and three other Justices (William Rehnquist, Anthony Kennedy, and Stephen Breyer), held in *Hamdi* that even assuming the 1971 Act applied to American citizens captured on the battlefield, the specific requirement of the Act—that the detention be authorized by statute— was satisfied. To that end, she relied upon a statute ('Authorization for the Use of Military Force') that was passed by Congress one week after September 11, and used by the Executive as the declaration of war

---

[10] Non-Detention Act of 1971,18 U.S.C. § 4001(a) (2000). On 3 April 2006, the court denied Padilla's petition.

[11] *Padilla*, 352 F.3d at 711.

against Afghanistan. It authorized the President to use all necessary and appropriate force against nations, organizations, or persons associated with the September 11 terrorist attacks.[12]

In a separate opinion in *Hamdi*, Justice David Souter, joined by Justice Ruth Bader Ginsburg, insisted that the requirement of the Non-Detention Act was not satisfied—the statute authorizing the use of military force against terrorism was far too general to count as the requisite statutory authorization for the detention. (Justice Souter also concluded that the 1971 Non-Detention Act governed prisoners taken on the battlefield and did not improperly interfere with the responsibilities of the President as Commander-in-Chief.) Yet in the interest of forming a majority, Justice Souter joined Justice O'Connor's opinion. Justice Souter said that by providing Hamdi with an opportunity to contest the factual predicate of the government's theory, the plurality's remand order was 'on terms closest to those [he] would impose'.[13] Justice Clarence Thomas embraced the government's position in its entirety, virtually denying any judicial review of the government's decision to detain Hamdi indefinitely,[14] while Justice Antonin Scalia and Justice John Paul Stevens took the opposite, view—because Hamdi was an American citizen, the only options for the government were to prosecute Hamdi in federal court for treason or some other crime or to let him go.[15]

In the United States and abroad, Justice O'Connor's opinion is best known for her statement that 'a state of war is not a blank check for the President when it comes to the rights of the Nation's citizens'.[16] In accordance with that aphorism, she did in fact place limits—procedural limits—on the President's capacity to detain citizens who had been captured on the battlefield and later detained in the United States.[17] She

---

[12] Authorization for the Use of Military Force, 107 Pub. L. No. 107-40, 115 Stat. 224. In its decision of 9 September 2005, rejecting Padilla's bid for freedom, the Fourth Circuit relied on the same reasoning.

[13] *Hamdi*, 542 US at 545-553 (Souter, J., concurring).

[14] Ibid., at 579 (Thomas, J., dissenting).

[15] The Justice Scalia and Justice Stevens opinions come close to endorsing the principle of freedom, but fall short of doing so by restricting their rule to American citizens and providing that American citizens cannot be held as enemy combatants. Ibid at 554 (Scalia, J., dissenting).

[16] Ibid., at 535.

[17] In Hamdi, Justice O'Connor says, 'Certainly, we agree that indefinite detention for the purposes of interrogation is not authorized'. Ibid., at 520. This sentence does not fit into the overall structure of the opinion, which is to impose procedural limitations on the government. But Ronald Dworkin reads it as imposing a substantive limitation, also rooted in due process, on the capacity of the government to detain enemy combatants who, like Hamdi, are American

required that Hamdi be given the opportunity to contest the government's claim that he was a soldier of the Taliban and thus an enemy combatant. This charge had been supported by an affidavit from the same official in the Department of Defense (Michael Mobbs) who gave the affidavit in *Padilla*, although Hamdi's father denied this allegation and said that his son went to Afghanistan in August 2001 to do relief work.

Justice O'Connor spoke to Hamdi's particular situation, but in effect crafted a more general procedural scheme. With that purpose in mind, she explained that the procedural rights of prisoners held as enemy combatants must be carefully tailored 'to alleviate their uncommon potential to burden the Executive at a time of ongoing military conflict'.[18] Accordingly, she allowed the government to support its charge that a prisoner is an enemy combatant by submitting an affidavit based on records maintained by the military of battlefield detainees. Such an affidavit would create a presumption, she said, that the prisoner is an enemy combatant and can be held on that basis. Then the prisoner would be given the opportunity to present evidence to rebut the presumption and to show that he is not an enemy combatant. The standard of proof Justice O'Connor contemplated remains unclear, but she did say that at this hearing Hamdi would have the assistance of counsel.

Justice O'Connor took up the counsel issue at the very end of her opinion. The entire discussion of this issue is one short paragraph following a sentence that, because of its emotional tone, reads as though it was to be the conclusion of her opinion. In that sense, the counsel paragraph seems like a postscript—as though all the hard issues had already been resolved. Most of the paragraph is devoted to explaining why the right to counsel issue is moot: although Hamdi was denied access to counsel, or for that matter anyone else, for a period of almost two years, following the grant of certiorari the government allowed Hamdi to meet with counsel without conceding any obligation to do so. Then this sentence appears, without any elaboration whatsoever: 'He unquestionably has the right to access to counsel in connection with the proceedings on remand'.[19]

A casual reader might think that the sentence was purely descriptive of Hamdi's situation and that the right to counsel to which Justice

---

citizens. According to Dworkin, American citizens can be held, not for coercive interrogation, but only to prevent them from returning to fight against the United States. Ronald Dworkin, *What the Court Really Said*, New York Review of Books, 12 August 2004, at 26, 29, *available at* http://www.nybooks.com/articles/17293.

[18] *Hamdi*, 542 U.S. at 533.

[19] Ibid., at 539.

O'Connor referred might be the right the government already allowed him as a discretionary matter. On reflection, however, it may well be that this 'right' to counsel applies more generally and has constitutional roots, not in the Sixth Amendment, which only applies to criminal prosecutions, but in the due process clause of the Fifth Amendment. The remand required the concurrence of Justice Souter, and he spoke of the plurality's 'affirmation' of Hamdi's right to counsel.[20] I therefore assume that Justice O'Connor and the three other Justices who joined her opinion intended to avoid a ruling on the right to counsel issue, but that they added the crucial sentence at the very last moment to secure Justice Souter's and Justice Ginsburg's votes.

Bargaining among the Justices had a less felicitous outcome with respect to the nature of the tribunal that must determine whether Hamdi is an enemy combatant. Throughout her opinion, Justice O'Connor made clear that the hearing must be held before 'a neutral decisionmaker'[21] or 'an impartial adjudicator'.[22] Clearly that standard would be satisfied by a federal district court passing on an application for habeas corpus. Indeed, the case before the Supreme Court had begun in such a manner—Hamdi's father acting as next friend filed a habeas petition in the federal district court with jurisdiction over the Norfolk brig. But Justice O'Connor created another alternative: a hearing before a military tribunal that would not be a prelude, but rather a substitute, for the hearing on the habeas petition in the federal district court. She wrote: 'There remains the possibility that the standards we have articulated could be met by an appropriately authorized and properly constituted military tribunal'.[23] She could not, however, obtain a fifth vote for this proposition. Justice Souter was explicit that in joining Justice O'Connor's plurality opinion he did not mean to imply 'that an opportunity to litigate before a military tribunal might obviate or truncate inquiry by a court on habeas'.[24]

Doubts can, of course, be raised as to whether a military tribunal can ever, no matter how it is constituted, have the 'neutrality' or 'impartiality'

---

[20] Ibid., at 553 (Souter, J., concurring).

[21] Ibid., at 535.

[22] Ibid., at 535.

[23] Ibid., at 538. Justice O'Connor did not rely upon *Ex Parte Quirin* for that proposition, and with good reason. *Quirin* involved seven German soldiers who were captured within the United States, which they had entered for purposes of sabotage. One of them claimed to be an American Citizen. The Supreme Court allowed all seven prisoners to be tried by military tribunal, but in contrast to *Hamdi*, in *Quirin* it was undisputed that the prisoners were German soldiers and thus enemy combatants. *Ex Parte Quirin*, 317 U.S. 1 (1942).

[24] Ibid., at 553 (Souter, J., concurring).

that fair procedure requires. After all, it is an act of the military that must be judged and a military tribunal is, as the name implies, staffed by members of the military. But Justice O'Connor's proposal—and that is all it is—can be faulted on more basic grounds. She does not fully grasp the significance of the issue to be resolved by the tribunal: the narrow technical issue is, as she says, whether the government has made a mistake in classifying Hamdi as an enemy combatant, but the stakes are much greater than she allows, because the classification of Hamdi as an enemy combatant is the basis for depriving him of the freedom that the Constitution guarantees. It is the basis for allowing the government to incarcerate Hamdi without charging or convicting him of a crime. Accordingly, Hamdi's claim that he was not an enemy combatant should have been tried by a federal court, not simply because such a court can achieve a measure of neutrality unavailable to a military tribunal, but also and more fundamentally because under our constitutional scheme it is the federal judiciary that has the responsibility of determining whether some individual has been deprived of a constitutionally guaranteed right, like the right to freedom. Federal judges are nominated by the President and confirmed by the Senate, and under our constitutional scheme are endowed with the authority to speak for the nation on the meaning of the Constitution.

The root of Justice O'Connor's error is clear. Much to the surprise of everyone, including the lawyers on both sides and some of her colleagues, she applied the *Mathews v. Eldridge*[25] formula to determine Hamdi's procedural rights. This formula was devised in the mid-1970s to determine whether an individual faced with the termination of welfare or disability benefits is, as a matter of due process, entitled to a hearing and what the character of that hearing must be. This formula requires a consideration of the benefits and costs of the proposed procedures and conceives of procedure as an instrument to arrive at correct decisions.[26] Although this formula has not been applied in recent decades to require elaborate procedural protections for welfare recipients, it has always been assumed that if a hearing were required before benefits were terminated that hearing need not be held before a federal judge. A supervisor in the welfare department would not suffice as a decisionmaker, because such an official would not possess the neutrality that fair procedure requires, but the hearing could be held before a member of the state civil service.[27]

---

[25] *Mathews v. Eldridge*, 424 U.S. 319 (1976).

[26] Owen Fiss, *The Law as It Could Be* 211 (2003).

[27] *Goldberg v. Kelly*, 397 U.S. 254 (1970).

In the case of Yaser Hamdi, however, the issue is entirely different from that presented in *Mathews v. Eldridge*: not the fairness of a procedure to determine whether the state was correctly classifying the individual as it did, but rather whether the prisoner is entitled to the substantive right to freedom guaranteed by the Constitution.

In saying this, I am not faulting Justice O'Connor, as some have, for eliding property and liberty. She understood that what is at stake is not a welfare cheque, disability benefits, or some other form of property, but rather Hamdi's liberty. Her error was to ignore the distinction between two types of liberties—those that are guaranteed by the Constitution itself, as for example, by the First Amendment or by what I have called the principle of freedom, and those liberties that people enjoy in society, but which are not constitutionally protected (one type of liberty can be called a constitutional liberty, the other a personal or social liberty).

A liberty of the latter type might be the liberty a parent has with respect to the control of his or her children. The Supreme Court had previously used the *Mathews v. Eldridge* formula to determine what procedures should be applied to deprive a person of such a personal liberty, as in *Lassiter v. Dept of Soc. Servs. of Durham County*.[28] Although I disagree with the result in that case—appointed counsel need not be provided to an indigent person whose parental rights are to be terminated—I acknowledge the applicability of the formula. Similarly, I would say that if all that were involved in Hamdi's case were a personal liberty, the *Mathews v. Eldridge* formula would be applicable, and from that perspective a hearing before a military tribunal might suffice, once again assuming that the tribunal possessed the requisite impartiality. The formula only requires fair procedures.

But for liberties of the first type—liberties guaranteed by the Constitution itself—the individual is entitled to a hearing before a federal court on his or her claim. Imagine a tenured professor being fired by a state university for criticizing some public official. He can challenge that action as a violation of the First Amendment and is entitled to have that action judged by a federal court, not simply some administrative tribunal within the university structure.[29] He is entitled to something more than fair procedure. Likewise, I maintain that Hamdi was entitled to a hearing before a federal court, not a military tribunal, on his claim that he was being denied the liberty provided by the principle of freedom—a liberty

---

[28] 452 U.S. 18 (1981); see also *MLB v. SLJ*, 519 U.S. 102 (1996).

[29] See *Perry v. Sindermann*, 408 US 593 (1972); *Bd. of Regents v. Roth*, 408 U.S. 564 (1972).

that can be traced to the Due Process Clause of the Fifth Amendment read in its substantive guise and the provision of Article I limiting the suspension of the writ of habeas corpus.[30]

The Supreme Court's failure in Hamdi's case is important but measured. Although the Court did not require a hearing before a federal court and thus did not honour the principle of freedom, it at least granted the prisoner some rights—an evidentiary hearing on the government's contention that he was an enemy combatant and access to counsel for such a hearing. The Court must also be credited for grounding these rights in the Due Process Clause, understood unfortunately not as a substantive guarantee of liberty, but only as a requirement of procedural fairness. In the third decision handed down on 28 June 2004, *Rasul v. Bush*, the Supreme Court also granted procedural rights to prisoners captured in the theatre of war and accused of having fought for the Taliban, but these rights were even more limited than in *Hamdi*.

Although the *Rasul* Court ruled that the prisoners had a right to file a habeas application in a federal district court and to require a response by the government, it did not specify what further rights—procedural or substantive—they had before that court. Even more significantly, the Court grounded the limited right it did provide in the federal habeas statute, not the Constitution, and left uncertain whether the prisoners had any constitutional rights that might be vindicated in the habeas proceeding it allowed. The Court simply granted the prisoners the right to file a piece of paper.

The first and most crucial difference between *Hamdi* and *Rasul* is that, unlike Yaser Hamdi, the prisoners in *Rasul* were not American citizens. Two were Australians and twelve were Kuwaitis (at one point, two British citizens were involved in the litigation, but due to intense diplomatic pressure, they were released after the grant of certiorari). All the prisoners denied that they took up arms against the United States and insisted that they were in the region for personal or humanitarian reasons. The second difference, which becomes of constitutional significance only because of the first difference, is that they were not held in Charleston or Norfolk, but rather were moved from the battlefield to the Guantánamo Naval Station and imprisoned there.

---

[30] After the Supreme Court's ruling, lawyers for Yaser Hamdi and the government began negotiations. On 11 October 2004, Hamdi was released from custody and transferred to Saudi Arabia. The release agreement requires Hamdi to renounce any claim to United States citizenship and to obey travel restrictions preventing him from travel to the United States, Afghanistan, Iraq, Israel, Pakistan, Syria, and the West Bank and Gaza Strip.

The Guantánamo Naval Station is a forty-five square-mile area on the southeastern coast of Cuba. It has been in the possession of the United States ever since the Spanish-American War of 1898, when Spanish dominion over the island was brought to an end. As a purely formal matter, the United States has possession of the territory by virtue of a 1903 lease (later modified in 1934). The lease reserves 'ultimate sovereignty' in Cuba, but also provides that 'so long as the United States of America shall not abandon the said naval station of Guantánamo or the two Governments shall not agree to a modification of its present limits, the station shall continue to have the territorial area that it now has'. The Guantánamo arrangement is a lease without a term, and given the allocation of power between the two nations, there is no doubt that the Naval Station is property within the exclusive control of the United States. Each year the United States tenders the rent, approximately $4,000. For the last forty years the Castro government has refused to accept it. The Naval Station is separated from the rest of Cuba by an extensive fencing system. It has its own stores, including a McDonald's and a Baskin-Robbins. With the exception of a handful of elderly Cuban employees, holdovers from another era, who enter the base for work, there is no exchange between the base and the rest of the island.

The federal habeas statute (28 U.S.C. § 2241) provides that the district courts can only grant habeas petitions 'within their respective jurisdictions'. The government argued that this statutory language means that a district court can only hear habeas petitions from prisoners being held within its jurisdiction and that because the prisoners were being held at Guantánamo they were not within the jurisdiction of the federal district court in which the habeas petition had been filed (the District of Columbia), nor indeed, the jurisdiction of any district court. The Supreme Court, in an opinion by Justice Stevens, rejected this argument and established the following scheme for § 2241: prisoners being held within the jurisdiction of a district court must apply for the habeas writ within the jurisdiction of that court. However, prisoners held outside the jurisdiction of any district court, such as those held in Guantánamo, can apply for a writ from any district court that has jurisdiction over their custodian.

Justice Stevens was helped to his conclusion by the spectre of having Americans citizens held at Guantánamo. As he put it, '[a]liens held at the base, no less than American citizens, are entitled to invoke the federal courts' authority under § 2241'.[31] Drawing a linkage between American

---

[31] *Rasul v. Bush*, 542 U.S. 466, 480 (2004).

citizens and aliens seems entirely appropriate as a technique of statutory interpretation: given that § 2241 does not distinguish between the petitions of citizens and those of non-citizens, a construction of § 2241 that accommodates the petitions of American citizens at Guantánamo should accommodate the petitions of non-citizens being held there. What the linkage overlooks, however, is that the right to file a habeas petition is meaningless unless the prisoner has constitutional rights, and the constitutional rights of aliens and citizens are, under established doctrine, conceived of in quite different terms.

Citizens can claim the protection of the Constitution no matter where they are held by United States agents—South Carolina, Guantánamo, or even, for example, Yemen. The situation with aliens is quite different. Location is all important. If the aliens live in South Carolina or any other state, they have the same constitutional rights as citizens. If they are being held in the South Carolina brig that contained Hamdi and Padilla, then presumably they too would be entitled to a due process right to a determination of their claim that they are not enemy combatants. Conversely, if they are being held by the United States government in a foreign country, for example, Yemen, they have, under established doctrine, no constitutional rights—not even a right to a due process hearing before some neutral tribunal to ascertain whether they are in fact enemy combatants.

Where does Guantánamo fit in this scheme? The Court put Guantánamo closer to the South Carolina side, and was quite right in this judgment. The forty-five square-mile area occupied by the Naval Base may, in some formal sense, belong to Cuba, but it is a territory over which the United States has exercised exclusive control for a century and has the right to do so forever. It is almost part of the United States. If the Court did not conceive of Guantánamo in this way, it is not clear to whom the prisoners might turn to challenge their detention. Their representatives might bring a legal proceeding in the country of their citizenship, but because they are being held in Guantánamo, not Kuwait or Australia, the courts of the countries of which they are citizens would not have the power or jurisdiction over the United States to order their release. As one Law Lord, writing extra-judicially, put it, a legal black hole would have been created.[32]

The Supreme Court discussed the status of Guantánamo in the context of interpreting the habeas statute. The Court of Appeals, which

---

[32] Johan Steyn, 'Guantánamo Bay: The Legal Black Hole', 53 *International and Comparative Law Quarterly* 1 (2004).

had held that the district court did not have jurisdiction to hear the prisoners' petitions, approached the problem from another perspective. Instead of starting with the statutory question of jurisdiction, the Court first looked to whether the prisoners had any underlying constitutional rights. The Court of Appeals read the prevailing Supreme Court precedents to mean that if the prisoners were held by United States agents in another country—even one that was not a battlefield, say Yemen—they would have no constitutional rights. The Court of Appeals was also of the view that Guantánamo was not part of the sovereign territory of the United States, but rather was like Yemen. Having reached this point in its analysis, the habeas proceedings made little sense to the Court of Appeals, even if the prisoners were, as a purely technical matter, deemed to be within the jurisdiction of the district court. As the Court of Appeals explained, 'We cannot see why, or how, the writ may be made available to aliens abroad when basic constitutional protections are not'.[33] In contrast, the Supreme Court first examined the statutory jurisdiction of the habeas court and in that context concluded that Guantánamo should be treated as part of the United States. It never reached the issue of what constitutional rights the prisoners enjoy and thus failed to engage the major premise of the Court of Appeals and the government. Seen in this way, Justice Stevens's opinion is not a tribute to judicial minimalism, but rather a contrived effort to make the case seem easier than it is—as though all that is at stake is a technical dispute over the jurisdictional requirements of § 2241.[34]

Justice Stevens was fully aware that in order to issue the writ under § 2241, the district court must not only have jurisdiction over the petition

---

[33] *Al Odah v. United States*, 321 F.3d 1134, 1141 (D.C. Cir. 2003).

[34] On 6 January, 2006, § 2241 was amended to deny the federal courts jurisdiction to hear the habeas petition of any alien detained by the Department of Defense at Guantánamo Bay. The new statute contemplates, however, that the claims of detainees at Guantánamo will be heard by a bureaucratic structure already in place: a Combatant Status Review Tribunal will determine whether a prisoner is an enemy combatant, a Detainee Administrative Review Board will review on an annual basis the need to continue the detention of an enemy combatant, and a Designated Civilian Official, acting on the recommendation of the review board, will make the final decision on continuing detention. Although the new statute abolishes habeas jurisdiction of such decisions, it vests in the United States Court of Appeals for the District of Columbia exclusive jurisdiction over the decision of the Designated Civilian Official that an alien is properly detained as an enemy combatant. The statute also prescribes the scope of review to be used in such proceedings (allowing it to determine, for example, whether the proceedings and standards used by the Guantánamo tribunals are consistent with the United States Constitution). Relying on the narrow scope of the *Rasul* decision, the new statute only affected § 2241, but did not purport to restrict the right to habeas corpus that emanates from the Constitution itself.

but must also determine that the detention violates the Constitution or laws of the United States. Of course, for the prisoners to have their constitutional rights violated, they must have constitutional rights in the first place. If the suit were filed by a United States citizen detained in Guantánamo, this would not be much of an issue because American citizens enjoy the protection of the Bill of Rights no matter where they are held, whether it be Guantánamo or Yemen or maybe even Afghanistan or Iraq (though in the latter cases exceptions could be made for the needs of the battlefield). But what about the constitutional rights of aliens, like the petitioners in *Rasul*, who never resided in the United States and had no other connection to it?

Justice Stevens addressed this question only in the most incidental way. In a footnote (n15) he lists five allegations that, if true, would render the detention of the prisoners before him, as he put it, 'unquestionably' unconstitutional or otherwise a violation of the laws or treaties of the United States: (1) the prisoners were not enemy combatants; (2) they were imprisoned for more than two years; (3) they were held in a territory subject to the long-term, exclusive jurisdiction of the United States; (4) they had no access to counsel; and (5) they were not charged with a crime.[35]

The meaning of this footnote is not at all clear. Not surprisingly, when the case returned to the trial level, two judges in the District Court for the District of Columbia, each presiding over different proceedings, read it differently. One judge granted the government's motion to dismiss the habeas petitions, concluding that the prisoners' reliance on footnote 15 was 'misplaced and unpersuasive'.[36] According to this judge, the Supreme Court 'had not concerned itself with whether the petitioners had any independent constitutional rights'.[37] He further concluded that based on prior doctrine, the prisoners had no underlying constitutional rights. This meant that although the prisoners had a statutory right to file a habeas petition—they had the right to file a piece of paper—the legal proceeding was of no practical import. The other district court judge denied the government's motion to dismiss.[38] On her reading, footnote 15 established that the prisoners had the same constitutional rights that they would have had if they were being held in Charleston—not a right to have a federal court ascertain their status as enemy combatants, for

---

[35] *Rasul*, 542 U.S. at 483.

[36] *Khalid v. Bush*, 355 F Supp 2d 311, 323 (D.D.C. 2005).

[37] Ibid., at 322.

[38] *In re Guantánamo Detainee Cases*, 355 F. Supp. 2d 443 (D.D.C. 2005).

even Hamdi did not have that right, but presumably a right to a hearing before some impartial tribunal with the assistance of counsel. On this interpretation the prisoners in Guantánamo—nationals of Australia and Kuwait—would be given the same rights as Hamdi.

This latter reading of footnote 15 would move the law in the right direction, but even with this gloss, the footnote remains troubling. First, it does no more than give the nationals of foreign countries a right to fair procedure to ascertain whether they are in fact enemy combatants—it does not afford them any of the substantive protections of the Constitution, including the right to freedom or any other rights embraced within the Bill of Rights, most notably the protection against cruel and unusual punishment. Second, this reading of footnote 15 makes location crucial—specifically the fact that the prisoners are being detained in Guantánamo, which has been under the exclusive control of the United States for more than a century. The *Rasul* prisoners are granted some protection, but those who are being held abroad—in Yemen, not to mention countries we are now occupying by force of our military power, like Iraq—could not claim the protection of the Constitution.

Sadly, this limitation in the law would mean that the prisoners abused and tortured by the United States military authorities at Abu Ghraib—fully disclosed to the world only weeks before the Supreme Court's decision in *Rasul*—could make no constitutional claims against the United States. In the months following this disclosure, Congress and the President apologized to the victims of torture at Abu Ghraib. The line officers immediately responsible for the torture have been disciplined. Victims of such abuses might even advance claims under various federal statutes.[39]

---

[39] These claims might be made under the Alien Torts Claims Act, 28 U.S.C. § 1350 (2000), on the theory that torture violates various treaties or international norms prohibiting torture. The Act, dating from the earliest days of the Republic, grants the district courts original jurisdiction of civil actions by aliens for torts committed in violation of the law of nations or a treaty of the United States. On 30 December 2005, a federal statute was passed providing: 'No individual in the custody or under the physical control of the United States Government, regardless of nationality or physical location, shall be subject to cruel, inhuman, or degrading treatment or punishment'. Department of Defense, Emergency Supplemental Appropriations to Address Hurricanes in the Gulf of Mexico, and Pandemic Influenza Act, 2006, Pub. L. No. 109-148,119 Stat. 2739 (2006). The means of enforcing this prohibition were not specified in the statute, and upon signing the legislation the President stated that he did not view the statute either to give rise to a private cause of action or to be enforceable through habeas corpus. The President further insisted that he will construe the statute in a manner consistent with his authority as Commander In Chief and the constitutional limitations on the judicial power. Statement on Signing the Department of Defense, Emergency Supplemental Appropriations to Address Hurricanes in the Gulf of Mexico, and Pandemic Influenza Act, 2006, 42 Weekly Comp. Pres. Doc. 1918 (Dec. 30, 2005). The new statute defines 'cruel, inhuman,

But they cannot, within the terms of settled doctrine, claim that officials of the United States violated the basic law of the nation—and that, in my view, is most unfortunate. Although it was no part of the business of the Supreme Court in *Rasul* to address the abuses in Abu Ghraib—the Court left the law where it found it—those events throw into bold relief the limitations of what the *Rasul* Court did in fact decide.

Footnote 15 ends with a reference to *United States v. Verdugo-Urquidez*[40]—one of the defining decisions of the modern period, and one of the cases upon which the Court of Appeals placed significant weight. *United States v. Verdugo-Urquidez* was decided in 1990—more than a decade before the Administration launched its 'War Against Terrorism' and invaded Afghanistan and then Iraq. The immediate context was a war of another type—the 'War Against Drugs'. But Chief Justice Rehnquist, the author of the Court's opinion, also expressed an interest in freeing the Executive from the shackles of the Bill of Rights in foreign military operations.[41] To that end, he denied the protection of the Fourth Amendment and perhaps the Bill of Rights in general to aliens living abroad.

René Martin Verdugo-Urquidez was a citizen of Mexico and the alleged violation of his rights occurred in Mexico. Federal drug enforcement agents, working with Mexican officials, searched his home in Mexico without a warrant and in the course of those searches seized certain documents. Prior to the search Verdugo-Urquidez had been arrested by Mexican authorities, transported to the Border Patrol station in southern California, and then turned over to United States Marshals. He was charged with being one of the leaders of an organization in Mexico that smuggled narcotics into the United States and was placed on trial in the United States for violating federal criminal statutes. In the course of the trial, Verdugo-Urquidez moved, on the basis of the Fourth Amendment,

---

or degrading treatment or punishment' as consisting of those punishments prohibited by the Fifth, Eighth, and Fourteenth Amendments of the Constitution. The statute further provides that the United States Reservations, Declarations and Understandings to the United Nations Convention Against Torture and Other Forms of Cruel, Inhuman or Degrading Treatment or Punishment shall be determinative of which punishments proscribed by those constitutional provisions are within the reach of the statute.

[40] 494 U.S. 259 (1990).

[41] Ibid., at 273 ('The United States frequently employs armed forces outside this country—over 200 times in our history—for the protection of American citizens or national security. Congressional Research Service, Instances of Use of United States Armed Forces Abroad, 1798-1989 (E. Collier ed. 1989). Application of the Fourth Amendment to those circumstances could significantly disrupt the ability of the political branches to respond to foreign situations involving our national interest').

to exclude the evidence seized in the raid on his Mexican residence. The Supreme Court held that the Fourth Amendment does not apply to a search by United States agents of a residence that is located in a foreign country and owned by an alien who did not reside in the United States and who did not otherwise voluntarily attach himself to the national community.

On a purely technical level, the Court's ruling was presented as a construction of the phrase 'the people' as it appears in the Fourth Amendment. The Fourth Amendment provides: 'The right of the people to be secure in their persons, houses, papers, and effects, against unreasonable searches and seizures, shall not be violated, and no Warrants shall issue, but upon probable cause, supported by Oath or affirmation, and particularly describing the place to be searched, and the persons or things to be seized'. Although the term 'the people' seems to be of universal scope, permitting no distinction between citizens and aliens, Chief Justice Rehnquist construed the phrase as a term of art that embraced only (a) citizens and (b) those aliens who have developed a sufficient voluntary connection with the United States to be considered part of the national community. Granted, Verdugo-Urquidez was being imprisoned in the United States, and tried in federal court for violating federal statutes, but this was not sufficient for the Chief Justice to place him within the scope of 'the people' protected by the Fourth Amendment.

Justice William Brennan dissented. In his dissent he convincingly showed that no evidence, either in the debates or in the general history surrounding the adoption of the Bill of Rights, indicates that the phrase 'the people' in the Fourth Amendment was meant to delineate a class of beneficiaries who would be protected by the Amendment. The phrase 'the people' was not a term of art, but rather, he insisted, merely a rhetorical device, to underscore the importance of the protection being granted. Justice Brennan also advanced a more cosmopolitan view of the Constitution, according to which the actions of the United States would be governed by the Constitution no matter where or against whom the United States acts. The Justice acknowledged that the meaning of the Constitution may vary from context to context; what the Fourth Amendment ban on unreasonable searches means in a suburban community in the United States differs from what it means on the battlefield, or for that matter, in a country that we occupy by virtue of our military power. But the actions of American officials would, according to Justice Brennan, always and everywhere be judged by the standards of the Constitution.

To defend his cosmopolitanism, Justice Brennan relied on the principle of mutuality: 'If we expect aliens to obey our laws, aliens should expect that we will obey our Constitution when we investigate, prosecute, and punish them'.[42] Such a principle seems unable to encompass all that Justice Brennan wanted—he was explicit that the Fourth Amendment applies to military activities abroad (though in such cases he would drop the warrant requirement and test the government's action only by the reasonableness requirement, which is necessarily sensitive to context). The principle of mutuality also suffers from a circularity, for the question is whether the government's action constitutes a violation of the Constitution. Justice Brennan may well be right in proclaiming that 'lawlessness breeds lawlessness',[43] but we cannot invoke that axiom to determine whether the government has acted lawlessly.

A more plausible account of Justice Brennan's cosmopolitanism, of great sway in the Warren Court era, identifies the nation with the Constitution and underscores the constitutive nature of that all-important law: the Constitution creates the structure of government and defines the limits of its authority.[44] The constitutive view of the relationship between the nation and the Constitution not only reflects the self understanding of the founders, but also and perhaps more importantly accords with the practice of constitutional adjudication over the last two hundred years. The doctrine of enumerated powers, the keystone of constitutional adjudication in the nineteenth century, was premised on the view that Congress had no authority other than that granted to it by the Constitution. In the twentieth century, the first question of constitutional adjudication shifted from whether the Constitution had granted the power to Congress to whether Congress or some other officer of the United States violated a particular constitutional prohibition. Still, it was assumed that the prohibitions on the government defined the outer limits of its authority, and that as a juridical entity, the United States has no existence outside of the Constitution.[45]

The limits on government authority can be derived from the terms upon which power was conferred on the new government, from certain prohibitions on the government contained in the body of the Constitution, notably Article IV, and above all, from the amendments to the Constitution adopted in 1791 and known as the Bill of Rights. For the

---

[42] Ibid., at 285 (Brennan, J., dissenting).

[43] Ibid., at 285 (Brennan, J., dissenting).

[44] See generally *Reid v. Covert*, 354 U.S. 1 (1957).

[45] *Downs v. Bidwell*, 182 US 244 (1901) (Harlan, J., dissenting). See generally Owen Fiss, *Troubled Beginnings of the Modern State, 1888-1910* at 225-56 (The Oliver Wendell Holmes Devise, History of the Supreme Court, Vol. VIII, 1993).

cosmopolitan, the Bill of Rights is conceived not as a testamentary document distributing a species of property to specific and limited classes of persons, but rather as a broad charter setting forth the norms that are to govern the operation of government. 'No person shall be deprived of life, liberty, or property without due process of law'. 'Congress shall make no law respecting the establishment of religion, or prohibiting the free exercise thereof; or abridging the freedom of speech'. 'Cruel and unusual punishment shall not be inflicted'. For the cosmopolitan, rights are not property belonging to particular people, but the concretization of these sweeping prohibitions of the Constitution.

This view of rights does not necessarily give the protections of the Constitution the universal scope that Justice Brennan demands. It still remains for the Court to apply the norm in some concrete case, and that necessarily entails a process of interpretation. The history or wording of the norm may delimit its scope, and the context will also determine the content of the right. All that can be said is that this way of viewing rights— as norms, not property—more easily accommodates cosmopolitanism and is more conducive to that orientation. It makes it more difficult for a justice to claim, as Chief Justice Rehnquist did, in *Verdugo-Urquidez*, that the Fourth Amendment affords protection only to citizens or those who voluntarily associate themselves with the national community. It renders the effort to limit the Bill of Rights in this way more implausible, and suggests that those limits are not based on a strict interpretation of the text, but on more extraneous or political considerations, like giving the Executive the flexibility Chief Justice Rehnquist believes is necessary to conduct foreign affairs effectively.

Chief Justice Rehnquist ended his opinion in *Verdugo-Urquidez* by proclaiming, '[f]or better or for worse, we live in a world of nation-states'.[46] The importance of the nation-state cannot be denied, even today, in the face of ever increasing globalization. The cosmopolitan view of the Constitution would not, however, deny the importance of the nation-state, but rather offer an alternative, and in my view, more appealing way of understanding the relation between the Constitution and the nation. Of course, non-citizens do not vote, and thus are not politically empowered to demand that the government justify its actions to them. But that does not mean that the government owes them no duties, as is indeed clear from the treatment of non-citizens who are residents of the country. They too cannot vote, but are protected by the Constitution. Similarly, although the government does not act in the name of non-citizens, those

---

[46] *Verdugo-Urquidez*, 494 U.S. at 275.

in whose name it does act—'we the people'—may demand that it proceed in a certain way whenever it acts and regardless of against whom it acts.[47] The key provisions of the Bill of Rights—including but in no way limited to the Fourth, Fifth, and Eighth Amendments—present themselves as universal prohibitions, and as such may be read as an expression of the demands by the founding generation as to the way the government they were creating must act.

Everyone who resides in the United States, aliens and citizens alike, are expected to obey the laws of the United States, and can be called upon to lend support to the government, through, say, the payment of taxes and perhaps even serving in the military. Yet as evident from the rules regarding the rights of those who flaunt the law, and who we can assume are justly convicted of doing so, the protection of the Constitution is not in any way limited to those who obey the laws or otherwise support the government. The obligations imposed on the government by the Bill of Rights are not a quid pro quo offered to its subjects, but the expression of principles of right behaviour.[48]

Chief Justice Rehnquist and Justice Brennan occupied polar positions in *Verdugo-Urquidez*. Justices Scalia, Thomas, and O'Connor joined Chief Justice Rehnquist's opinion without comment. Justice Thurgood Marshall joined Justice Brennan's opinion in a similar fashion. The remaining three Justices—John Paul Stevens, Harry Blackmun, and Anthony Kennedy—were arrayed between the poles. None of these three believed that only those persons who voluntarily affiliated themselves with the national community were protected by the Fourth Amendment. Justices Blackmun and Stevens stressed the fact that Verdugo-Urquidez had been placed on trial in the United States for violating its criminal laws and as a result the Fourth Amendment was applicable. Justice Blackmun dissented because, although he agreed with Chief Justice Rehnquist that there was no need for a warrant to search the residence of an alien outside the country, he insisted that to be valid under the Fourth Amendment the search must be reasonable, and thought that the case should be remanded to the lower court to make the reasonableness determination. Justice Stevens, like Justice Blackmun, applied the reasonableness standard, but on the

---

[47] But see Thomas Nagel, *The Problem of Global Justice*, 33 Phil. & Pub. Aff. 113, 121 (2005) (discussing 'the political conception of justice', which asserts that 'justice is something we owe through our shared institutions only to those with whom we stand in a strong political relation'). Ibid., at 121.

[48] But see Gerald L. Neuman, *Strangers to the Constitution: Immigrants, Borders, and Fundamental Law* 54-56 (1996) (discussing the Federalist's argument that aliens have no constitutional rights as they are not parties to the Constitution).

record before him thought there was sufficient basis to conclude that the search of Verdugo-Urquidez's house was reasonable. He concurred in the judgment.

The position of Justice Kennedy—then a very recent appointee to the Court—is harder to characterize. He was the crucial fifth vote that Chief Justice Rehnquist needed to endow his opinion with the status of law, and Justice Kennedy obliged him. Justice Kennedy began his separate concurrence by announcing that he joined the Chief Justice's opinion. He also said that his views did not depart in 'fundamental respects' from those expressed by the Chief Justice,[49] but one is left to wonder whether this was in fact the case. Although he rejected the view that the Fourth Amendment's warrant requirement should be applied to the search of a foreign home of a non-resident alien, his reason was quite different from Chief Justice Rehnquist's. He did not read the phrase 'the people' as a restriction on the universe of persons protected. As he put it, 'explicit recognition of "the right of the people" to Fourth Amendment protection may be interpreted to underscore the importance of the right, rather than to restrict the category of persons who may assert it'.[50] In contrast to Chief Justice Rehnquist, Justice Kennedy simply posited that adherence to the Fourth Amendment warrant requirement abroad would be 'impracticable and anomalous'.[51]

Even more importantly, Justice Kennedy seemed to give a certain measure of extraterritorial force to the Constitution. He began from the proposition that 'it is correct . . . that the government may act only as the Constitution authorizes, whether the actions in question are foreign or domestic'.[52] Yet, building on a view articulated by the second Justice John Harlan, he maintained that this does not require that the government necessarily apply each and every provision of the Constitution abroad. Rather, the constitutionality of the government's actions abroad should be judged by a flexible standard based on some notion of fundamental fairness. In conducting searches of the homes of non-citizens abroad the Constitution does not require federal agents to obtain: a warrant, as the Fourth Amendment might be read to require, but only that non-citizens be treated fairly. Justice Brennan's constitution would also allow adjustments to be made as to how the Bill of Rights is applied abroad, but, as with the doctrine of selective incorporation, always within the disciplining force

---

[49] *Verdugo-Urquidez*, 494 US at 275 (Kennedy, J., concurring).

[50] Ibid., at 276 (Kennedy, J., concurring).

[51] Ibid., at 278 (Kennedy, J., concurring).

[52] Ibid., at 277 (Kennedy, J., concurring).

of the text of the amendments themselves. Justice Kennedy's constitution is more flexible, and thus less clear. My hunch is that Justice Brennan's approach would yield results more approximating justice than Justice Kennedy's, but both describe a constitution without borders.

Such a view of the Constitution makes an appearance in *Rasul*, though in the most oblique way. When Justice Stevens cited *Verdugo-Urquidez* in footnote 15 in *Rasul*, he referred only to Justice Kennedy's concurring opinion in that case, not Chief Justice Rehnquist's opinion for the Court. The significance of that selective reference is not clear to me. Perhaps Justice Stevens meant to embrace Justice Kennedy's constitutional cosmopolitanism. Or, conceivably the reference was offered as an inducement for Justice Kennedy to join the majority opinion. As it turned out, however, Justice Kennedy did not join Justice Stevens's opinion, but wrote a short separate concurrence. In it, he applied the same flexible approach outlined in his concurrence in *Verdugo-Urquidez*, again expressing unease with creating 'automatic' rules.[53]

Like Justice Stevens, Justice Kennedy acknowledged the unique status of Guantánamo—that for all practical purposes it was a territory of the United States. Yet he refused to treat the case as though it were nothing more than an exercise in statutory interpretation. Justice Kennedy understood that the petitioners had to have some constitutional rights in order for there to be any point in the habeas proceeding at all. Although he cautioned against judicial interference with the rightful prerogatives of the President acting as Commander-in-Chief, Justice Kennedy recognized that 'there are circumstances in which the courts maintain the power and the responsibility to protect *persons* from unlawful detention even where military affairs are implicated', (emphasis added).[54] The touchstone for Justice Kennedy was 'military necessity'[55]—only exigencies of war would prevent the exercise of the judicial power implicit in the writ of habeas corpus. He also believed that the government's insistence on military necessity in the case at hand was contradicted by the fact that prisoners were being held indefinitely (justified by the government on the theory that they were illegal enemy combatants, comparable to members of irregular militias, and thus not entitled to the usual protections of the Third Geneva Convention for prisoners of war, including repatriation at the end of the hostilities). Justice Kennedy wrote, '[p]erhaps, where detainees are taken from a zone of hostilities, detention without proceed-

---

[53] *Rasul v. Bush*, 542 U.S. 466,488 (2004) (Kennedy, J., concurring).

[54] Ibid., at 487 (Kennedy, J., concurring) (emphasis added).

[55] Ibid., at 488 (Kennedy, J., concurring).

ings or trial would be justified by military necessity for a matter of weeks; but as the period of detention stretches from months to years, the case for continued detention to meet military exigencies becomes weaker'.[56] Such a flexible or variable approach has its pitfalls, all of which are well known, but at least one can see within it the possibility of confronting on a constitutional basis possible government abuse of alien prisoners who are not American citizens, such as occurred at Abu Ghraib, provided of course that Justice Kennedy's insistence upon fundamental fairness is not conditioned upon the anomalous territorial status of Guantánamo.

No one else joined Justice Kennedy's opinion. The timidity of the majority in *Rasul*, as well as that of the majorities responsible for *Padilla* and *Hamdi*, is no accidental quality, but largely a product of the situation in which the Justices found themselves. Faced with the events of September 11, and then the invasions of Afghanistan and Iraq and the military occupations of these countries, the demands for power by the President and his Administration must have pressed heavily on the Justices. Although the Justices are committed to the rule of law and the protection of the Constitution, they also see themselves as responsible for protecting the interests of the nation they serve. The Justices are practical people. So they searched for ways to honour the Constitution without compromising vital national interests. As a result, they told Jose Padilla to start over in another court, provided Yaser Hamdi with an opportunity to contest the legality of his classification but made it possible for that hearing to be conducted by a military tribunal, and allowed the prisoners in Guantánamo to begin habeas proceedings without telling them in any clear way what rights they might assert in those proceedings. What is missing from this calculus, and in my judgment from all three of these much celebrated cases, however, is a full appreciation of the value of the Constitution—as a statement of the ideals of the nation and as the basis of the principle of freedom—and even more, a full appreciation of the fact that the whole-hearted pursuit of any ideal requires sacrifices, sometimes quite substantial ones. It is hard for the Justices, or for that matter anyone, to accept that we may have to risk the material well-being of the nation in order to be faithful to the Constitution and the duties it imposes. Still, it must be remembered that the issue is not just the survival of the nation—of course the United States will survive—but rather the terms of survival.

---

[56] Ibid., at 488 (Kennedy, J., concurring).

V

The Fragility of Law[1]

Fiss has also criticized the Bush Administration for directing the National Security Agency to intercept electronic communications by telephone and e-mail between the United States and foreign countries without warrants or probable cause and for the torturing of prisoners.[2] He correctly sees both of these activities as constitutional violations. As he notes, however, these actions are not only an abuse of executive power. Both Congress and the courts are complicit in these clear violations of the rule of law.

In December 2005, the New York Times reported that the National Security Agency was intercepting electronic communications by telephone and e-mail between the United States and foreign countries without probable cause and without obtaining judicial warrants.[3] The Bush Administration acknowledged this revelation and strongly defended this warrantless wiretapping as necessary to our national security.[4] On several occasions, then Attorney General Gonzales boldly stated that there may be other warrantless eavesdropping beyond what had already been disclosed and reported in the media. Unfortunately, that has proved accurate. For example, on September 9, 2007, the New York Times reported that the Federal Bureau of Investigation (FBI) used secret demands for records to obtain data not only on individuals it saw as targets but also details on what their documents referred to as the targets' "community

---

[1] Owen M. Fiss, *The Fragility of Law*, 54 Yale L. Rep. 40 (2007).

[2] *See* discussion *supra* Introduction. Fiss elaborated his views on the issue of torture in a recent article. *See* Owen Fiss, *The Example of America*, 119 Yale L.J. Pocket Part 1 (2009), http://yalelawjournal.org/content/view/764/1/.

[3] *See* James Risen & Eric Lichtblau, *Bush Lets U.S. Spy on Callers Without Courts*, N.Y. Times, Dec. 16, 2005, at A1 (article based on James Risen, State of War: The Secret History of the CIA and the Bush Administration (2005)).

[4] *See, e.g.*, Eric Lichtblau, *Bush Defends Spy Programs and Denies Misleading Public*, N.Y. Times, Jan. 2, 2006, at A11.

interest." This community included the network of people the target was in contact with during the course of the warrantless and ostensibly illegal and unconstitutional wiretapping.[5] As Fiss notes, these activities are clearly violations of the Fourth Amendment, which under prevailing doctrine requires a judicially approved warrant.[6] Federal statutes also require the government to obtain a warrant either from a federal district court or from the Foreign Intelligence Surveillance Court (FISC) before it can engage in electronic eavesdropping.[7] President Bush has claimed two sources of power for engaging in warrantless surveillance: his power as Commander in Chief and his authority under the Authorization for the Use of Military Force Joint Resolution (AUMF),[8] enacted after September 11. Neither of these arguments or "claims of power," of course, authorize warrantless electronic surveillance.

The scope of President Bush's argument is breathtaking and far reaching. It suggests that the President can legally authorize violations of the Bill of Rights. The President, even in his role as Commander in Chief, has no legal authority, inherent or otherwise, to violate any provision of the Bill of Rights. Under the Bush Administration's reasoning, the President could authorize executive branch officials to coerce confessions out of people in clear violation of the Fifth Amendment, or could authorize searches of homes without complying with the Fourth Amendment, or suspend freedom of speech in violation of the First Amendment. The AUMF, of course, does not provide such a basis for presidential power. Under the AUMF, Congress authorized the use of troops and arms to respond to the threat of terrorism. The resolution makes absolutely no reference to eavesdropping.

It is beyond doubt that authorizing military force does not include any and every other action that the government wishes to take in the name of the war on terrorism. The Supreme Court strongly made this point in *Hamdan v. Rumsfeld*.[9] In that case, the Supreme Court ruled that there was not adequate statutory authority for the military commissions created

---

[5] Erik Lichtblau, *F.B.I. Data Mining Reached Beyond Initial Targets*, N.Y. Times, Sept. 9, 2007, at A1. The community of interest data sought by the FBI is central to a data-mining technique called link analysis. In addition to monitoring these "threats," the Bush Administration has been eavesdropping on the lawyers representing terrorism suspects. Philip Shenon, *Lawyers Fear Monitoring in Cases on Terrorism*, N.Y. Times, Apr. 28, 2008, at A14.

[6] U.S. Const. amend. IV.

[7] 18 U.S.C. § 25511(2)(f) (2006).

[8] Authorization for Use of Military Force, Pub. L. No. 107-40, 115 Stat. 224 (2001).

[9] 548 U.S. 557 (2006).

by President Bush's executive order.[10] The Court unequivocally stated that it did not need to consider whether the President may constitutionally convene military commissions "without the sanction of Congress."[11] In a footnote, the Court further explained: "Whether or not the President has independent power, absent congressional authorization, to convene military commissions, he may not disregard limitations that Congress has, in proper exercise of its own war powers, placed on his powers .... The Government does not argue otherwise."[12]

Justice Stevens, writing for the majority, concluded that two statutory provisions, Articles 21 and 36 of the Uniform Code of Military Justice (UCMJ),[13] limited the President's authority. The Court explained that Article 21 expressly conditioned the President's use of military commissions on compliance with the "law of war" which includes the four Geneva Conventions.[14]

The government argued that there was statutory authority for the military commissions. Specifically, the government argued that authority was provided for in the presidential executive order, especially under AUMF, adopted after September 11.[15] The government also argued that the Detainee Treatment Act authorized the military commissions.[16] The Supreme Court expressly rejected these arguments. The Court stated: "[T]here is nothing in the text or legislative history of the AUMF even hinting that Congress intended to expand or alter the authorization set forth in Article 21 of the UCMJ."[17]

The *Hamdan* Court's reasoning is significant because, along with many other arguments, the Bush Administration has continued to argue that the AUMF authorizes its actions in the war on terrorism. The Bush Administration has, of course, even claimed that the AUMF authorizes the executive to engage in warrantless electronic eavesdropping. Justice Steven's majority opinion convincingly demonstrates that the Supreme Court is unwilling to read the AUMF as authority for presidential actions that

---

[10] *Id.* at 567.

[11] *Id.* at 592 (internal quotations omitted).

[12] *Id.* at 593, n.23.

[13] *Id.* at 592-93, 621-22 (quoting 10 U.S.C § 836(b) and concluding that the statute did not authorize a sweeping presidential mandate and that the executive branch's determination of practicability under this section was simply insufficient to justify military tribunals).

[14] *Id.* at 600-02.

[15] *Id.* at 593-615.

[16] *Id.*

[17] *Id.* at 594.

are clearly inconsistent with statutory provisions.[18] Moreover, warrantless electronic eavesdropping is simply unnecessary because the government can easily go to the FISC and obtain a warrant.[19] The major argument that the Administration has given for not going to the FISC is that FISC warrants require too much paperwork.[20] This is complete nonsense. In any event, the claim that requiring a warrant harms administrative efficiency, of course, can never justify violating either the Constitution or a congressional enactment.

While the Supreme Court has rejected the Bush Administration's arguments, which that Administration could have used in support of its electronic surveillance activities, Congress has undermined the Court's conclusions. On July 10, 2008, President Bush signed legislation which for the first time provided a legal framework for much of the surveillance without warrants that has been conducted in secret by the NSA and outside FISA.[21] This bill makes it much easier to spy on Americans at home, greatly reduces the FISA court's power, and grants immunity to the companies that turn over Americans' private communications without warrant. For example, the bill allows the government to avoid the FISA court and collect untold amounts of Americans' communications without a warrant simply by claiming that it is doing so for national security reasons. Moreover, the bill defines national security so broadly that the term could be interpreted to mean anything a president wants it to

---

[18] Unfortunately, Congress has been complicit in allowing warrantless electronic surveillance. See *supra* text accompanying notes 62-74 (Introduction).

[19] Between 1978 and 1999, the FISC granted all 11,833 warrant requests. It denied none! Lawrence D. Sloan, *Echelon and the Legal Restraints on Signals Intelligence: A Need for Reevaluation*, 50 Duke L.J. 1467, 1496 (2001). Moreover, over the past thirty years, the FISA court has approved nearly 20,000 warrants while rejecting perhaps a half dozen. Editorial, *Compromising the Constitution*, N.Y. Times, July 8, 2008, at A22. Furthermore, FISC denied a request by the ACLU to release portions of its past rulings to explain how it has interpreted the FISA. *See The Court that May Not Be Heard*, N.Y. Times, Dec. 15, 2007, at A34.

[20] *See* Press Briefing by Attorney General Alberto Gonzales & General Michael Hayden, Principal Dir. For Nat'l Intelligence (Dec. 19, 2005), *available at* http://www.whitehouse.gov/news/releases/2005/12/20051219-1.html (stating that Bush Administration continues to "go to FISA court and obtain orders," but because FISA requires court orders "[they] don't have the speed and agility that [they] need, in all circumstances, to deal with this new kind of enemy"); *see also* Dep't of Justice, Legal Authorities Supporting the Activities of the National Security Agency Described by the President (discussing basis for authorizing NSA's interception of international communication linked to Al Qaeda, *available at* http://www.usdoj.gov/opa/whitepaperonnsalegalauthorities.pdf, at 5. "FISA, by contrast, is better suited 'for long-term monitoring'" *Id.* (quoting Press Conference by President George W. Bush (Dec. 19, 2005)).

[21] Foreign Intelligence Surveillance Act of 1978 Amendments Acts of 2008, H.R. 6304, 110th Cong. (2008) (enacted) *available* at http://thomas.loc.gov/cgi-bin/bdquery/z?d110:HR6304. See *supra* text accompanying notes 62-74 (Introduction).

mean. The bill also fails even to mention counterterrorism and deletes the significant "foreign power" provision from FISA. It also greatly expands the government's power to invoke emergency wiretapping procedures.

Fiss argues that the prohibition against torture, which derives from the Eighth Amendment's bar against cruel and unusual punishment and our participation in the Convention Against Torture,[22] has also been violated by the Bush Administration. These actions include the despicable treatment of prisoners at Abu Ghraib prison in Iraq, the treatment of prisoners at Guantánamo and other prisons, and the program of "extraordinary rendition" in which American officials have sent suspected Al Qaeda operatives to countries that engage in torture.

In August 2002, the Department of Justice, Office of Legal Counsel, issued a memorandum boldly stating that the President could authorize torture of human beings in violation of treaties ratified by the United States and federal statutes that prohibit such conduct.[23] The infamous, so-called "Torture Memo" argued that the anti-torture statutes did not prohibit the President from ordering the use of torture in interrogations because such a prohibition would violate the President's constitutional powers.[24] The memorandum based this conclusion, of course, on an overly broad assertion of presidential war powers. It claimed that neither statutes nor treaties could limit those powers.[25] Top officials of government were claiming that the government could torture human beings, notwithstanding laws and treaties specifically forbidding torture. This is an assertion of executive power that has no precedent in American history. It is an argument for absolute power without any limits or check and balances. It is the assertion of one who believes not in the rule of law, but in the rule of the dictator.[26]

---

[22] United Nations Convention Against Torture and Other Cruel, Inhuman or Degrading Treatment or Punishment, Dec. 10, 1984, 1465 U.N.T.S. 85.

[23] See Memorandum from Jay S. Bybee, Assistant Attorney Gen., to Alberto R. Gonzales, Counsel to the President (Aug. 1, 2002), in THE TORTURE PAPERS: THE ROAD TO ABU GHRAIB 218 (Karen J. Greenberg & Joshua L. Dratel eds., 2005) [August 2002 Torture Memorandum]. On October 15, 2008, the Washington Post reported that the Bush Administration issued two secret memoranda to the C.I.A. in 2003 and 2004 that explicitly endorsed the agency's use of interrogation techniques, such as waterboarding, against al-Qaeda suspects. Joby Warrick, CIA Tactics Endorsed in Secret Memos, WASH. POST, Oct. 15, 2008, at A1.

[24] See memorandum from Jay S. Bybee, supra note 23, at 39-46.

[25] Id. at 36-39.

[26] On December 5, 2007, a Congressional conference committee voted to outlaw the harsh interrogation techniques used by the C.I.A. against suspected terrorists. See Scott Shane, Lawmakers Back Limits On Interrogation Tactics, N.Y. TIMES, Dec. 7, 2007, at A14. On March 8, 2008, President Bush used his executive power to veto the Congressional effort to

The "Torture Memo" argued that only causing pain "equivalent in intensity to the pain accompanying physical injury, such as organ failure, impairment of bodily function, or even death" fell within the definition of torture. The Department of Justice later withdrew the "Torture Memo."[27] A subsequent Department of Defense Memorandum, issued in December 2002, however, suggested that the use of scenarios to convince the prisoner that death was imminent and the use of a wet towel and dripping water to induce fear of suffocation, "may be legally available" even though forbidden "as a matter of policy for the time being."[28] The withdrawing memorandum, however, does not even question the substance of the "Torture Memo's" position on the question of presidential power.

In another Justice Department memorandum,[29] dated March 14, 2003, the Justice Department's Deputy Assistant Attorney General tells the Pentagon's senior leadership that inflicting pain would not be torture unless it caused "death, organ failure or permanent damage." As with the "Torture Memo," the March 14, 2003 memorandum notes that the presidential wartime powers would not be limited by United Nations ("U.N.") treaties. But this memorandum goes further, arguing explicitly that the President's war powers could trump any international law against torture, which it said could not constitutionally be enforced if a law interferes with the President's—the Commander in Chief's—orders. According to the memorandum, "previous opinions [of the Justice De-

---

limit the C.I.A.'s latitude to utilize torture techniques while interrogating terrorism suspects. The House of Representatives failed to override the veto. Mark Mazzetti, *Officials Say C.I.A. Kept Qaeda Suspect in Secret Detention*, N.Y. TIMES, Mar. 15, 2008, at A6. The law required the C.I.A. and all intelligence services to abide by the restrictions on holding and interrogating prisoners contained in the United States Army Field Manual. The bill explicitly prohibited many coercive interrogation techniques. Steven Lee Myers and Mark Mazzetti, *Bush Vetoes Bill on C.I.A. Tactics, Affirming Legacy*, N.Y. TIMES, Mar. 9, 2008, at A1. In addition to a blanket prohibition on torture, these prohibitions included forcing a prisoner to be naked, perform sexual acts or pose in a sexual manner; placing hoods or sacks over the heads of a prisoner, and using duct tape over the eyes; applying beatings, electric shocks, burns or other forms of physical pain; waterboarding; using military working dogs; inducing hypothermia or heat injury; conducting mock executions; and depriving a prisoner of necessary food, water, or medical care. Editorial, *Horrifying and Unnecessary*, N.Y. TIMES, Mar. 2, 2008, at WK 10. These practices have, of course, long been prohibited by American laws and international treaties. President Bush, however, does not think it necessary to live up to the rule of law.

[27] *See* Memorandum from Daniel Levi, Acting Assistant Attorney Gen., Office of Legal Counsel, to James Corney, Deputy Attorney Gen. (Dec. 30, 2004), *available at* http://www.usdoj.gov/olc/18usc23402340a2.htm.

[28] Owen Fiss, *The Fragility of Law*, 54 YALE L. REP., 40, 41 2007.

[29] *See* Memorandum from John C. Yoo, Deputy Assistant Attorney General, U.S. Justice Department Office of Legal Counsel, to William J. Haynes II, General Counsel of the Department of Defense (Mar. 14, 2003).

partment] make clear that customary international law is not federal law and that the President is free to override it at his discretion." Opinions drafted by the Office of Legal Counsel are binding on the Defense Department. The opinion memorandum effectively sidelined military lawyers who adamantly opposed harsh interrogation methods. Although this memorandum was rescinded in December 2003, it reveals that the abuse of prisoners in custody may have involved not-so-subtle signals from high ranking Bush Administration and Pentagon officials, and was not simply irresponsible actions by low level personnel. Indeed, it has now been acknowledged by President Bush that some of the very highest officials in his Administration not only approved the abuse of prisoners, but directly participated in the detailed planning of harsh interrogations and helped create the legal structure used to justify these techniques and protect those who followed the orders. In April 2008, Mr. Bush stated that he knew of these meetings and approved of the result.[30]

Much of the Bush Administration's constant arguments that this government does not torture people are apparently mere smokescreens. The Bush Administration has never abandoned its assertion of unlimited presidential power to order brutal interrogations amounting to torture under international and domestic definitions of torture.[31] On October 4, 2007, the New York Times revealed that, in two separate secret legal opinions, written in 2005, the Justice Department had authorized the harshest interrogation techniques ever used by the Central Intelligence Agency (C.I.A.).[32] These secret memoranda provided explicit authority for government agents to use painful physical and psychological interrogation methods, including head slapping, simulated drowning, and frigid temperatures. The secret opinions were written just months after a Justice Department opinion, issued in December 2004, declared torture "abhorrent." The second secret opinion authorizing torture was written a short time after Congress moved toward outlawing "cruel, inhuman,

---

[30] Editorial, *The Torture Sessions*, N.Y. TIMES, Apr. 20, 2008, at WK 9. On April 16, 2009, the Justice Department made public other memoranda written in 2002 and 2005 which described in detail the brutal methods approved by the Bush Administration and used by the C.I.A. to extract information from senior Al Queda operatives. Mark Mazzetti & Scott Shane, *Memos Spell Out Brutal C.I.A. Mode of Interrogation*, N.Y. TIMES, Apr. 17, 2009, at A1.

[31] Even after the Supreme Court and Congress made clear that this Administration must adhere to the Geneva Convention Standards, the Bush Administration continued to argue that intelligence operations attempting to disrupt terrorist attacks may legally use interrogation methods that are prohibited under international law. Mark Mazzetti, *Letters Outline Legal Rationale for C.I.A. Tactics*, N.Y. TIMES, Apr. 27, 2008, at A1.

[32] Scott Shave, David Johnston & James Risen, *Secret U.S. Endorsement of Severe Interrogations*, N.Y. TIMES, Oct. 4, 2007, at A1.

and degrading treatment." This secret opinion stated that none of the C.I.A. interrogation methods violated that standard. Congress was never informed about these two secret opinions.[33] The Bush Administration has not only condoned torture and abuse at secret prisons, but this Administration has conducted a systematic campaign to mislead Congress, the American people, and the world about these policies.

On April 30, 2008, in what appears to be a partial concession to Congressional pressure, the Bush Administration agreed to show the Senate and House Intelligence Committees these secret Justice Department legal opinions justifying torture. This may, however, be a pyrrhic victory for Congress. It is not clear whether the Bush Administration will turn over the complete and unredacted opinions or merely selected parts of the memoranda. Moreover, the White House has agreed to give the memoranda only to the House and Senate Intelligence Committee. It refuses to give them to the Senate Judiciary Committee, which has supervisory power over the Justice Department. One of that committee's major functions is to determine the legality of government policies. The Bush Administration continues to use the false claim of secrecy to bar the documents from the public, which, of course, has an absolute right to know what the law requires.[34]

Not only has the President given orders that allow people to be tortured, but it appears the Supreme Court condones this policy. On October 9, 2007, the Supreme Court refused to hear an appeal filed on behalf of a German citizen of Lebanese descent who claims he was abducted by United States agents and tortured by them while imprisoned in Afghanistan.[35] Without comment, the Justices let stand an appeals court

---

[33] *Id.*

[34] Editorial, *Notes From the War on Terror,* N.Y. Times, May 2, 2008, at A22. Moreover, two Bush Administration lawyers who provided important legal justifications for harsh interrogation methods that condone torture recently testified in front of a House Judiciary subcommittee to support their positions. The lawyers, John Yoo, the former Justice Department official who wrote several legal opinions on torture, and David S. Addington, who as Vice-President Dick Cheney's legal advisor provided support for the harsh interrogation policies, vigorously defended these policies. They also testified that higher level officials approved these "techniques." Scott Shane, *2 Testify on Their Support For Harsh Interrogation,* N.Y. TIMES, June 27, 2008, at A15. The Bush Administration continues to assert the legality and authority to use harsh interrogation techniques violative of international law. In recent letters, the Justice Department has informed Congress that American intelligence operatives attempting to avert terrorist attacks can legally use interrogation methods that might otherwise be prohibited under international law. Mark Mazzetti, *C.I.A. Interrogation Tactics Get Legal Rationale,* N.Y. TIMES, Apr. 27, 2008, at A1.

[35] El-Masri v. U.S., 479 F.3d 296 (4th Cir. 2007), *cert denied,* 76 U.S.L.W. 3663 (U.S. Oct. 9, 2007) (No. 06-1613).

ruling that the state secrets privilege, a judicially created doctrine that the Bush Administration has invoked to win dismissal of lawsuits that touch on issues of national security, protected the government's actions from court review. The claim is that allowing the case to go forward would put national security secrets at risk. In effect, the Supreme Court has granted the government immunity for subjecting Mr. El-Masri to "extraordinary rendition," the morally and legally unsupportable practice of transporting foreign nationals to be interrogated in other countries known to use torture and lacking basic legal protections.

Nevertheless, the Bush Administration has been put on notice by an objective source—the International Committee for the Red Cross—that its interrogation techniques constitute torture. In a secret report issued in 2007 and shared with President Bush and Secretary of State Condoleeza Rice, the Red Cross concluded that the C.IA.'s interrogation methods for high-level Al-Qaeda prisoners "categorically" constitute torture, which is, of course, illegal under both American domestic law and international law. The report also warned that these activities could make the Bush Administration officials who approved them—even the President—guilty of war crimes, and subject to prosecution.[36] The secret report was revealed in a recently published book, *The Dark Side: The Inside Story of How the War on Terror Turned into a War on American Ideals*,[37] by Jane Mayer, who writes on counterterrorism for the New Yorker. The book states that the interrogators confined one of the prisoners in a box so small as to require him to double up his limbs in a fetal position, slammed some prisoners against walls, waterboarded other prisoners, subjected some to prolonged sleep deprivation, kept at least one prisoner naked for more than a month subjecting him to extreme temperature changes, from

---

[36] Moreover, on December 11, 2008, a bipartisan Senate Armed Services Committee issued a report which makes a strong case for bringing criminal charges for authorizing these interrogation tactics against former Defense Secretary Donald Rumsfeld; his legal counsel, William J. Haynes; and potentially other top officials, including the former White House counsel Alberto Gonzales and David Addington, Vice President Cheney's former chief of staff. Senate Armed Services Committee, 110th Cong., Inquiry into the Treatment of Detainees in U.S. Custody (Dec. 11, 2008), *available at* http://www.levin.senate.gov/newsroom/. The report details how the actions of these men led directly to the abuses at Abu Ghraib, in Afghanistan, in Guantánamo Bay, Cuba, and in secret C.I.A. prisons. The report makes clear that these officials methodically introduced interrogation practices based on illegal torture devised by Chinese officials during the Korean War. Their only use in the United States, before the Bush Administration took office, was to train soldiers to resist what might happen to them if they were captured by a ruthless enemy. These same officials then issued morally and legally questionable documents—discussed above in the text—to justify their actions.

[37] JANE MAYER, THE DARK SIDE: THE INSIDE STORY OF HOW THE WAR ON TERROR TURNED INTO A WAR ON AMERICAN IDEALS (2008).

suffocating heat to painfully cold temperatures, and shackled prisoners to the ceiling for periods up to eight hours.[38]

The use of torture has weakened, not strengthened, our ability to stop future terrorist attacks. This is not just because Abu Ghraib photographs have been used as recruitment tools by jihadists. Perhaps even more destructive are the false confessions inevitably elicited from tortured prisoners. The huge amount of misinformation has compromised prosecutions, allowed other guilty parties to escape, and sent the American military off on wild-goose chases, including the war in Iraq.[39]

---

[38] Scott Shane, *Book Cites Secret Red Cross Report of C.I.A. Torture of Qaeda Captives*, N.Y. TIMES, July 11, 2008, at A9.

[39] Frank Rich, *The Real-Life '24' of Summer 2008*, N.Y. TIMES, July 13, 2008, at WK 12. In addition to the questions about torture, the Bush Administration has argued that the President has the legal power to order the indefinite detention of civilians captured in the United States. In a 5 to 4 decision issued on July 15, 2008, the Court of Appeals for the Fourth Circuit agreed with the President. Al-Marri v. Pucciarelli, No. 06-7427, 2008 WL 2736787 (4th Cir. July 15, 2008). The court held that if the government's allegations about Ali al-Marri, a citizen of Qatar now in military custody in Charleston, South Carolina, are true, Congress has empowered the President to detain him as an enemy combatant. But a second, overlapping 5 to 4 majority of that court ruled that al-Marri must be given an additional opportunity to challenge his detention in federal court. The court ruled that an earlier court proceeding, in which the government had only presented a sworn statement from a defense intelligence specialist, was inadequate process. Soon after President Obama came into office, the Justice Department decided to move the case into a civilian court. On March 6, 2009, the Supreme Court vacated the lower court ruling and remanded the case with instructions to dismiss the appeal as moot. Al-Marri, v. Spagone, No. 08-368, 2009 WL 564940 (U.S. March 6, 2009). The Supreme Court ruling thus leaves open the question of whether detention of resident aliens can ever be constitutional.

THE FRAGILITY OF LAW*

The phrase "War Against Terrorism" has no discrete legal content. It was politically inspired, and used to mobilize American society. Yet the declaration of the "War Against Terrorism" marked the beginning of a unique challenge to the rule of law that began on September 11, 2001, and continues to this very day.

In speaking of the rule of law, I refer not to the statutes and regulations that serve the purposes of the state, but rather to the Constitution itself, which creates the public morality of the nation. The Constitution is not exhausted by the words appearing in the document executed in 1787 and its twenty-seven amendments. It also includes principles, such as the separation of powers or the right to travel, that are inferred from the overall structure of the Constitution, and certain enactments of Congress—the Civil Rights Act of 1964, for example—that articulate the governing principles of American society. These principles are laden with a special normative value that derives from the role they play in defining our national identity—what it means to be American.

Since September 11, at least three of these principles have been put in issue. The first is the prohibition against torture, derived, as I see it, from the Eighth Amendment and our participation in the Convention Against Torture. The challenge comes not so much from the grotesque treatment of prisoners at the Abu Ghraib prison in Iraq, where disciplinary proceedings were brought against those responsible, but from the Administration's actions in the war against Al Qaeda itself.

In order to broaden the range of techniques that interrogators can use against prisoners allegedly linked to Al Qaeda, an August 2002 Department of Justice memorandum argued that only acts causing pain "equivalent in intensity to the pain accompanying physical injury, such as organ failure, impairment of body function, or even death" fell within the legal definition of torture. The Department of Justice later distanced itself from this definition, but a separate December 2002 Department

---

* Owen M. Fiss, The Fragility of Law, 54 YALE L. REP. 40 (2007). This article uses the footnote numbers and citation form of this particular publication.

of Defense memorandum establishing guidelines for the interrogation of prisoners held at Guantánamo suggested that two practices almost universally understood as torture—the use of scenarios designed to convince detainees that death was imminent, and use of a wet towel and dripping water to induce fear of suffocation—though forbidden "as a matter of policy for the time being," nonetheless "may be legally available."

The program of "extraordinary renditions," in which American officials have abducted suspected Al Qaeda members and transferred them to countries that routinely engage in torture, suggests a similar disregard for the principle against torture. Indeed, it has become an open question whether the President even believes himself bound by the principle. In December 2005, when he signed a statutory ban on torture, President Bush said that he intended to construe the ban as consistent with his constitutional powers as Commander in Chief and his duty to protect against terrorist attacks, a statement that has been widely understood as indicating that he may not feel bound by the act's language. The President is entirely correct that statutes cannot constitutionally interfere with his powers as Commander in Chief, but the statutory ban on torture merely codifies an underlying constitutional prohibition that is, of course, superior to the President's power to lead the military. As such, it is fully binding on his actions.

The second principle that has been put into doubt is the right of the people to communicate without fear of government eavesdropping. This freedom is rooted in the Fourth Amendment and is not absolute: the Fourth Amendment only prohibits unreasonable searches. Courts have historically protected this freedom by requiring the government, if at all possible, to apply for a judicial warrant before listening in on private conversations.

In 2005, news media revealed that soon after the September 11 attacks the President had authorized the National Security Agency (NSA) to intercept communications between persons in the United States and persons abroad if the NSA believed that one of the parties was linked to Al Qaeda. This program has proven enormously controversial, and much of the controversy has centered on whether it violated a 1978 law, the Foreign Intelligence Surveillance Act (FISA), that prohibits such governmental surveillance without authorization by a special court. In a 2006 legal memorandum defending the program, the Attorney General argued that the wiretaps were much like any other strategic engagement with the enemy, exclusively within the President's powers as Commander in Chief, and not subject to statutory regulation. This past January, the Attorney General modified his position, perhaps in a nod to critics or to an unfavorable lower court decision denying the government's motion to dismiss a challenge to the NSA program. The Attorney General indicated that he had, for the first time, begun to obtain judicial approval of the wiretaps under FISA. But he did not concede the issue of presidential power, and left unresolved important questions about the scope of judicial oversight. The Attorney General did not disclose, for example, whether the special court is approving wiretaps on an individual basis, or whether it is granting blanket authorizations that cover multiple wiretaps.

To my mind the focus of the inquiry should not be on whether the NSA program violates FISA, but rather whether it violates the Fourth Amendment itself. Admittedly, the Supreme Court has never spoken directly to the issue of whether the government must obtain a warrant before intercepting communications like those at issue in the NSA program, but the very reasons that the Supreme Court has imposed a warrant requirement in other wiretapping cases—including those involving domestic threats to public order—are fully applicable. A warrant requirement does not prevent the President from thwarting terrorist attacks, but minimizes abuses and avoids the impairment of communicative freedom that comes from knowing that the President could tap the phone of anyone he claims is linked to Al Qaeda.

A third principle challenged by the "War Against Terrorism" is what I call the principle of freedom. This principle is rooted in the constitutional guarantee of the writ of habeas corpus and due process, and denies the government the power to incarcerate anyone without charging them with a crime and swiftly bringing them to trial. This principle contains an exception for the exigencies of war: as a matter of necessity, enemy combatants can be seized on the battlefield and imprisoned for the duration of hostilities.

In the midst of the Afghanistan War, the President declared that alleged soldiers of the Taliban and Al Qaeda captured anywhere in the world were not ordinary prisoners of war but rather "illegal enemy combatants." This special designation allows the military to interrogate them on a protracted basis, to incarcerate them indefinitely, even beyond the duration of hostilities, to put them on trial before military commissions, and to punish them for the simple act of fighting. Traditionally the designation of "illegal enemy combatant" applied to individual spies or saboteurs, or to irregular militias, never to entire armies.

Because they are being held as "illegal enemy combatants," prisoners at Guantánamo have had little ability to press their claim for freedom. Some insisted, for example, that they never fought for the Taliban or Al Qaeda, but had been wrongly seized by local authorities or bounty hunters. At first there was no procedure to adjudicate these claims, but in July 2004 the Administration established a system of administrative tribunals to review individual cases. These tribunals were staffed by the military, freed of many of the ordinary rules of evidence, and though military personnel serve as personal representatives, the prisoners were not allowed the assistance of counsel.

The Administration is now putting some of the Guantánamo prisoners on trial, using military commissions instead of courts martial or ordinary civilian courts. Traditionally military commissions were used to try persons caught red-handed in a theater of war, and, in response to litigation challenging their use at Guantánamo, the Supreme Court expressed the fear that the Administration had transformed them "from a tribunal of true exigency into a more convenient adjudicatory tool." But the Court stopped short of declaring these tribunals an offense to due process, holding only that they conflicted with a statute. In October 2006, Congress responded to this decision by enacting a law specifically granting the Administration authority to continue with its use of military tribunals. This statute came on the heels of an earlier use of administrative tribunals to review the status of the Guantánamo prisoners and denied them the right to petition for a writ of habeas corpus.

The Administration has not been content to confine the "illegal enemy combatant" designation to those seized in Afghanistan or another theater of armed conflict. The war against Al Qaeda knows no bounds, and the Administration has thus invited us to view the United States itself as a battleground and subject to the same rules. As a result, a citizen of Qatar studying at Butler University in Indiana (Ali Saleh Kahlah al-Marri) was seized and is now being held incommunicado at a naval brig in South Carolina. Similarly, an American citizen (Jose Padilla) was arrested at O'Hare airport and held in the same brig for more than three years before being charged with a crime in federal court.

One could accept that the war against Al Qaeda is a war, and resist the conclusion—that the United States is a battleground similar to Afghanistan—not just as a matter of ordinary usage, but because of the consequences that conclusion would have for American society. To treat the United States as a battleground in the same sense as Afghanistan would threaten the fabric of ordinary life and put the exception to the principle of freedom for enemy combatants in the position of eating up the rule. The Administration would be able to imprison anyone living within our midst—citizens and non-citizens alike—without ever charging them with a crime and putting them on trial.

Many have decried these developments as an abuse of executive power. Yet while the Executive Branch is the driving force, the other branches are complicit in these challenges to the rule of law. When Congress enacted the 2005 statute affirming the ban against torture, legislators failed to provide any remedy for violations. Congress has not taken any steps to stop the NSA wiretapping program, though the Administration's about-face in January 2007 made such measures less urgent. When it comes to the principle of freedom, Congress became a full partner with the Administration, passing legislation to deny aliens deemed "illegal enemy combatants" access to the protection of the writ of habeas corpus and authorizing their trial by military commissions.

The Supreme Court's performance has been no better. Its decisions have caught the headlines because they rebuffed the Administration, but they are hardly victories for the Constitution. In one case, the Court ruled that an American citizen (Yasser Hamdi) held as an illegal enemy combatant in the South Carolina naval brig was entitled to the assistance of counsel and an evidentiary hearing regarding his claim that he had not taken up arms against the United States. This ruling was based on due process, yet it left the prisoner to carry most of the evidentiary burden and four Justices expressed their view that a military tribunal offered a sufficient forum for the prisoner to press his claim for freedom.

In other cases, the Court's performance has even been more timid. When Jose Padilla challenged his detention, the Supreme Court refused to rule on the merits and instead held that he had initially filed his habeas petition in the wrong court. Even more significantly, the Court has refused, at least so far, to address a ruling that the Court of Appeals in Washington, D.C., first advanced in 2003 and reaffirmed this February, that aliens held at Guantánamo do not have any constitutional rights that can be vindicated by the writ of habeas corpus. On April 2, 2007, the Supreme Court denied a writ of certiorari seeking review of this judgment. In so doing, the Court allowed the program of the elected branches to run its course, but it failed, yet again, in its duty to safeguard the Constitution and the values it embodies.

CONCLUSION

President Bush's drive for the greatest expansion in executive power since the Nixon era and perhaps in the history of our nation is too slowly grinding to a halt after years of challenges—some of which were half-hearted—by Congress, the courts, and finally by the political calendar. Yet that does not mean that his assertion of power has in any shape or form been pushed back to September 10, 2001.

The United States Supreme Court has recently ruled against the Bush Administration in several cases, including its decision allowing the detainees at Guantánamo to contest their detention in court. However, these decisions are somewhat limited in scope. Congress has allowed some key Administration actions which are constitutionally unacceptable to continue. These include the use of harsh interrogation techniques—torture—by the CIA and broad authority to eavesdrop on Americans. Mr. Bush has also abused the use of "signing statements" to accompany bills that become law. He has used those statements to reserve the right not to enforce any laws he thinks violate the Constitution,[1] harm national security, or impair foreign relations. The Bush Administration's unprecedented and frequent use of those statements has been one front in the battle between the President and Congress over the power of the executive branch.

As a result, President Obama has inherited executive powers which have been greatly expanded since the September 11, 2001, terrorist attacks. What can we expect from President Obama, who will clearly face extreme pressure both to pre-empt aggressively another terrorist attack and to protect civil liberties? Given the abuses of the Bush Administration, it is difficult to put too much trust in the hope that Mr. Bush's successor will be highly protective of our civil liberties. Those in power abuse it. In addition to these pressing issues, American society will continue to confront other serious problems, including issues of race and questions about the proper functioning of our democratic institutions. These are

---

[1] President Bush's primary use of signing statements are often meant to dispute any limits on his overly expansive view of presidential powers.

some of the major reasons to rely on the constitutional vision of Owen Fiss.

For four decades, Owen Fiss has been a leading intellectual and moral force in the law. His values were shaped in the Civil Rights Movement of the so-called Second Reconstruction. That movement was both legal and political—it was a struggle for group justice for African-Americans. To Fiss, the claim for group justice was legal because the end of law is justice.

He later became interested in international human rights concerns. His work in Argentina and the Middle East helped him to develop strong positions in the struggle between terrorism and civil liberties. His nuanced analysis of the Supreme Court's terrorism cases reflect these experiences and the moral force of his quest for justice through law.

As this book demonstrates, Owen Fiss's work has forged new ground in many different fields—from equality and freedom of speech to the role of the judiciary and the War on Terrorism. In several of these areas—particularly in the Equal Protection and Free Speech areas—he has been extremely creative, suggesting entirely new paradigms in which to view the field. The boldness and public-spirited nature of his scholarship inspires people to take risks, to think large, and to take on the injustices of the modern world. He has even moved on to speak about the role of the law in the international human rights movement and in the transition from dictatorship to democracy. He has been a role model to countless students, scholars, and activists. As his scholarship demonstrates, Owen Fiss's involvement in the law reflects the broadest boundaries of the social imagination that define the institutional and personal arrangements within which we organize our social world. He is a hero of the law, pushing us to recognize what the law has become and demanding that we try to ensure through our work what the law should be.

About the Author

Irwin P. Stotzky is Professor of Law at the University of Miami School of Law and the Director of the University of Miami Center for the Study of Human Rights. He received his J.D. from the University of Chicago Law School in 1974. In 1986–87, he was a Visiting Scholar at the Yale Law School. In 1991–92, he was a Fulbright Scholar in Argentina. For the past thirty-five years, he has represented Haitian and other refugees on constitutional and human rights issues in many cases, including several cases in the United States Supreme Court. He has worked extensively with advisors to the Alfonsin regime in Argentina on what steps to take, including human rights trials, against those who committed massive human rights abuses during the so-called "dirty war," and on other issues related to the transition to democracy. He has served as an attorney and advisor to Haitian President Jean-Bertrand Aristide, and as an advisor to President Renè Preval's administration. He has published numerous articles and books on democracy and human rights, criminal law and procedure, and the role of the judiciary in the transition to democracy. His books include THE THEORY AND CRAFT OF AMERICAN LAW: ELEMENTS (with Soia Mentschikoff) (1981), TRANSITION TO DEMOCRACY IN LATIN AMERICA: THE ROLE OF THE JUDICIARY (1993), and SILENCING THE GUNS IN HAITI: THE PROMISE OF DELIBERATIVE DEMOCRACY (1997). Another book, entitled IMMIGRATION LAW: CASES AND MATERIALS, is scheduled to be published in 2010.

For his representation of refugees in a series of cases before the United States Supreme Court and his human rights work abroad, he received human rights awards from the American Immigration Lawyers Association and the Haitian Refugee Center. For his work in investigating human rights abuses worldwide and his scholarship, he received the *Inter-American Law Review's* 1997 Lawyer of the Americas award.